Confronting

FEAR

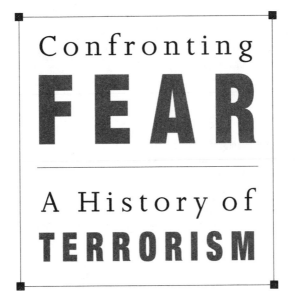

Confronting FEAR

A History of TERRORISM

Edited and with an introduction by

ISAAC CRONIN

Thunder's Mouth Press
New York

CONFRONTING FEAR: *A History of Terrorism*

Compilation © 2002 by Isaac Cronin
Introductions © 2002 by Isaac Cronin

Published by
Thunder's Mouth Press
An Imprint of Avalon Publishing Group Incorporated
161 William St., 16th Floor
New York, NY 10038

Library of Congress Cataloging-in-Publication Data

Confronting fear: a history of terrorism / edited by Isaac Cronin.
    p. cm.
ISBN 1-56025-399-1 (trade paper)
1. Terrorism—History. 2. Terrorism—History—Sources. I. Cronin, Isaac, 1948-

HV6431 .C6473 2002
303.6'25–dc21   2002018005

9 8 7 6 5 4 3 2 1

Interior Design by Sue Canavan

Printed in the United States of America
Distributed by Publishers Group West

To my children, Scarlet and Beau, who, along with the rest of us, will have to live in this brave new world, a world that will require all the honesty, compassion, and clarity that we can bring together.

Contents

RELIGIOUS TERRORISM

Introduction

The events of September 11, 2001, have placed the brutal realities of terrorism in front of the entire world. The most effective way to view the recent attack is to see it as part of an unfolding historical process. Terrorism is a form of warfare that has evolving causes, motivations, and objectives.

We begin at the beginning, with a working definition of terrorism that encompasses the broad range of activities included in this book.

Terrorism: Violence perpetrated by either individuals or groups against a more powerful opponent, usually a government (and/or its citizenry), the goal of which is to disrupt normal functioning by the dissemination of fear and intimidation, thereby forcing a change in the policy or approach of that opponent in the direction of the terrorists' political or social program or viewpoint. Terrorist acts include assassination, bombing, kidnapping, hijacking, and the use of weapons of mass destruction.

Terror: A systematic policy of violence and intimidation by an existing government intended to further the domination and control of its own population. The word terror entered modern usage just after the end of the French Revolution. Recent examples include Nazi Germany, the Pol

Pot regime in Cambodia, and Stalinist Russia (see *A History of Terrorism*, page 4).

It is useful to distinguish between terrorism and openly declared warfare between formally constituted governments. While guerilla movements and coup d'états seek to replace an existing government with another regime, they may employ terrorism along with other tactics of traditional warfare (see *Minimanual of the Urban Guerilla*, page 57).

Based on the breadth of the material in this book and in keeping with the perspective of researchers such as Walter Laqueur, terrorism can be divided into four categories that are based on the type of perpetrator.

1. Individual Acts of Terror: Individuals generally commit terrorist acts because they believe there is no other effective way to communicate their dissatisfaction to the world (see *Understanding Terrorist Behavior*, page 506). Usually they do not have a specific political or social agenda but rather an overall viewpoint they believe is irreconcilable with the world order (see *The Unabomber's Manifesto*, page 486, and *President McKinley Shot*, page 22).

2. Acts Committed by Groups: Terrorist cells and organizations have been motivated by beliefs across the ideological spectrum, from anarchist to fascist, Christian to Muslim. They often recruit individuals who already display criminal or antisocial behavior. Organizations frequently harness this individual discontent in the service of an often vaguely articulated political or social program, creating militants and militancy directed by a leadership cadre (see *Abu Nidal*, page 184; *Televisionaries*, page 94; and *My People Shall Live*, page 160).

3. State-Sponsored Terrorism: States have sponsored surrogate groups to do their terrorist bidding since at least as far back as the Roman Empire.

It is a less risky, less visible alternative to declared warfare that allows denial in the face of a difficult to prove chain of responsibility. Recent practitioners have included Russia, Syria, Iraq, Libya, and East Germany. When the United States supports repressive regimes in Latin America and elsewhere, this policy constitutes, arguably, state-sponsored terror (see *The New Terrorism*, page 253).

4. State Terrorism: Through acts of subterfuge, states have impersonated their internal radical oppositions, committing acts of terror they make sure are ascribed to their opponents in order to discredit the rebels and defuse a social crisis (see *On Terrorism and the State*, page 75).

This collection attempts to convey the broad range and complexity of the motivations and justifications for terrorism. It provides a look at the methodology of those who hunt terrorists and those who attempt to elude capture. It chronicles the rise and fall of cunning strategists (see *The New Jackals*, page 378) and sociopaths (see *Jackal: The Complete Story of the Legendary Terrorist*, page 111). It traces the failure of geopolitical strategies (see *Dollars for Terror: The United States and Islam*, page 326) and the success of brilliantly executed special operations assaults (see *The Hunt for the Engineer*, page 304).

One of the essential tools for confronting terrorism on an individual and collective level is understanding: when and why terrorism arises, how it functions, what its weaknesses are. The goal of this collection is to provide the reader with a broad overview that is often lacking in the short-term reactions of politicians, diplomats, and security officials as well as in the communications of terrorists themselves. The history of terrorism contains a great deal of tragedy; it may also contain the key to moving beyond this fear-based form of mass manipulation.

—*Isaac Cronin*

PRE-HISTORY

Pre-History

We can divide the prehistory of terrorism into two epochs. According to Walter Laqueur, the first begins with the earliest known terrorists, the Zealots, who slit the throats of their enemies in broad daylight in the marketplaces of Palestine in A.D. 66 (see *A History of Terrorism*, page 4), and the second starts with the bomb throwers and assassins of the extreme left and the extreme right who agitated for revolution beginning in the 1870s.

The second period was certainly more smoke than fire. For all the radical rhetoric and establishment counter-rhetoric, the fiery manifestos (see *The Science of Revolutionary Warfare*, page 17), and the political persecutions, the period between the 1870s and the Russian Revolution in 1917 saw fewer than 50 people killed through terrorist acts in all of Europe and America. Frequently the terrorists themselves were the ones who died or who were injured because of the primitive nature of their weapons (see *Propaganda by Deed—The Greenwich Observatory Bombing of 1894*, page 33; and *The Secret Agent*, page 36). The literary and journalistic notoriety of these terrorists far surpassed their practical effect.

The failure of the First International in 1868 (led by Marx and Engels, among others) to bring about a communist revolution was a major factor in the rise of the "propaganda by the deed" movement, as the proletarian provocateurs became known. For example, the bloody defeat of the Paris Commune in 1871, an attempt at workers' self-rule after the defeat of the French in their war with the Prussians, was followed closely by the appearance of lone wolf anarchists such as Ravachol and Emile Henry, who used the bomb as their voice in the absence of any organized alternative. The failure of a popular antiestablishment political movement leading to scattered acts of terrorism by desperate extremists was a pattern to be repeated in Europe and America a century later.

From 1917 to 1941, the Russian Revolution and its massive backlash distracted extremists from venturing into the terrorist arena. At the same time, terror-based totalitarian regimes in Spain, Germany, Italy, and, ultimately, Russia apparently left little room for the possibility of terrorism. These states enjoyed a monopoly on violent assault as they mercilessly suppressed any form of opposition.

The violence of World War II was so global and massive it would have rendered terrorist acts irrelevant had there been any. The various partisan resistance movements that attacked occupying armies in Europe and elsewhere using terrorist means were, in fact, acting as unofficial arms of governments in exile or in hiding.

The ill-planned and reluctant end of the European colonial regimes in the 1950s then set in motion forces that would lead to the next chapter in this book ("Political Terrorism," page 43).

excerpt from:

A History of Terrorism
by Walter Laqueur

Walter Laqueur is the head of the International Research Council for Strategic and International Studies in Washington, D.C., and is considered to be the dean of American terrorism experts. He has undertaken seminal research on terrorism from its earliest days just after the birth of Christ in the form of the Zealot movement of Palestine through the end of the 19th century with its idealistic French and Spanish anarchists who assassinated several political leaders. This selection focuses on the 19th century, a period characterized by conditions of intense exploitation and by passionate popular movements whose extremist fringe occasionally employed assassination and bombs in an attempt to galvanize "the masses." This era produced the phrase "propaganda by the deed," still used as a synonym for terrorism.

Terrorism "from below" has emerged in many different forms and out of such various motivations as religious protest movements, political revolts and social uprisings. One of the earliest known examples of a terrorist movement is the *sicarii*, a highly organized religious sect consisting of men of lower orders active in the Zealot struggle in Palestine (A.D. 66–73). The sources telling of their activities are sparse and sometimes contradictory, but it is known from Josephus that the *sicarii* used unorthodox tactics such as attacking their enemies by daylight, preferably on holidays when crowds congregated in Jerusalem. Their favorite weapon was a short sword *(sica)* hidden under their coats. In the words of the expert in De Quincey's club considering murder as a fine art: "Justly considering that great crowds are in themselves a sort of darkness by means of the dense pressure, and the impossibility of finding out who it was that gave the blow, they mingled with crowds everywhere . . . and when it was asked, who was the murderer and where he was—why, then it was answered 'Non est inventus'." They destroyed the house of Ananias, the high priest, as well as the palaces of the Herodian dynasts; they hurried the public archives, eager to annihilate the bonds of moneylenders and to prevent the recovery of debts.

A similar mixture of messianic hope and political terrorism was the prominent feature of a much better known sect—the Assassins, an off-shoot of the Ismailis who appeared in the eleventh century and were sup-pressed only by the Mongols in the thirteenth. The Assassins have fascinated Western authorities for a long time and this interest has grown in recent times, for some of the features of this movement remind one of contemporary terrorist movements. Based in Persia the Assassins spread to Syria, killing prefects, governors, caliphs and even Conrad of Montferrat, the Crusader King of Jerusalem. They tried twice to kill Saladin but failed. Their first leader, Hassan Sibai, seems to have realized early on that his group was too small to confront the enemy in open battle but that a planned, systematic, long-term campaign of terror carried out by a small, disciplined force could be a most effective political weapon. They always operated in complete secrecy; the terrorist fighters (fidaíin) were disguised as strangers or even Christians. The Assassins always used the dagger, never poison or missiles, and not just because the dagger was considered the safer weapon: murder was a sacramental act. Contemporary sources described the Assassins as an order of almost ascetic discipline; they courted death and martyrdom and were firm believers in a new mil-lennium. Seen in historical perspective, the terrorist struggle of the Assassins was a fruitless attempt by a relatively small religious sect to defend its religious autonomy (and way of life) against the Seljuqs who wanted to suppress them. But the means they used were certainly effective for a while, and the legends about the Old Man from the Mountain deeply impressed contemporaries and subsequent generations.

Secret societies of a different kind existed for centuries in India and the Far East. The Anglo-Indian authorities denied the existence of the Thugs until Captain (subsequently Major General) William Sleeman studied the subject and ultimately destroyed the sect. The Thugs strangled their victims with a silk tie; Europeans were hardly ever affected, but otherwise their choice of victims was quite indiscriminate. Its devotees thought the origin of Thuggee was derived from an act of sacrifice to the goddess Kali. It had a fatal attraction. In the, words of Feringea, a captured Thug: "Let any man taste of that *goor* [sugar] of the sacrifice, and he will be a Thug, though he know all the trades and has all the wealth in the world. . . . I have been in high office myself and became so great a favorite wherever I went that I was sure of promotion. Yet I was always miserable when away from my gang and obliged to return to Thuggee." The Thugs had contempt for death. Their political aims, if any, were not easily discernible; nor did they want to terrorize the government or population.

Systematic terrorism begins in the second half of the nineteenth century and there were several quite distinct categories of it from the very beginning.

Of all these movements the *Narodnaya Volya* was the most important by far, even though its operations lasted only from January 1878 to March 1881. The armed struggle began when Kovalski, one of its members, resisted arrest; it continued with Vera Zasulich's shooting of the governor general of St. Petersburg and reached a first climax with the assassination of General Mezentsev, the head of the Third Section (the Tsarist political police) in August 1878. In September 1879 Alexander II was sentenced to death by the revolutionary tribunal of the *Narodnaya Volya*. Even before, in April of that year, Solovev had tried to kill the tsar, but this had been a case of failed private initiative. Further attempts were no more successful;

they included an attempt to blow up the train in which the tsar traveled and the explosion of a mine in the Winter Palace. Success came on 1 March 1881, paradoxically after most of the members of the group had already been apprehended by the police. This was the apogee of the terror and also its end for more than two decades.

The high tide of terrorism in Western Europe was the anarchist "propaganda of the deed" in the 1890s. The exploits of Ravachol, Auguste Vaillant and Emile Henry between 1892 and 1894 created an enormous stir, and because the bomb throwing by individuals coincided with a turn in anarchist propaganda favoring violence, the impression of a giant international conspiracy was created, which in actual fact never existed. Ravachol was in many ways an extraordinary villain, a bandit who would have killed and robbed even if there had been no anarchist movement in France; Vaillant was a Bohemian and Emile Henry an excited young man. An analysis of the statistics of urbanization in nineteenth-century France would not add much to the understanding of their motives. The public at large was fascinated by the secret and mysterious character of the anarchist groups; anarchists, socialists, nihilists and radicals were all believed to be birds of one feather. Governments and police forces who knew better saw no reason to correct this impression.

There were a great many attempts on the lives of leading statesmen in Europe and America between the 1880s and the first decade of the twentieth century. Presidents Garfield and McKinley were among the victims; there were several unsuccessful attempts to kill Bismarck and the German emperor; French President Carnot was assassinated in 1894; Antonio Canovas, the Spanish prime minister, was murdered in 1897, Empress Elisabeth (Zita) of Austria in 1898 and King Umberto of Italy in 1900. But inasmuch as the assassins were anarchists—and quite a few were not—they all acted on their own initiative without the knowledge and support of the groups to which they belonged. It was conveniently forgotten at the time that there had been a long tradition of regicide, and attempted regicide, in Europe and that there had been countless attempts to kill Napoleon and Napoleon III. As a contemporary observer, who had little sympathy for anarchism, noted: "It is difficult to assign to them [the anarchists] any participation in the various outrages, notably the assassination of rulers."

The year of the revolution, 1848, also gave fresh impetus to the concept of terrorism, expressed most succinctly perhaps in an essay entitled "Murder" *(Der Mord)* written by the German radical democrat Karl Heinzen (1809–1880). He argued that while murder was forbidden in principle this prohibition did not apply to politics. The physical liquidation of hundreds or thousands of people could still be in the higher interests of humanity. Heinzen took tyrannicide as his starting point; he pointed out that such acts of liberation had been undertaken at all times and in all places. But it soon emerged that he was willing to justify terrorist tactics on a much more massive scale: "If you have to blow up half a continent and pour out a sea of blood in order to destroy the party of the barbarians, have no scruples of conscience. He is no true republican who would not gladly pay with his life for the satisfaction of exterminating a million barbarians." There could be no social and political progress unless kings and generals, the foes of liberty, were removed.

Seen in retrospect, Karl Heinzen was the first to provide a full-fledged doctrine of modern terrorism; most elements of latter-day terrorist thought can be found in the writings of this forgotten German radical democrat. It was a confused doctrine, to be sure; on one hand he argued that killing was always a crime, but on the other hand he claimed that murder might well be a "physical necessity," that the atmosphere or the soil of the earth needed a certain quantity of blood. (*Die Evolution,* January 26, 1849). He maintained that it was absolutely certain that the forces of progress would prevail over the reactionaries in any case but doubted whether the spirit of freedom and the "good cause" would win without using, dagger, poison and explosives: "We have to become more energetic, more desperate." This led him into speculations about the use of arms of mass destruction. For the greater strength, training and discipline of the forces of repression could be counterbalanced only by weapons that could be employed by a few people and that would cause great havoc. These weapons, Heinzen thought, could not be used by armies against a few individual fighters. Hence the great hopes attached to the potential of poison gas, to ballistic missiles (known at the time as Congreve rockets) and mines which one day "could destroy whole cities with 100,000 inhabitants" (*Die Evolution,* February 16, 1849). Heinzen blamed the revolutionaries of 1848 for not having shown sufficient ruthlessness; the party of freedom would be defeated unless it gave the highest priority to the development of the art of murder. Heinzen, like Most after him, came to see the key to revolution in modern technology: new explosives would have to be invented, bombs planted under pavements, new means of poisoning food explored. To expedite progress he advocated prizes for research in these fields. Heinzen's subsequent career was not, however, in the field of professional terrorism; he did not blow up half a continent but migrated to the United States and became an editor of various shortlived German-language newspapers, first in Louisville, Kentucky, and eventually in Boston—"the most civilized city in America."

The demand that the revolutionary should have but one thought day and night, that is, merciless destruction, recurs in the most famous document of the period, the "Revolutionary Catechism." [by Sergei Nechaev—ed.] The Catechism has frequently been quoted and a short summary will suffice for our purposes. It opens with a general list of rules for organization and then characterizes the attitude of the revolutionary toward himself and others. He is a lost man, without interests, belongings, personal ties of his own—not even a name. (The idea of the nameless soldier of the revolution was later to recur in many terrorist organizations as far afield as Ireland and Serbia where members were known by number rather than by name.) He must be absorbed by a single interest, thought and passion— the revolution. He has broken with society and its laws and conventions; he must eschew doctrinairism and despise public opinion, be prepared for torture and death at any time. Hard toward himself, he must be hard toward others, leaving no place for love, friendship, gratitude or even honor—room was to be spared only for the cold passion of the revolutionary cause whose success was to give him his pleasure, gratification and reward.

Tactical advice follows: in order to effect merciless destruction, the revolutionary has to pretend to be what he is not, to infiltrate the Church, the world of business, the bureaucracy and army, the secret police and even the royal palace. Bakunin [Michael Bakunin, one of the founders of anarchism and Nechaev's associate at the time—ed.] divided "society" into six categories: intelligent and energetic individuals, particularly dangerous to the revolutionary organization, were to be killed first, for their sudden and violent death would inspire fear among the government; secondly there were those, albeit no less guilty, whose lives should be temporarily spared, for their monstrous crimes objectively fomented revolution. The third category consisted of the high-ranking, the rich and powerful; they were mere "animals," neither particularly intelligent nor dynamic, who should be duped and blackmailed. Use should be made of ambitious politicians, including the liberals among them. The revolutionaries should conspire with them, pretending to follow them blindly, but at the same time ferreting out their secrets, thereby compromising them to such a degree as would cut off their retreat from the struggle against the authorities. The fifth category, the loudmouths, those platonic advocates of revolution, should be engineered into making dangerous declarations; most would perish in the struggle but a few might become authentic revolutionaries. Finally, the women: some were useless and stupid and were to be treated like categories three and four; others were capable, passionate and devoted even though they might not yet have acquired full revolutionary consciousness. The sixth category comprised those who had completely thrown in their lot with the revolutionaries; they were the most precious possession of the revolutionary party, and their aid was absolutely essential. In its final section, the Catechism emphasizes the need for total revolution: institutions, social structures, civilization and morality were to be destroyed, root and branch. A closing reference is made to the world of brigands, the only real revolutionaries who, once united, would bring into being a terrible and invincible power.

Only in 1878, after Vera Zasulich's shooting of General Trepov, the governor of the Russian capital, did terrorism as a doctrine, the Russian version of Propaganda by Deed, finally emerge. The Tsarist authorities explained this sudden upsurge of terrorism as a result of the Narodniks' failure to "go to the people"; the peasants had been unresponsive, the workers had informed on the "apostles of future happiness." After their lack of success in mobilizing the masses, the authorities maintained, the revolutionaries had come to regard terror as the only effective means of discrediting the government and proving to society at large that a revolutionary party not only existed but was growing stronger. This interpretation was not far from the truth. Plekhanov took virtually the same view when he wrote that terror was the product of the revolutionary party's weakness and followed on its realization that it could not stage a peasant uprising.

Morozov described how the revolutionaries had advanced from self-defense to attack. The government with its guns, prisons, spies and millions of soldiers could easily defeat any frontal assault, but it was powerless against terrorist attacks. The only thing that the terrorists had to fear was lack of caution on the part of their own members. Terrorism, according to

Morozov, was an altogether new fighting method, far more "cost-effective" than an old-fashioned revolutionary mass struggle. Despite insignificant forces, it would still be possible to concentrate every effort upon the overthrow of tyranny. Since there was no limit to human inventiveness, it was virtually impossible for the tyrants to provide safeguards against attacks. Never before were conditions so auspicious from the point of view of the revolutionary party, and once a whole series of terrorist groups came into being, they would spell the final days of the monarchy. Terrorist attempts in the past had been acts of despair and frequently of suicide. This tragic element no longer existed: the terrorists simply carried out a death sentence which had been imposed by their tribunals and there was every reason to assume that the executioners would not be apprehended and would disappear without trace. Victory was inevitable sooner or later. In order to blunt the terrorist struggle and win over the bourgeoisie, the government was quite likely to grant a constitution. But the terrorist struggle could be conducted not only against tyranny but also against a constitutional oppression such as in Germany.

Romanenko's views were on similar lines: terrorism was not only effective, it was humanitarian. It cost infinitely fewer victims than a mass struggle; in a popular revolution the best were killed while the real villains looked on from the sidelines. The blows of terrorism were directed against the main culprits; a few innocent people might suffer, but this was inevitable in warfare. Terrorism, then, was the application of modern science to the revolutionary struggle. He interpreted Russian history since the days of the Decembrists as a duel between the intelligentsia and the regime. It was pointless asking the people to rise against their oppressors for the masses were insufficently strong. It was wrong to regard systematic terror as immoral, since everything that contributed to the liberating revolution was *a priori* moral. The same idea of cost-effectiveness and, in particular, the humanitarian character of terrorism was also voiced by Zhelyabov, the central figure of the Narodnaya Volya and, most outspokenly, in a pamphlet by Lev Sternberg (1861–1927), *Politicheski Terror v Rossii*. Terrorism, in Sternberg's view, was a safety valve; if there was no terror there would be a terrible explosion from below. It was the historical mission of the intelligentsia to prevent—or, to be precise, to preempt—this uncontrolled explosion.

Thus the Anarchist appeals had no serious consequence other than alarming the general public. There is evidence that in their endeavor to penetrate the ranks of the Anarchists the police actually provided money for Anarchist publications and, in some cases, apparently also for terrorist operations. One of the most bloodcurdling appeals was published in a police-sponsored French-language periodical in London: it called for blows against the left, right and center, against religion and patriotism. Theft, murder and arson were legitimate means in the struggle and so, of course, was the great friend, the "thunder of dynamite." In 1880 the French Anarchist journal *La Révolution Sociale* began publishing instructions for the fabrication of bombs. At the time this paper was edited by Serreaux, a police spy, with money provided by Louis Andrieux, the prefect of the Paris police, who thoughtfully left us with detailed memoirs. On the other hand, the bomb, "the last weapon of revolt," was also praised in bona fide Anarchist publications such as Most's *Freiheit, La Lutte Sociale*, and Swiss publications. Advice was given to place bombs or inflammable materials near storehouses where cotton or alcohol were kept. Chemical formulae for making *produits anti-bourgeoises* were published. Of course, one could not be too specific: '*L'action ne se conseille, ni ne se parle, ni ne s'érit—elle se fait.*" Marie Constant, a revolutionary Paris shoemaker, composed a popular song ending

> *Maintenant la danse tragique*
> *vent une plus forte musique:*
> *Dynamitons, dynamitons.*

• • •

After the execution of Ravachol, a new verb came into being, *ravacholiser;* the *Ravachole* was sung to the tune of the *Carmagnole, Vive le son de l'ex-plosion.* A Ravachol cult caused considerable accession of strength to Anarchism. Among the more far-fetched suggestions was advice to domestic servants to poison their employers, to churchgoers to poison clerics, to soak rats in petrol, set them on fire and then let them loose in buildings marked for destruction. Anarchist journals called on their followers to arm themselves with every weapon provided by science, to destroy the criminal institutions of society based on the most extreme egoism: "*Pillons, brûlons, détrusions.*" The new revolutionary strategy, it was announced, was no longer based on open, frontal battles, "*mais une guerre des partisans menés de façon occulte.*"

Terrorist acts in the United States resembled those in Spain insofar as there was a tradition of violence and a long history of stormy, often bloody, labor disputes. This was particularly true among the miners, and continued from the days of the Molly Maguires to the Western Federation of Miners under Bill Haywood and the IWW. Following the arrival of German and later of East European proponents of "propaganda by deed," an ideological element was infused which did not exist in southern Europe. The antiparliamentarian International Working People's Association, founded in Pittsburgh in 1883, was syndicalist in character and advocated violence in the form of mass strikes and sabotage rather than acts of terror. Chicago was the center of these activities.

But as the industrial conflicts worsened and tempers rose, the *Alarm* and the *Chicagoer Arbeiterzeitung* became advocates of individual as well as mass terror. Dynamite was the great social solvent, the emancipator, and instruction was freely offered to workers on how to handle arms: "The Weapons of the Social Revolutionist Placed within the Reach of All." Dynamite, a reader wrote, "of all good stuff, this is *the* stuff . . . . It is something not very ornamental but exceedingly useful. It can be used against persons and things, it is better to use it against the former than against bricks and masonry." C. S. Griffin argued that no government can exist without a head, and "by assassinating the head just as fast as a government head appeared, the government could be destroyed, and, generally speaking all governments be kept out of existence. Those least offensive to the people should be destroyed last." Albert Parsons, one of the accused in the Haymarket affair, editor of Alarm and former chief deputy collector of Internal Revenue in Austin, Texas, defended the use of dynamite even in court: it was democratic, it made everybody equal. It was a peacemaker, man's best friend. As force was the law of the universe, dynamite made all men equal and therefore free. But Parsons denied that he had anything to do with throwing the bomb. Those allegedly involved in the Haymarket affair were the contemporaries and pupils of Johann Most, for many years the high priest of terrorism in America.

In the 1890s, younger and even more radical activists such as Emma Goldman and Alexander Berkman came to the fore. In July 1892, Berkman tried to shoot Henry C. Frick of the Carnegie Company, whom he regarded responsible for the outrages committed during the Homestead strike earlier that year. Aged twenty-one at the time, Berkman had arrived in the United States five years previously. He was an enthusiast; Bazarov, Hegel, "Liberty" and Chernishevski (apparently in this order) were his idols. As he saw it, only the toilers, the producers, counted; the rest were parasites who had no right to exist. All means were justifiable, nay advisable, in the fight against them: the more radical the treatment, the quicker the cure. Society was a patient, sick constitutionally and functionally; in the circumstances surgical treatment was imperative. The removal of a tyrant was an act of liberation, the highest duty of any revolutionary.

Lucien de la Hodde, writing in 1850, provides a most interesting analysis of the social composition of the secret societies in Paris in the first half of the last century, groups who from time to time engaged in terrorist actions. He listed nine categories of participants: first, and above all, the students. There was a rebellious tradition among students dating back to the Middle Ages. De la Hodde made it clear, however, that he did not have in mind the students who studied but those who thought all bourgeois ideas ridiculous and who had a weakness for *le bruit, les coups, les évènements.* The author admired the British for their political wisdom in having set up their universities outside the capital. Secondly, de la Hodde lists *les impuissants*—advocates without clients, physicians without patients, writers without readers, merchants without buyers, and all unsophisticated souls who saw themselves as statesmen, having studied politics in the newspapers. In short: the educated, or semieducated, *déclassés*, who have always constituted the backbone of such groups. De la Hodde further lists *les bohêmes, une classe de fantaisistes ayant horreur de la vie ordinaire,* mainly to be found in the capital, hardly ever outside it. Furthermore, *le peuple souverain,* i.e., the working class, *les gobe-mouche*—the simpletons, well-meaning but naïve and credulous people (and true believers, the permanently discontented, political refugees; and lastly the bandits, the criminal elements.

excerpt from:

The Science of Revolutionary Warfare

by Johann Most

The subtitle of this little pamphlet written by German anarchist Johann Most in 1881 says it all: *Handbook of Instruction Regarding the Use and Manufacture of Nitroglycerine, Dynamite, Gun-Cotton, Fulminating Mercury, Bombs, Arsons, Poisons, etc.* Most left England in 1882 after a sixteen-month jail sentence for advocating the assassination of the Russian Tsar. Deciding that five stays in European prisons were enough, he immigrated to America where he wrote this text. Most, a skilled orator and propagandist, organized the International Anarchist Congress in Pittsburgh in 1883, advocating "Establishment of a free society based upon co-operative organization of production."

Today, the importance of explosives as an instrument for carrying out revolutions oriented to social justice is obvious. Anyone can see that these materials will be the decisive factor in the next period of world history.

It therefore makes sense for revolutionaries in all countries to acquire explosives and to learn the skills needed to use them in real situations.

It seems to us that far too much time and money has been wasted on false approaches to this objective.

Many people obtained expensive textbooks meant for professional chemists and not for the layman, and were unable to understand them.

Some individuals may have learned a little in this way, especially in cases where they were able to consult an expert. Everything learned is worth something, so their time was not entirely wasted.

We, along with some other people, went a step further, and arranged for popularized versions of technical papers on the production of explosives to be published. However, we found that these also were not well understood.

Here and there, people started experimenting on the basis of this material, but the results were usually not very encouraging. The equipment they worked with was expensive and fragile, and easily damaged beyond repair when used by unskilled people. The necessary raw materials, when bought from ordinary retailers, usually turned out to be of inferior quality. Upgrading or purifying these raw materials would once again have called for expensive equipment and economic demands beyond the means of the man in the street. It would have been still more difficult to make the materials, both for financial reasons and due to the lack of expertise. We do know some people who have made something resembling gun cotton. Some have even succeeded—after their fifth or sixth mixing rig blew up—in making small quantities of nitroglycerine, and converting it into dynamite.

These fortunate ones were then faced with the fact that all their efforts and sacrifices had resulted in something of theoretical value only, since one cannot accomplish much with *small* quantities, and the method was too expensive anyway.

To manufacture large quantities of dynamite, one must have a rather expensive setup. Several rooms are needed, so it cannot be done in a private apartment. In fact, it is necessary to locate the workshop away from any neighbors, because dynamite manufacture produces a strong smell that would soon betray the operation.

Although people have not given up experimenting, we conclude that the demand for dynamite and other explosives required for revolutionary purposes cannot be met on a do-it-yourself basis, and that it is a much better idea to obtain it ready-made, from regular industrial sources.

Not an ounce of the dynamite that has actually been used by revolutionaries anywhere in the world was home-made.

Imperial, royal and republican (government) arsenals have had to do the providing. No matter how well-guarded they are, the authorities can never completely prevent the disappearance of some of their stores, generally before the material is actually delivered and locked up in the arsenal.

On the other hand, dynamite is used for many purposes, so that it is nonsense to believe that it cannot be obtained from conventional suppliers.

Everything can be had for money, and that includes dynamite. Revolutionaries with money will be able to get it, and without money they can neither buy it nor make it. So the slogan is, "Save your pennies!!" You may object that nothing can be made out of nothing, and that resources are in the hands of others. This becomes a question of appropriating them . . .

Once we are in an era when things are really happening, it would be stupid to consider amateur dynamite production. Dynamite factories and explosives warehouses can be seized just like anything else. The skilled workers there would work just as well for us as for anyone else, if we pay them properly.

Summing up, we shall from now on *not* focus our attention on making dynamite, about which there has been so much talk and so little to be seen, and occupy ourselves with how to obtain large quantities of ready-made dynamite.

For the sake of completeness, however, the plan to include a description of the simplest methods of making explosives. For the moment, we propose to discuss a much more important aspect: the effects of explosives, and how to use them. A great many mistakes have been made in this context, through ignorance.

Many people believe that dynamite is to be handled like gun-powder. They try to make it explode with a simple fuse, or even with relatively crude kindling materials. It's not so bad when they try this experimentally, because then they see that it doesn't work. The worst situations arise when they attempt this as a part of a serious action, resulting in a fiasco.

It is indeed possible for dynamite to explode when exposed to hot sparks, flames, or a burning fuse, but it happens so very rarely that this procedure is not worthy of consideration as an explosive technique. When dynamite comes into contact with flames or a glowing substance, it usually catches fire and burns up, without any other result.

A violent shock or jolt is the only reliable way to make dynamite explode. For this reason, one should be cautious when transporting it, avoiding sharp jolts and careless handling. This doesn't mean that dynamite will inevitably explode if it gets banged around a little. You could, perhaps, throw a pound of dynamite against the wall 99 times without any trouble. Accidentally knocking it off the table, so that it just drops to the floor, might then cause an explosion.

When frozen, dynamite is less able to withstand shocks, i.e. it explodes more readily than when it is not in a frozen condition. Note that dynamite freezes at a relatively high temperature, at which water is still completely fluid. On the other hand, dynamite can tolerate quite warm temperatures, without any danger of exploding. The heat would have to become intense—corresponding to the temperature of the metal shelf in a heated oven before one might expect an explosion.

Dampness has no effect at all on dynamite, as its main component (nitroglycerine) is extremely fatty.

These preliminary notes should be sufficient for the layman. Now we can move on to the main subject.

...

'In giving dynamite to the downtrodden millions of the globe, science has done its best work. The dear stuff can be carried in the pocket without danger, while it is a formidable weapon against any force of militia, police or detectives that may want to stifle the cry for justice that goes forth from plundered slaves. It is something not very ornamental, but exceedingly useful. It can be used against persons and things. It is better to use it against the former than against bricks and masonry . . . A pound of this stuff beats a bushel of ballots all hollow—and don't you forget it.'

President McKinley Shot, The Trial and Execution of Leon Czolgosz

Leon Czolgosz, a laborer and a self-proclaimed disciple of anarchist Emma Goldman, shot President McKinley in Buffalo, New York, on September 6, 1901. Excerpts include the original newspaper article, a transcript of the assassin's court testimony and an account of the execution.

PRESIDENT M'KINLEY SHOT AT PUBLIC RECEPTION IN THE TEMPLE OF MUSIC
ONE BULLET PASSED THROUGH STOMACH— WOUND CRITICAL—NOT NECESSARILY FATAL
RAGING MOBS ATTEMPT TO LYNCH ANARCHIST— SIXTY-FIFTH REGIMENT IS UNDER WAITING ORDERS
"I DID MY DUTY," EXCLAIMS THE ASSASSIN WHO SAYS HE IS A DISCIPLE OF EMMA GOLDMAN

While extending in friendly greeting his hand of fellowship, in the Temple of Music at the Pan-American Exposition, William McKinley, President of the United States, was shot down at the hands of either an Anarchist or a lunatic, a few minutes after 4 o'clock yesterday afternoon.

The assassin was captured and is safely in custody, while the President has undergone an operation and is at the home of President Milburn of the Pan-American Exposition, whose guest he has been. Grave fears are entertained as to his recovery, the second bullet having entered the abdomen, completely penetrating the stomach. It has not been found and further search for it has been abandoned for the present. The first bullet struck the breast and did not penetrate. When Mrs. McKinley was told of the tragedy she was at the home of Mr. Milburn and it was reported that she bore up well although still an invalid.

The World's Anxiety

The world is pouring its messages of regret into the doorway of the Milburn home. Thousands of telegrams have been received, and an effort has not yet been made to open them, but they all go to show the effect of the tragedy has had upon the entire world.

Buffalo is now undergoing the most trying ordeal in its history. Her guest of honor, the nation's ruler and the respected colleague of the rulers of all civilized nations, lies between life and death within her own doors. No adequate description may be attempted of the impression this tragedy has made upon the people of Buffalo. Everywhere people are so horrified that the crime is discussed in the shortest sentences, and many are the expressions of revenge.

Militia On Waiting Orders

Exciting mobs have gathered about the 1st Precinct Police Station, wherein the assassin is a prisoner, and the police have been kept busy all night dispersing them. Fearing the worst might come, the militia had been ordered into readiness. Governor Odell has arrived and the 65 Regiment is under waiting orders. A few minutes after the President was shot, the Midway closed and last night the entire Exposition grounds were in darkness and deserted.

Assassin's Confession

The assassin, in a confession made to the District Attorney, court officials and the police at midnight, said that his name was Leon Czolgosz, that he was 28 years old, a blacksmith, and that he had come to Buffalo from his

home in Cleveland three days ago with the express intention of assassinating the President. He said he had been a student of Emma Goldberg,
the Anarchist, had approved her doctrines and did not believe in this form
of government. He described with accuracy and with seeming pride the
preparations he had made to kill the President, how he had practiced in
folding the handkerchief about his hand so as to conceal the revolver, and
described how he had shot the President.

To a Courier reporter District Attorney Penney gave the substance of
Czolgosz's confession as follows:

> *"This man has admitted shooting the President. He says he
> intended to kill; that he has been planning to do it for the last
> three days since he came here. He went into the Temple of
> Music with murder in his heart, intending to shoot to kill.
> He fixed up his hand by tying a handkerchief around it and
> waited his turn to get near the President, just as the newspa-
> pers have described. When he got directly in front of the
> President he fired. He says he had no confederates, that he
> was entirely alone in the planning and execution of his dia-
> bolical act."*

This in substance is the confession made by Czolgosz, who is a German-
Pole and says his home is in the vicinity of Cleveland, Ohio. He is 28 years
old, unmarried, and has seven brothers and two sisters living there. He
worked for a time in the wire mills at Newark, Ohio. He exhibits no signs
of contrition and acts as if he had done a praiseworthy, instead of a das-
tardly, act.

The President, with Mrs. McKinley, had been to Niagara Falls up until
3:30 o'clock, when his special train brought them to the Exposition.
There, Mrs. McKinley took a carriage to the Milburn home, she feeling
fatigued. The President and his party were driven to the Government

building, where a light lunch was served, and then the President, accompanied only by President Milburn, Secretary Cortelyou and the Secret Service men, drove to the Temple of Music, where it had been arranged to have a public reception.

Numerous Soldiers

The President had taken his position under a bower of palms, and to his left was President Milburn, to his right Secretary Cortelyou, and opposite them Secret Service operatives Ireland and Foster. They were so arranged that the crowd would have to pass in single file. Along the aisle down which the public must pass were numerous soldiers from the 73rd Sea Coast Artillery and guards from the Exposition police.

The President was never in a better mood; he was smiling from the moment he stepped into the building, and when he announced that he was ready for the doors to be thrown open, he appeared as though the coming on-slaught of handshaking was to be a long-looked-for pleasure.

Music of the Organ

Two hundred people had not passed the President when the tragedy which was to startle the world turned the joyous scene into one of indestructible excitement, assault and pandemonium. Organist Gomph had reached the highest notes in one of Bach's masterpieces on the great pipe organ, and as he stopped at the height to let the strains reverberate through the auditorium the two shots rang out.

THE TRIAL AND EXECUTION OF LEON CZOLGOSZ

When Leon Czolgosz was removed from the Temple of Music and taken to Buffalo Police Headquarters, he was in near death condition. Having suffered a terrible beating at the hands of President McKinley's military escort and the secret service, it was questioned as to whether or not he would survive to go to trial. The police had a terrible time trying to keep the angry mobs of Buffalo away from Czolgosz. If given the chance the mobs would tear him apart, so security and protection for the assassin was a constant problem.

On September 27, 1901, Czolgosz was moved from Buffalo to Auburn prison where he was to receive the punishment for his crime. When he arrived at Auburn, he came into contact with more people than he ever had during the entire ordeal. At 3:10 a.m., his train arrived at the prison and he was brutally dragged from the train and shoved through a crowd of three hundred people who were constantly mauling him. Czolgosz was handcuffed and the continuous beatings made it almost impossible for him to walk. The prison guards were caught completely off guard by the crowd's reaction and had to use clubs and revolver butts to keep the mobs back. Many times he was knocked to his knees so the guards found it necessary to drag him up the stairs to the prison office. He was thrown to the ground upon reaching the office and cried out in terror, frothing at the mouth and uttering the most horrible sounds.

He stumbled into a cane seat and lay there moaning in terror, while the crowd hung on the iron gates outside and chanted, "GIVE HIM TO US! GIVE HIM TO US!" Shivering uncontrollably, Czolgosz nearly jumped out of his skin when a guard approached him and removed the handcuffs. He was then dragged through heavy oaken, iron-barred doors that led to the warden's office; in fact, he was carried. Four husky guards held his shoulders and arms. They dumped him in a chair; a limp, disheveled figure, his cries echoing down the long corridors and arousing all the other convicts. Czolgosz was in a state of absolute collapse, and when left alone rolled onto the floor, convulsing uncontrollably.

Two guards grabbed him and ripped him off the floor. Unable to stand, he quickly collapsed, screaming in pain. The angry cries from the crowd outside could be heard from the open window in the office.

"Shut up! You're faking!" said Dr. Gern, the prison physician. Czolgosz obeyed the order, but still continued to moan quietly and writhe in agony. Two prison guards stripped him of his clothing and placed a prison uniform on him. He was then removed to his cell where he would not emerge again until his execution.

The trial of Leon Czolgosz began at 10:00 in the morning on September 23, 1901, at Buffalo's Supreme Court with Justice Truman C. White on the bench. After various witnesses were called to testify as to the events of the tragedy on September 6, Czolgosz was finally called to the stand by Clerk Martin Fisher. He placed his hand on the Bible and nodded his head in agreement with the words to the oath. However, he did not say, "I do."

District Attorney Thomas Penney began Czolgosz's interrogation by first asking, "What is your name?"

"Leon Czolgosz," came the weak response, scarcely audible to the Judge.

"What is your age?"

"Twenty-eight," after some hesitation.

"Where were you born?"

"In Detroit."

"Where did you last reside?"

"In Buffalo," whispered Czolgosz. His voice seemed husky and his mouth dry. He didn't make an effort at all to speak loudly and moved about nervously while the questions were being asked.

"Where did you live in Buffalo?"

"On Broadway."

"Where on Broadway?" insisted Penney. No answer. "At Nowak's?"

"Yes," after a pause.

"What is your occupation? Do you understand the question?"

Czolgosz shook his head. It seemed as though he was hard of hearing and not understanding of all that was asked of him. Penney repeated the question distinctly and in a loud voice. Czolgosz responded as if half-stupefied.

"Yes, sir; I was a laborer."

"Are you married or single?"

"Single," came the ready response.

"Are your parents living or dead?"

"No, sir," was the answer.

"You don't understand me quite," said Penney. "Is your father living?"

"Yes, sir."

"Is your mother living?"

"No sir," Penney gave a tired glance at the jury.

"Mr. Czolgosz, have you been temperate or intemperate in the use of intoxicating liquors?" No reply.

"You don't understand the question?"

"No, sir. I don't."

Penney took a few steps toward Czolgosz and glared at him. "Do you drink much?"

"No, sir."

"Ever been drunk?" Again there was no response. "Come on, man! Do you drink much?"

"Mr. Penney, please pass on to something else," interrupted Judge White.

Penney slowly turned and gave a slight bow to the judge acknowledging his request. "Mr. Czolgosz, were you ever before convicted of a crime?"

"No, sir."

Clerk Fisher then asked, "Have you any legal cause to show now why the sentence of the court should not now be pronounced against you?"

"I cannot hear that," replied the prisoner.

The Clerk repeated the question, and Czolgosz replied, "I'd rather have this gentleman here speak," looking toward District Attorney Penney. "I can hear him much better." At this point, Judge White told all those in the courtroom to be quiet or they would be removed.

Mr. Penney then asked the prisoner, "Czolgosz, the court wants to know if you have any reason to give as to why sentence should not be pronounced against you. Have you anything to say to the judge? Say yes or no."

Czolgosz did not reply, and Judge White addressed him, saying, "In that behalf, what you have a right to say relates explicitly to the subject in hand here. What we are asking you is if there are any reasons why we should not proceed with your trial. The first being that you claim insanity, the second being that you have good cause to offer either in arrest of the judgment about to be pronounced against you or for a new trial. Those are the grounds specified by the statute in which you have a right to speak at this time, and you are at perfect liberty to do so if you wish."

Czolgosz appeared dazed. "I have nothing to say about that."

The judge then said to Penney, "Are you ready?" Penney nodded that he was.

"Have you anything to say?" Judge White asked Czolgosz.

"Yes," replied the prisoner.

Czolgosz was then permitted to make a brief statement to the court. "There was no one else but me. No one else told me to do it, and no one paid me to do it."

"Anything further, Czolgosz?" asked Judge White.

"No, sir," he replied.

Judge White then turned in his seat and looked directly into the prisoner's eyes. "Czolgosz, in taking the life of our beloved President, you committed a crime which shocked and outraged the moral sense of the civilized world. You have confessed that guilt, and after learning all that at this time can be learned from the facts and circumstances of the case, twelve good jurors have found you guilty of murder in the first degree.

"You have said, according to the testimony of credible witnesses and yourself, that no other person aided you in the commission of this terrible act. God grant it may be so. The penalty for the crime for which you stand is fixed by this statute, and it now becomes my duty to pronounce this judgment against you. The sentence of the court is that the week beginning October 28, 1901, at the place, in the manner and means prescribed by law, you suffer the punishment of death. May God have mercy on your soul. Remove the prisoner."

Czolgosz stood erect as the sentence was pronounced to him. He did not tremble. In fact, he never moved a muscle. His execution would be carried out by the electric chair at Auburn Prison.

Statistics show that by 1901, Leon Czolgosz was the 50th person to die in the electric chair in the state of New York. Those assigned to guard him while he was in Buffalo, and later at Auburn, were relieved when the prison physician approached the lifeless body and proclaimed that he was dead. However, the events that ultimately led up to his execution were without incident. Members of the press were denied interviews and were not permitted to witness the execution. There was no formal ceremony at the prison.

The images showing the execution of Leon Czolgosz are from a collection of original films shot by Thomas Edison at the Pan-American. However the "execution" shown in these films is actually a reenactment and does not depict the actual death of Czolgosz.

On October 29, 1901, Leon Czolgosz was led from his cell and slowly walked the twenty feet down the corridor to the door of the death room. He stumbled when his feet touched the stone pavement of the room and again when he got onto the platform that held the chair. It was there that he got the first look at the instrument that was about to take his life.

The electric chair was a plain looking, but heavy piece of furniture. It was decorated with wide leather straps and heavy buckles. From the ceiling came a coil of wire no wider than a common pencil to which the electrode for the head-piece would attach. Electric lamps were along the wall behind the chair and about the ceiling. The chair was large enough to hold a man much heavier than Czolgosz, so a broad plank was placed on its edge across the seat and against the back of the chair, that there might not be any movement of the prisoner's body to break the circuit.

Just before the electrocution was to begin, a leather-backed sponge soaked with salt water was tightly buckled below the knees, and on the head was placed a helmet, the top of which was filled with a wet sponge. The top of Czolgosz head was shaved so that perfect electrical contact could be made.

As he was being strapped into the chair, Czolgosz blurted out, "I killed the President because he was the enemy of the good people! I did it for the help of the good people, the working men of all countries!" The guards quickly finished preparing him. Then they slowly stepped away from the platform, turned, and walked away.

After what seemed like an eternity, the signal was given to throw the switch and send the current through his body. Czolgosz immediately gave a gurgled cry and his body lunged upward. He seemed to tremble with a slight rigidity as his body was converted into a piece of iron. As the 1,700 volts of raw energy exploded into his body, Czolgosz arched his body backwards and remained still. The current flowed for a full minute and was gradually backed down to 200 volts. After the electricity was turned off, some time passed without anyone saying a word. Then one of the prison officials said, "Give him another poke."

The current was turned on at 1,700 volts for another full minute without any reaction from Czolgosz's body. After this round was finished, the medical examiner went up to the lifeless body and pronounced Czolgosz dead. His eyes were open and seemed to be staring out at everyone in the room. The matter was finished. Justice was served.

Back at the Pan-American Exposition, the Temple of Music stood quiet and empty. The fair long since over. The crowds long gone. All around were signs that the elements had begun to lay claim on the buildings as pieces of plaster and wood lay scattered in every direction.

The Temple was an empty shell. Chairs were littered all about and a musty smell hung in the air. A small fence was built to surround the spot where President McKinley had been assassinated. Only a month prior, McKinley uttered the words, "Expositions were the timekeepers of progress." Now, the only progress that needed doing was the removal of the Pan-American Exposition. Buffalo had a black spot on its history. The Rainbow City was now an abandoned eyesore that many wished would go away.

Propaganda by Deed—
The Greenwich Observatory Bomb
of 1894

In this London Royal Observatory web site document we learn about a
French anarchist, Martial Bourdin, who blew himself up with a bomb
outside the observatory. No one could discern the bomber's motivation.
To this day his act remains unexplained. This speculation was continued
in Joseph Conrad's *Secret Agent,* a portion of which is included in this
collection.

Working life at the Royal Observatory, Greenwich in the 1890s must
have been generally uneventful. An endless series of transit observations were done by duty observers at night, with a team of
human 'computers' working through the day on data reduction and pre-
dictions. This routine existence was shattered one Thursday afternoon in
February 1894 by a totally unexpected event, which put the Observatory
into the headlines for days afterwards.

In the last two decades of the 19th century, a series of anarchist
inspired terrorist attacks hit many European countries. One of the earliest
and most spectacular was the bomb assassination of the Russian Tsar
Alexander in 1881 which inspired anarchists to many other similar attacks
on the rulers and aristocracy. By late 1893 anarchist terrorists were particularly active in France, culminating in the bombing of the Chamber of
Deputies in Paris in December. Auguste Vaillant was convicted and executed for this crime in early February 1894, with a particularly futile

'reprisal' for the execution following close after when a bomb exploded in a Paris Cafe on February 12, 1894. Up until then, Britain remained unaffected by the anarchist campaign, although Irish Fenian bomb attacks had occurred in England as early as the 1860's.

In Greenwich, on the afternoon of February 15th, 1894, two members of the Observatory staff were still in the building at 4.45 p.m. This they described as working 'late'—all the other staff had left by that time. Mr Thackeray and Mr Hollis were both in the Lower Computing Room when they were startled by a 'sharp and clear detonation, followed by a noise like a shell going through the air'. They looked out to see the door porter running across the courtyard and rapidly followed him so as to be able to look down the hillside North of the Observatory into Greenwich Park. They saw a park-warden and some school-boys running towards a figure that appeared to be crouched on the zig-zag path below the Observatory.

Racing down, their first thought was that the man had shot himself, but the scene they encountered was unexpected and horrific. The park-warden was holding a man who, despite massive injuries, was still alive and able to speak. The man's left hand was completely missing and he had a gaping hole in his stomach. Soon a doctor and stretcher were fetched from the nearby Seaman's Hospital, to where he was carried. The man died about 30 minutes later, having said nothing about who he was or what had happened.

Messrs Hollis and Thackeray searched the area between where the man was found and the Observatory wall and recovered numerous fragments of the man's hand, including a 2 inch piece of bone. A trail of blood and fragments were spread over a distance of nearly 60 yards towards the Observatory wall. As the two shocked Observatory staff went home that day, the identity of the man and the reason for the explosion was still a mystery to them.

Police investigators soon learned that his name was Martial Bourdin. That afternoon the 26 year old Frenchman left his room in Fitzroy Street, and took a tram from Westminster that took him all the way to Greenwich.

On leaving the tram he was observed to be carrying a parcel as he made his way to Greenwich Park. What happened a few minutes later, no one knows, but it appears that due to "some mischance or miscalculation or some clumsy bungling" the bomb exploded in his hand. He had a considerable amount of money on him, which led investigators to believe that he was intending to leave for France immediately.

Later on the day of the explosion, police raided the Club Autonomie in London, arrested all of those inside and discovered that Bourdin had been a member of this club which had attracted mainly foreign anarchists. Many were deported but no charges were made. The funeral of Martial Bourdin became a rallying point for anarchist sympathisers in London and attracted huge crowds.

A mystery remains—why did Bourdin pick such an unlikely target as the Observatory? The small bomb was unlikely to cause any serious damage there and it was a very different target from the crowded opera houses and cafes favoured by the terrorists in France. Some believe that Bourdin was duped into carrying the bomb or that he was on the way to France and wanted to dump it in the Park. The true reason will never be known. His brother in law was widely believed to be a police informer and anarchist writers in the years following the bombing always claimed that the whole episode had been inspired by this agent provocateur.

The French anarchist campaign reached a climax soon afterwards with the assassination of the French President, leading to a ruthless clampdown by the French authorities which effectively ended the terrorist campaign in France.

excerpt from:

The Secret Agent
by Joseph Conrad

Joseph Conrad took on the sordid relationship between the police, agents
provocateur, and anarchistic extremists in this dark and probing novel
about London lowlife near the turn of the century. Beginning with the
news account of Martin Bourdin, the bomber, Conrad creates an inspired
explanation for the observatory bombing. His one-hundred-year-old novel
still holds valuable lessons for understanding the mind of the contemporary terrorist and the police who hunt them. In this excerpt we meet
Verloc, a provocateur and spy hired by the French Embassy, and his boss,
the embassy first secretary Mr. Vladimir, who is seeking to get the British
government to take the threat of a violent worker's opposition more seriously. It is Vladimir who suggests that an attack on the Royal
Observatory may both perplex and terrify the Crown. Verloc is in danger
of losing his job; he is vulnerable to the secretary's designs.

What we want is to administer a tonic to the Conference in Milan," he
said, airily. "Its deliberations upon international action for the suppression of political crime don't seem to get anywhere. England lags.
This country is absurd with its sentimental regard for individual liberty. It's
intolerable to think that all your friends have got only to come over, to—"

"In that way I have them all under my eye," Mr. Verloc interrupted,
huskily.

"It would be much more to the point to have them all under lock and
key. England must be brought into line. The imbecile bourgeoisie of this
country make themselves the accomplices of the very people whose aim is
to drive them out of their houses to starve in ditches. And they have the

political power still, if they only had the sense to use it for their preserva-
tion. I suppose you agree that the middle classes are stupid?"

Mr. Verloc agreed hoarsely.

"They are."

"They have no imagination. They are blinded by an idiotic vanity.
What they want just now is a jolly good scare. This is the psychological
moment to set your friends to work. I have had you called here to develop
to you my idea."

And Mr. Vladimir developed his idea from on high, with scorn and con-
descension, displaying at the same time an amount of ignorance as to the real
aims, thoughts, and methods of the revolutionary world which filled the
silent Mr. Verloc with inward consternation. He confounded causes with
effects more than was excusable; the most distinguished propagandists with
impulsive bomb throwers; assumed organization where in the nature of
things it could not exist; spoke of the social revolutionary party one moment
as of a perfectly disciplined army, where the word of chiefs was supreme, and
at another as if it had been the loosest association of desperate brigands that
ever camped in a mountain gorge. Once Mr. Verloc had opened his mouth
for a protest, but the raising of a shapely, large white hand arrested him. Very
soon he became too appalled to even try to protest. He listened in a stillness
of dread which resembled the immobility of profound attention.

"A series of outrages," Mr. Vladimir continued, calmly, "executed here
in this country; not only *planned* here—that would not do—they would
not mind. Your friends could set half the Continent on fire without influencing the public opinion here in favour of a universal repressive legisla-
tion. They will not look outside their backyard here."

Mr. Verloc cleared his throat, but his heart failed him, and he said
nothing.

"These outrages need not be especially sanguinary," Mr. Vladimir went
on, as if delivering a scientific lecture, "but they must be sufficiently
startling—effective. Let them be directed against buildings, for instance.

What is the fetish of the hour that all the bourgeoisie recognize—eh, Mr. Verloc?"

Mr. Verloc opened his hands and shrugged his shoulders slightly.

"You are too lazy to think," was Mr. Vladimir's comment upon that gesture. "Pay attention to what I say. The fetish of to-day is neither royalty nor religion. Therefore the palace and the church should be left alone. You understand what I mean, Mr. Verloc?"

The dismay and the scorn of Mr. Verloc found vent in an attempt at levity.

"Perfectly. But what of the Embassies? A series of attacks on the various Embassies," he began; but he could not withstand the cold, watchful stare of the First Secretary.

"You can be facetious, I see," the latter observed, carelessly. "That's all right. It may enliven your oratory at socialistic congresses. But this room is no place for it. It would be infinitely safer for you to follow carefully what I am saying. As you are being called upon to furnish facts instead of cock-and-bull stories, you had better try to make your profit of what I am taking the trouble to explain to you. The sacrosanct fetish of to-day is science. Why don't you get some of your friends to go for that wooden-faced panjandrum—eh? Is it not part of these institutions which must be swept away before the F. P. comes along?"

Mr. Verloc said nothing. He was afraid to open his lips lest a groan should escape him.

"This is what you should try for. An attempt upon a crowned head or on a president is sensational enough in a way, but not so much as it used to be. It has entered into the general conception of the existence of all chiefs of state. It's almost conventional—especially since so many presidents have been assassinated. Now let us take an outrage upon—say a church. Horrible enough at first sight, no doubt, and yet not so effective as a person of an ordinary mind might think. No matter how revolutionary and anarchist in inception, there would be fools enough to give such an outrage the character of a religious manifestation. And that would detract from the especial alarming significance we wish to give to the act. A murderous attempt on a restaurant or a theatre would suffer in the same way from the suggestion of non-political passion; the exasperation of a hungry man, an act of social revenge. All this is used up; it is no longer instructive as an object lesson in revolutionary anarchism. Every newspaper has ready-made phrases to explain such manifestations away. I am about to give you the philosophy of bomb throwing from my point of view; from the point of view you pretend to have been serving for the last eleven years. I will try not to talk above your head. The sensibilities of the class you are attacking are soon blunted. Property seems to them an indestructible thing. You can't count upon their emotions either of pity or fear for very long. A bomb outrage to have any influence on public opinion now must go beyond the intention of vengeance or terrorism. It must be purely destructive. It must be that, and only that, beyond the faintest suspicion of any other object. You anarchists should make it clear that you are perfectly determined to make a clean sweep of the whole social creation. But how to get that appallingly absurd notion into the heads of the middle classes so that there should be no mistake? That's the question. By directing your blows at something outside the ordinary passions of humanity is the answer. Of course, there is art. A bomb in the National Gallery would make some noise. But it would not be serious enough. Art has never been their fetish. It's like breaking a few back windows in a man's house; whereas, if you want to make him really sit up, you must try at least to raise the roof. There would be some screaming of course, but from whom? Artists—art critics and such like—people of no account. Nobody minds what they say. But there is learning—science. Any imbecile that has got an income believes in that. He does not know why, but he believes it matters somehow. It is the sacrosanct fetish. All the damned professors are radicals at heart. Let them know that their great panjandrum has got to go, too, to make room for the Future of the Proletariat. A howl from all these intellectual idiots is bound to help forward the labours of the Milan

Conference. They will be writing to the papers. Their indignation would be above suspicion, no material interests being openly at stake, and it will alarm every selfishness of the class which should be impressed. They believe that in some mysterious way science is at the source of their material prosperity. They do. And the absurd ferocity of such a demonstration will affect them more profoundly than the mangling of a whole street—or theatre—full of their own kind. To that last they can always say: 'Oh! it's mere class hate.' But what is one to say to an act of destructive ferocity so absurd as to be incomprehensible, inexplicable, almost unthinkable; in fact, mad? Madness alone is truly terrifying, inasmuch as you cannot placate it either by threats, persuasion, or bribes. Moreover, I am a civilized man. I would never dream of directing you to organize a mere butchery, even if I expected the best results from it. But I wouldn't expect from a butchery the result I want. Murder is always with us. It is almost an institution. The demonstration must be against learning—science. But not every science will do. The attack must have all the shocking senselessness of gratuitous blasphemy. Since bombs are your means of expression, it would be really telling if one could throw a bomb into pure mathematics. But that is impossible. I have been trying to educate you; I have expounded to you the higher philosophy of your usefulness, and suggested to you some serviceable arguments. The practical application of my teaching interests *you* mostly. But from the moment I have undertaken to interview you I have also given some attention to the practical aspect of the question. What do you think of having a go at astronomy?"

For sometime already Mr. Verloc's immobility by the side of the armchair resembled a state of collapsed coma—a sort of passive insensibility interrupted by slight convulsive starts, such as may be observed in the domestic dog having a nightmare on the hearthrug. And it was in an uneasy, doglike, growl that he repeated the word:

"Astronomy."

• • •

"There could be nothing better. Such an outrage combines the greatest possible regard for humanity with the most alarming display of ferocious imbecility. I defy the ingenuity of journalists to persuade their public that any given member of the proletariat can have a personal grievance against astronomy. Starvation itself could hardly be dragged in there—eh? And there are other advantages. The whole civilized world has heard of Greenwich. The very boot-blacks in the basement of Charing Cross Station know something of it. See?"

POLITICAL TERRORISM

Political Terrorism

Political terrorism in the period from 1960 to 1987 was the responsibility mainly of the radical left. Globally, the groups were heavily influenced by anticolonial struggles in Cuba, Vietnam, and Algeria (see *The Wretched of the Earth*, page 47). In Europe and the United States, these movements began in the mid-1960s as popular revolts centering on antiwar protest and social experimentation. This move toward terrorism coincided with a different development in Palestine, where the impulse for revenge was spurred by the humiliating defeat of the Six Day War of 1967 and the desire to reclaim physical territory lost during that conflict. Along with Europe, the Middle East, and North America, activity also began in Latin America. Militants mounted an assault against authoritarian regimes, many of them military dictatorships. These groups all shared a loosely fashioned and vaguely defined socialist ideology that identified the enemy as the "imperialist power" and put forward the necessity of a vanguard party to lead the "masses."

For a brief period between 1970 and 1974, terrorist acts often took on an international cast as tactical alliances proliferated: The Libyans gave guns to the IRA; a Nicaraguan partnered with Palestinian Leila Khaled in the failed hijacking of an El Al aircraft; the German Baader-Meinhof group trained briefly in Palestine; Carlos the Jackal and his German comrades kidnapped the OPEC ministers and flew them to Algeria; Japanese militants gunned down tourists at the El Al counter in Rome. They all religiously studied the writings of a Brazilian Marxist, Carlos Marighella, who transposed Che Guevara's and Mao Tse-tung's theories of rural warfare to an urban setting (see *Minimanual of the Urban Guerilla,* page 57).

The three social factors that contributed most to the rapid growth of terrorism in this period were: (1) The increased availability and growing lethality of arms such as automatic weapons and the presence of products with broad applications including aviation equipment, computers, and cell phones. (2) The spread of mass communication, which increased the impact of terrorist attacks by almost instantaneous worldwide broadcast. The kind of simplistic message created by terrorists was ideally suited for the small screen, which works best when communicating emotional content. (3) A decline in the importance of ideology and intellectual debate in all societal circles in favor of the simplistic sloganeering and cynical techniques of manipulation that terrorists had learned to master.

Terrorist groups were hierarchically organized with a rigid command structure and strict division of labor. Typically in a terrorist organization there was a separation between the above-ground political wing, or front, and the terrorist cells themselves. The groups had slightly different agendas, though within the group the terrorists were usually viewed as the most committed and the most heroic of the members. As these movements expanded, the demands of planning and completing attacks often eclipsed the original purpose and platform. For the political militant, terrorism was a tactic that became a strategy, a strategy that became a reason for being. It moved from being a tool to a method to a way of life without gaining in lucidity, coherence, or depth. These groups eventually collapsed under the weight of their own inadequacy, unable to accomplish the broad social task that their terrorist tactic was never meant to achieve (see *Abu Nidal,* page 184).

By 1977, with a few minor exceptions, the European and U.S. terrorist movements had lost most of their influence, not only because of this inescapable internal dynamic, but also due to legal persecution and a general lack of interest on the part of the citizenry. Groups based in Palestine continued until 1989 when the fall of the Soviet Union and of socialist ideology in general, as well as their failure to alter the Middle East peace process, led to the gradual dissolution of leftist-based terrorist groups. The formerly secular PLO, for example, had to take on trappings of Muslim fundamentalism to help it remain viable.

Indeed, with leftist terrorism, when the flame appears to burn brightest, it is often about to go out. Rather than being an early or a middle stage, terrorism has often been the concluding phase—or even the last gasp—of a popular movement. Terrorism usually arrives when broad-based parties are on the wane, and only the hard-core leadership and their militant followers remain. The Weather Underground and the Baader-Meinhof group emerged after the anti-Vietnam war movement had succeeded in encouraging the United States to withdraw from the war, and the New Left was drifting without clear direction or purpose. These groups needed a new sales pitch to get attention for a program that had been largely rendered irrelevant. Terrorism seemed to fit the bill. Rather than attempt to analyze why the Left had lost support, they falsely assumed that success would result from being more aggressive in attacking the "system."

excerpt from:

The Wretched of the Earth
by Frantz Fanon

This explosive analysis of the colonizer/colonized relationship influenced Leftists from Tokyo to Berlin to Berkeley. Frantz Fanon was an Algerian psychiatrist whose discussion of the violence inherent in the Third World and the violence it evoked was the most influential text of the anti-imperialist movement. Part of the force of Fanon's writing stemmed from the insights he gained from his experience as a doctor working with colonial patients during a period of overwhelming tension and violence. In other texts he eloquently summoned the weight of historical inevitability, attempting to unite what had seemed like isolated national struggles the Third World (the so-called underdeveloped nations) into a global movement. Fanon provided the ideological basis for German, Palestinian, Nicaraguan, and Irish terrorist groups to form an alliance, however superficial and temporary.

The violence which has ruled over the ordering of the colonial world, which has ceaselessly drummed the rhythm for the destruction of native social forms and broken up without reserve the systems of reference of the economy, the customs of dress and external life, that same violence will be claimed and taken over by the native at the moment when, deciding to embody history in his own person, he surges into the forbidden quarters. To wreck the colonial world is henceforward a mental picture of action which is very clear, very easy to understand and which may be assumed by each one of the individuals which constitute the colonized people. To break up the colonial world does not mean that after the frontiers have been abolished lines of communication will be set up between the two zones. The destruction of the colonial world is no more and no less that the abolition of one zone, its burial in the depths of the earth or its expulsion from the country.

The natives' challenge to the colonial world is not a rational confrontation of points of view. It is not a treatise on the universal, but the untidy affirmation of an original idea propounded as an absolute. The colonial world is a Manichean world. It is not enough for the settler to delimit physically, that is to say with. the help of the army and the police force, the place of the native. As if to show the totalitarian character of colonial exploitation the settler paints the native as a sort of quintessence of evil.* Native society is not simply described as a society lacking in values. It is not enough for the colonist to affirm that those values have disappeared from, or still better never existed in, the colonial world. The native is declared insensible to ethics; he represents not only the absence of values, but also the negation of values. He is, let us dare to admit, the enemy of values, and in this sense he is the absolute evil. He is the corrosive element, destroying all that comes near him; he is the deforming element, disfiguring all that has to do with beauty or morality; he is the depository of maleficent powers, the unconscious and irretrievable instrument of blind forces. Monsieur Meyer could thus state seriously in the French National Assembly that the Republic must not be prostituted by allowing the Algerian people to become part of it. All values, in fact, are irrevocably poisoned and diseased as soon as they are allowed in contact with the colonized race. The customs of the colonized people, their traditions, their myths—above all, their myths—are the very sign of that poverty of spirit and of their constitutional depravity. That is why we must put the DDT which destroys parasites, the bearers of disease, on the same level as the Christian religion which wages war on embryonic heresies

*We have demonstrated the mechanism of this Manichean world in *Black Skin, White Masks* (New York: Grove Press, 1967).

and instincts, and on evil as yet unborn. The recession of yellow fever and the advance of evangelization form part of the same balance sheet. But the triumphant *communiqués* from the missions are in fact a source of information concerning the implantation of foreign influences in the core of the colonized people. I speak of the Christian religion, and no one need be astonished. The Church in the colonies is the white people's Church, the foreigner's Church. She does not call the native to God's ways but to the ways of the white man, of the master, of the oppressor. And as we know, in this matter many are called but few chosen.

At times this Manicheism goes to its logical conclusion and dehumanizes the native, or to speak plainly, it turns him into an animal. In fact, the terms the settler uses when he mentions the native are zoological terms. He speaks of the yellow man's reptilian motions, of the stink of the native quarter, of breeding swarms, of foulness, of spawn, of gesticulations. When the settler seeks to describe the native fully in exact terms he constantly refers to the bestiary. The European rarely hits on a picturesque style; but the native, who knows what is in the mind of the settler, guesses at once what he is thinking of. Those hordes of vital statistics, those hysterical masses, those faces bereft of all humanity, those distended bodies which are like nothing on earth, that mob without beginning or end, those children who seem to belong to nobody, that laziness stretched out in the sun, that vegetative rhythm of life—all this forms part of the colonial vocabulary. General de Gaulle speaks of "the yellow multitudes" and François Mauriac of the black, brown, and yellow masses which soon will be unleashed. The native knows all this, and laughs to himself every time he spots an allusion to the animal world in the other's words. For he knows that he is not an animal; and it is precisely at the moment he realized his humanity that he begins to sharpen the weapons with which he will secure its victory.

As soon as the native begins to pull on his moorings, and to cause anxiety to the settler, he is handed over to well-meaning souls who in cultural congresses point out to him the specificity and wealth of Western values. But every time Western values are mentioned they produce in the native a sort of stiffening or muscular lockjaw. During the period of decolonization, the native's reason is appealed to. He is offered definite values, he is told frequently that decolonization need not mean regression, and that he must put his trust in qualities which are well-tried, solid, and highly esteemed. But it so happens that when the native hears a speech about Western culture he pulls out his knife—or at least he makes sure it is within reach. The violence with which the supremacy of white values is affirmed and the aggressiveness which has permeated the victory of these values over the ways of life and of thought of the native mean that, in revenge, the native laughs in mockery when Western values are mentioned in front of him. In the colonial context the settler only ends his work of breaking in the native when the latter admits loudly and intelligibly the supremacy of the white man's values. In the period of decolonization, the colonized masses mock at these very values, insult them, and vomit them up.

This phenomenon is ordinarily masked because, during the period of decolonization, certain colonized intellectuals have begun a dialogue with the bourgeoisie of the colonialist country. During this phase, the indigenous population is discerned only as an indistinct mass. The few native personalities whom the colonialist bourgeois have come to know here and there have not sufficient influence on that immediate discernment to give rise to nuances. On the other hand, during the period of liberation, the colonialist bourgeoisie looks feverishly far contacts with the elite and it is with these elite that the familiar dialogue concerning values is carried on. The colonialist bourgeoisie, when it realizes that it is impossible for it to maintain its domination over the colonial countries, decides to carry out a rearguard action with regard to culture, values, techniques, and so on. Now what we must never forget is that the immense majority of colonized peoples is oblivious to these problems. For a colonized people the most essential value, because the most concrete, is first and foremost the land:

the land which will bring them bread and, above all, dignity. But this dignity has nothing to do with the dignity of the human individual: for that human individual has never heard tell of it. All that the native has seen in his country is that they can freely arrest him, beat him, starve him: and no professor of ethics, no priest has ever come to be beaten in his place, nor to share their bread with him. As far as the native is concerned, morality is very concrete; it is to silence the settler's defiance, to break his flaunting violence—in a word, to put him out of the picture. The well-known principle that all men are equal will be illustrated in the colonies from the moment that the native claims that he is the equal of the settler. One step more, and he is ready to fight to be more than the settler. In fact, he has already decided to eject him and to take his place; as we see it, it is a whole material and moral universe which is breaking up. The intellectual who for his part has followed the colonialist with regard to the universal abstract will fight in order that the settler and the native may live together in peace in a new world. But the thing he does not see, precisely because he is permeated by colonialism and all its ways of thinking, is that the settler, from the moment that the colonial context disappears, has no longer any interest in remaining or in co-existing. It is not by chance that, even before any negotiation* between the Algerian and French governments has taken place, the European minority which calls itself "liberal" has already made its position clear: it demands nothing more nor less than twofold citizenship. By setting themselves apart in an abstract manner, the liberals try to force the settler into taking a very concrete jump into the unknown. Let us admit it, the settler knows perfectly well that no phraseology can be a substitute for reality.

Thus the native discovers that his life, his breath, his beating heart are the same as those of the settler. He finds out that the settler's skin is not of any more value than a native's skin; and it must be, said that this discovery

---

*Fanon is writing in 1961.—*Trans.*

shakes the world in a very necessary manner. All the new, revolutionary assurance of the native stems from it. For if, in fact, my life is worth as much as the settler's, his glance no longer shrivels me up nor freezes me, and his voice no longer turns me into stone. I am no longer on tenterhooks in his presence; in fact, I don't give a damn for him. Not only does his presence no longer trouble me, but I am already preparing such efficient ambushes for him that soon there will be no way out but that of flight.

But let us return to that atmosphere of violence, that violence which is just under the skin. We have seen that in its process toward maturity many leads are attached to it, to control it and show it the way out. Yet in spite of the metamorphoses which the colonial regime imposes upon it in the way of tribal or regional quarrels, that violence makes its way forward, and the native identifies his enemy and recognizes all his misfortunes, throwing all the exacerbated might of his hate and anger into this new channel. But how do we pass from the atmosphere of violence to violence in action? What makes the lid blow off? There is first of all the fact that this development does not leave the settler's blissful existence intact. The settler who "understands" the natives is made aware by several straws in the wind showing that something is afoot. "Good" natives become scarce; silence falls when the oppressor approaches; sometimes looks are black, and attitudes and remarks openly aggressive. The nationalist parties are astir, they hold a great many meetings, the police are increased and reinforcements of soldiers are brought in. The settlers, above all the farmers isolated on their land, are the first to become alarmed. They call for energetic measures.

The authorities do in fact take some spectacular measures. They arrest one or two leaders, they organize military parades and maneuvers, and air force displays. But the demonstrations and warlike exercises, the smell of gunpowder which now fills the atmosphere, these things do not make the people draw back. Those bayonets and cannonades only serve to reinforce their aggressiveness. The atmosphere becomes dramatic, and everyone wishes to show that he is ready for anything. And it is in these circumstances that the guns go off by themselves, for nerves are jangled, fear reigns and everyone is trigger-happy. A single commonplace incident is enough to start the machine-gunning: Sétif in Algeria, the Central Quarries in Morocco, Moramanga in Madagascar.

The repressions, far from calling a halt to the forward rush of national consciousness, urge it on. Mass slaughter in the colonies at a certain stage of the embryonic development of consciousness increases that consciousness, for the hecatombs are an indication that between oppressors and oppressed everything can be solved by force. It must be remarked here that the political parties have not called for armed insurrection, and have made no preparations for such an insurrection. All these repressive measures, all those actions which are a result of fear are not within the leaders' intentions: they are overtaken by events. At this moment, then, colonialism may decide to arrest the nationalist leaders. But today the governments of colonized countries know very well that it is extremely dangerous to deprive the masses of their leaders; for then the people, unbridled, fling themselves into *jacqueries*, mutinies, and "brutish murders." The masses give free rein to their "bloodthirsty instincts" and force colonialism to free their leaders, to whom falls the difficult task of bringing them back to order. The colonized people, who have spontaneously brought their violence to the colossal task of destroying the colonial system, will very soon find themselves with the barren, inert slogan "Release X or Y."* Then colonialism will release these men, and hold discussions with them. The time for dancing in the streets has come.

* It may happen that the arrested leader is in fact the authentic mouthpiece of the colonized masses. In this case colonialism will make use of his period of detention to try to launch new leaders.

In certain circumstances, the party political machine may remain intact. But as a result of the colonialist repression and of the spontaneous reaction of the people the parties find themselves out-distanced by their militants. The violence of the masses is vigorously pitted against the military forces of the occupying power, and the situation deteriorates and comes to a head. Those leaders who are free remain, therefore, on the touchline. They have suddenly become useless, with their bureaucracy and their reasonable demands; yet we see them, far removed from events, attempting the crowning imposture—that of "speaking in the name of the silenced nation." As a general rule, colonialism welcomes this godsend with open arms, tranforms these "blind mouths" into spokesmen, and in two minutes endows them with independence, on condition that they restore order.

So we see that all parties are aware of the power of such violence and that the question is not always to reply to it by a greater violence, but rather to see how to relax the tension.

What is the real nature of this violence? We have seen that it is the intuition of the colonized masses that their liberation must, and can only, be achieved by force. By what spiritual aberration do these men, without technique, starving and enfeebled, confronted with the military and economic might of the occupation, come to believe that violence alone will free them? How can they hope to triumph?

It is because violence (and this is the disgraceful thing) may constitute, in so far as it forms part of its system, the slogan of a political party. The leaders may call on the people to enter upon an armed struggle. This problematical question has to be thought over. When militarist Germany decides to settle its frontier disputes by force, we are not in the least surprised; but when the people of Angola, for example, decide to take up arms, when the Algerian people reject all means which are not violent, these are proofs that something has happened or is happening at this very moment. The colonized races, those slaves of modern times, are impatient. They know that this apparent folly alone can put them out of reach of colonial oppression. A new type of relations is established in the world. The underdeveloped peoples try to break their chains, and the extraordinary thing is that they succeed. It could be argued that in these days of sputniks it is ridiculous to die of hunger; but for the colonized masses the argument is more down-to-earth. The truth is that there is no colonial power today which is capable of adopting the only form of contest which has a chance of succeeding, namely, the prolonged establishment of large forces of occupation.

We have said that the native's violence unifies the people. By its very structure, colonialism is separatist and regionalist. Colonialism does not simply state the existence of tribes; it also reinforces it and separates them. The colonial system encourages chieftaincies and keeps alive the old Marabout confraternities. Violence is in action all inclusive and national. It follows that it is closely involved in the liquidation of regionalism and of tribalism. Thus the national parties show no pity at all toward the raids and the customary chiefs. Their destruction is the preliminary to the unification of the people.

At the level of individuals, violence is a cleansing force. It frees the native from his inferiority complex and from his despair and inaction; it makes him fearless and restores his self-respect. Even if the armed struggle has been symbolic and the nation is demobilized through a rapid movement of decolonization, the people have the time to see that the liberation has been the business of each and all and that the leader has no special merit. From thence comes that type of aggressive reticence with regard to the machinery of protocol which young governments quickly show. When the people have taken violent part in the national liberation they will allow no one to set themselves up as "liberators." They show themselves to be jealous of the results of their action and take good care not to place their future, their destiny, or the fate of their country in the hands of a living god. Yesterday they were completely irresponsible; today they mean to understand everything and make all decisions. Illuminated by violence, the consciousness of the people rebels against any pacification. From now on the demagogues, the opportunists, and the magicians have a difficult task. The action which has thrown them into a hand-to-hand struggle confers upon the masses a voracious taste for the concrete. The attempt at mystification becomes, in the long run, practically impossible.

excerpt from:

Minimanual of the Urban Guerilla
by Carlos Marighella

Carlos Marighella, a Brazilian Marxist, based his how-to manual on
Guerilla Warfare written by Che Guevara, who had learned from his
own experience in the Cuban countryside. Realizing that the developing
Latin American countries were increasingly more urban, and that a revolution could be fought there, he created a concise guidebook that was
widely read and used by radicals in Europe and became the subject of
intense debate among Leftists in the United States at the time of the
rise of the Weather Underground.

A Definition of the Urban Guerrilla

The chronic structural crisis characteristic of Brazil today, and its
resultant political instability, are what have brought about the upsurge of
revolutionary war in the country. The revolutionary war manifests itself
in the form of urban guerrilla warfare, psychological warfare, or rural
guerrilla warfare. Urban guerrilla warfare or psychological warfare in the
city depends on the urban guerrilla.

The urban guerrilla is a man who fights the military dictatorship with
arms, using unconventional methods. A political revolutionary and an
ardent patriot, he is a fighter for his country's liberation, a friend of the
people and of freedom. The area in which the urban guerrilla acts is in the
large Brazilian cities. There are also bandits, commonly known as outlaws,
who work in the big cities. Many times assaults by outlaws are taken as
actions by urban guerrillas.

The urban guerrilla, however, differs radically from the outlaw. The outlaw benefits personally from the action, and attacks indiscriminately without distinguishing between the exploited and the exploiters, which is why there are so many ordinary men and women among his victims. The urban guerrilla follows a political goal and only attacks the government, the big capitalists, and the foreign imperialists, particularly North Americans.

Another element just as prejudicial as the outlaw and also operating in the urban area is the right-wing counterrevolutionary who creates confusion, assaults banks, hurls bombs, kidnaps, assassinates, and commits the worst imaginable crimes against urban guerrillas, revolutionary priests, students, and citizens who oppose fascism and seek liberty.

The urban guerrilla is an implacable enemy of the government and systematically inflicts damage on the authorities and on the men who dominate the country and exercise power. The principal task of the urban guerrilla is to distract, to wear out, to demoralize the militarists, the military dictatorship and its repressive forces, and also to attack and destroy the wealth and property of the North Americans, the foreign managers, and the Brazilian upper class.

The urban guerrilla is not afraid of dismantling and destroying the present Brazilian economic, political, and social system, for his aim is to help the rural guerrilla and to collaborate in the creation of a totally new and revolutionary social and political structure, with the armed people in power.

The urban guerrilla must have a certain minimal political understanding. To gain that he must read certain printed or mimeographed works such as:

> *Guerrilla Warfare* by Ché Guevara
> *Memories of a Terrorist*
> *Some Questions about the Brazilian Guerrilla Operations and Tactics*
> *On Strategic Problems and Principles*

Political Terrorism

Certain Tactical Principles for Comrades Undertaking Guer-
rilla Operations
Organizational Questions
O Guerrilheiro, newspaper of the Brazilian revolutionary groups.

Personal Qualities of the Urban Guerrilla

The urban guerrilla is characterized by his bravery and decisive nature. He must be a good tactician and a good shot. The urban guerrilla must be a person of great astuteness to compensate for the fact that he is not suffi-ciently strong in arms, ammunition, and equipment.

The career militarists or the government police have modern arms and transport, and can go about anywhere freely, using the force of their power. The urban guerrilla does not have such resources at his disposal and leans to a clandestine existence. Sometimes he is a convicted person or is out on parole, and is obliged to use false documents.

Nevertheless, the urban guerrilla has a certain advantage over the con-ventional military or the police. It is that, while the military and the police act on behalf of the enemy, whom the people hate, the urban guerrilla defends a just cause, which is the people's cause.

The urban guerrilla's arms are inferior to the enemy's, but from a moral point of view, the urban guerrilla has an undeniable superiority.

This moral superiority is what sustains the urban guerrilla. Thanks to it, the urban guerrilla can accomplish his principal duty, which is to attack and to survive.

The urban guerrilla has to capture or divert arms from the enemy to be able to fight. Because his arms are not uniform, since what he has are expropriated or have fallen into his hands in different ways, the urban guerrilla faces the problem of a variety of arms and a shortage of ammu-nition. Moreover, he has no place to practice shooting and marksmanship.

These difficulties have to be surmounted, forcing the urban guerrilla to be imaginative and creative, qualities without which it would be impossible for him to carry out his role as a revolutionary.

The urban guerrilla must possess initiative, mobility, and flexibility, as well as versatility and a command of any situation. Initiative especially is an indispensable quality. It is not always possible to foresee everything, and the urban guerrilla cannot let himself become confused, or wait for orders. His duty is to act, to find adequate solutions for each problem he faces, and not to retreat. It is better to err acting than to do nothing for fear of erring. Without initiative there is no urban guerrilla warfare.

Other important qualities in the urban guerrilla are the following: to be a good walker, to be able to stand up against fatigue, hunger, rain, heat. To know how to hide and to be vigilant. To conquer the art of dissembling. Never to fear danger. To behave the same by day as by night. Not to act impetuously. To have unlimited patience. To remain calm and cool in the worst conditions and situations. Never to leave a track or trail. Not to get discouraged.

In the face of the almost insurmountable difficulties of urban warfare, sometimes comrades weaken, leave, give up the work.

The urban guerrilla is not a businessman in a commercial firm nor is he a character in a play. Urban guerrilla warfare, like rural guerrilla warfare, is a pledge the guerrilla makes to himself. When he cannot face the difficulties, or knows that he lacks the patience to wait, then it is better to relinquish his role before he betrays his pledge, for he clearly lacks the basic qualities necessary to be a guerrilla.

The Urban Guerrilla's Arms

The urban guerrilla's arms are light arms, easily exchanged, usually captured from the enemy, purchased, or made on the spot.

Light arms have the advantage of fast handling and easy transport. In general, light arms are characterized as short barrelled. This includes many automatic arms.

Automatic and semiautomatic arms considerably increase the fighting power of the urban guerrilla. The disadvantage of this type of arm for us is the difficulty in controlling it, resulting in wasted rounds or in a prodigious use of ammunition, compensated for only by optimal aim and firing precision. Men who are poorly trained convert automatic weapons into an ammunition drain.

Experience has shown that the basic arm of the urban guerrilla is the light machine gun. This arm, in addition to being efficient and easy to shoot in an urban area, has the advantage of being greatly respected by the enemy. The guerrilla must know thoroughly how to handle the machine gun, now so popular and indispensable to the Brazilian urban guerrilla.

The ideal machine gun for the urban guerrilla is the Ina 45 calibre. Other types of machine guns of different calibres can be used—understanding, of course, the problem of ammunition. Thus it is preferable that the industrial potential of the urban guerrilla permit the production of a single machine gun so that the ammunition used can be standardized.

Each firing group of urban guerrillas must have a machine gun managed by a good marksman. The other components of the group must be armed with .38 revolvers, our standard arm. The .32 is also useful for those who want to participate. But the .38 is preferable since its impact usually puts the enemy out of action.

Hand grenades and conventional smoke bombs can be considered light arms, the defensive power for cover and withdrawal.

Long barrel arms are more difficult for the urban guerrilla to transport and attract much attention because of their size. Among the long barrel arms are the FAL, the Mauser guns or rifles, hunting guns such as the Winchester, and others.

Shotguns can be useful if used at close range and point blank. They are useful even for a poor shot, especially at night when precision isn't much help. A pressure air gun can be useful for training in marksmanship. Bazookas and mortars can also be used in action but the conditions for using them have to be prepared and the people who use them must be trained.

The urban guerrilla should not try to base his actions on the use of heavy arms, which have major drawbacks in a type of fighting that demands lightweight weapons to insure mobility and speed.

Homemade weapons are often as efficient as the best arms produced in conventional factories, and even a cut-off shotgun is a good arm for the urban guerrilla.

The urban guerrilla's role as gunsmith has a fundamental importance. As a gunsmith he takes care of the arms, knows how to repair them, and in many cases can set up a small shop for improvising and producing efficient small arms.

Work in metallurgy and on the mechanical lathe are basic skills the urban guerrilla should incorporate into his industrial planning, which is the construction of homemade weapons.

This construction and courses in explosives and sabotage must be organized. The primary materials for practice in these courses must be obtained ahead of time to prevent an incomplete apprenticeship—that is to say, so as to leave no room for experimentation.

Molotov cocktails, gasoline, homemade contrivances such as catapults and mortars for firing explosives, grenades made of tubes and cans, smoke bombs, mines, conventional explosives such as dynamite and potassium chloride, plastic explosives, gelatine capsules, ammunition of every kind are indispensable to the success of the urban guerrilla's mission.

The method of obtaining the necessary materials and munitions will be to buy them or to take them by force in expropriation actions especially planned and carried out.

The urban guerrilla will be careful not to keep explosives and materials that can cause accidents around for very long, but will try always to use them immediately on their destined targets.

The urban guerrilla's arms and his ability to maintain them constitute his fire power. By taking advantage of modern arms and introducing innovations in his fire power and in the use of certain arms, the urban guerrilla can change many of the tactics of city warfare. An example of this was the innovation made by the urban guerrillas in Brazil when they introduced the machine gun in their attacks on banks.

When the massive use of uniform machine guns becomes possible, there will be new changes in urban guerrilla warfare tactics. The firing group that utilizes uniform weapons and corresponding ammunition, with reasonable support for their maintenance, will reach a considerable level of efficiency. The urban guerrilla increases his efficiency as he improves his firing potential.

Characteristics of the Urban Guerrilla's Technique

The technique of the urban guerrilla has the following characteristics:

(a) it is an aggressive technique, or in other words, it has an offensive character. As is well known, defensive action means death for us. Since we are inferior to the enemy in fire power and have neither his resources nor his power force, we cannot defend ourselves against an offensive or a concentrated attack by the gorillas. And that is the reason why our urban technique can never be permanent, can never defend a fixed base nor remain in any one spot waiting to repel the circle of reaction;

(b) it is a technique of attack and retreat by which we preserve our forces;

(c) it is a technique that aims at the development of urban guerrilla warfare, whose function will be to wear out, demoralize, and distract the enemy forces, permitting the emergence and survival of rural guerrilla warfare which is destined to play the decisive role in the revolutionary war.

On the Types and Nature of Action Models for the Urban Guerrilla

In order to achieve the objectives previously enumerated, the urban guerrilla is obliged, in his technique, to follow an action whose nature is as different and as diversified as possible. The urban guerrilla does not arbitrarily choose this or that action model. Some actions are simple, others are complicated. The urban guerrilla without experience must be incorporated gradually into actions and operations that run from the simple to the complex. He begins with small missions and tasks until he becomes a completely experienced urban guerrilla.

Before any action, the urban guerrilla must think of the methods and the personnel at his disposal to carry out the action. Operations and actions that demand the urban guerrilla's technical preparation cannot be carried out by someone who lacks that technical skill. With these cautions, the action models which the urban guerrilla can carry out are the following:

(a) assaults;

(b) raids and penetrations;

(c) occupations;

(d) ambush;

(e) street tactics;

(f) strikes and work interruptions;

(g) desertions, diversions, seizures, expropriations of arms, ammunition, explosives;

(h) liberation of prisoners;

(i) executions;

(j) kidnappings;

(k) sabotage;

(l) terrorism;

(m) armed propaganda;

(n) war of nerves.

Assaults

Assault is the armed attack which we make to expropriate funds, liberate prisoners, capture explosives, machine guns, and other types of arms and ammunition.

Assaults can take place in broad daylight or at night.

Daytime assaults are made when the objective cannot be achieved at any other hour, as for example, the transport of money by the banks, which is not done at night.

Night assault is usually the most advantageous to the urban guerrilla. The ideal is for all assaults to take place at night when conditions for a surprise attack are most favorable and the darkness facilitates flight and hides the identity of the participants. The urban guerrilla must prepare himself, nevertheless, to act under all conditions, daytime as well as nighttime.

The most vulnerable targets for assault are the following:

(a) credit establishments;

(b) commercial and industrial enterprises, including the production of arms and explosives;

(c) military establishments;

(d) commissaries and police stations;

(e) jails;

(f) government property;

(g) mass communication media;

(h) North American firms and properties;

(i) government vehicles, including military and police vehicles, trucks, armored vehicles, money carriers, trains, ships, and planes.

The assaults on establishments are of the same nature because in every case the property and buildings represent a fixed target.

Assaults on buildings are conceived as guerrilla operations, varied according to whether they are against banks, a commercial enterprise, industries, military camps, commissaries, prisons, radio stations, warehouses for imperialist firms, etc.

The assaults on vehicles—money-carriers, armored cars, trains, ships, airplanes—are of another nature since they are moving targets. The nature of the operations varies according to the situation and the possibility—that is, whether the target is stationary or moving.

Armored cars, including military cars, are not immune to mines. Obstructed roads, traps, ruses, interception of other vehicles, Molotov cocktails, shooting with heavy arms, are efficient methods of assaulting vehicles.

Heavy vehicles, grounded planes, anchored ships can be seized and their crews and guards overcome. Airplanes in flight can be diverted from their course by guerrilla action or by one person.

Ships and trains in movement can be assaulted or taken by guerrilla operations in order to capture the arms and munitions or to prevent troop deployment.

The Bank Assault as a Popular Model

The most popular assault model is the bank assault. In Brazil, the urban guerrilla has begun a type of organized assault on the banks as a guerrilla operation. Today this type of assault is widely used and has served as a sort of preliminary examination for the urban guerrilla in his apprenticeship for the techniques of revolutionary warfare.

Important innovations in the technique of assaulting banks have developed, guaranteeing flight, the withdrawal of money, and the anonymity of those involved. Among these innovations we cite shooting the tires of cars to prevent pursuit; locking people in the bank bathroom, making them sit on the floor; immobilizing the bank guards and removing their arms, forcing someone to open the coffer or the strong box; using disguises.

Attempts to install bank alarms, to use guards or electronic detection devices of U.S. origin, prove fruitless when the assault is political and is carried out according to urban guerrilla warfare technique. This technique tries to utilize new resources to meet the enemy's tactical changes, has access to a fire power that is growing every day, becomes increasingly astute and audacious, and uses a larger number of revolutionaries every time; all to guarantee the success of operations planned down to the last detail.

The bank assault is a typical expropriation. But, as is true in any kind of armed expropriatory action, the revolutionary is handicapped by a two-fold competition:

(a) competition from the outlaw;

(b) competition from the right-wing counterrevolutionary.

This competition produces confusion, which is reflected in the people's uncertainty. It is up to the urban guerrilla to prevent this from happening, and to accomplish this he must use two methods:

(a) he must avoid the outlaw's technique, which is one of unnecessary violence and appropriation of goods and possessions belonging to the people;

(b) he must use the assault for propaganda purposes, at the very moment it is taking place, and later distribute material, leaflets, every possible means of explaining the objectives and the principles of the urban guerrilla as expropriator of the government, the ruling classes, and imperialism.

Raids and Penetration

Raids and penetrations are quick attacks on establishments located in neighborhoods or even in the center of the city, such as small military units, commissaries, hospitals, to cause trouble, seize arms, punish and terrorize the enemy, take reprisal, or rescue wounded prisoners, or those hospitalized under police vigilance.

Raids and penetrations are also made on garages and depots to destroy vehicles and damage installations, especially if they are North American firms and property.

When they take place on certain stretches of the highway or in certain distant neighborhoods, the raids can serve to force the enemy to move great numbers of troops, a totally useless effort since he will find nobody there to fight.

When they are carried out in certain houses, offices, archives, or public offices, their purpose is to capture or search for secret papers and documents with which to denounce involvements, compromises, and the corruption of men in government, their dirty deals and criminal transactions with the North Americans.

Raids and penetrations are most effective if they are carried out at night.

Occupations

Occupations are a type of attack carried out when the urban guerrilla stations himself in specific establishments and locations for a temporary resistance against the enemy or for some propaganda purpose.

The occupation of factories and schools during strikes or at other times is a method of protest or of distracting the enemy's attention.

The occupation of radio stations is for propaganda purposes.

Occupation is a highly effective model for action but, in order to prevent losses and material damage to our ranks, it is always a good idea to count on the possibility of withdrawal. It must always be meticulously planned and carried out at the opportune moment.

Occupation always has a time limit and the faster it is completed the better.

• • •

Street Tactics

Street tactics are used to fight the enemy in the streets, utilizing the participation of the masses against him.

In 1968 the Brazilian students used excellent street tactics against police troops, such as marching down streets against traffic, utilizing slings and marbles as arms against the mounted police.

Other street tactics consist in constructing barricades; pulling up paving blocks and hurling them at the police; throwing bottles, bricks, paper-weights, and other projectiles from the tops of apartment and office buildings against the police; using buildings under construction for flight, for hiding, and for supporting surprise attacks.

It is equally necessary to know how to respond to enemy tactics. When the police troops come protected with helmets to defend themselves against flying objects, we have to divide ourselves into two teams: one to attack the enemy from the front, the other to attack him in the rear, withdrawing one as the other goes into action to prevent the first from becoming a target for projectiles hurled by the second.

By the same token it is important to know how to respond to the police net. When the police designate certain of their men to go into the masses to arrest a demonstrator, a larger group of urban guerrillas must surround the police group, disarming and beating them and at the same time letting the prisoner escape. This urban guerrilla operation is called the *net within the net*.

When the police net is formed at a school building, a factory, a place where the masses assemble, or some other point, the urban guerrilla must not give up or allow himself to be taken by surprise. To make his net work the enemy is obliged to transport the police in vehicles and special cars to occupy strategic points in the streets in order to invade the building or chosen locale. The urban guerrilla for his part, must never clear a building or an area and meet in it without first knowing its exits, the way to break the circle, the strategic points that the police might occupy, and the roads that inevitably lead into the net, and he must hold other strategic points from which to strike at the enemy.

The roads followed by the police vehicles must be mined at key points along the way and at forced stopping points. When the mines explode, the vehicles will fly into the air. The police will be caught in the trap and will suffer losses or will be victims of ambush. The net must be broken by escape routes unknown to the police. The rigorous planning of the retreat is the best way of frustrating any encircling effort on the part of the enemy.

When there is no possibility of a flight plan, the urban guerrilla must not hold meetings, assemblies, or do anything else since to do so will prevent him from breaking through the net the enemy will surely try to throw around him.

Street tactics have revealed a new type of urban guerrilla, the urban guerrilla who participates in mass demonstrations. This is the type we designate as the urban guerrilla demonstrator, who joins the ranks and participates in popular marches with specific and definite aims.

These aims consist in hurling stones and projectiles of every type, using gasoline to start fires, using the police as a target for their fire arms, capturing police arms, kidnapping agents of the enemy and provocateurs, shooting with careful aim at the henchmen torturers and the police chiefs who come in special cars with false plates in order not to attract attention.

The urban guerrilla demonstrator shows groups in the mass demonstration the flight route if that is necessary. He plants mines, throws Molotov cocktails, prepares ambushes and explosions.

The urban guerrilla demonstrator must also initiate the net within the net, going through government vehicles, official cars, and police vehicles before turning them over or setting them on fire, to see if any of them have money and arms.

Snipers are very good for mass demonstrations and, along with the urban guerrilla demonstrators, can play a valuable role.

Hidden at strategic points, the snipers have complete success, using shotguns, machine guns, etc. whose fire and ricocheting easily cause losses among the enemy.

Execution

Execution is the killing of a North American spy, of an agent of the dictatorship, of a police torturer, of a fascist personality in the government involved in crimes and persecutions against patriots, of a stool pigeon, informer, police agent, or police provocateur.

Those who go to the police of their own free will to make denunciations and accusations, who supply clues and information and finger people, must also be executed when they are caught by the urban guerrilla.

Execution is a secret action in which the least possible number of urban guerrillas are involved. In many cases, the execution can be carried out by one sniper, patiently, alone and unknown, and operating in absolute secrecy and in cold blood.

Kidnapping

Kidnapping is capturing and holding in a secret spot a police agent, a North American spy, a political personality, or a notorious and dangerous enemy of the revolutionary movement.

Kidnapping is used to exchange or liberate imprisoned revolutionary comrades, or to force suspension of torture in the jail cells of the military dictatorship.

The kidnapping of personalities who are known artists, sports figures, or are outstanding in some other field, but who have evidenced no political interest, can be useful form of propaganda for the revolutionary and patriotic principles of the urban guerrilla provided it occurs under special circumstances, and the kidnapping is handled so that the public sympathizes with it and accepts it.

The kidnapping of North American residents or visitors in Brazil constitutes a form of protest against the penetration and domination of United States imperialism in our country.

Sabotage

Sabotage is a highly destructive type of attack using very few persons and sometimes requiring only one to accomplish the desired result. When the urban guerrilla uses sabotage the first phase is isolated sabotage. Then comes the phase of dispersed and generalized sabotage, carried out by the people.

Well-executed sabotage demands study, planning, and careful execution. A characteristic form of sabotage is explosion using dynamite, fire, and the placing of mines.

A little sand, a trickle of any kind of combustible, a poor lubrication, a screw removed, a short circuit, pieces of wood or of iron, can cause irreparable damage.

The objective of sabotage is to hurt, to damage, to make useless, and to destroy vital enemy points such as the following:

(a) the economy of the country;

(b) agricultural or industrial production;

(c) transport and communication systems;

(d) the military and police systems and their establishments and deposits;

(e) the repressive military-police system;

(f) the firms and properties of North Americans in the country.

The urban guerrilla should endanger the economy of the country, particularly its economic and financial aspects, such as its domestic and foreign commercial network, its exchange and banking systems, its tax collection systems, and others.

Public offices, centers of government services, government warehouses, are easy targets for sabotage.

Nor will it be easy to prevent the sabotage of agricultural and industrial production by the urban guerrilla, with his thorough knowledge of the local situation.

Industrial workers acting as urban guerrillas are excellent industrial saboteurs since they, better than anyone, understand the industry, the factory, the machine, or the part most likely to destroy an entire operation, doing far more damage than a poorly informed layman could do.

With respect to the enemy's transport and communications systems, beginning with railway traffic, it is necessary to attack them systematically with sabotage arms.

The only caution is against causing death and fatal injury to passengers, especially regular commuters on suburban and long-distance trains.

Attacks on freight trains, rolling or stationary stock, stoppage of military transport and communication systems, these are the major sabotage objectives in this area.

Sleepers can be damaged and pulled up, as can rails. A tunnel blocked by a barrier after an explosion, an obstruction by a derailed car, cause tremendous harm.

The derailment of a cargo train carrying fuel is of major damage to the enemy. So is dynamiting railway bridges. In a system where the weight and the size of the rolling equipment is enormous, it takes months for workers to repair or rebuild the destruction and damage.

As for highways they can be obstructed by trees, stationary vehicles, ditches, dislocation of barriers by dynamite, and bridges blown up by explosion.

Ships can be damaged at anchor in seaports and river ports or in the shipyards. Airplanes can be destroyed or sabotaged on the ground.

Telephonic and telegraphic lines can be systematically damaged, their towers blown up, and their lines made useless.

Transport and communications must be sabotaged at once because the revolutionary war has already begun in Brazil and it is essential to impede the enemy's movement of troops and munitions.

Oil lines, fuel plants, depots for bombs and ammunition, powder magazines and arsenals, military camps, commissaries must become targets par excellence in sabotage operations, while vehicles, army trucks, and other military and police cars must be destroyed wherever they are found.

The military and police repression centers and their specific and specialized organs, must also claim the attention of the urban guerrilla saboteur.

North American firms and properties in the country, for their part, must become such frequent targets of sabotage that the volume of actions directed against them surpasses the total of all other actions against vital enemy points.

Terrorism

Terrorism is an action, usually involving the placement of a bomb or fire explosion of great destructive power, which is capable of effecting irreparable loss against the enemy.

Terrorism requires that the urban guerrilla should have an adequate theoretical and practical knowledge of how to make explosives.

The terroristic act, apart from the apparent facility with which it can be carried out, is no different from the other urban guerrilla acts and actions whose success depends on the planning and determination of the revolutionary organization. It is an action the urban guerrilla must execute with the greatest cold bloodedness, calmness, and decision.

Although terrorism generally involves an explosion, there are cases in which it may also be carried out by execution and the systematic burning of installations, properties, and North American depots, plantations, etc. It is essential to point out the importance of fires and the construction of incendiary bombs such as gasoline bombs in the technique of revolutionary terrorism. Another thing is the importance of the material the urban guerrilla can persuade the people to expropriate in moments of hunger and scarcity resulting from the greed of the big commercial interest.

Terrorism is an arm the revolutionary can never relinquish.

excerpt from:

On Terrorism and the State
by Gianfranco Sanguinetti

Gianfranco Sanguinetti was a member of the Situationist International,
a European-based group that spent as much time criticizing the Left as
it did attacking capitalism. Sanguinetti provides a theoretical context in
which to examine the maneuvers of the Italian State as it infiltrated
Leftist groups and drove the population back into the arms of the government by carrying out terrorist attacks in the name of radicalism. Dozens of
books and articles have been published linking the CIA, particularly Naval
Intelligence, to this policy, known as the "strategy of tension." Journalists
such as Phillip Willan (in his book *Puppetmasters*) have posited that right-
wing paramilitary groups hired by the Italian government were responsible
for all of these bombings. Sanguinetti's perspective allows us to see how
the threat of terrorism works to make both the government and the citizenry more conservative, discouraging critical thinking and dissent. The
events he refers to are: Piazza Fontana (a bombing that killed 16 at the
Banca della Agricoltura in Milan), Brescia (a bombing in Piazza della Loggia
that killed 8 and wounded 103) and Italicus (an attack on the Rome-
Munich train that killed 12). These events changed the Italian political landscape, taking the momentum out of a growing movement. Also mentioned
are: Pinelli, (An anarchist accused of the Piazza Fontana bombing and subsequently killed by the Italian police. His purported suicide was presented
as proof of his guilt. However, he had already been murdered when his
body was dumped out of an upper-story window), and Valpreda (arrested
at the same time as Pinelli and released three years later without ever
being charged.) Aldo Moro was the former prime minister of Italy kidnapped in 1978 and then killed many months later. His body was found in a
car trunk in Rome. Moro's murder, originally attributed to the Red Brigade,
was also linked to government surrogates by Sanguinetti and others.

All acts of terrorism, all the attacks that have assaulted and assault the imaginations of men, were and are today either offensive or defensive actions. If they comprise part of an offensive strategy, experience, over a long period of time, has shown that they are destined to fail. If, on the other hand, they comprise part of a defensive strategy, experience demonstrates that these acts can expect some success, which is however, only temporary and precarious. The attempts of the Palestinians and the Irish, for example, are offensive terrorism, by contrast, the Piazza Fontana bombs and the kidnapping of Aldo Moro are defensive acts.

However, it is not only the strategy that changes, shaping whether these actions are offensive or defensive in nature, but also the strategists. The desperate and the deluded resort to offensive terrorism . . . In contrast it is *always* and *only* States that resort to defensive terrorism, either because they are mired in some deep crisis, like the Italian State, or else they fear one, like the German State.

The defensive terrorism of States is undertaken either *directly* or *indirectly*, with their own weapons or with those of others. If States resort to *direct* terrorism, these acts must be directed against the people—as happened, for example, with the massacre at Piazza Fontana, with that of Italicus, and with that of Brescia. If, however, States decide to rely on *indirect* terrorism, it must appear to be directed against them, as happened for instance in the Moro affair.

The attacks undertaken directly by undercover agents and by parallel services of the State are not usually claimed by anyone, but are assigned and attributed to one or another convenient "culprit" like Pinelli or Valpreda. Experience shows that this is the weakest moment of this kind of terrorism determining the extreme fragility of its political usefulness. Moving on from the outcome of these same events, the strategists of the parallel services of the State, try to lend greater credibility, or at least less realism, to their own actions either by claiming them directly though such and such acronyms of a phantom group, or by claiming them on behalf of an existing group, whose militants apparently are, and sometimes believe themselves to be, unaware of the intentions of the State.

All terrorist cells are organized and directed by a clandestine hierarchy of militants who specialize in clandestinity, accurately reflecting the division of labor and of roles appropriate to this social organization: the leadership plans and the base executes their orders. Ideology and physical discipline protect the leadership from all risk, and the base from all suspicion. Any secret service can create an acronym for a revolutionary group, and undertake a few attacks that the press will publicize. After which, it will be easy to gather a small band of naïve, easily manipulated militants. But in the case of a tiny spontaneously formed, terrorist group, nothing is simpler than for State agents to infiltrate, and based on the material means at their disposal and because of the total freedom of action they enjoy, to get to the leaders, substituting themselves, either by specific arrests at the right moment, or through the assassination of the original hierarchy, which, as a rule, occurs after a firefight with the "forces of order", who have been forewarned about this event by their infiltrators.

From that point on, the State's parallel services have at their disposal an extremely efficient organism comprised of naïve or fanatical militants, who ask nothing more than to be given instructions. The original little terrorist cell, created out of the illusions of its militants about the possibility of carrying out an effective offensive strategy, changes strategists, and becomes nothing more than a *defensive* appendage of the State, maneuvering with the utmost agility and ease, according to the necessities of the moment, or according to what it believes are its own necessities.

From Piazza Fontana to the kidnapping of Aldo Moro, only the short term objectives that defensive terrorism accomplished have changed, but what can never change is the *goal*. And the goal from December 12th 1960 through March 16th 1978 to today, has always remained the same, that is to make the entire population—that henceforth doesn't support this State or is struggling against it—believe that it *has at least one enemy in common* with the State, and which the State defends it against on the condition that it is no longer called into question by anyone. The people, who are generally hostile to terrorism and not without reason, must agree that at least in this regard, they need the State, to which it must delegate the broadest possible powers so that it can vigorously take on the arduous task of a unified defense against an enemy that is obscure, mysterious, treacherous, merciless and, in a word, phantasmal. Confronted by a terrorism that is always presented as the *absolute* evil in-itself and for-itself, all other evils, as real as they are, fade into the background, and *can even be forgotten; because the fight against terrorism embodies the* common interest; it is already the *common good*, and the State which magnanimously conducts this war is good in-itself and for-itself. Without the wickedness of the devil, the infinite goodness of God could not appear and be appreciated for what it is.

The State, extremely weakened by all the attacks it has undergone for the last ten years from the proletariat on the one hand and from the incompetence of its managers on the other, can silence both by solemnly taking on the staging of the spectacle of the united and holy defense against the terrorist monster, and, in the name of this pious mission, can take away from its subjects a remaining piece of their tiny bit of freedom, enforcing police control over the entire population. "We are at war", and at war with an enemy so powerful that any disagreement or conflict would constitute an act of sabotage or desertion: it is only when one opposes terrorism that one has the right to call a general strike. Terrorism, and "the emergency", a state of continuous emergency and "vigilance", these are the only real problems, at the very least the only ones that one has a right to be concerned with. Nothing else exists, or is forgotten, and in any case moves away, is repressed in the social unconscious, in the face of the seriousness of the issue of "public order." And faced with the universal necessity for its defense, everyone is encouraged to inform on others, to be afraid, to be mean: cowardice becomes, for the first time in history, a sublime quality, fear is always justified. The only "courage" that is not contemptible is based on approving and supporting all the lies, all the abuses and all the loathsomeness of the State. Because the present crisis spares no nation in the world, no geographic border of peace or war, of truth or freedom, this border moves inside each country, and each State arms itself and declares war on the truth.

Perhaps, one of you doesn't believe in the occult power of the terrorists. He will change his mind when he sees the subtly filmed images showing three German terrorists about to get into a helicopter, so powerful that they even succeeded in escaping from the German secret service, better able to film their prey than to capture them.

Perhaps, one of you doesn't believe that one or two hundred terrorists are capable of delivering a mortal blow to our institutions. Well, let him see what five or six of them are capable of doing to Moro and his escort, and he will acknowledge that the threat to our institutions (so beloved by 50 million Italians) is a real and credible threat. Perhaps one of you still wants to object. Are you an accomplice of the terrorists? Everybody will agree that the State can not let itself be brought down without defending itself: and, whatever it costs, this defense is a sacred and necessary duty for everyone. And this because the Republic is public, the State is for all, everyone is the State and the State is all, because everyone enjoys its advantages equally: isn't that democracy. And this is why the people rule, but beware if they don't defend their reign.

excerpt from:

No One a Neutral
by Norman Antokol and Mayer Nudell

Morris Nudell and Norman Antokol are former U.S. diplomats who currently work as consultants in the fields of security and political training.
They define hostage-taking as the political form of kidnapping in which
individuals are taken captive to make political demands. The chief distinction between kidnapping and hostage-taking is that terrorists want
their acts to be communicated as broadly as possible. Hostage-taking
was, for two decades, the terrorists' best attention-getter, the longer
the duration of the event the greater the notoriety (e.g. the U.S.
hostages in Iran in 1979). From 1970 to 1988 there were 169 plane
hijackings and 1,408 terrorist abductions committed worldwide, most
of them political.

The earliest contemporary political kidnappings, which took place
during Castro's struggle in Cuba, were undertaken almost entirely
for publicity; no specific demands were made. In 1958, race driver
Juan Manuel Fangio was abducted just before he was to participate in a
race. The incident generated the desired publicity, and Fangio was
released unharmed. Shortly after, forty-five U.S. citizens were taken
hostage under the direction of Raul Castro to protest the U.S. maintenance of the Batista government's planes at Guantanamo. As in the previous case, no demands were made and the hostages were released
unharmed.

Castro eventually realized that taking hostages *en masse* was more efficient than capturing them singly, and this, coupled with his recognition of
the vulnerability of civil aviation, led to the first Cuban hijackings. Three

planes were hijacked during this period, but again there were neither ransoms nor releases demanded. (Airplane hijacking ultimately became a major part of the strategy of some groups, particularly after its adoption by Palestinian terrorists. Prior to Marighella's codification of urban guerrilla operations, it was only a minor piece of the overall picture.)

Given that the intellectual founder of this new approach was a Brazilian, it is perhaps not surprising that the first successful application of Marighella's theories was the kidnapping of the U.S. ambassador to Brazil, Charles Burke Elbrick, on September 4, 1969.[1] Ambassador Elbrick was taken from his car by four men on a street in downtown Rio de Janeiro. The kidnappers left behind a ransom note demanding the publication of its manifesto, the release of fifteen prisoners by the Brazilian government, and provision for their flight to another country. If these demands were not met within forty-eight hours, the note said, Ambassador Elbrick would be "executed."

The kidnapping was carried out by two left-wing Brazilian groups, the *Movimiento Revolucionario do Outubre 8* (MR-8) and the *Acao Libertadora*

---

[1] Hostage-taking as part of a terrorist strategy actually made its first appearance in two separate incidents in Guatemala in 1968, but we relegate these to a footnote because, in both cases, the intended hostages were killed without actually being kidnapped. On January 16, 1968, U.S. Army Colonel John D. Webber and U.S. Navy Lieutenant Commander Ernest A. Munro were shot to death from a passing car. Webber was commander of the U.S. Military Group in Guatemala and Munro headed its naval section. The episode is believed to have been the responsibility of the *Fuerzas Armadas Rebeldes* (FAR), which claimed responsibility for the killings the following day.

On August 28, 1968, U.S. ambassador to Guatemala, John G. Mein, was en route to the Embassy when his car was forced to the curb, blocked in, and surrounded by several young men with weapons. Ambassador Mein jumped from the car, but was shot down as he tried to escape. A communique issued by the FAR the next day stated that the ambassador was killed "while resisting political kidnapping." It is believed that the FAR had intended to try to exchange Mein for their imprisoned Commandant Camilo Sanchez.

While both these incidents pre-date the kidnapping of Ambassador Elbrick, neither actually brought about a genuine hostage situation, with demands for ransom or release of prisoners. We therefore consider the Brazilian episode as the beginning of the application of Marighella's theory.

Nacional (ALN). The Brazilian government gave in to their demands and, on September 5, broadcast the groups' manifesto. The next day, the fifteen prisoners were released and flown to Mexico. The following day, Ambassador Elbrick was released by his captors, whom he described as having been fully prepared to carry out their threats had their demands not been met. The theories of Carlos Marighella had been shown to work.

The lesson learned, it quickly was put into practice in various parts of Latin America. On March 6, 1970, U.S. labor Attaché Sean Holly was seized by the *Fuerzas Armadas Rebeldes* (FAR) on a main street in Guatemala City. The terrorists demanded the release of four of their imprisoned comrades in return for Holly's release. The government of Guatemala quickly agreed, and within two days, two of the four were released and given political asylum in the Costa Rican Embassy. All four received safe conduct to Mexico.[2] Holly was held for a total of thirty-nine hours, then released at a church in a working-class district of the city. The whole affair took less than two days, but once again the taking of a hostage had proven to be an effective tactic in the "revolutionary struggle."

Emboldened by success, the FAR kidnapped the West German ambassador to Guatemala, Count Karl von Spreti, a mere three weeks later. On March 31, Ambassador von Spreti was forced from his car by armed men in downtown Guatemala City. This time, the terrorists demanded the release of seventeen political prisoners, including five who were charged with responsibility for the earlier kidnapping of Sean Holly. The other twelve included prisoners accused of killing several politicians and policemen. The Papal Nuncio was contacted to serve as intermediary.

On April 2, the Guatemalan government announced that it would not agree to the kidnappers' demands; no prisoners would be released. Indeed, since some of the prisoners had already been tried and con-

---

[2] The kidnappers were incorrect in thinking that all four were in jail in the first place. Even terrorists apparently can make mistakes.

victed, the government argued that they couldn't be released by executive order in any event. Instead, political and labor activities were ordered suspended, personal rights were shoved aside, and the military was authorized to interrogate anyone it considered suspicious.

The West German government protested this refusal to accede to the kidnappers' demands, and on the morning of April 3, a delegation of foreign ambassadors met with the Guatemalan Foreign Minister to urge that the prisoners be released. Meanwhile, the FAR upped its price to twenty-five prisoners and a ransom of seven hundred thousand dollars. The West German government reportedly offered to provide the money, but the Guatemalan government remained adamant. On April 5, the body of Ambassador von Spreti was found in an abandoned house, fatally shot in the head.

While the results were disastrous for Count von Spreti, and almost as bad for relations between West Germany and Guatemala, it was hardly a victory for the theories of Carlos Marighella. The FAR found itself isolated from the masses it had expected to incite, and it became the target of a crackdown by the authorities. The fate of urban guerrilla warfare in Guatemala suggested that the theory would have to be refined and adapted somewhat more carefully.

Meanwhile, in the three weeks between the release of Sean Holly and the murder of Count von Spreti, there were three more political kidnappings in Latin America. Two of these, in Brazil and the Dominican Republic, achieved their aims, while the third, in Argentina, failed.[3]

---

[3] There was a fourth attempt, also in Argentina, on March 29, when the Soviet Assistant Commercial Attaché was overpowered in a garage in Buenos Aires. Fleeing from the police, the terrorists' car collided with another vehicle and the attempt was foiled. Since one of the kidnappers was a Deputy Police Inspector, however, and the plot was the brainchild of a Soviet-hating right-wing organization, it is difficult to know precisely what the group intended. This incident does not fit in with the others detailed here, but it is interesting to note how tactics and ideas can be copied—even by organizations with radically different goals.

The first of these incidents, just three days after Holly's release in Guatemala, took place—perhaps not surprisingly—in Brazil. On March 11, the Japanese Consul General in São Paulo, Nobico Okushi, was taken from his car en route to his home. The kidnappers, who identified themselves as members of the Popular Revolutionary Vanguard *(Vanguarda Popular Revolucionaria)*, demanded the release of five individuals from prison and their safe conduct to another country. They also demanded that the government call off the manhunt it had begun or Okushi would be killed.

As in the Burke case six months earlier, the Brazilian authorities announced that they would meet the terrorists' demands. They further agreed to an additional demand, a guarantee of humane treatment for all prisoners in Brazilian jails. On March 4, the five prisoners were released and allowed to leave for Mexico. Ten hours later, Okushi was released unharmed. The doctrine of Marighella was two-for-two in his native Brazil.

Ten days later, the U.S. Air Attaché in the Dominican Republic, Air Force Lieutenant Colonel Donald J. Crowley, was kidnapped from a polo field next to a hotel in Santo Domingo. The abductors, who identified themselves as members of the United Anti-Reelection Command (a group attempting to keep incumbent President Joaquin Balaguer from serving another term), demanded that twenty-one prisoners be released in a public ceremony in Santo Domingo's main square. Crowley's release would take place ten hours after the ceremony, the kidnappers' note promised.

The Dominican Republic's government agreed to the release of the prisoners, but it refused both the public ceremony and the ten-hour delay preceding Crowley's release. The two sides eventually reached a compromise, and twenty prisoners were placed on board an airplane under the protection of the Mexican Embassy, accompanied by the auxiliary Archbishop of Santo Domingo, to be permitted to leave only upon the appearance of Lt. Col. Crowley. On March 26, Crowley was released unharmed, and the twenty former prisoners took off for Mexico. In light of this and the Okushi incident, it is hardly surprising that the FAR thought it could get away with the demands it presented for the return of Ambassador von Spreti only a week later in Guatemala.

The Tactic Spreads

While the successes of these few weeks in March 1970 marked a turning point in the history of political hostage taking, there was one notable exception. On March 24, the same day that Lt. Col. Crowley was being abducted in the Dominican Republic, a left-wing guerrilla group in Argentina tried its hand at a terrorist kidnapping. The *Frente Argentina de Liberación* (Argentine Liberation Front), a splinter group of the Argentine Communist Party, abducted Paraguayan Consul Waldemar Sanchez in the town of Ituzaingo. His safety was promised in exchange for the release of two of the group's imprisoned members, and a deadline was set for 10:00 p.m. the following night.

The Argentine government refused these demands, apparently with the approval of Paraguayan President Stroessner (who had arrived in Argentina on March 25 to begin a scheduled vacation). The government insisted that one of the alleged prisoners was not even in custody, while the other was a criminal and could not be released. The kidnappers responded that if their terms were not met they would not only kill Sanchez, but also undertake the "execution" of "all managers of American businesses." The Argentine authorities stood firm, repeatedly broadcasting over the next two days that they would not be coerced into releasing prisoners. Faced with this intransigence, the kidnappers released Sanchez on March 28, explaining this action in "humanitarian" terms. The emerging tactic of political kidnapping was still gaining strength in Latin America, but Argentina and Guatemala were not yet fertile breeding grounds.

Had all the responses to the demands of terrorists been so uncooperative, it is impossible to guess what the ultimate outcome would have been. There were other failures as well, but there were enough successes along the way to encourage practitioners of this new revolutionary credo. In Brazil particularly, political kidnapping became a specialty of left-wing revolutionary organizations. An attempt was made on April 5 to abduct U.S. Consul General Curtis Cutter in Porto Alegre. Although the attempt was unsuccessful, Cutter was shot in the back and only narrowly escaped fatal injury.

Undaunted, terrorists struck again in Brazil on June 11, this time kidnapping West German Ambassador Ehrenfried von Hollenben. The terrorists, members of the Popular Revolutionary Vanguard and the National Liberation Action, demanded the release of forty prisoners in return for the Ambassador. The Brazilian government agreed, and von Hollenben was released on June 16. The lesson learned—at least as far as operations in Brazil were concerned—the same two groups attacked the Swiss Ambassador, Giovanni Enrico Bucher, on December 7 of the same year. This time, they demanded the release of seventy prisoners. Once again, the Brazilian government acceded to the kidnappers' demands, and the seventy were released on January 14, 1971, and given political asylum in Chile. Ambassador Bucher was released two days later, after nearly six weeks of captivity.

The implications of the Brazilian experience, if not that of Argentina, were soon felt in neighboring Uruguay. On July 31, 1970, the *Movimiento de Liberatión Nacional* (MLN) undertook three simultaneous and separate kidnappings. (The MLN is better known as the *Tupamaros*; they were named after the leader of the last Inca revolt against the Spaniards during the late eighteenth century, Tupac Amaru.) One of the three captives taken that day was U.S. diplomat Michael Gordon Jones. He managed to leap from the kidnappers' vehicle and make it to safety, thereby escaping the fate which befell the others. The second victim was Brazilian Consul Aloysio Mores Dias Gomides. The third victim was U.S. Public Safety Adviser Daniel A. Mitrione. Both originally were offered in exchange for the release of approximately 150 imprisoned *Tupamaros*.

The Uruguayan government, however, had apparently been more impressed by the Argentine example than the Brazilian, and absolutely refused to negotiate. Instead, the police launched a massive manhunt throughout Montevideo and arrested twenty accused terrorists. The *Tupamaros* announced they would "execute" Mitrione if their demands were not met, and to strengthen their hand, they abducted another American, Claude Fly, on August 7. Fly, an agricultural adviser, was taken from his office in the Ministry of Agriculture on the outskirts of Montevideo.

In the face of continued governmental intransigence, the *Tupamaros* realized that they would have to either back down or carry out their threats. As a result, Mitrione's body was found in an abandoned car on August 10, his wrists bound with wire and several bullets in his back and neck. A *Tupamaro* leader later explained that they "had to" kill him in order to preserve the taking of hostages as a political tool. Thus was demonstrated one of the practical drawbacks of the new urban guerrilla theory: if the other side won't negotiate, a terrorist group may feel compelled to take an action which it neither intends nor wants.

The killing of Daniel Mitrione was a major setback for the Uruguayan left (and, as it turned out, for democracy in that country as a whole). The *Tupamaros* previously had enjoyed a rather romantic image—men whose ends were admirable even if their means were violent. The murder of an innocent man, who left behind a wife and nine children, shocked the public's sensibilities and vastly undercut the *Tupamaros'* popular support. With Fly and Dias Gomides still in the kidnappers' hands, the Uruguayan legislature voted to temporarily suspend many individual rights, and a massive search for Mitrione's murderers was begun. In September, the *Tupamaros* issued a statement rather lamely attempting to justify their actions, but it was clear that the tide of public opinion was turning against them.

Making the best of a bad job, the kidnappers dropped their demand for the release of prisoners (which by now clearly was not a possibility), and asked instead for a ransom of two hundred fifty thousand dollars for the safe return of the Brazilian Consul. The money was paid, and Dias Gomides finally was released on February 21, 1971. Claude Fly, meanwhile, suffered a heart attack during his captivity, and the *Tupamaros* (after abducting a cardiologist from a medical convention in Montevideo to examine him) released him on March 2. Another death at that point was the last thing they needed.

However, the *Tupamaros* still had one outstanding practical problem. During the negotiations over Fly and Dias Gomides, the group had attempted to gain greater leverage by kidnapping the British ambassador, Sir Geoffrey Jackson, on January 8, 1971. By March it was obvious that no prisoners were going to be released. The other hostages had all been either killed or freed, and the government was continuing its crackdown. The *Tupamaros* had little hope of receiving any concessions, yet they could neither kill Jackson nor return him without suffering a devastating loss of face.

The situation dragged on like this for more than eight months. Finally, in early September, 106 of the prisoners on the *Tupamaros'* list somehow escaped on their own. Three days later, undoubtedly relieved to have been shown a way out of the impasse, the kidnappers released Ambassador Jackson. They quickly explained that there was no longer any reason to hold their hostage, as their comrades were no longer in prison. The net result of all this was a public relations disaster for the *Tupamaros*. Unsuccessful as hostage-takers, they turned, in 1972, to a campaign of murderous assaults on police and military personnel. The government declared an "internal state of war" and virtually wiped out the entire *Tupamaro* network. Nonetheless, despite the magnitude of these setbacks, the tactics of Marighella had shown enough success in Latin America to have become an entrenched part of the political landscape by 1972.

Strategic and Tactical Modifications

The experience of Argentina suggests the flexibility of this new approach and the adaptability of its advocates. As we have seen, the Argentine government had shown itself unwilling to exchange prisoners for hostages, so the local terrorist groups changed both their targets and their demands. The forerunner of the new strategy was the kidnapping of an executive at the Swift Meat Packing plant in Rosario, Stanley Sylvester. He was also the British honorary consul in that city. Sylvester was taken outside his home by the *Ejército Revolucionario Popular* (ERP) on May 23, 1971. The kidnappers demanded not a prisoner exchange this time, but $62,500 in "gifts" of food and clothing to the poor. The Swift Company agreed, and Sylvester was released unharmed a week later.

The implications of this victory, when coupled with the defeat suffered in the earlier Sanchez case, was not lost on Argentina's terrorists. Large companies were easier to do business with than was the government, and money ransoms were easier to obtain than were political concessions. This doesn't really seem much different from the actions of any number of common criminals over the years, considerably pre-dating the revolutionary theories of Guevara and Marighella, but the rhetoric remained political. Money was to be taken in exchange for hostages in order to "finance the revolution" and help "alleviate the suffering of the masses."

On March 22, 1972, the ERP attempted to combine fundraising with political demands in the kidnapping of Oberdan Sallustro, a Fiat executive in Buenos Aires. The demands for Sallustro's release included a ransom of one million dollars (to be paid in the form of "gift packages" to poor school children around the country), the release of fifty imprisoned comrades, safe passage to Algeria, and the reinstatement of some 250 employees who had lost their jobs as the result of their participation in a labor dispute at the Fiat factory in Cordova. Fiat was willing to pay the ransom, but was prevented from doing so by the Argentine government, which decided on a much tougher line.

Argentine authorities warned the Fiat Company that they would be prosecuted if they didn't immediately break off ransom negotiations with the ERP. A manhunt was then mounted and, on April 10, police found the hideout where Sallustro was being held. A shootout took place, resulting in the arrest of four terrorists. Unfortunately, moments before the police could effect his rescue, Sallustro was murdered by his captors. This failure notwithstanding, the willingness of Fiat to come to terms and the near-payment of such a large ransom virtually ensured that Argentine terrorists would soon try again.

Almost a year to the day later, on April 2, 1973, a U.S. executive was kidnapped on the outskirts of Buenos Aires. Anthony R. DaCruz, a technical operations manager for the Eastman Kodak Company, was taken from his car at gunpoint. This time the kidnappers, who identified themselves as members of a guerrilla organization without volunteering which one, ignored the question of jailed revolutionary comrades altogether. They demanded instead a then-record $1.5 million ransom. Kodak quickly agreed, and DaCruz was released unharmed on April 7.

It didn't take long for the lesson to sink in. On May 22, 1973, an attempt was made to kidnap Luis V. Giovanelli, an executive with the Ford Motor Company in Buenos Aires. Plant security guards intervened, and Giovanelli and another employee were seriously wounded in the ensuing exchange of gunfire. In an effort to recoup something from the fiasco, the ERP released a communique through a local newspaper which announced that the victims were shot because they had resisted. They then demanded that Ford pay them a million dollars in protection money to avoid repetition of such an attempt. That money wasn't paid, but the terrorists were sure they were on to something anyway.

The same day the communique was released, May 23, the ERP kidnapped an Argentine executive, Aaron Bellinson, from his home in Buenos Aires and demanded a ransom of one million dollars "to help finance the revolutionary struggle." Bellinson's company paid what was believed to be the equivalent of a million dollars and he was released unharmed on June 3. Just three days later, the ERP struck again. This time, the victim was an executive of an Argentine affiliate of Britain's Acrow Steel Company, Charles Lockwood, and the ransom demanded was two million dollars. On July 30, Lockwood was released, after payment of a sum estimated to have been very close to two million dollars. The revolutionary terrorist business clearly was turning out to be very profitable, at least in Argentina.

Given the relative vulnerability of businessmen in Argentina, and the spiraling ransom demands that were being paid, it would have been surprising if the kidnappings had stopped. On June 18, 1973, while negotiations were still going on for the release of Charles Lockwood, the ERP abducted John R. Thompson, the American president of Firestone's Argentine operations. Although Firestone officials refused to comment, the media reported that the ransom demand this time was for three million dollars. Negotiations took place over the next two weeks or so, and an undisclosed figure was agreed upon. Whatever the final amount, it was reported that huge piles of five-hundred-peso notes were delivered in an armored car, which the terrorists thoughtfully provided. Thompson was released unhurt three days later, on July 6.

Worldwide Application

There are numerous other examples, but we think the point is made. The shift in focus from Guevara to Marighella meant a shift in political violence from the countryside to the cities, and the birth of what came to be known as modern terrorism. The taking of hostages proved successful for several groups in Latin America, and the idea spread from country to country. By the early 1970s there were hostage incidents occurring in other parts of the Western Hemisphere, even where there had been no previous tradition of rurally based guerrilla warfare.

For example, two incidents occurred in Canada in October 1970, just five days apart. On October 5, James R. Cross, the British Trade

Commissioner in Quebec, was abducted from his home in Montreal by members of the *Front de Liberation du Quebec* (FLQ). In exchange for his safe return, the group demanded the release of thirteen of its members from prison, a ransom of $500,000 in gold, publication of an FLQ manifesto, reinstatement of jobs to recently dismissed postal workers, and the name of an informant against whom the group wanted revenge. Canadian authorities rejected these demands outright.

The group then kidnapped Pierre LaPorte, Minister of Labor in the Quebec government, and announced that it would kill both men unless its terms were met. The government again refused, but offered the terrorists safe conduct out of Canada if Cross and LaPorte were set free. On October 18, LaPorte's body was found in the trunk of a car in Montreal. The government responded with a massive manhunt, culminating in the arrest of more than four hundred FLQ members and sympathizers. Agreement was reached for the safe return of Cross, and on December 3, 1970, he was released. In return, the kidnappers were flown to Cuba on a Canadian military aircraft. Two FLQ members ultimately were arrested and convicted of LaPorte's murder, but it was clear that the tactics of modern "urban guerrilla warfare" were not going to remain confined to the countries of Latin America.

Within just a few years, the fever spread and the stakes increased. On January 23, 1973, the U.S. ambassador to Haiti, Clinton Knox, was briefly taken hostage, along with his consul general, Ward Christensen. The kidnappers originally demanded the release of thirty prisoners and the payment of one million dollars. They settled for twelve prisoners (which were all of the thirty that Haitian authorities were holding) and seventy thousand dollars. The money, which was all that could be raised within the terrorists' four-hour deadline, was paid, and the twelve released prisoners were flown to Mexico. Knox and Christensen were then freed, on January 24. This was the second incident involving a U.S. ambassador, and the first to result in concessions.

Only a few weeks later, on March 1, 1973, the U.S. ambassador to the Sudan, Cleo A. Noel, Jr., was taken hostage by members of the Black September group. Also captured were his deputy chief of mission, G. Curtis Moore, and Belgian *Chargé d'Affaires* Guy Eid, and a number of other diplomats from various countries. The terrorists barricaded themselves in the Saudi Arabian Embassy (where the kidnapping took place during a diplomatic reception) and demanded the release of sixty Palestinian guerrillas plus freedom for Sirhan Sirhan, the assassin of Robert Kennedy. When these terms were refused, they murdered the three diplomats. After the terrorists surrendered to Sudanese authorities, they were granted safe passage out of the country.

It is not unreasonable to suppose that the successes of terrorist groups in Latin America had a significant influence on groups in Canada, Haiti, and the Sudan. Applying the new revolutionary theories of Carlos Marighella, they consistently had won freedom for many of their imprisoned comrades, to say nothing of the huge ransom payments some had achieved. Once the strategy had been shown to work, it was natural that it should be copied by other would-be revolutionaries. The taking of hostages for the accomplishment of political objectives, once limited mainly to soldiers and loyal families, was extended to private citizens, and the modern era of terrorism was under way.

This is not the complete answer, however. The shift in focus among Latin American guerrillas, and their early successes with political kidnapping, provide part of the explanation of this phenomenon. But other, seemingly unrelated events were taking place in another part of the world at just about the same time. In 1967, the loss of a war in the Middle East—many miles distant from the cities of Latin America and light years away in political terms—would combine with the new guerrilla theories to visit a plague of terrorism and hostage-taking on the modern world.

excerpt from:

Televisionaries

by Tom Vague

The Baader-Meinhof group (aka The Red Army Faction) was the most
active Marxist terrorist group in Europe during the 70s. They trained with
the PLO in Jordan, although differences surfaced over whether the
German women should be permitted to sunbathe in the nude. They
funded their operation by robbing a series of banks. Thirteen American soldiers were injured and one was killed by three pipe bombs placed in an
officers' mess in Frankfurt. A bomb exploded in the car of a judge active
on Baader-Meinhof cases. His wife was seriously injured. Two car bombs
went off outside the European headquarters of the U.S. Army in
Heidelberg, killing three GIs and wounding five. A few weeks later,
founding member Andreas Baader was arrested. The rest of the leaders
(Enslin, Raspe and Meinhof) were jailed soon after. The CEO of Daimler
Benz, Hanns-Martin Schlyer, was kidnapped by Red Army members and
the liberation of the RAF prisoners was demanded. When this failed to
produce the desired result ,a Lufthansa jet was hijacked in Mallorca. The
Arab hijackers insisted on the release of the Baader-Meinhof members, as
well as two Arabs held in jail, and demanded fifteen million American dollars. Schlyer was to be freed if these demands were met. After many stops
in the Middle East, the plane landed in Mogadishu, Somalia. German
Special Forces, who had been following from city to city, stormed the
plane and killed all but one of the hijackers. All the passengers exited the
plane safely. That night the four imprisoned Germans purportedly committed suicide, though it appeared that one or more of them may have
been murdered. Schlyer was executed in response. This excerpt narrates
many of these events and captures the manic desperation of a group that
naively believed it was carrying the weight of the world on its shoulders.

JUNE 8: The Horst Mahler group (Hans-Jürgen Bäcker, Monika Berberich, Brigitte Asdonk, Manfred Grashof, Petra Schelm and Mahler) fly to Beirut from East Berlin. From Beirut they intend to go on to an Al Fatah training camp in Amman, Jordan; but their flight's delayed due to fierce fighting between the PLO and King Hussein. This means the Germans have to pass through the Lebanese checkpoint, and some of them only have Berlin ID cards. The official on duty decides to impound all their papers and holds the group in the customs office. After a while the official knocks off for the day and locks the Germans' papers in his desk.

Time for another blundering phone-call from Horst Mahler: this time to the French embassy, who he thinks are looking after East German interests. They are in fact only looking after West German interests. Mahler announces who and where he is before Petra Schelm realises who's at the other end and cuts him off. The French embassy duly inform the BRD, who order the Lebanese to arrest the group. However the Lebanese stall, not particularly wanting to upset the Palestinians, and a PLO troop arrive at the airport and release the Germans. Some fedayeen go to the house of the official, beat him up and demand the key to the desk. But someone else has it so they load the whole desk into a truck and take it with them.

Then the Mahler group are put in the Beirut Strand for the night. And that's where the Lebanese militia arrest them a few hours later, before returning them to the airport, where once again they are rescued by the Palestinians, who this time take them across the Syrian border to Damascus. There they receive some firearms training from the fedayeen before being driven on to Amman.

JUNE 21: A second group including Baader, Ensslin and Meinhof take the U-bahn to Friedrichstr and cross over into East Berlin. There they disguise themselves as Arabs and proceed to Schönefeld airport. The PLO liaison man, Said Dudin brings United Arab Emirates passports this time, but they're still delayed and don't reach Damascus until the following afternoon. Then the Syrians refuse to let them in, but once again the Palestinians intervene and escort them over the Jordanian border.

At Amman the advance party greet them with hugs and kisses. Horst Mahler, sporting a Castro-style beard and cap, is very much the leader of the guerrilla band. But not for long: Baader immediately gives him a dressing down for making their trip frontpage news back in Germany. Mahler might have been a brilliant lawyer but he's no match for his venomous former client, and soon concedes leadership.

Then PLO basic training begins with a sort of revolutionary tourist programme (which many legal parties of European students undertook at the time). But the Baader/Mahler group insist on getting some real military training. Everyone is issued with combat gear (except Andreas Baader, who goes through basic training in skintight trousers) and armed with a Kalashnikov, because the camp is under constant threat of attack. (A few weeks after the embryonic RAF leave Amman, the camp and most of its occupants are wiped out in 'Black September'.)

Baader soon makes sure that the training is altered to suit 'The Job', as he calls their proposed urban guerrilla activities. This includes instruction in 'How to rob a bank', which the Algerian camp commandant, Achmed has first hand experience of in the Algerian war of independence. But it doesn't take long for Baader and Achmed to fall out. Baader demands to be treated on an equal footing to the Palestinian leader Abu Hassan. When Achmed ignores this demand, Baader calls a training strike.

During the strike some of the German girls sunbathe naked on the roof of their quarters. This causes some consternation among the young fedayeen, most of whom have never seen a woman naked before. Achmed puts his foot down, shouting "What do you think this is? This isn't a tourist beach!" To which Baader counters "The anti-imperialist struggle and sexual emancipation go hand in hand, fucking and shooting are the same thing!"

But for once Baader has met his match and the strike is called off. Then Abu Hassan visits the camp to attempt to give a lecture on the Palestinian struggle. He doesn't get very far before he's interrupted by shouts of new demands. Hassan tells Achmed not to stand for anymore of it and the next day, when the Germans complain about their training again, Achmed acts. That night a group of fedayeen storm the Germans' quarters and disarm them.

Also, within the group, a conflict develops between Baader and Peter Homann, the man suspected of being the masked gunman who freed Baader. The two are old acquaintances but during the training they fall out drastically. Homann starts to hang out with Achmed and the fedayeen. This arouses suspicion amongst his countrymen, he's called a traitor and there's talk of a tribunal and liquidation. Finally the Palestinians have to take Homann out of the camp and give him a minder.

The PLO get Homann to write a report about the group and the political situation in the BRD, then Abu Hassan takes him for a meal and arranges a meeting with the others. Homann listens in from another room as Hassan guarantees everybody a safe passage back to Germany, and arms possibly, but ignores Gudrun Ensslin's accusation that Homann is an Israeli spy and should be shot. Gudrun also makes a peculiar request on behalf of Ulrike Meinhof: could her children be brought up in one of the Palestinian orphan camps. Hassan says sure, if that's what she wants, but she'll never see them again.

AUGUST 9: The group return to West Berlin via the East without a hitch. Peter Homann decides to go his own way, the PLO give him an Arab passport (in the name of Omar Sharif), $200 and a ticket for a flight from Beirut to Rome. He arrives in Rome a week after the others return to Berlin and gets on a train to Hamburg.

This is where 'Baader-Meinhof Group' author, Stefan Aust comes back into his own story. After the springing of Baader, Aust is commissioned by (the German) 'Panorama' to do a documentary on Ulrike Meinhof. In the course of his research he unsuccessfully tries to contact Peter Homann (who lived with Meinhof for a while in Berlin). When Homann returns from the Middle East he contacts Aust and tells him of the plans for Ulrike Meinhof's children.

After Ulrike went underground, friends had smuggled her kids through France and Italy to a hippy colony near Mount Etna. Peter Homann subsequently makes contact with a woman who'd looked after them and she tells him someone is coming from Berlin to take them to Jordan. She also gives Homann the password, 'Professor Schnase' and a phone number, which Homann rings and says someone will be at Palermo airport the next day to pick up the girls. Then Aust flies down to Sicily, takes the girls off the hands of the Mount Etna hippies and returns them to their father, his old boss Klaus Rainer Röhl.

This lands Aust in hot water with the subjects of his future book. When the Berlin group call Sicily and find the children already gone, they inevitably find the woman who'd told Homann and Aust and come looking for them. Fortunately for Aust, when Baader and Mahler call on him one day, another old friend of his persuades them to let him check for police first. Aust manages to slip out the back, takes an extended holiday and goes around armed for some time after. Peter Homann eventually turns himself in (when he's no longer suspected of being the masked man) and is released after a brief spell remanded in custody.

MAY 29: Horst Herold calls together the leaders of all the regional commissions to announce a nationwide sweep-search on May 31. 'Operation Watersplash' is to involve the entire BRD police force, but when Herold's big break comes it isn't as a result of the search; it comes in the form of an anonymous tip-off that young people in big cars are bringing gas cylinders to a garage in the Hofeckweg district of Frankfurt. BKA men locate the garage and check it out. Substances they find which are confirmed to be explosives are replaced by bonemeal and the garage staked out.

JUNE 1: 5.50am. A Porsche Targa pulls up outside the garage and three men get out. Two of the men, Holger Meins and Andreas Baader go into the garage, the third man, Jan-Carl Raspe stays outside by the car and soon becomes aware that he is not alone. In fact police are swarming all over the place. Then Jillian Becker ('Hitler's Children') predictably claims Raspe tries to leg it; but Stefan Aust has a squad car approaching him first, Raspe drawing his gun and two more policemen rushing him. Then Raspe takes flight firing off a shot, only to be captured in a nearby garden. (At the same time, a male nurse on his way to work is also pounced upon and arrested before he can explain who he is.)

Following Raspe's arrest, a surveillance car is pushed up against the garage doors and Baader fires a shot through the side. Then holes are knocked through the thick glass panels at the back of the garage. At this point, Baader and Meins are laughing and waving their guns at the police. Next tear gas grenades are shot through the holes and the top BKA man at the scene tells them to throw out their guns, take off their outer clothing and come out with their hands up. Baader and Meins push one side of the doors out and the police, thinking they're about to surrender, remove the car. Thereupon, Baader flings the tear gas grenades back at the police.

7.45am. An armoured car is driven into the garage doors and more tear gas fired into the garage. Then Det. Sgt. Bernhard Honke gets access to an overlooking apartment, gets Baader in his sights and shoots him in the leg. Shortly after that, Holger Meins comes out with his hands up; he's ordered to strip to his underpants, then he walks towards the police line.

Ten minutes later, the armoured car goes in again, this time supported by police in bullet-proof vests. They find Andreas Baader, hair dyed with peroxide, lying bleeding still clutching his gun. One of the policemen kicks it out of his hand then four of them drag him away, still struggling, on a stretcher. These events are relayed live across the BRD by a Frankfurt TV crew, who stopped off on their way to a race track.

After the arrest of Baader, Meins and Raspe, Gudrun Ensslin joins Ulrike Meinhof, Klaus Jünschke and Gerhard Müller in Hamburg. Spirits are understandably low, as Jünschke puts it, "It was like going downhill out of control, if you jump out you're done for, if you carry on you're done for just the same."

JUNE 7: Ensslin is being driven through Hamburg by Jünschke. She thinks he's driving erratically, so they switch to a taxi. Then the taxi driver looks at her suspiciously, so panicking, Gudrun goes to a boutique to buy new clothes. While she's trying something on, a sales girl moves her jacket and sees her gun. The manageress subsequently calls the police and delays her until they arrive. Thereupon, Gudrun makes calmly for the door but gets grabbed before she reaches it. A desperate struggle ensues and two policemen end up on the ground, before Gudrun Ensslin is finally overpowered.

> Police report of apartment search (key to which found on Gudrun Ensslin at time of her arrest) 'Re: Hunt for violent anarchist criminals. Subject: Conspirators' apartment at 71 Seidenstr. Stuttgart. Attached: 22 Mickey Mouse comic books were found in the above mentioned apartment. There are good grounds for suspecting that these Mickey Mouse books were read by the gang member Andreas Baader.'

JUNE 9: Brigitte Mohnhaupt and Bernhard Braun (SPK/J2M) are arrested in Berlin.

JUNE 15: The schili finally turn on and turn in Ulrike Meinhof. Fritz Rodewald, a left-wing teacher living in Hannover is asked to put up two people, who turn out to be Ulrike Meinhof and Gerhard Müller. He agrees but has second thoughts and calls the police. (True to trendy lefty form, he later donates the reward money to the RAF defence fund.)

Not long after plain clothes police arrive at the building, Gerhard Müller goes out to make a phone call and is promptly nabbed. Reinforcements are called but there's to be no repeat of the Frankfurt siege. Ulrike Meinhof is arrested without much of a struggle, when she answers the door to the apartment. However once she's captured Ulrike causes quite a commotion and struggles for hours; hence the unflattering, swollen faced pictures that will be used for posterity. To give Andreas Baader his due, he still looks cool in dark glasses and peroxide hair when he's dragged out of the garage.

JUNE 25: Police raid another apartment in Stuttgart and Scottish ex-pat Ian MacLeod is shot dead. Nothing but the most tenuous rumours link MacLeod with the RAF. He's merely an unfortunate statistic on Herold's computer whose apartment may or may not have been used by the group.

JULY 7: Klaus Jünschke and Irmgard Möller are arrested in Offenbach, after being set up by new RAF member Hans-Peter Konieczny.

SEPTEMBER 5: A 'Black September' commando unit climb the fence of the Olympic Village in Munich and shoot their way into the Israeli team quarters. Two Israeli athletes are killed and 9 more taken hostage. Then, after a day's televised bargaining, the commando unit and their hostages are driven to Fürstenfeldbruck airport. They are all to be flown to Cairo, but as the Palestinians board their plane police marksmen open fire. In the ensuing gun battle all the Israeli athletes (11 in all), one of the police and five of the Palestinians are killed; leaving three to carry the can.

RAF prisoners spend the first year of imprisonment in separate jails, isolated not only from ordinary prisoners but from each other. Ulrike Meinhof spends a year in almost complete acoustic isolation before bad publicity forces prison authorities to move her. She describes the experience as: 'The feeling that your head is exploding . . . The feeling of your spinal chord being pressed into your brain . . . Furious aggression for which there is no outlet. That's the worst thing. A clear awareness that your chance of survival is nil.'

> RAF code of conduct in jail: 'Not a word to the pigs, in whatever guise they may appear, particularly as doctors. Not a single word. And naturally we give them no assistance, never lift a finger to help them. Nothing but hostility and contempt . . . No provocation; that's important. But we will defend ourselves implacably, relentlessly, with what human methods we have.'

NOVEMBER 26: 'Action Winter Journey' police raids throughout BRD; 80 apartments are raided, including RAF lawyers' offices from which trial documents are taken; 50 arrests are made but no significant ones.

Meanwhile, the hunger strike starts falling apart; Gerhard Müller, Margrit Schiller and Irene Goergens all come off. Ulrike Meinhof and Ingrid Schubert sympathise with Goergens, but Gudrun Ensslin condemns her as a sellout. Relations between Meinhof and Ensslin are at an all-time low. Baader remains remarkably neutral (and relatively un-misogynist), calling them both 'grotesque madwomen'.

DECEMBER: Gudrun Ensslin suggests, through the info-system, that somebody commits suicide every month until the isolation ends. Klaus Croissant has a more subtle (dare I say, existential) idea. He arranges for Jean-Paul Sartre to visit Stammheim, to interview Baader. The interview is never to be published—Sartre finds the RAF 'a danger to the Left' and

Baader, like a true Punk Rocker, just finds Sartre 'OLD'—but the press presence assures plenty of publicity for the hunger strike.

DECEMBER 20: 'Baader-Meinhof Law' passed by the Bundestag, allowing the trial to continue in the absence of the defendants (if they have made themselves unfit to appear) and to bar lawyers suspected of 'supporting a criminal association'. Defence lawyer Ströbele is barred merely for describing himself as a socialist. Croissant, Groenewold and Lang are also barred, even though they've already been sacked by their clients.

FEBRUARY 2, 1975: Third RAF hunger strike called off after 140 days and the deaths of Holger Meins and Judge von Drenkmann. The RAF prisoners have now drawn out the battle lines for the next two years. The RAF, inside and out, will now devote all its time and energy to freeing the prisoners.

Baader, Ensslin, Meinhof and Raspe are now allowed several hours together each day and almost daily visits from their lawyers. On the outside, Red Aid activists Angelika and Volker Speitel take over the running of the info-system from Klaus Croissant. After the death of Holger Meins, they go underground and join the remnants of the '4.2 Group' (Second generation RAF/SPK named after the date most of them got busted). From Stammheim the word comes out that this time they want to see less planning and more action.

FEBRUARY 27: Three days before the Berlin mayoral elections, Peter Lorenz, the leading Christian Democrat (CDU) candidate is kidnapped by J2M.

FEBRUARY 28: Along with a photo of Lorenz (with 'Prisoner of J2M' notice round his neck) the kidnappers demand: amnesty for those arrested at 'Avenge Holger' demos; the release of Horst Mahler, Verena Becker, Gabi Kröcher-Tiedemann, Ingrid Siepmann, Rolf Heissler and Rolf Pohle; to be accompanied to their destination by former Mayor Albertz (of Shah's visit fame); and while negotiations are in progress, a police cease fire—otherwise Lorenz will end up the same as von Drenkmann.

The demands are reasonable enough. Nobody convicted of murder is on the list; and there's no mention of the Stammheim Four, except a footnote: 'To our comrades in jail. We would like to get more of you out, but at our present strength we're not in a position to do it.' Horst Mahler is the only non-J2M member and he elects to stay put.

MARCH 2: Former Mayor/Pastor Albertz flies to Frankfurt, where he meets the J2M prisoners (and is bugged doing so, against his will) in a room under the airport complex. Then they all board a Lufthansa Boeing 707, each of the former prisoners is given $20,000 spending money and the take-off is shown live on TV.

MARCH 3: After being refused permission to land in Libya, the plane comes down at Aden in Yemen, and Pastor Albertz returns to Germany.

MARCH 4: Albertz appears on TV, giving the all clear line, 'a wonderful day like today', and Peter Lorenz walks free in the Berlin Volks Park with some small change to call his family. However, all the niceties stop there. An immediate nationwide search is launched for the J2M. Gerald Klopper and Ronald Fritsch are arrested merely for 'supporting the kidnapping'. And in return a J2M leaflet is circulated, detailing Lorenz's corrupt career plus information extracted during his imprisonment in a Kreuzberg basement. (By the way, Lorenz receives 43% of the vote but loses the election which is held during his captivity.)

APRIL 25: As the finishing touches are given to the specially constructed courthouse at Stammheim, six former SPK members (Siegfried Hausner, Hanne-Elise Krabbe, Karl-Heinz Dellwo, Lutz Taufer, Bernhard-Maria Rössner and Ullrich Wessel) enter the West German Embassy in Stockholm.

Once inside, they produce guns, obtain the keys to the upper floors and take 11 embassy officials hostage. Swedish police subsequently occupy the ground floor and prepare to move up. Then one of the guerrillas calls down to the police, telling them to get out immediately or the German military attache will be shot. The police stay put. This is to be a lot messier affair than the Lorenz kidnapping.

At mid-day the RAF/SPK group call the German Press Agency and announce: "The Holger Meins Commando is holding members of the embassy staff in order to free prisoners in West Germany. If the police move in we shall blow the building up with 15 kilos of TNT." Then they repeat their demand to the Swedish police down below. There's still no response, so the German Military Attache, Baron von Mirbach is made to walk out onto the landing and shot. Two Swedish policemen (stripped to their underpants to show they're unarmed) drag the dying attache downstairs; and only then do the police retreat to the building next door.

After that the group contact the German Press Agency again and specify their demands. They want 26 prisoners freed in all, this time including Baader, Ensslin, Meinhof and Raspe. Chancellor Helmut Schmidt hears the news at Palais Schaumburg, and informs the assembled 'Crisis Staff' that he isn't prepared to deal this time. Then he gives the go-ahead for an assault on the embassy by a special antiterrorist squad. So that leaves the Swedish Minister of Justice nothing to negotiate with but safe conduct. The kidnappers aren't interested, and insist they'll shoot a hostage every hour until their demands are met.

10.20pm. The Economic Attache Hillegaart appears at a window, three shots are fired and the old man slumps forward. The Swedish police prepare to fire K62 stun gas into the upper floors, before storming the building. But before anybody has a chance to do anything the building is rocked by a series of explosions. The force of the blast throws three policemen to the ground and, along with window frames, guttering and office chairs, Ullrich Wessel is blown out into the embassy grounds. All the kidnappers and the hostages are badly burnt, but Wessel is the only one to die in the blast. However, despite particularly severe burns, Siegfried (no pun intended) Hausner is flown back to the BRD, where he dies of his injuries in Stammheim, evening the score. (It's later proved that the TNT was set off accidentally.)

MAY: Red lawyer Siegfried Haag, former partner of Klaus Croissant, and Elisabeth von Dyck arrested for smuggling arms out of Switzerland.

MAY 9: Karl-Heinz Roth (who warned Stefan Aust about Baader/Mahler), Werner Sauber and Roland Otto arrested after a shootout at a roadblock in Cologne. Sauber's wounds also prove fatal.

MAY 21: DAY 1 of the trial of Baader, Ensslin, Meinhof and Raspe begins at Stammheim. First of many objections to the court appointed defence lawyers raised by Ulrike Meinhof.

JUNE 5: DAY 2: Baader, still without a defence lawyer of his own choice, petitions for suspension of the trial until he's found one; and is allowed unsupervised conversations with lawyers. (Baader's claim that the prosecution is bugging cells used for lawyers' visits is scoffed at. But later the state has to admit that cells were bugged at the time of the Lorenz kidnapping and the Stockholm siege: 'two cases of justifiable emergency.')

JUNE 11: DAY 4: Baader allows Hans Heinz Heldmann to represent him. Heldmann immediately applies for a ten day adjournment to talk to his client and study the case files he hasn't yet been issued with. Then Otto Schily, defending Ensslin, asks for an adjournment on the grounds that the defendants are no longer fit to stand trial. When both applications are rejected, all the chosen defence lawyers walk out. Presiding Judge Prinzing then adjourns.

JUNE 15: DAY 5: Despite extensive cross-examination by Schily, Heldmann and Baader, prison doctor Henck maintains that the defendants are fit to stand to trial. After an adjournment there's more court-appointed defence lawyer baiting, ending in an uproar that the defendants have to create in order to leave the court.

JUNE 18: DAY 6: Baader reads out a statement on 'Fitness to stand trial': "The basic problem, on this point too, is the antagonism that calls for the state machine to make re-education, or brain washing, a legitimate project. That is, in order to subdue the subject the state machine must be able to constitute it. The cause at issue between the repressive state machine and the capturred revolutionary, however, is that both know that in their irreconcilability, as in their relationship, they express the maturity of the development wherein the contradiction between productive forces and the circumstances of production becomes antagonistic in the final crisis of capital, and thus the expression of the trend whereby the legitimisation of the bourgeois state has fallen apart."

Judge Prinzing withdraws Baader's permission to speak. Then Ulrike Meinhof applies for an examination by an independent doctor because she is finding it difficult to follow the proceedings. Her application is, needless to say, denied.

JUNE 23: Klaus Croissant and Hans-Christian Ströbele are arrested. Croissant's Stuttgart office is raided and documents taken away, causing a five day delay of the trial.

JULY 3: DAY 13: Jan-Carl Raspe makes the first of many challenges to Prinzing and the court on grounds of bias.

AUGUST 5: DAY 23: Application after application has been made by the defendants and their lawyers in order to raise the trial to a political level. To get more directly to the point, Baader quotes an Interior Minister's definition of terrorism: 'The basic rule of terrorism is to kill as many people as possible. Numb horror is the state of mind terrorists obviously wish to produce in more and more people throughout the world.'

Baader continues: "I would say that is the precise definition of Israel's policy towards the Palestinian Liberation Movement, that is the precise definition of the USA's policy in Vietnam, until its defeat . . . Numb horror is, in fact, exactly the state of mind the Federal Prosecutor's Office wants to produce in more and more people by having more and more 'dead sections' built in prisons . . . "

Ulrike Meinhof warms to this 'state monopoly on terror' line:

"Terrorism is the destruction of utilities such as dykes, waterworks, hospitals, power stations. All the targets at which the American bomb attacks on North Vietnam were systematically aimed from 1965 onwards. Terrorism operates amidst the fear of the masses. The Urban Guerrilla Movement, on the other hand, carries fear to the machinery of the state."

The defendants are removed from court.

AUGUST 19: DAY 26: The defendants, having been expelled from the courtroom for causing another disturbance, are recalled individually to have their personal data examined. Judge Prinzing has been trying to get to this initial stage of the trial (which comes before the reading of the charges) since Day 1.

Jan-Carl Raspe is dragged into the courtroom by two prison guards.

Prinzing: "Please sit down."

Raspe: "I won't sit down."

Prinzing: "Then I must draw the following points to your attention. We now intend to proceed to the examination of personal data."

Raspe: "That doesn't interest me."

Prinzing: "At this point you have an opportunity to give your own account of yourself. The consequence of your failing to do so will be that we must proceed with the trial."

Raspe: "All I have to tell you is that I've been dragged in here by force. In the circumstances I'm not giving an account of myself. I'm going down again now, and naturally you'll continue with this spectacle."

Prinzing: "It is your duty, as a defendant, to remain here."

Raspe: "If you won't expel me from court anyway, I'll climb out over this balustrade somehow."

Attempts to do so, but guards prevent him. Thereupon Prinzing decides to have Raspe removed. A few minutes later, Ulrike Meinhof is carried into the courtroom by four prison guards.

Prinzing: "Please sit down, Frau Meinhof."

Meinhof: "I've no intention of sitting down."

Prinzing: "You have no intention of sitting down. Would you at least make use of the microphone, so that we can hear what you have to say?"

Meinhof: "I don't want anything to do with this. I'm in no position to defend myself, and naturally I can't be defended either."

Prinzing: "Will you give an account of your personal details?"

Meinhof: "In these circumstances I will not give any account of my personal details."

Makes to leave the dock, but is stopped by the guards.

Meinhof: "I want to go."

Prinzing: "It is your duty, as a defendant, to remain here."

Meinhof: "I'm not letting anyone force me, you arsehole!"

Prinzing: "Frau Meinhof, I observe that you have just addressed me as 'arsehole', as 'you arsehole'."

Meinhof: "Perhaps you'll take note of that."

Prinzing, after consulting his colleagues: "The defendant is expelled from court for the rest of today's hearing for calling the presiding judge, 'You arsehole'."

Andreas Baader is brought in and refuses to sit down.

Baader: "Get on with it and expel me, will you?"

Prinzing: "Herr Baader, this is not a question of your own wishes."

Baader: "Then list all the disturbances, or do I have to call you names? I'm finding this very difficult. You want to force me to stay here?"

Prinzing: "It's not that I want to; I must."

Baader: "What are you waiting for, do you want to provoke abuse or what?"

Prinzing: "I don't want to provoke anything, I would far rather you refrained from abuse."

Baader: "I shall disrupt the trial, this manoeuvring of yours is a dirty trick."

Prinzing: "There is no dirty trick involved. The rules of procedure oblige me to act as I do."

Baader: "So what do you want? Are you set on having physical violence here, or what?"

Prinzing: "I want you to sit down and take part in the hearing in an orderly manner."

Baader: "Hell, it's filthy manipulation, the way you're forcing me to spend five minutes insisting you expel me. I simply want to be out of here."

Prinzing: "It is not a question of your personal wishes. Your duty as a defendant is to remain here."

Baader: "Oh, alright, carry on with your ridiculous procedure. I shall create a disturbance."

Prinzing: "So far you are creating no disturbance."

Baader: "Well, let me tell you, Prinzing, you'd better expel me now or I'll find myself forced to abuse you."

Prinzing: "Herr Baader."

Baader: "Are you set on hearing it then? Alright, you can have it, you can have it all sorts of ways."

Prinzing: "I do not wish to hear it."

Baader: "Well, you can hear me tell you you're a Fascist arsehole."

excerpt from:

Jackal

by John Follain

Carlos and Carlos the Jackal were the *noms de guerre* of Ilich Ramirez Sanchez, a manic Venezuelan-born terrorist best known for kidnapping eleven OPEC oil ministers in Vienna and flying with them to Algeria in 1975. Carlos was trained in Russia and later in Palestine, and became part of a new generation of careerists whose interest in terrorism seems to have had no ideological component despite his red diaper youth as the son of a prominent Communist party member. He worked for whoever would sponsor him, including East Germany, Iraq, Syria and Libya. He was paid handsomely for his labor, allowing him a lavish life style of three-star restaurants, swank townhouses and numerous mistresses. Among his "accomplishments": planting lethal bombs on two high-speed French trains, killing dozens; randomly destroying several Paris cafes; and assassination attempts in London. In this excerpt, we read how Carlos and his associates pull off the kidnapping of the century at the Vienna OPEC meeting. At the height of his power in the early 80s he had an inner circle of forty members and several hundred others on his payroll, most of whom were from Arab nations. He was captured by the DST in 1994 and is serving a life sentence in a French prison. Today the Jackal seems to have been, along with Abu Nidal, a secular model for the current wave of professional terrorists based in Afghanistan and elsewhere, who, whatever their religious or political motivations and justifications, willingly choose terror as a way to make a living and see it as a lifelong calling. John Follain is a former Reuters reporter who has written about the Mafia. He currently covers Italy for the AP.

On the morning of Sunday, 21 December Carlos trimmed his goatee, moustache and sideburns. He dressed in khaki trousers, a light grey pullover, and a brown Pierre Cardin leather jacket. He wore his beret at a not-too-jaunty angle. Weapons, as well as ammunition, explosives, fuses and detonators, were stuffed into Adidas sports bags which Carlos, Klein, Kröcher-Tiedemann and the three Arab members of the group slung over their shoulders.

The six left the flat and took a tramway along the Dr Karl Lueger Ring west of the city centre and got off close to the Christkindlmarkt, the traditional Christmas market which the previous night had done a brisk trade in grilled Austrian sausages and festive knick-knacks as seasonal carols blared out over loudspeakers. The market was quiet as the team stepped on to the slippery, snow-packed pavement. Clad in raincoats or light coats, they caught the blast of an icy wind. Weighed down by their heavy bags, they slowly made for the OPEC headquarters further down the avenue. they reached the seven-storey building, which also housed the Canadian embassy and a branch office of the Texaco company, just after half past eleven.

Klein breezily greeted the young policeman guarding the entrance of the glass and concrete building who barely nodded in reply. All through the morning ministers and their retinues had been arriving and leaving, and there was no reason to check this particular group, or so the policeman thought. The start of the session and the possibility of catching ministers on their way in had drawn some thirty journalists. Although no dramatic announcement was expected, the oil-producers' lobby had been news ever since it had jacked up prices in recent years. But after the talks resumed behind closed doors at half past ten, only a handful of reporters had stayed. When Carlos walked in, three news agency correspondents to whom stoic door-stepping 'on the offchance' was second nature were sheltering in the hallway from the cold outside.

Carlos asked them in English if the OPEC meeting was still on. The answer was yes, and his unremarkable party started up the stairs to the first floor. They looked a little shabby, as if they were junior members of some unimportant delegation. No one thought the short girl wearing a long skirt and a woollen hat worth a second look. Several of them looked swarthy, and Barthelémy Healey of Associated Press quipped as they went on their way, 'There goes the Angolan delegation.' Out of sight at the top of the stairs, Carlos and his team unzipped their sports bags, drew their guns out and then broke into a run. Klein donned a balaclava.

The ministerial session was still under way, but a few delegates were milling around the first-floor reception area and the corridor that led to the conference room. Only two plainclothed police officers were on duty on the first floor, Austrian Inspectors Anton Tichler and Josef Janda. They were among the first to see Carlos and his commando, clutching guns and grenades, burst through the red steel doors that led off the building's main stairway. Carlos's team started shooting.

Klein's orders were to take control of the telephone switchboard, and to search people in the reception area to make sure they were unarmed. The plan made no allowance for the no-nonsense temperament of the young blonde and bespectacled receptionist, Edith Heller. Squatting behind the reception desk which faced the stairway doors and the lifts, she managed to dial the police immediately and report, 'This is OPEC. They're shooting all over the place.' Klein realised what Heller was doing, ran up to her and aimed his pistol at the young woman's head. Heller felt as if her head had exploded when, after shifting his pistol very slightly, he fired a bullet through the telephone handset she was holding.

'I tried to signal to the operator that she must stop telephoning,' Klein related later. 'As she didn't react, I started shooting at the phones. But she was a hell of a woman, it was incredible. Each time I shot at a phone with my Beretta, a big automatic pistol, it made a huge racket. As for her, she would pick up another phone, so I tried to put a stop to it. I emptied my charger on the switchboard.'

On reaching the reception area, Carlos had immediately turned to his right and run towards the corridor that led to the conference chamber. Inspector Tichler, with a dexterity that belied his sixty years—he was due to retire in two months—lunged forward and managed to grab the barrel of Carlos's machine-pistol. But Carlos broke free. It was left to Kröcher-Tiedemann to deal with Tichler. Kröcher-Tiedemann paused only long enough to ask him, 'Are you a policeman?' The inspector had his hands up and was in no position to risk reaching for the Walther PPK automatic nestling in its holster on his belt. He started to turn away from the girl who was standing very close, just over a metre away. His answer that yes, he was a police officer, earned him a bullet which entered the back of his neck and ripped through his throat. Kröcher-Tiedemann shoved the fatally injured Tichler into one of the three lifts that opened on the reception area and pressed the button for the ground floor.

Moments later, Kröcher-Tiedemann spotted a broad-shouldered man who was walking backwards away from her, his hands in the air, and making for the steel doorway that led to the stairs. Klein saw him too—'a great hulking brute'—and thought, 'So much the better, one less to look after.' But Kröcher-Tiedemann strode up to the escapee, an Iraqi security guard called Hassan Saeed Al Khafari, and, undaunted by the fact that he dwarfed her, shoved her pistol into his chest. The Iraqi instantly threw his arms around her, and clasped her in a tight embrace. He began dragging her towards the doorway, the gun pressed tightly between them. The struggling couple disappeared out of Klein's view.

When Klein next saw the security guard, his brain lay spattered across the floor. Kröcher-Tiedemann had managed to draw another pistol. She later apologised to an Iraqi diplomat for the murder. The killing had been necessary, she explained, because the man had tried to take her weapon from her. She showed the diplomat her torn jacket. 'She behaved the way Carlos had ordered,' Klein observed.

After shaking off Inspector Tichler, Carlos seized hold of the brawny Inspector Josef Janda and dragged him down the corridor towards the conference hall. Janda, a Second World War veteran, had sized up the attackers, and realised it would be suicidal for him to draw his Walther PPK automatic. He offered little resistance to Carlos, who did not know he was a police officer. Moments later, Carlos threw the unharmed inspector into one of the side offices that lined the corridor. The recording of Janda's telephone call to Vienna's police headquarters, which he made at 11.44 following the set formula he had been trained to use, caught not only his voice—'Criminal Officer Janda, Department One. OPEC attack. Shooting with machine-pistols'—but also more shots, the sound of an execution carried out by Carlos.

A one-man offensive by a Libyan economist, Yousef Ismirli, had almost proved Carlos's undoing. Carlos was still in the corridor, which by then stank of gunsmoke and was half darkened as several lights had been shot to pieces, when the unarmed Ismirli—by all accounts a placid character—seized Carlos's weapon. The Libyan however did not know how to work the Beretta and fumbled with it ineffectually. Meanwhile Carlos drew an automatic pistol from underneath his leather jacket. A single shot would have been enough to put Ismirli out of action. But Carlos shot him first in the hand, making him drop the Beretta, then in a leg and in the stomach, before squeezing off a final shot into the back of the neck. 'I was furious, and what's more, I had to set an example,' Carlos coldly explained later. This was in line with one of his favourite mottoes: 'To achieve things, you have to walk on bodies." Klein thought otherwise. 'It was a massacre,' he concluded, 'pure showing off, a gratuitous act, because the man was out of the fight.'

• • •

In the wood-panelled conference room an argument with millions of dollars at stake was in progress when Carlos's group walked into the building. Patience among the eleven Oil Ministers was running low, with everyone feeling put out by the failure to sign an agreement on oil prices two days earlier on Friday, as originally planned.

Shortly after the sixty or so people in the conference room heard the first shots being fired, two masked gunmen strode in and fired a volley of shots into the ceiling. With little regard for protocol or ministerial dignity, one of them ordered everyone to lie on the carpet and stay there. Sheikh Yamani's first thought was that he was the victim of an attack by Europeans seeking revenge for the oil price rises for which OPEC had been responsible. Convinced he was going to die, the forty-five-year-old Yamani began reciting to himself a verse from the Koran: 'To the righteous soul will be said: O thou soul, in complete rest and satisfaction. Come back to thy lord, well content thyself and well-pleasing unto him. Enter thou, then, among thy devotees. Yea, enter thou my Heaven.'

From their low vantage point, the Oil Ministers and officials stared at the tall man with a pale round face and an aquiline nose who ordered, 'Yussef! Put down your explosives!' speaking Arabic with a heavy foreign accent. Carlos then asked in English 'Have you found Yamani?' There was nowhere to hide. 'I'm here,' said the minister. He later recalled how 'the gunman scanned our faces and as his eyes met mine he greeted me sarcastically and identified me to his colleagues.'

It was soon afterwards, when Carlos sought out the Venezuelan Oil Minister, Valentin Hernandez Acosta, that the penny dropped—chillingly so for Yamani: 'The leader began talking to the Venezuelan minister in kindly fashion. That convinced us that the leader was the well-known terrorist, Carlos. This came as an unpleasant shock to me, for when the French government had raided his apartment last summer and he escaped, papers and documents were found there—and among them a plan to assassinate me.'

Klein had stationed himself in the corridor leading to the conference room with Joseph, who according to Klein had until that moment been hiding somewhere, probably to avoid getting hurt. As far as Klein could tell the team was now in control of the first floor and of everyone on it. 'That must have been clear even to people outside,' he reflected. 'You could have heard a pin drop in OPEC headquarters.' Unknown to Carlos's team, and within seconds of receiving Inspector Janda's telephone call, the duty officer at police headquarters had called out Vienna's Special Command unit. Minutes later, by which time Carlos was in the conference room, three of the squad's steel-helmeted men stormed into the foyer on the ground floor, brandishing Uzi submachineguns and wearing bullet-proof vests. They halted only long enough to make sure it was too late to save Inspector Tichler, whose body sprawled half in, half out of the lift, before charging up the stairs. A barrage of gunfire greeted them when they reached the reception area on the first floor.

Klein and Joseph were covering the corridor and reception area. The squad's commander Kurt Leopolder managed to make them out down the poorly lit corridor and returned fire. A bullet bounced off the wall and hit Klein in the stomach, while another grazed his thigh and a third hit his pistol. Leopolder was stopped from pressing his advantage when he was shot in the backside. Klein, who felt little pain from his stomach wound, threw a grenade, but clumsily. It exploded only four metres or so away from him, and six metres away from its target, Leopolder. Klein had dived to the floor in time and most of the shrapnel embedded itself in the walls.

The grenade, together with Klein's repeated shouts—'Get out or everybody will be killed!'—convinced the Austrians that retreat was the best option. Klein walked into a kitchen next to the corridor, lit a cigarette and rolled up his sweater to examine his injury. He was surprised to see no blood flowing from the neat hole in his stomach. When Klein entered the conference room to show Carlos his wound and tell him about the injured Austrian in the reception area, Carlos gave him a comforting pat on the head and told him to sit down and help guard the hostages. Kröcher-Tiedemann also reported back to Carlos, sauntering up to him with a smirk: 'I've killed two,' she said. Carlos smiled and answered, 'Good. I've killed one myself.' She asked him about Yamani, and Carlos pointed the minister out to her.

There was plenty for Carlos to smile about. By midday, after an attack that lasted less than half an hour, he had pulled off the first part of his mission. His group had seized control of the OPEC offices, and taken sixty-two hostages. From the windows of the conference chamber, Carlos could see Special Command units, equipped with machine-guns and tear gas, who had massed around the building. The units made no move to attack.

Carlos ordered his hostages to get up. As they dusted down their suits, the ministers and their delegations were told to stand in three separate groups: 'liberals and semi-liberals', 'criminals', and 'neutrals'. Algeria, Iraq, Libya and Kuwait counted as liberals and their representatives were shepherded to the far side of the oval conference table by the windows, uncomfortably close to where Yussef was stacking the gelignite explosive and connecting it to electronic detonators. Officials from the neutral camp—Ecuador, Gabon, Indonesia, Nigeria and Venezuela—were placed on the other side of the table. Saudi Arabia, Iran, Qatar and the United Arab Emirates, whose ambassador Carlos had planned to kidnap in London, were criminals. Turning to Yamani, Carlos said; 'I am Carlos. You know me.'

'Very well,' Yamani answered evenly.

Carlos felt he owed his hostages an explanation. In less than fluent Arabic, he announced he was at the head of a Palestinian commando and that its main targets were Saudi Arabia and Iran. If everyone cooperated, he promised, no one would be killed. Carlos then made a young British secretary, Griselda Carey, copy out a note written in approximate English. Carlos's message was terse and to the point:

• • •

To the Austrian Authorities

We are holding hostage the delegations to the OPEC Conference. We demand the lecture of our communique on the Austrian radio and television network every two hours, starting two hours from now.

A large bus with windows covered by curtains must be prepared to carry us to the airport of Vienna tomorrow at 7.00, where a full-tanked DC9 with a crew of three must be ready to take us and our hostages to our destination.

Any delay, provocation or unauthorised approach under any guise will endanger the life of our hostages.

The Arm of the Arab Revolution

Vienna 21/XII/75

Carlos also made Carey copy, this time in French, a rambling, seven-page communiqué which carried Haddad's stamp. The Arab people, the manifesto proclaimed, were under threat from a violent plot which would culminate in a victory for Zionism. The plotters were American imperialism, Zionist aggressors and several Arab governments, and they aimed to break the resistance of the Palestinian revolutionaries and to sow disunity in the Arab world. The communique also demanded that there should be no negotiation, no treaty and no recognition for Israel; no capitulation, tacit or otherwise, in the face of Israeli occupation of 'Palestinian Arab land'. It insisted there must be an Egyptian army offensive on Israel, with Syria, Iraq and the Palestinians forming a common front north-east of Israel. It also demanded the relaunch of Arab unification and, finally, that oil resources be handled 'for the benefit of the Arab people and other peoples of the Third World'.

When Carey had finished writing, Carlos told her to take the letter and the manifesto to the Austrian authorities. On her way, she should help out of the building the wounded policeman in the reception area. It was a daunting task for Carey. Clutching Carlos's messages, she had to make her way down the darkened corridor, managing to locate the injured Leopolder despite the lack of light. The terrorists, she told him, had agreed to his leaving the building but only on condition that his unit cease firing. Leopolder, whose men had retreated down the stairway, had no choice but to accept. Her job accomplished, Carey emerged at last into the cold air, trembling and shouting, 'Don't shoot! Don't shoot!'

As Carlos waited for an answer to his letter, he felt confident enough to ignore the rules he had tried to drum into Klein and allowed an Austrian secretary in hysterics to walk free. Moments later, Carlos casually left a loaded Beretta on a table close to several ministers and walked away, carrying only his machine pistol. Had anyone been so foolish as to try to grab it, Carlos would have shot him and probably wounded others as well. 'I wanted to find out who the security guards were,' Carlos justified himself later. It was typical of the games Carlos liked to play, as he blew hot and cold on his hostages' fate. 'At times we believed our lives would be spared and at other times we thought our execution was a certainty,' recalled the Venezuelan minister Hernandez Acosta, who asked Carlos to pick up the gun he had left behind. Another delegate compared their plight to 'some awful party which you couldn't leave'.

With the hostages held at gunpoint, and the conference room wired with explosives, the Austrians had little choice but to start negotiating. Belaïd Abdessalam, the Algerian Oil Minister who was also a doctor, relayed to the officials waiting on the ground floor Carlos's demand that Klein should be taken to hospital for urgent treatment. Carlos emptied Klein's pockets so the police would have no clue as to his identity. The Algerian minister then escorted Klein down the staircase, holding Klein's hands up in the air as they walked.

As Klein was carried to a waiting ambulance on a stretcher, right hand clutching his wound and left hand masking his face, a policeman asked him in German: 'Are you a hostage?' Klein answered in the best English he could muster: 'My fight-name is Angie.' It was only then that he lost consciousness. He had been extraordinarily resilient. On the operating table, surgeons found that the bullet, which had broken up inside him, had pierced not only his colon, but also his pancreas and duodenal artery.

Carlos requested that the Libyan ambassador to Vienna act as mediator, but he was away in Hungary. The Iraqi chargé d'affaires in the city, Riyadh Al-Azzawi, volunteered his services and he proved acceptable to both the Austrians and Carlos. The diplomat was greeted with bravado. 'Tell them I'm from Venezuela and my name is Carlos. Tell them I'm the famous Carlos. They know me.' From then on, negotiations were conducted through Al-Azzawi who relayed the kidnappers' demands to Austrian officials on the ground floor of the OPEC building. The only telephone available there was in the porter's lodge. The negotiators were reduced to making long-distance calls to the organisation's various members one at a time.

Carlos hammered home his demands: a plane and crew; the return of the injured Klein who would travel with them; a radio; and twenty-five metres of rope and five pairs of scissors. If the demands were not met, or if government forces were foolish enough to storm the building, he would start shooting the hostages. The mediator reported to Carlos that doctors at the Allgemeines Krankenhaus hospital, where Klein had had his fingerprints taken and was photographed by police, estimated that he needed a month to recover. He added that Klein was being kept alive with a breathing apparatus. Carlos turned to consult his companions. They were unanimous. 'I don't care if he dies on the flight,' Carlos said. 'We came together and we will leave together.'

Carlos's demands were passed on to the Austrian Chancellor, socialist Bruno Kreisky, who had been plucked by an air force helicopter from his Christmas holiday in the mountain resort of Lech some six hundred kilometres away to confront what he later laconically termed 'a particularly difficult situation'.

At three o'clock in the afternoon, more than three hours after the first shots had rung out, Carlos motioned Yamani outside the conference chamber and into a smaller room. Of all the hostages, Yamani was the most famous. As a chief architect of the oil embargo that had led to crippling fuel price rises, he was for many years a bogey-man for the West. But the decision to lift the embargo in the spring of 1974 brought down on him the wrath of Palestinian extremists. The Popular Front had hoped the embargo would be used to isolate Israel from allies such as Washington. Notoriety in the West and Haddad's hatred for Yamani combined to make him an ideal target.

Yamani believed his execution was about to take place, out of sight of the other officials. So he was surprised to hear Carlos talking to him in a reassuring tone, even singing his praises. But the mask soon dropped. Carlos said he planned to make an example of Yamani in protest against the policies of Saudi Arabia. Much as he personally respected the sheikh, he insisted he had no alternative than to kill him. If the Austrian government failed to have the communiqué read on the radio and to supply the plane, his execution would take place at six o'clock that evening, and his body would be thrown into the street. A man of Yamani's intelligence and courage, Carlos concluded with a flourish, would bear no resentment against his executioners, and would understand the nobility of their objectives and intentions.

'How can it be that you tell me that you will kill me and then ask me not to feel bitterness towards you?' the sheikh asked. 'You must be trying to force me to do something.'

'You! Why should I put pressure on you?' Carlos exclaimed. 'I am putting pressure on the Austrian government to get out of this place. So far as you are concerned I am just making you aware of the facts.'

As the Sunday afternoon wore on, Carlos relaxed. The ministers and officials were free to walk from the conference room to the toilets across the corridor without having to seek permission. The rope supplied by the Austrians was abandoned in a corner of the room. A radio which the Iraqi mediator had fetched from his home played in another corner, as Carlos's team took turns at listening to news reports about their coup and to find out whether Kreisky would broadcast their statement. Carlos chatted amicably, switching between Arabic, French and Spanish. He understood German, but the only time he spoke in that language was when he politely asked one of the officials, 'Would you like some more cigarettes?'

Carlos told his hostages that he was at war with capitalist society, styling himself a leader who must marshal his troops to final victory. 'Me, I'm a soldier and I live under the tent,' Carlos proclaimed. When a Gabonese delegate told him his nationality, Carlos reassured him: 'Don't worry, we have nothing against you. You are the defenders of the Third World.' Carlos also told the Iranian Oil Minister that the OPEC raid would not be his last, and boasted that he had forty trained commandos ready to launch attacks across the world.

At five o'clock the communiqué had still not been read out. Carlos walked up to Yamani and, with a smile, reminded him of their chat. 'My feelings had changed and there was less terror in my heart,' Yamani recalled. 'I began to think, not of myself but of my family, my children, my relatives and those for whom I had responsibility. I wrote a farewell letter to them, explaining what I wanted done.'

The Austrian Chancellor agreed to have the statement broadcast for the first time at 6.22 p.m. It cannot have made a great impression upon its Austrian audience, although it expressed 'regrets for the predicament in which our operation has placed the peace-loving Austrian people'. The statement was read by a solemn Austrian announcer in laughable French every two hours until four o'clock the following morning.

Chancellor Kreisky had made one concession, but now he insisted on consulting the hostages before going any further. At Kreisky's request, a total of thirteen ministers and senior officials wrote letters addressed to him, and Carlos made a great show of respecting their confidentiality. All appealed to Kreisky to grant Carlos's demands, and wrote that they were willing to leave Austria under his guard. Yamani's letter urged Austria to accept Carlos's requests to spare any unnecessary bloodshed.

To feed his team and the hostages, none of whom had eaten since that morning, Carlos requested a hundred sandwiches and fruit. The Austrians promptly supplied these, but many of the sandwiches contained ham. As most of those held in the conference room were Moslem, Carlos rejected the delivery. He requested chicken and chips instead. The Hilton solved the problem. The hotel had planned to serve a banquet on its premises in OPEC's honour that evening. Although the reception was unavoidably cancelled the food was sent to the OPEC building at ten o'clock. As many of the conference room's lights had been shot at, the ministers and officials picked at the food by candlelight. Carlos showed no regret for the blood shed that morning. Perhaps the Libyan economist whom he had slain had taken him for a Mossad agent. 'It's not my fault if I look Jewish,' Carlos joked loudly.

After a midnight Cabinet meeting at the Chancellery, a strained-looking Kreisky announced that an agreement with Carlos had been reached by his government and OPEC officials. Austria caved in, hoping to prevent any more bloodshed, in return for a pledge that the hostages would be freed on arrival at their destination. To one reporter who challenged his decision, Kreisky snapped: 'What kind of alternative do you want? A storm attack on the building? That's no alternative . . . We can't be generous with the lives of others.'

Later, the Chancellor cited the killings at the outset of the raid, the explosives laid around the conference room, and Carlos's insistence on taking the badly wounded Klein with him even though he might die on the flight as evidence that the gang had no regard for human life. Algeria, one of the countries that Carlos had accepted as a possible destination, was willing to receive the planeload of hostages and their kidnappers. Kreisky saw no reason not to take up the offer, but insisted that Carlos should release all OPEC employees before leaving Vienna.

The Chancellor's condition infuriated Carlos. He shouted at the Iraqi intermediary: 'I command Kreisky and everybody else here. I decide who shall go and who shall stay.' But he then calmed down and added petulantly: 'I don't intend to take them. But I don't want people to tell me who to take and who not to take.' As for where to take them, Carlos had apparently not yet decided. In the small hours of Monday morning he asked the Iraqi mediator which Arab states were prepared to receive him.

The hostages had an uncomfortable night, settling down as best they could in the chairs around the conference table, or on the floor. The body of the Libyan economist who had made his one man stand against Carlos was left close to where he had fallen.

At twenty to seven the following morning, a yellow Austrian post office bus—the only bus equipped with curtains that the authorities had been able to find at short notice—drew up outside the rear entrance of the OPEC building. 'We could have made Kreisky dance on the table,' Carlos bragged. Standing in the snow by the bus, like a schoolteacher on an outing cheerfully directing his flock, Carlos gave those whom he had agreed to free a hearty handshake or a playful tap on the shoulder. In full view of television crews, he even made to embrace one hostage, but the Beretta slung across his chest got in the way. Carlos complied with Kreisky's request, but this still left forty-two hostages.

Wary of triggering a massacre similar to that which had claimed the lives of the Israeli athletes at the Munich Olympics three years earlier, the Austrians made no attempt to shoot at Carlos or his accomplices during the hour or so that they spent out in the open. As the bus, its curtains drawn, started down the Dr Karl Lueger Ring, an ambulance and two police cars with flashing blue warning lights led it slowly through the Monday morning traffic. Standing by the driver at the front of the bus, Carlos waved to people in the streets. '*Sonderfahrt*' (Special trip) read the sign behind the windscreen. Earlier, another ambulance had ferried Klein, and a doctor who had volunteered to accompany him on the flight, to the getaway Austrian Airlines DC9 at Vienna's airport.

The plane was ready to leave when Austrian Interior Minister Otto Roesch, a former member of the Hitler Youth who had helped the ministers abroad, made to shake hands with Carlos. Carlos caught his own hand in the shoulder strap of his machine-pistol but still managed to give the Austrian a clumsy handshake. 'Handshake of Shame', headlined the newspapers the next day as Roesch was castigated for his gesture towards a man whose accomplice had shot dead an Austrian police inspector. (More than twenty years later, Austrian police officers questioning Carlos refused to shake his hand, saying that they did not want to attract the same criticism as Roesch had.)

As he organised the hostages in the plane's cabin, Carlos segregated Amouzegar, Yamani and his deputy. Explosives were placed under their seats. According to Klein, Amouzegar was on the blacklist because he had headed the shah's internal security and secret police, the Savak—a role which Amouzegar denies having played. Created with a helping hand from the CIA and Mossad, the Savak rooted out dissent at home and abroad with its army of 30,000, and a vast number of collaborators. For Haddad, the fact that the shah had granted Israel diplomatic recognition was enough to justify Amouzegar's elimination.

Carlos began to relax once the plane took off just after nine o'clock on Monday, 22 December, its destination unknown to the hostages. Machine-pistol resting in his lap, he talked calmly and courteously with Amouzegar and Yamani. He even gave Yamani his mother's telephone number in Venezuela, asking him to ring her and tell her that her son was fine. 'We talked about everything, including his private life, his youth, his studies in London,' Yamani recalled. 'He was a man who loved life, running after girls and having fun. He was also very well dressed in luxury clothes. He chatted and joked, but I couldn't stop myself thinking that he had promised me he would kill me in cold blood.'

Sheikh Yamani took advantage of Carlos's bonhomie to seek some clues about their fate. The plane would fly to Algiers, spend a couple of hours there, and then move on to Tripoli. Yamani asked if he expected any problems in Libya. Carlos looked surprised: 'On the contrary, the Prime Minister will be there to receive us, and a Boeing plane will be ready to take us to Baghdad.' When Yamani asked if a stop in Damascus was on the cards, Carlos replied: 'They have become deviationists and dangerous, and I will not set foot on their soil.'

On the flight Carlos handed out autographs, 'like a film-star', recalled the Venezuelan minister Hernandez Acosta. The one Carlos gave a Nigerian official read simply, 'On flight Vienna–Algiers. Carlos 22/XII/75', with his name underlined. Carlos boasted to Hernandez Acosta that he was the man who, in his phrase, had 'liquidated' the French counter-intelligence officers and Moukharbal in Paris that June. When it was suggested to Amouzegar some time later that the autographs, and the way Carlos had previously waved to people from the bus, smacked a little of Robin Hood, the Iranian agreed. Carlos wanted to be loved, and felt that he was fighting for the poor, Amouzegar remarked.

During the flight to Algiers Kröcher-Tiedemann squatted by Klein's side at the back of the plane, wiped the sweat off his brow, moistened his cracked lips with water and whispered words of comfort in his ear. She broke off looking after Klein to regale the hostages with an account punctuated by laughter of how she had shot dead 'the old man' (Inspector Tichler). Then she broke down and wept.

The red and white twin-engined plane touched down at the Dar El Beida airport outside Algiers after a two-and-a-half-hour flight. Carlos, still clad in his beret but now sporting sunglasses, emerged from the plane unarmed. A smiling Abdel Aziz Bouteflika, Algeria's long-serving Foreign Minister, embraced Carlos and patted him on the back as they walked to the VIP lounge. A Red Crescent ambulance took Klein away, and when he regained consciousness he found himself back in hospital.

With the jet's engines still running, a cigar-smoking Carlos negotiated with Bouteflika and the Algerian Oil Minister, Belatd Abdessalam, for the better part of five hours. In the aircraft, his hostages sat with the blinds pulled down. The atmosphere, as Yamani described it, was one of 'silent horror,' caused by the alertness and anxiety of the terrorists' while everyone awaited the outcome.

Carlos agreed at the airport to release most of the non-Arab hostages, some thirty ministers and delegation officials. Carlos's countryman Hernandez Acosta, who was among those freed, asked before leaving: 'Tell me, Carlos, would you really have shot us?'

'Oh we wouldn't have shot you until the very last,' was the comforting retort.

Yamani and Amouzegar, together with senior officials from the other Arab delegations—a total of fifteen hostages—were told to remain on the plane. 'I am going to kill you,' Carlos told Yamani. 'I may not get you now, but I am going to kill you. You are a criminal, it won't be long before you are killed.'

Despite the initial warmth of his hosts, the talks with the Algerian authorities did not go as well as Carlos had hoped: 'We demanded another plane but they refused, saying there were none available. We were in a DC9, which is worth nothing for long distances.' On Monday afternoon Carlos decided to try his luck in another Arab state. The plane was refuelled and then flew from Algiers to Tripoli. But the reception did not live up to Carlos's expectations. The Libyan authorities ordered the plane to stop close to the runway and refused to give Carlos a red-carpet welcome. Frustrated and dismayed, Carlos protested that he had spent a month preparing the OPEC attack and that he could not work with the undisciplined Libyans.

Fanned by Carlos's nervousness, the atmosphere on board turned ominously tense. One of the exhausted guerrillas was taken ill and began vomiting in a corner. After talks with the Austrian ambassador to Libya who was acting as a go-between, Carlos set free the Libyan and Algerian ministers and five other delegates in the early hours of Tuesday, 23 December. One of the two Saudi officials released, who had tried to stay with his minister, said to Carlos as he left: 'For God's sake, do not harm Yamani.' Carlos replied: 'I have received instructions here in Libya from my bosses not to do any harm to him or to the Iranian minister, and I can now promise you that they will be safe. I could not make that promise to the Algerians.' Yamani, who overheard the remark, was unsure whether to believe him.

The second stage of Carlos's mission, as planned by Haddad, was unravelling. Libya refused to supply a longer-range plane. Saudi Arabia, with Yamani's safety a key concern, also refused to oblige. Only Austria had broadcast the commando's political statement. The city-hopping tour of Middle East capitals—to drop ministers off on their front doorstep or to blow their brains out, whichever the governments decided—was on the verge of being abandoned.

The plane took off from Tripoli at one o'clock in the morning, bound again for Algiers. But as it flew over Tunis the radio crackled and air traffic control there refused them permission to land. Carlos had sought no such authorisation, and the veto provoked him into defiance. He ordered the captain to descend towards the airport, but the runway lights were promptly turned off. 'We knew that a battle would probably break out on our arrival [in Tunis],' a still embittered Carlos recounted. 'It was a stupid gesture on the part of the Tunisians . . . The pilot was tired, and so we told him to go back to Algiers. We too were tired. We hadn't slept in four days, our nerves were stretched, rest was imperative.'

At 3.40 a.m. the DC9 landed once more at Dar El Beida airport outside Algiers. Carlos again isolated himself with the Algerian Foreign Minister Bouteflika, who was less than pleased at his return. Shortly afterwards Carlos walked back to the plane. He sat next to the hostages he despised the most, Yamani and Amouzegar: 'I do not know what I should do. I am a democrat and you do not know the meaning of democracy. I shall have a meeting now with my colleagues and consult them on what to do about your case. I shall inform you later about the decision taken.'

The ministers were unable to follow Carlos's discussion with his accomplices at the front of the cabin, but they could see that Kröcher-Tiedemann and Khalid were angry about something. The ministers sat in silence. Eventually Carlos returned: 'We have finally decided to release you by midday and with that decision your life is completely out of danger.'

'Why wait till then?' Yamani asked. 'It is late at night and if you release us now both you and ourselves can have some rest which we badly need.' Carlos replied that he wanted the excitement to last until noon. 'We shall turn off the lights and pull down the blinds,' he proposed. 'You will sleep peacefully knowing that your lives are no longer in danger.' Carlos's solicitude enraged Kröcher-Tiedemann, who it seems was against sparing the lives of the two ministers. 'Fuck you!' she yelled at Carlos.

The Algerians then recontacted Carlos and asked him to return to the VIP lounge for more talks. Two hours later Carlos came back to the plane and strode up to Yamani and Amouzegar. Yamani noted that Carlos's attitude had changed a great deal—possibly under pressure from the Algerians. 'I am leaving the plane now, and you can come out in five minutes,' Carlos announced. Carlos's team followed him out of the plane. Yamani wondered whether the jet was about to blow up. After waiting for the five minutes to elapse, he decided to leave, but his deputy volunteered to go first: 'I will go, they may be waiting at the bottom of the steps aiming to shoot you'.

When the last of the remaining hostages finally found the courage to abandon the plane and walk to the VIP lounge to which police directed them, they found themselves sharing it with the guerrillas who had seized them forty-four hours earlier. Suddenly, Haddad's orders came very close to being carried out. As Yamani and Amouzegar sat down to talk over their ordeal with the Algerian minister Bouteflika, a distraught-looking Khalid approached and began threatening them, his right hand scratching nervously at his chest. Bouteflika thrust a glass of fruit juice into Khalid's hand, giving Algerian policemen time to approach and frisk him. They found that Khalid, apparently reluctant to follow Carlos's orders, had hidden a gun under his arm. 'I came here to carry out the agreed execution of these criminals. But you have prevented me,' Khalid told the policemen.

Carlos stage-managed a lingering curtain-call. On the way out of the airport a black official car drove up to where a few journalists were standing and stopped while Carlos, lounging in the passenger seat, stared fixedly at them for a full minute or so. The three-car convoy bearing him and his team then swept away.

It was Hernandez Acosta who confirmed to the waiting world that the leader of the Vienna hostage-taking and the Venezuelan guerrilla known as Carlos the Jackal were one and the same man. Passing through Charles de Gaulle airport near Paris after flying in from Algiers, he quoted Carlos's boast about the shooting of the DST officers, and showed French police a letter that Carlos had handed him. It was addressed to 'Sra Elba Sánchez, Apt 2B, Residencia Las Americas, Av Las Americas, Caracas'.

The French Interior Ministry, embarrassed that positive identification of the letter's author would force Paris to put pressure on the friendly Algerian government and seek Carlos's extradition, hurriedly denied that any such document existed. 'There is no positive proof,' an Interior Ministry statement insisted, 'that the letter really exists, and certainly there is no copy in the possession of the police chiefs in the French capital.' A few hours later the Interior Ministry admitted it had lied, saying that Hernandez Acosta had allowed police to photocopy the letter. This too was untrue. Hernandez Acosta believed that his integrity demanded that he respect the privacy of the letter's author, whom he described as 'young, spontaneous and talking a lot'. He refused to let the police photocopy the letter, as the police report drawn up at the time which only contains a copy of the envelope shows.

According to the Interior Ministry, a graphology expert failed to establish a definite link with the notes found in Carlos's arms cache in Paris. But within hours, Scotland Yard brushed aside the reservations of its French colleagues and insisted that the writing on the envelope was identical to that on papers found in the London flat of Angela Otaola. The writer, and the master of the Vienna coup, was definitely Ilich Ramírez Sánchez, alias Carlos the Jackal.

Handing the letter to the Venezuelan minister was a typically flamboyant, but ultimately foolish act by Carlos. There was no need to ask Hernandez Acosta to act as a courier. Carlos could simply have stuck a stamp on the envelope and sent the letter from the nearest post office, and the police forces hunting him would have been none the wiser. But, as he had shown in handing out his autographs, Carlos felt the need, literally, to sign the OPEC raid.

'With hindsight,' said Klein, 'I think that what motivated Carlos was adventure, followed by money.' Vienna supplied plenty of both as sparing the lives of Yamani and Amouzegar made Carlos a rich man. Twenty million dollars richer according to Western intelligence estimates. And once again, Carlos got away with murder.

excerpt from:

The Dirty War
by Martin Dillon

The conflict in Northern Ireland is one of the bloodiest and most complex civil wars in recent times, and the only one in Western Europe in
the post-World War II era. What rarely surfaces in political commentary
about the IRA is the inhumanity conveyed by the randomness of so
many murders, and the cynicism and despair displayed by supposedly
ordinary citizens "in the line of patriotic duty." As we begin this selection, set in 1970, the English troops have arrived in Northern Ireland en
masse, dramatically changing the nature of the conflict. The IRA goes on
the offensive, deciding that the easiest way to kill ordinary soldiers and
to frighten their comrades was literally to seduce them. Martin Dillon is
a BBC journalist, television documentary producer and terrorism expert.

The arrival of the Provisionals on the scene in 1970 transformed the
situation on the streets and ended the honeymoon for British
troops who had arrived in August 1969 as defenders of the Catholic
population. Events in 1970 changed the manner in which the troops operated and heralded the difficulties they would face in later years. It was in
1970 that the Provisionals began preparing for a war with the British
Army—planning arms shipments, training volunteers and moulding their
organisation into an urban guerrilla force. The Provisionals' Chief of Staff,
Sean MacStiofan, told other members of the Army Council that once
units were equipped with modern weaponry the war with the traditional
enemy, the British, would begin in earnest. What he really meant was that
when the time was right the IRA would start killing soldiers on the streets
of Northern Ireland. The IRA campaign in 1970 amounted to bombing

commercial targets and the killing of two policemen in a booby-trap explosion close to the border. While the Provisionals busied themselves devising a political language of revolution through the IRA newspaper *Republican News*, a series of events on the streets coalesced to harden attitudes within the Catholic community towards the British Army and to ignite the traditional Republican methods espoused by the Provisionals.

In May the Conservative administration of Edward Heath replaced the Labour government at Westminster and led to a change in military strategy in Northern Ireland. Encouraged by the presence of the Tories in power, the British Army believed the new government would support a change of Army policy from the peacekeeping role to a more assertive one of seeking out the troublemakers in both communities. In June the Army illustrated its willingness to adopt an aggressive posture by dealing harshly with rioters and seeking out IRA weapons. As a result of a tip-off, soldiers entered the Lower Falls area of Belfast on 3 July and in a house search they uncovered a quantity of pistols, a sub-machine-gun and explosives; the weapons belonged to the Official IRA. The seizure led to crowd reaction and within a short time a full-scale riot was in progress. The area was an Official IRA stronghold, and at the height of the disturbance the Provisionals pulled their men out and left the Officials to face the full force of the British Army. In this way the Provos avoided losing what few weapons they had in a confrontation which could only end in disaster. As the Officials engaged the troops, the narrow streets of the Lower Falls became a battleground, with guns being fired and grenades thrown. The rioting began at 6.00 p.m. and within four hours, as the area was shrouded in CS gas, the Army general, Sir Ian Freeland, placed a curfew on the area. The general later explained it was not in fact a curfew but merely a 'movement restriction on the population of that area for their own safety and the safety of the soldiers'. His decision also had the effect of clearing the area of the media. Those few journalists who were unable to avoid the imposition of the curfew were arrested and charged with breaking the curfew order, though the charges were later dropped. However, without the media there to observe their activities soldiers undertook a search operation which went beyond the rules of normal Army conduct. Hundreds of homes were damaged and several pubs and business premises were looted. The search did yield a massive quantity of weapons, ammunition and explosives, but it also allowed soldiers to behave with reckless abandon and thereby served to signal a change in Army strategy. Four people were shot dead, one man was killed when he was hit by an armoured personnel carrier, and sixty people were injured, fifteen of them soldiers. The Army were judged by many nationalist politicians to have overreacted. The quantity of CS gas, 1600 canisters, was considered to be excessive in a small area which housed a lot of elderly people and children.

The Provisionals, who were suspected of starting much of the trouble, benefited from the outcome. That episode and others where the Provisionals were the instigators in 1970 fuelled a resentment towards the Army within Catholic areas and reinforced the Provisional IRA philosophy that the soldiers were the traditional enemies of the nationalist population. Some observers saw the Army's developing role of aggression as a policy of attrition in keeping with the thoughts of Brigadier Frank Kitson, who believed that riots provided the ideal opportunity for seeking out and arresting the extremists. By the end of 1970 the Provisionals were ready for their own war of attrition. As the Army was announcing that rioters were liable to be shot, the Provisionals were planning to kill soldiers but not during riots. The Provisionals had learned one important lesson from the Lower Falls curfew: that the British Army was a formidable enemy in open warfare. Some IRA members decided that other methods were required to kill soldiers. Those Provisionals who decided to devise new and what would eventually be considered dirty tactics were influenced in their thinking by the volunteers in Cumann na mBann, the female wing of the IRA.

The role of women in the shadowy world of espionage and terror has been depicted in novels and movies as glamorous and deadly. In reality that imagery holds certain truths, but in the world of terrorism women tend to be more deadly than glamorous. Exceptions to the rule have been the Irish terrorist Maria Maguire, who was in the headlines in the early 1970s as a pretty, miniskirted gunrunner, and Leila Khaled, the first female hijacker, whose smouldering attractiveness made her a Palestinian pin-up.

The IRA always recognised the deadly capabilities of its female members but traditionally refused to permit girls and women to play a prominent role in the expression and execution of terror. The supportive role of women in IRA history until 1971 mirrored the role of women in Irish society. The male adopted the dominant, overt role, while the female was subservient. Women were only allowed to act as couriers or to help move guns and explosives. It was unthinkable to the IRA that women should be in the front line of the war killing soldiers. The image of Leila Khaled hijacking a plane over London on 6 September 1970 may well have been a signal to the Provisionals that the time had come for women to play a prominent role in guerrilla warfare. It was also a time when well-educated young women such as the Price sisters were joining the Provisionals and asserting their right to be at the forefront of the conflict. It was younger women within the IRA who recognised that the 'honeytrap', the use of sexual entrapment, was a way of luring soldiers to their deaths. Such a tactic would never have been contemplated by the IRA in other decades, but by the end of 1970 and the beginning of 1971 there were younger IRA commanders who were prepared to consider any tactic which would deliver soldiers to their deaths. These younger elements were not rooted in the old Catholic IRA tradition and their hatred of the British Army was so intense that it disposed of previous IRA principles and tactics. A new type of war was taking shape. There was a great deal of bitterness within the minds of many young people—resentment of a system which the British had kept in place for fifty years, anger against soldiers who were behaving with heavy-handedness towards the Catholic population, and a general feeling that the Provisionals were right in maintaining that the Army was in place to deal with only one section of the population, the nationalists. The Provisionals opened up old historical wounds, and no one in military or political circles had the foresight to realise what was happening or to seek to develop a different military or political strategy to counter the rise of romantic nationalism. Kitson did recognise one of the difficulties facing the Army: that the Protestant population was always 'leaning on us' to do something about the Republicans.

In this atmosphere the IRA began planning the murder of off-duty soldiers. The British Army had failed to learn the lessons of Palestine and allowed young soldiers to drink while off-duty in pubs in Belfast city centre and in town centres such as Lisburn. Cumann na mBann argued that soldiers were easily identified because of their regular Army hairstyles and they were vulnerable because they were unarmed. The proposal made to the IRA was that the soldiers could be lured from bars by the offer of sex, and then taken to a convenient place and shot.

On 9 March 1971 three young Scotsmen from the Royal Highland Fusiliers decided to spend an off-duty day in Belfast city centre. Two of the soldiers, seventeen-year-old John McCaig and his brother Joseph, aged eighteen, were new to Army life and on their first tour of duty. They knew little of the background to the conflict in Northern Ireland and did not regard themselves as being at risk. Another member of their unit, twenty-three-year-old Dougald McCaughey, agreed to join them on a pub crawl to alleviate their boredom and to seek out female companionship. At that time the city centre had not yet become a target for bombers and a nightly haunt of sectarian assassins, and it was regarded as a neutral area of Belfast which offered a lively nightlife. The three young Scotsmen were based at Girdwood Barracks on Belfast's Antrim Road, half a mile from the city's main shopping precinct.

On 9 March the McCaig brothers from Ayr and McCaughey from Glasgow travelled into town in much the same way as they did in their home towns. They were casually dressed, and aside from their accents and short hairstyles they did not appear at first sight to be off-duty soldiers. They visited several bars in the vicinity of High Street and Royal Avenue and in one of them they were singled out for attention by two female IRA volunteers in their early twenties who were searching bars for soldiers. On that day there were many off-duty soldiers in town, and one can only speculate that the youth and demeanour of the teenage McCaigs suggested that they were vulnerable. Until now it was always believed that IRA men apprehended the three soldiers, but that is not true. The female terrorists followed the three soldiers to Mooney's Bar in Cornmarket and befriended them there; doubtless they chose their moment to approach the soldiers after a considerable quantity of alcohol had been consumed. At some stage in the evening, one of the women made a pre-arranged phone call to an IRA safe-house in Ardoyne and confirmed that a car and assistance were required. A short time later, three men from the IRA's 3rd Battalion arrived in Mooney's. The two women welcomed them as friends and introduced them to the soldiers. The three IRA men were from Ardoyne. One of them was Paddy McAdorey, who was shot dead by the Army later that year. Another man, whom I cannot name for legal reasons, is, I believe, living in the Irish Republic and was known as a professional killer who bragged about his exploits. However, to the young soldiers the IRA men must have appeared pleasant and friendly.

As the evening progressed, the soldiers became intoxicated and the IRA women invited them to a party which they said was being held on the outskirts of Belfast. The IRA men said they had two cars and they would drive everyone there. As closing time approached the IRA team and the soldiers left the bar. McCaughey and the McCaig brothers followed, carrying their pint beer glasses, and walked to a nearby street where the IRA team had left two cars. The IRA leader and the two women got into one car and the other IRA men and the three soldiers climbed into the other. The vehicle carrying the women contained two weapons.

It was driven towards North Belfast and the Crumlin Road while the other car travelled behind at a short distance. Both cars proceeded countrywards and left the city limits. On the Hightown Road the first vehicle came to a halt when the car behind sounded its horn. The IRA leader left his vehicle and was told by his accomplices that the three Scotsmen needed to urinate. The soldiers left the car, each of them with a beer glass in one hand, and began to urinate at a ditch by the roadside. At this stage the IRA men took the guns from the first vehicle. Joseph McCaig was shot three times through the back of the head. His brother was struck with the butt of a pistol and shot twice in the head. McCaughey was shot once through the back of the head.

It was a professional execution which shocked Catholics as well as Protestants in Ireland. To the Army it was a warning that was not fully heeded. Since it was believed that the soldiers had been picked up by IRA men, the IRA could use the same ploy again. No one was ever charged with the killings. The IRA leader was one of the toughest and most infamous IRA men in the Ardoyne district, and regarded by the Army as a hardened terrorist. His accomplices left Northern Ireland for the safety of the Irish Republic in the mid-seventies. One of them was a ruthless killer who enjoyed killing at close quarters and who shot a policeman at point-blank range with a carbine before fleeing to the Republic. . . . The names of the three killers were made known to the Army in 1972 by the SDLP councillor Paddy Wilson; his revelation was made to a masseuse in an Antrim Road massage parlour and tape-recorded by Army intelligence, who were running their own honeytrap as part of the MRF operations.

The Army's failure to discover the role of IRA women in the soldiers' deaths and their reluctance to curtail the off-duty activities of soldiers was to have fatal consequences. As a result of the killing of the three Fusiliers, Belfast city centre was made out of bounds to off-duty soldiers, but this policy served to encourage soldiers to frequent pubs and hotels on the periphery of the city and near the town of Lisburn, which was predominantly Protestant and the site of Army headquarters. The change of habit did not go unnoticed in IRA circles, particularly in Ardoyne, where Martin Meehan was in control of the 3rd Battalion and on the Belfast Brigade Staff. The Brigade Staff were told that it was possible to lure soldiers from a well-known hotel near Lisburn and that the 3rd Battalion could handle such an operation, since they had proved their ability to do so by killing the Scots soldiers. The Provisionals' Belfast Brigade gave permission for a similar operation, even though it might well take place within an area covered by the 1st Battalion, whose responsibility extended outwards towards Finaghy and Lisburn. As with the Four-Square Laundry operation the Brigade Staff were consulted because of the IRA's strict rule that volunteers or active service units should operate only in those areas defined for their units, companies and battalions. If the Belfast Brigade were prepared to bend the rules, that implies that the 3rd Battalion was offering to use the same team as in the murder of the Scottish soldiers. I do not know if the same team was indeed used, but I leave the reader to make a judgment based on the facts.

During March 1973 two IRA women paid daily visits to the lounge bar of the Woodlands Hotel outside Lisburn. It was a favourite drinking haunt for off-duty soldiers from Army HQ and was deemed to be a safe haven. The two women introduced themselves to soldiers as Jean and Pat, names which would not have appeared to be Catholic and therefore did not arouse suspicion about their origins. They appeared to be aged between eighteen and twenty-two. One of them was of slim build with thin features and shoulder-length mid-brown hair. Her companion was well built and attractive, with a small upturned nose and dark wavy hair. Both were smartly dressed and about 5ft 7ins tall. By 24 March they had made friends with five NCOs from Army HQ. On that day the soldiers met the women at the Woodlands and were invited to a party in their flat on Belfast's Antrim Road, in a part of the road which the girls said was safe. As an enticement the two terrorists told the soldiers they would be inviting other female friends, that the flat was already prepared for a party and food had been cooked for the occasion. One of the NCOs decided for personal reasons not to go, but his four colleagues were keen to enjoy an evening with attractive women who were making their flat available for what appeared to be an interesting party restricted to eight people.

One of the NCOs, Staff Sergeant Penrose, phoned his wife from the hotel to say he was planning to have a quiet drink in the mess and watch television. Instead he accompanied the girls and his three colleagues in a car which took them to no. 358 Antrim Road. The IRA women led the soldiers to a ground-floor flat. Inside a fire was lit and food and drinks were laid out on a table. As the soldiers poured themselves a drink one of the women said she would drive to a house nearby and pick up two friends. While the unsuspecting soldiers were making themselves comfortable, two gunmen burst into the flat, frogmarched the soldiers into a bedroom and ordered them to lie face downward on a bed. The gunmen then opened fire, raking the bed and its occupants. Two soldiers died instantly and a third died later from his wounds. One soldier survived, possibly because he moved as soon as the first shot was fired. Nevertheless he was shot in the neck and part of his tongue was blown away. After the gunmen fled, he managed to crawl out of the flat and was seen by a young girl in an upstairs flat who raised the alarm.

The soldiers who died were Michael Muldoon, aged twenty-five, Barrington Foster, twenty-eight, and Thomas William Penrose, also twenty-eight. The soldier who survived was never named on the grounds that he might some day be called to identify the killers and until then he remains a target as the only witness of the savagery.

The Army was quoted as saying that it was reviewing its policy about the movement and conduct of off-duty soldiers. A military source was reported to have remarked that the dead soldiers had been based at Army HQ for some time and were aware of the risks. In fact they had been allowed to be exposed to an unforeseen risk. The IRA had hired the Antrim Road flat some time prior to the murders and left it vacant until the moment when the two female terrorists knew they were ready to lure soldiers to it.

The NCO who had declined the invitation to the flat was able to provide detailed descriptions of the women and within days photofit pictures were on the front pages of many newspapers. Journalists speculated about the incident, and Simon Hoggart, writing in the *Guardian*, claimed the Army reckoned the killers were 'members of the Provisionals acting with or without authority from the Belfast Brigade'. Within seventy-two hours of the murders Army and police raids took place in the Antrim Road and New Lodge Road areas. Five days after the killings, morning newspapers carried a photograph of a woman whom police said they were seeking to interview in connection with the murders. Although they were not prepared to name her, the police did tell journalists that she was known to them in connection with militant Republican activities. The photograph was of Roisin McLaughlin, a thirty-year-old housewife from Clifton Drive, about a quarter of a mile from the scene of the murders. What journalists did not know was that police had raided the McLaughlin home the day before and removed the photograph from Mrs McLaughlin's bedroom.

Roisin McLaughlin was not at home, but her husband, William, was arrested and taken to Glenravel Street police station where he was interviewed by Chief Inspector Abbott. William McLaughlin told Abbott that the murders had nothing to do with him. Abbott replied: 'They have plenty to do with your wife.' A member of military intelligence who was present said: 'Look, McLaughlin, you are not helping yourself or your cause by adopting your attitude that you don't know anything. We know that your wife is involved in IRA intelligence and is a party to these murders.' McLaughlin replied that Roisin was primarily a housewife but also did voluntary work for the Northern Ireland Civil Rights Association and the Association for Legal Justice. The English intelligence officer retorted:

'You must be bloody naive to think that we believe that. We know about her work in the IRA and the part she has played in these killings.' McLaughlin pointed out that neither he nor his wife was involved in any conflict with the police or Army. He was told he was free to leave the police station.

Two months later, Roisin McLaughlin was arrested in Cork in the Irish Republic, 300 miles from her home in Belfast from which she had vanished after 24 March, the day of the murders. Gardai swooped on a car in which she was a passenger. Her companions were her husband and Matt Fitzpatrick, who was due to appear in court to answer a charge of membership of the IRA. Mrs McLaughlin was no longer a brunette and had dyed her hair blonde. She was wearing brown trousers and a white coat. Later that day she appeared in a district courthouse looking very composed. An extradition warrant was granted and she was remanded in custody with the right to appeal against the court's decision at the Dublin High Court. On 30 May she appeared before Mr Justice Finlay in Dublin and was granted bail after arguing that she was the mother of a twelve-year-old boy and she believed her incarceration was having a 'deleterious effect on his welfare'.

Roisin McLaughlin was again before the Dublin High Court on 19 December, 1974, and it was expected that the matter of her extradition would be finally resolved. Detective Inspector Matchett of the Royal Ulster Constabulary told the court that he had led the inquiry, and that he believed that Mrs McLaughlin was involved in the murder of the soldiers and that she was the woman who left the flat and returned with the gunmen. Detective Inspector Matchett's evidence was ably expressed, but some of his statements indicated that he was aware that the extradition warrant was being contested on the basis of unconstitutionality and the assertion that Mrs McLaughlin was being sought for a political offence which the Irish judiciary was unlikely to deem sufficient for extradition. Matchett said there was no reason to believe Mrs McLaughlin was a member of the IRA or that she was associated with any group engaged in political activity intended to effect a change of government in Northern Ireland. He was assuring the court that if she was returned to Northern Ireland she would be charged only with offences relating to this particular incident and that those offences would be concerned with murder and attempted murder. RUC headquarters, he maintained, had confirmed that she would not be either interned or detained.

This aspect of Matchett's evidence was clearly designed to circumvent a situation in which people who claimed they were involved in politically motivated events were able to avoid extradition from the Irish Republic. That situation has since been relaxed rather than changed, but in 1974 Matchett was fighting a losing battle, and his statements that Roisin McLaughlin's alleged involvement was not political and that the RUC did not believe her to be a member of the IRA represented half-truths. His evidence conflicted with the media reports which followed the murder of the soldiers and the statements being made privately to journalists by both the RUC and the Army.

William McLaughlin also gave evidence and was asked by Counsel for the State if he had ever been a member of the IRA. The judge instructed McLaughlin that he was not obliged to answer the question and could simply say that he did not wish to reply. McLaughlin took Mr Justice Finlay's advice. He was also asked if he believed his wife was a member of the IRA and he replied that he could not 'state that'.

Counsel for Mrs McLaughlin told the court that he was unwilling to call her to give evidence because he might expose her to the risk of incriminating herself either in respect of the offence of murder as charged in the extradition warrant or in respect of some other offence in 'this jurisdiction or the jurisdiction of Northern Ireland'. The judge remarked that he could not in this case, any more than in others, have regard to the reasons for not calling a party to give evidence, nor could he fill any gap arising from the absence of such evidence.

Reviewing Detective Inspector Matchett's assertion that he had an open mind about whether the crime was motivated and carried out by the IRA because they had not claimed responsibility for it, Mr Justice Finlay declared it was most unlikely that the murders resulted from personal revenge, robbery or crime of passion. With regard to what constituted a political offence, the judge stressed that if such a murder as that of the soldiers was carried out by or on behalf of an organisation which by such methods sought to overthrow the government, then there could be no doubt that it was political. He added that in relying on Matchett's evidence he was obliged to conclude that the murders of unarmed soldiers were part of a paramilitary organisation's aim to overthrow the government of Northern Ireland. It was, in his opinion, a matter of probability that the offence named in the warrant was a political one, and on that basis he was refusing to order Mrs McLaughlin's extradition. Finally, Mr Justice Finlay pronounced that, in view of the fact that Roisin McLaughlin did not give evidence on the grounds that she might incriminate herself, he would not allow her to claim for the cost of her legal defence.

Roisin McLaughlin walked from the court to freedom in the Irish Republic knowing that if she ever sets foot on British soil she will be arrested and charged. An unnamed soldier remains a witness to the Antrim Road massacre and he may some day face her across a courtroom, though that is unlikely to happen while extradition remains a political issue. Roisin McLaughlin is only one of hundreds who are sought by the British authorities.

The Antrim Road killings forced the Army radically to review the activities and freedom of movement of off-duty soldiers. However, as in all wars, it is virtually impossible to guard constantly against terrorism. In 1981 the IRA learned that soldiers were regularly frequenting a disco at the Robin's Nest pub adjacent to the railway station in the town of Lisburn. Once again they prepared a honeytrap, a device they had not used successfully for eight years. When I was researching the role of female terrorists, I was told that on several occasions between 1973 and 1978 efforts were made to lure soldiers from licensed premises in the Lisburn area, but all attempts failed because previous murders such as the Antrim Road killings had generated fear and caution among off-duty members of the military. The IRA say they abandoned several honeytrap operations 'at the last moment'. Lisburn was the ideal place for the IRA to seek out soldiers who were out on the town looking for easy sex, for girls who were willing to invite them to parties or to their flats. The women of the IRA knew exactly what some soldiers had in mind and were prepared to offer sex to lure soldiers to a place where they could be murdered. Lisburn was regarded as a relatively safe area for soldiers because the majority of its inhabitants are Protestants and it is close to Thiepval Barracks (Army HQ). However, these reasons for assuming it to be safe did not deter the IRA in 1973. I believe the Army authorities, for the sake of expediency and to create an element of normality in the lives of serving soldiers, were prepared to take a calculated risk by not declaring Lisburn pubs out of bounds. A similar policy was applied to other towns with a majority Protestant population such as Holywood, but events indicate that the risks for off-duty soldiers in a dirty war may be too high.

They certainly were too high on 4 September, 1981, when two privates, twenty-year-old Sohan Singh Virdee and twenty-one-year-old John Lunt, both of the Royal Pioneer Corps, decided to spend the evening in Lisburn town centre. After visiting two pubs they made their way to the Robin's Nest, where they knew there would be a disco and the opportunity for picking up females, and in a short time they were joined by two young women who engaged them in conversation.

The women asked Virdee and Lunt if they were soldiers, but both replied that they were not in any way connected with the military, and they gave their names as Fred and Wally. The women said they were nurses and lived in a flat in the Stranmillis area of Belfast, a quiet, middle-class neighbourhood adjacent to the Malone Road. It was they who bought the first round of drinks, and Virdee and Lunt began to feel so much at ease that each indicated to the other without words which of the women he wished to make his 'pick-up' for the evening. Considering the history of the Northern Ireland conflict, it is astonishing that neither Virdee nor Lunt—who were willing to disguise their true identity—was suspicious of two women who were prepared to lead the conversation, buy the first round of drinks and enquire if 'Fred and Wally' were soldiers. Perhaps it is a measure of the male ego, sexual demands or the vulnerability of men in stressful jobs that security can so easily be eroded, particularly in pubs and after drinking alcohol. Eventually Virdee and Lunt's female companions suggested that they should all return for late-night drinks to the Stranmillis flat. When the girls explained that they did not have a car, 'Fred and Wally' replied that they could supply one.

The four left the Robin's Nest and walked to Lunt's car. Initially the car would not start and Virdee and the girls proceeded to push it. A patrol of military police appeared on the scene and asked Lunt what was happening. He informed them of his identity and told them that he was giving the girls a lift to their flat. The military police accepted the explanation and left. Their role at that time was to patrol Lisburn to ensure that soldiers were safe and were not disturbing the peace. As Lunt drove towards Belfast he had to stop at a filling station to buy petrol. One of the women handed him money and asked him to buy some bread for making sandwiches at the flat. This further reassured the soldiers of the normality of the situation. When the four arrived at the flat, which was on the first floor of a large terraced house in Stranmillis Park, the girls told Virdee and Lunt to make themselves comfortable. Lunt informed police of his reaction on entering the flat:

> As I walked up the hall I could see Fred sitting on the
> settee in a room to my left. The girl with me told me to
> go in and sit down and she would join me soon. I sat
> beside Fred. I can't remember where the girl went at that

stage and I did not see the girl Fred had been with. I was sat on the right-hand side of the two-seater settee. Fred had just spoken a few words of conversation to me when two dark figures burst through the door in front of us. I could see that both of these persons had hand-guns and were holding them in a two-handed grip and pointing them directly at us. The next thing I knew there was a burst of shots, not automatic shots but single shots in quick succession. I would say five to six shots were fired. Both of us slumped over the settee. I remember feeling pain in my arms. I got the impression the figures were masked, were wearing dark clothes and were not very big. These two figures rushed out of the door from which I had come in and, at the same time, I saw a third gunman emerge from the door in front me. He was slightly bigger than the two previous ones and was dressed in a lightish cream-coloured suit. He carried a revolver in a two-handed grip similar to the first two gunmen. At that stage I had got up on my feet in front of this man who fired approximately three to four shots at me, some of which struck me. I collapsed to the floor. As this man ran out the door the girl I had been with appeared in the doorway. She screamed or shouted something at me before running out of the room in the same direction as the gunmen—that was into the hall and out the front door. My mate Fred was lying slumped on the settee, motionless. I remember I got up and walked around a bit but I'm not quite sure to where. The next thing I knew, a lady came into the room and said, 'Oh, my God'. She went to get an ambulance. I was shot in both arms, left shoulder and right leg.

His companion was not so lucky. He was found to be dead on arrival at hospital. Fortunately Lunt was able to provide police with descriptions of the girls who lured him and his colleague to the flat.

> The one to whom I was speaking was mid-twenties and about 5ft 8ins. She had a nice figure, medium build, shoulder-length hair parted in the middle, ginger to blonde; pale face with freckles, clean, straight teeth, eye shadow and thin oval face. She spoke with a quiet pleasant voice and on occasions used phrases such as 'here's me' and 'so am I'. She was wearing a lightish-coloured blouse buttoned down the front but opened at the neck to such an extent that one could see part of her breasts.

He also remarked to police that the other girl's breasts were large and she had a 'rounded sort of big backside'.

His description of both women shows plainly their physical attractions for him and, presumably, his unfortunate friend. He indicated that they were dressed in a provocative manner and that they talked to the soldiers about sharing supper and possibly breakfast, thereby creating the impression that both girls were available for the night. This ensured that Lunt and Virdee were more interested in sexual enticements than their safety. Lunt was unable to tell police the names of the girls, though he mentioned that they only used Christian names and that one of them 'had a daft name like Ethel'.

Investigating detectives were particularly interested in one piece of detail about the woman who accompanied Virdee. Lunt remembered that she had tattoos on her right forearm. They were smallish, and it was his impression that one was a 'short name' and the other was composed of dots in the shape of lines.

Within less than a year the RUC arrested two young women on the evidence of a supergrass and charged them with the murder of Private Sohan Singh Virdee. They were twenty-one-year-old Alice Martha Taylor from Broadway in the Falls area of Belfast and Maureen O'Neill, aged twenty-four, from Joy Street in the Markets area close to Belfast city centre.

At an identification parade Lunt picked out O'Neill but not Taylor. When the trial began, the case against Taylor was based on a statement she made to police within one hour of her arrest in May 1982, but she denied that she had voluntarily made the statement. O'Neill argued in court that she was in Kerry in the Irish Republic when the murder took place and had a range of people to confirm her alibi. The Crown argued that hair found in Lunt's car matched hers but produced no forensic evidence to substantiate the claim. The Crown case against O'Neill was also based on Lunt's identification and on the fact that she had tattoos on her arm. However, her counsel argued that the tattoos were typical of those sported by many girls of her age. O'Neill, he added, had the tattoos painted on her arm while at school and the defence could produce nine other girls with similar markings.

The case against O'Neill collapsed not only on the issue of the tattoos but when Alice Taylor was judged to be guilty by the Diplock court. At that point defence counsel saw an opportunity to damage the Crown case. O'Neill's lawyer pointed out that Lunt's identification evidence against her was weakened by the fact that he was unable to select Taylor at an identification parade, and yet it was alleged that Taylor was the woman with whom he had spent most time on the night of the murder.

Mr Justice McDermott accepted O'Neill's defence because, he stated, there was a reasonable doubt that she was not the person described in court as 'Virdee's girl' and Lunt had identified her not by visual recognition but by a heart-shaped tattoo on her arm. 'As a reasonable number of girls are tattooed this leaves me less than satisfied that Private Lunt's identification is sound,' the judge remarked. He did not, however, accept her alibi that she was in Kerry.

As for Alice Martha Taylor, Mr. Justice MacDermott gaoled her for life. She had actively aided the gunmen and the judge was in no doubt that she possessed the necessary intent, as well as being aware of the nature of what she was doing in 'bringing the Brits to the flat'. The judge departed from rebuking Taylor only to remark that he felt she had shown remorse since the murder.

Taylor's statement was legally an admission of guilt, though she attempted to suggest that she was an unwilling accomplice; that the operation was haphazard; and that she did not realise that the soldiers were to be shot. She also failed to name her accomplices. However, it is an example of the ease with which murder can be committed when women are used as bait:

> Sometime around the end of May 1981 I was asked by a man to check to see if there were any Security Forces between Beechmount and the Springfield Road. I assumed this was a member of the IRA and the arrangement was that I was to walk in front of him and if there were any police or army about, I was to bend down and he would know to turn back. I only knew this man to see. I did this for him and there was no one about. The man went on up to Kashmir. I was going to my cousin's house on the Kashmir Road at the time. About the end of June 1981 the same man approached me in the Iveagh Club which is off Broadway. I was there with a friend at a dance. He came over to me and asked me outside to speak to him. When I went out he asked me to do a job and I said I would. He told me he would see me later and make arrangements. A couple of days later he called at my

house at 43 Broadway. There was no one in the house but me and I asked him in. He told me that he wanted me to go along with another girl to bring a couple of Brits back to a flat. I asked him when he wanted me to do this. He told me some time in the near future and he would be in touch with me some time in August. The same man came back to my house, picked me up in a car and drove me over to Stranmillis. He parked the car in Stranmillis Park and described the flat to me. He explained that I would meet another girl in the bus station at the back of the Europa Hotel. He would tell me later when we would be going on the job and it would be a Friday night. He also told me we would be going to a pub in Lisburn to pick up Brits and bring them back to the flat about midnight. This man called back at my house. I'm not sure whether it was the Friday we brought the Brits back or the day before. He told me the job was on that Friday night and that I was to meet the other girl as planned. I think it was just after eight o'clock when I went to the bus station. I was approached by a girl. I knew her face but I don't wish to mention her name. We got on the bus to Lisburn and got off at Lisburn's railway station. On the journey we talked about the pub we were going to and that it was full of Brits. The girl seemed to know it well and told me it was the Robin's Nest.

Taylor added that she and her friend talked to several soldiers until they were joined by Lunt and Virdee; her friend bought most of the drinks. She did not tell police that she and her accomplice talked of supper and breakfast. At the end of her statement she declared that she allowed her friend and the soldiers to enter the flat, closed the door behind them, then walked into the street and heard shots coming from the flat: 'I'm glad I wasn't in the flat when the Brits were shot and I'm sorry it ever happened at all. I knew I was bringing these Brits to the flat for the IRA but I didn't think they were going to be shot.'

Taylor's attempt to abdicate responsibility for her actions was absurd and impossible to believe, since she was a member of the IRA's female wing, Cumann na mBann, a grouping much more secretive than any other within the IRA. She was not chosen at random for such an operation and she knew her associates. Members of Cumann na mBann have included the Price sisters, Mairead Farrell and many others who were central to the planning and execution of major operations. Their most successful roles have been in luring soldiers to their deaths and in accompanying IRA operatives abroad to create an image of young couples on holiday. Unlike the IRA, Cumann na mBann does not give interviews and its members are rarely observed in action, but it is no less an effective terrorist grouping. One can only guess at the number of soldiers who ignored the charms of provocative females in Northern Ireland pubs or turned down offers of supper and breakfast.

excerpt from:

ETA: Profile of a Terrorist Group

by Yonah Alexander, Michael Swetnam, and Herbert M. Levine

The ETA (Euskadi Ta Askatasuna, "Basque Homeland and Liberty"), the Basque separatist movement, was formed in 1962. Its members come from the Basque provinces of Spain and France, and its goals are stated as Basque self-rule and the socialization of resources. Its method is "armed fight." The ETA began terrorist activity in 1965 and since than has killed more than 800 people. Its tactics include bombings, assassinations, kidnappings and extortions. It has frequently funded its activities by demanding money from prominent citizens, threatening to kill them if they fail to comply. The letter excerpted here demanding payment of protection money was sent to one of Spain's most celebrated soccer players, Bixente Lizarazu, in September of 2000. He did not accede to the request but was not subsequently pursued. Recent attempts to negotiate an end to Basque terror have failed. A car bombing in November of 2001, an apparent failed assassination attempt of a local politician, injured dozens.

1992	Because of cooperation between French and Spanish security forces, many arrests are made of ETA leaders.
January 1996	ETA kidnaps José Antonio Omega Lara, a prison official, and holds him under torturous conditions, until he is freed by the Civil Guard in 1997 after 532 days of captivity.
June 1996	ETA declares a one-week truce.
July 1997	ETA assassinates Miguel Angel Blanco Carrido, a councillor from Ermua, near San Sebastian, by first kidnapping him and then tying him to a tree in the forest and shooting him in the head. The murder provokes many millions of Spanish citizens to demonstrate in protest against ETA. Six other councillors, all members of the People's Party, were later assassinated by ETA.
December 1997	Spanish judges sentence 23 Herri Batasuna leaders to seven years in prison for making a video that allegedly supported ETA terrorism. But the Spanish Supreme Court overturns the sentences in July 1999.
February 1998	An ETA gunman shoots and kills Alberto Himnas Becerril, a politician from the Popular Party in Seville, and his wife.

• • •

September 1998   ETA declares an indefinite truce in the hope of win-
                  ning electoral support.

November 1999   ETA formally ends the truce.

December 1999   United States extradites Ramón Aldasoro Magunace-
                 laya. He is the first alleged member of ETA to be
                 extradited from the United States to Spain.

January 2000   ETA claims responsibility for gunning down Jesus
                 Maria Pedrosa Urkiza, a local councillor of the
                 ruling Popular Party, in Urkiza.

May 2000   ETA murders journalist José Luis Lopez de la Calle
                 in Andoain, Guipúzcoa.

October 2000   ETA murders José Francisco Querol Lombardero, a
                 judge of the Fifth Military Division of the Supreme
                 Court of justice, in a car bomb attack in Madrid. Also
                 killed in the attack are his police guard and driver.

November 2000   ETA murders former socialist Health Minister
                 Ernest Lluch in his home in Barcelona.

December 2000   ETA kills Francisco Cano Consuegra, a Popular
                 Party councilman in Viladecavalls when an explo-
                 sive device in his car blows up.

March 2001   ETA announces that it will target tourists to Spain
                 in a bombing campaign.

                             • • •

March 2001   ETA car bomb at a tourist site in Spain's northeast Costa Brava coast kills a policeman. A tourist bus and several cars are destroyed by the blast.

Letter of Extortion to Football Player Vicente Lizarazu (Translated and edited)

Euskal Herria (Basque Country), September 2000.

To the attention of Mr. Bixente Lizarazu:

The ETA organization had decided to contact you in order to transmit to you its views on different issues. You may probably be surprised to see to what extent we are following your sports career. However, you should know that in our opinion, we need every effort of all the Basque citizens wherever they are in our fight for Euskal Herria.

In this sense, as a well-known personality you often act as a representative of a people who are not yours, on behalf of a state that oppresses Euskal Herria. As you know, all the things personalities do and say are often an example to a large sector of society, and in your case you have a great influence on young people. So, working "for the state," you are arousing contradictory feelings by Basque youngsters and citizens. On the one hand, they are proud and glad to see a Basque national at the top of a high-level sport; and on the other hand, they feel anger and pain to see a fellow national defending ideas and colors that are not his.

Spain and France are continuously oppressing Euskal Herria. In the last years, many Basque citizens have risen against them, some even paid with their lives; others have been imprisoned for many years, and some are living in exile. They are all committed to fighting for Euskal Herria, which means obviously doing as much as you can in your public and private life, rather than joining ETA.

We are aware of how difficult it is nowadays to defend the colors of Euskal Herria as well as of the kind of "retaliation" this may entail. It is common knowledge what those who have kept a coherent position have received, and sometimes the professional career of sports aces was disrupted. Moreover, there could be a better sports federation in Euskal Herria even before achieving independence, and the possibility of organizing national teams without permission of France or Spain. There are many examples of this worldwide in different sports (the national teams of Wales and Scotland . . .). Why don't Basque people have the opportunity of greeting their sports aces working for their country? Why don't you have the right to compete on behalf of your people, besides those occasional friendly competitions? Why do Basque players have to fight each other for Spain and France?

The answers to those questions are clear to us: because our people's rights are not respected. But also, because nowadays autonomous leaders are not interested at all in changing the current situation by taking the necessary steps. We do not consider that you or other sports leaders have no responsibility for this situation. You simply cannot sit down and wait while others are fighting. Your example and your fame may be useful to take positive steps, since many people hear what you say.

Having said all this, we must transmit to you our concern and anger. You have defended the colors of a country hostile to Euskal Herria in the European football cup not long ago. In your fight to defend that flag, you may have possibly used, either publicly or privately, any of the following statements:

1. You do not feel Basque at all, and that is why you have chosen to defend a state that oppresses Euskal Herria.
2. You did it for the sake of money.
3. You thought it might be a good opportunity for your professional career.

• • •

In the above lines, we have clearly stated our position. So we are not going to discuss the reasons for your decision to align yourself with the enemies of Euskal Herria and, at the same time, find an excuse to improve your image or to have a clear conscience, or both. However, a citizen cannot serve two homelands. You have therefore chosen to turn your back on Euskal Herria.

ETA has decided to get in touch with you considering your economic value.

Apart from all you can do for Euskal Herria from the point of view of sports, you know the requirements of the fight for Euskal Herria. Financial demands are not small. The Spanish state wants to dominate economically our people, imposing huge efforts on it (. . .). Over the past years, all the projects that prospered in Euskal Herria were financed with money from the pockets of Basque citizens, and thanks to it the Basque language and culture have a future nowadays. Today, we have huge economic necessities as regards the fight for the independence of Euskal Herria.

We are demanding from you, Mr. Bixente Lizarazu, all the money you have earned from your participation on an enemy of Euskal Herria's national team, as a contribution to our cause. You have different options to channel your help: either into ETA or into different movements and organizations that are working for the national build-up of Euskal Herria (*Udalbiltza* [local councils], *Ikastolas* [schools with only the Basque language], Basque mass media, etc.).

In case you do not respond to our demand, ETA should start the necessary actions against you and your possessions.

Looking forward to hearing from you,

ETA

excerpt from:

My People Shall Live

by Leila Khaled

Leila Khaled was the most notorious woman active in the Palestinian
terrorist movement. Shocked and angered by the Six Day War, she
sought out the terrorist organization Fatah and spent several years in
training camps in the Middle East preparing for duty as a guerrilla in
the People's Army. Khaled participated in two airline hijackings, the first
one successful, the second one, narrated here, ending in her capture.
She was subsequently set free after another hijacking forced her
English captors to let her go. Ms. Khaled's autobiography describes the
hardships of Palestinians living in Jordan and documents the rise of
the PLO and the Fatah. Khaled wrote her autobiography, excerpted
here, in 1972. Her story recalls an era of naive idealism fueled by a
simplistic political ideology now totally discredited.

O ur study group was rapidly mastering the strategy and ideology of
the PF and moving towards the cell stage. On the advice of Abu
Nidal we were studying more advanced radical books and broad-
ening our horizons when another Palestinian woman revolutionary made
world headlines and shook our movement.

The morning of Februay 18 was just another day for me. As usual I got
up at five-thirty a.m. to prepare breakfast and listen to the BBC news. Suddenly I heard over the air the name of Amina Dhahbour. She had been in
on an attack on an El-Al plane at Zurich. She was the first woman to participate in a foreign operation. The news struck me like lightning. A Palestinian woman, a revolutionary, in the citadel of financial capitalism!

Fortunately the BBC announcers regularly repeat the major news items and read them over in detail for I wasn't certain at first whether I was hearing or imagining.

I ran out in my pyjamas screaming throughout the dormitory. "She did it! She did it! Palestine will be free!" Everyone thought that I had gone mad. But I made sure that everyone got the message: A Palestinian woman was fighting while we were talking in far-away Kuwait. Within a few minutes we were all celebrating the liberation of Palestine and the liberation of women. Fateh and PF women embraced and danced the Palestine *Debke* together in the corridors of El-Shaab. The PFLP had earned its way to the El-Shaab teaching staff and their wallets. We decided that henceforth all funds collected must be distributed equally between Fateh and the PF. The Fateh sisters acquiesced; they had no choice. The school became a beehive for the resistance. Even the pupils were turned into revolutionary salesmen and fundraisers. We indoctrinated them so well that some of them turned out to be more effective supporters of the resistance than many of us.

That same day I called comrade Abu Nidal and informed him that I wanted to join the Special Operations Squad. He agreed. From then on I received advanced, highly specialised training. It was now only a matter of time until I participated in a foreign military operation. The hour of reckoning was drawing closer for me.

We must grow tough, but without ever losing our tenderness.
                                                    Che Guevara, 1967

The Arab people are frequently accused by their opponents and sometimes by their friends of being too emotional. I, as a Palestine Arab woman, have something to be legitimately emotional about: the loss of my home and community and the denial of my present and future. But I am not going to succumb to emotionalism and allow my feelings to blind my reason and undermine my confidence in the capacity of my people to liberate their land. In spite of the power of the enemy, I intend to rely on revolutionary ideology and strategy and mass mobilisation to achieve our objectives. In my work I have chosen to be the ally of reason, not passion, and my party, the Popular Front, also analyses and reasons before acting.

We do not embark haphazardly on adventurous and romantic individualistic projects to fulfil "individual needs" or "act out of frustrations and hostilities" as Western "scientific" psychologists hypothesise. We act collectively in a planned manner either to neutralise a prospective friend of the enemy or to expose a vital nerve of the enemy and, above all, to dramatise our own plight and to express our resolute determination to alter "the new realities" that Mr. Moshe Dayan's armies have created. Generally, we act not with a view to crippling the enemy—because we lack the power to do so—but with a view to disseminating revolutionary propaganda, sowing terror in the heart of the enemy, mobilising our masses, making our cause international, rallying the forces of progress on our side, and underscoring our grievances before an unresponsive Zionist-inspired and Zionist-informed Western public opinion. As a comrade has said: We act heroically in a cowardly world to prove that the enemy is not invincible. We act "violently" in order to blow the wax out of the ears of the deaf Western liberals and to remove the straws that block their vision. We act as revolutionaries to inspire the masses and to trigger off the revolutionary upheaval in an era of counter-revolution. Dr. Habash, the Secretary General of the PFLP, has stated our human dilemma and our ethical view thus:

> After 22 years of injustice and inhuman living in camps
> with nobody caring for us, we feel that we have the very

full right to protect our revolution, we have *all* the right to protect our revolution. Our Code of Morals is Our Revolution. What helps our revolution, what protects our revolution is right, is very right and honourable and very noble and very beautiful, because our revolution means justice, means having our homes back, having back our country, which is a very just and noble aim.

(June 12, 1970)

I do not see how my oppressor could sit in judgment on my response to his oppressive actions against me. He is in no position to render an impartial judgment or to accuse me of air piracy and hijacking when he has hijacked my home and hijacked me and my people out of our land. If the enemy defines morality and legality in his own terms and decides to apply his ethical and legal doctrines against me because he has the power as well as the means of communications to justify his inhumanity, I am under no moral obligation to listen, let alone obey his dictates. Indeed, I am under a moral obligation to resist and to fight to death the enemy's moral corruption. My deed cannot be evaluated without examining the underlying causes. The revolutionary deed I carried out on August 29, 1969 was an assertion of my spurned humanity, a declaration of the humanity of Palestinians. It was an act of protest against the West for its pro-Zionist (therefore anti-Palestinian) posture. The list of the sins of the West is overwhelming.

Early on the morning of August 29, I checked out of the hotel and caught a bus to Fiumicino Airport on the outskirts of Rome. Happily, the only snag was a half-hour flight delay. My associate, whom I recognised only from a photograph, appeared on schedule and we exchanged pre-arranged signals. His name was Salim Issawi; he was a Palestinian from Haifa who had been raised in Syria. Salim sat quietly nearby and we tried to ignore each other.

All was going smoothly when suddenly the human element threatened our careful planning. A few seats away there was a little girl with a button on her dress cheerfully proclaiming "Make Friends". That message brought me up short, forced me to remind myself, as I watched her playing with her little sister, that this child had committed no crime against me or my people. It would be cruel to imperil her life by hijacking a plane, the symbolic meaning of which she had no conception—a plane that could explode during our attempted seizure or be blown up by Israeli anti-aircraft fire when we entered the "Israeli airspace".

While these qualms pricked my conscience, the whole history of Palestine and her children came before my eyes. I saw everything from the first day of my exile. I saw my people homeless, hungry, barefoot. The twice "refugee" children of Bagan camp near Amman seemed to stand, a humiliated multitude, in front of me saying, "We too are children and we are a part of the human race." The scene strengthened me enormously. I said to myself, "What crime did I and my people perpetrate against anyone to deserve the fate we have suffered?" The answer was "None". The operation must be carried out. There can be no doubt or retreat. My children have spoken.

On the bus across the field to the Boeing 707, another unscheduled problem developed. A handsome man in his early thirties came up to me and said "Hello" in a most jovial, enthusiastic manner. "Hello," I replied nonchalantly, as I calmly tried to read *My Friend Che* by Ricardo Rojo. He seemed very eager to talk and asked me who I was and where I was going. I couldn't very well repeat the marriage tale and couldn't invent anything quickly enough. I said, "Guess."

He tried, "Greek, Spanish, Italian?" I asked him where he was from. "I am from Chicago," he answered, and continued his questioning. "You wouldn't be South American, would you?" Now that I knew where he was from, I figured it was safe to say that I was a South American. I thought it might end his questioning, at least. "From Brazil?" he asked, looking admiringly at me, and ogling my whole body. "You're getting closer," I said.

"Bolivia?" "Yes," I replied, "but how did you know?" "It's your book that gave you away," he declared. I asked him what he thought of Che. "Good man," he said. "Where are you going?" I countered, trying to change to a less controversial topic. "To Athens, to see my mother. I haven't seen her in fifteen years. I bet she's there already, waiting for me at the airport." I was astounded, and almost told him, "You bloody fool, you'd better get off this plane, because it isn't going to Athens." I tried to ignore him and closed my ears to keep his voice from penetrating my inner conscience. I plunged into a nervous reading of *My Friend Che.*

This encounter made me stop and think, because I understood the longing for one's own country. However, I rationalised his plight by making a distinction between his "exile", which was voluntary, and mine, which was forced. But these human encounters made me decide to be extra careful not to jeopardise the lives of the passengers unnecessarily. Their welfare, however, did not and could not cripple my operation. The deed had to be carried out. There was no turning back.

The plane was airborne for only twenty minutes before the hostesses were graciously trying to serve their five first-class passengers. Neither Salim nor I was anxious to eat. The stewardesses were very solicitous. They offered us drinks and peanuts. Anything we wanted. I settled for a coffee, Salim for a beer. But they made us nervous, as they kept returning and asking us if we wanted anything else. I pretended that I had a stomach ache and asked for a blanket. I innocently placed it over my lap, so I could take my hand grenade out of my purse and put my pistol right in the top of my trousers without being noticed. Salim asked for an aspirin tablet. I was afraid the stewardess might suspect something had she realised that two passengers opposite each other in the first row were sick. In any case, I dreaded the prospect of having a companion with a headache, so was relieved when he merely pocketed the aspirin. Seconds after the only other male passenger in the first class section returned from the small lounge, I gestured to Salim to proceed to the cockpit. Just at that moment, another hostess carrying the crew's lunch trays was opening the door of the cockpit. Salim seized the opportunity and leapt in ahead of her. She screamed, "Oh no!" and her trays flew in the air, causing much noise but no injury. I was behind Salim and ordered the stewardess to get out of the way. She did, quivering and watching us over her shoulder. Salim was so huge that he blocked my view, and I couldn't see the reaction of the crew. I could, however, hear him say that the plane had been taken over by the Che Guevara Commando Unit of the PFLP, and announce that the new captain was Shadiah Abu Ghazalah.

In the middle of his speech, my pistol slipped down the leg of my trousers and, as I bent down to pick it up, I saw the bewildered looks on the crew's faces. I suppose all they could see was part of my wide-brimmed chic hat. I felt ridiculous for a moment, laughed at my inept-ness, put the pistol away, and entered the cockpit solemnly brandishing my hand grenade and declaring I was the new captain. The crew were completely shocked to see me there, but they showed no fear. To demon-strate my credibility, I immediately offered my predecessor, Captain Carter, the safety pin from the grenade as a souvenir. He respectfully declined it. I dropped it at his feet and made my speech. "If you obey my orders, all will be well; if not, you will be responsible for the safety of pas-sengers and aircraft."

"Go to Lydda," I instructed. "To Lod?" he queried, using the Israeli name. "You understand English, don't you?" I said curtly. "You just listen to my orders and don't ask silly questions." Since I knew the plane carried fuel for almost three hours and 45 minutes, I decided to reaffirm my authority by testing the flight engineer. I turned towards him and asked,

"How much fuel do you have, flight engineer?" "For two hours," he promptly replied, without even looking at the fuel gauge. "Liar," I shouted, and told him that I knew just as much as he did about the Boeing, and that if he ever lied to me again I'd break his neck. The pilot tried to calm me down. He thought I was angry, but I was actually overjoyed. He warned the crew not to be obstinate in dealing with their new captain.

Realising that he was prepared to co-operate, I asked Captain Carter to radio Rome so that I could explain my action to the Italian people. He explained that we were too far away. I insisted that he try. He did. We had no luck. I asked a steward to bring our hand luggage forward, and then ordered him and the other first-class passengers to move to the tourist section. Next I demanded that the intercom system be turned on. All orders were complied with, and I read the following message to the passengers:

> Ladies and gentlemen, your attention please. Kindly fasten your seat belts. This is your new captain speaking. The Che Guevara Commando Unit of the Popular Front for the Liberation of Palestine which has taken over command of this TWA flight demands that all passengers on board adhere to the following instructions.
>
> Remain seated and keep calm.
>
> For your own safety, place your hands behind your head.
>
> Make no move which would endanger the lives of other passengers on this plane.
>
> We will consider all your demands within the safe limits of our plan. Among you is a passenger responsible for the death and misery of a number of Palestinian men, women and children, on behalf of whom we are carrying out this operation to bring this assassin before a revolu-

tionary Palestinian court. The rest of you will be honourable guests of the heroic Palestinian people in a hospitable, friendly country. Every one of you, regardless of religion or nationality, is guaranteed freedom to go wherever he pleases as soon as the plane is safely landed.

Our destination is a friendly country, and friendly people will receive you.

As I completed reading the message, I observed that the plane had swerved off the course I charted for it. I ordered the captain not to play games if he wanted to reach our destination safely and put him on course again. Then Salim reminded me that fifteen minutes had elapsed since the passengers were asked to hold their hands behind their heads. I quickly advised them to relax and to drink champagne if they so desired, and offered an apology for inconveniencing them.

Shortly afterwards, a stewardess came in and explained that most of the passengers didn't understand English, didn't know what we had said, and would like us to repeat the message. She even offered to translate it into French for them. I repeated the message and assured them that everything was normal, that there was only one person on the plane we were after. Later, this was interpreted by the press as indicating that we were after the Israeli ambassador to the US, General Itzhak Rabin of June War fame. We were not, and if we had been, I would not have boarded flight 840 at Rome, since I saw all the passengers and knew that Rabin was not among them. Saleh Al Moualim, an Israeli Arab on board, must have thought that he was the person we meant, because he became very jittery and frightened. The selective terror tactic worked; the passengers' fear diminished and everyone co-operated with us. In explaining the message to the passengers, I told them that we detested the American government's Middle East actions, and held no grudge against any individual person. They were frightened, however, when I announced that we intended to blow up the plane upon arrival in a friendly country. I announced this only an hour before reaching Damascus.

Meanwhile, I resumed radio contact with the ground, sending messages of solidarity to the Greek revolutionaries and to the people of South Europe. I demanded that the Greek colonels release our imprisoned revolutionaries, and said that the CIA plotters would be toppled by the Greek people. All went according to plan, until we got the Egyptian observation tower on our wave-length. I identified myself to the controller in Arabic and asked him to convey to the Egyptian people the greetings of the Palestinian revolution. I advised him that I was going to Lydda, and his voice crackled: "Allah, to Lydda, what will you do there?" "Visit the fatherland," I said. "Are you sure of that?" "I certainly am," I replied enthusiastically. He tried to tell me that it was too dangerous. I switched him off, then relented momentarily as he screamed, "Oh Front, Oh Popular, Oh Arab Palestine!" but the rest of the appeal was too incoherent and inaudible.

Within minutes, I could see the coast of my Palestine in the haze. As we approached the land of my birth, it seemed that my love and I were racing towards each other for an eternal embrace. I rushed towards my beloved and saw Palestine for the first time since my forced exile in 1948. I was lost in a moment of passion and meditation. Then I remembered the mission and ordered the pilot to descend, and I addressed a message in Arabic to my fellow exiles in occupied Palestine, telling them we shall return and we shall recover the land. I advised them to remain steadfast and promised to smash the Zionist fortress of conceit. I told Lydda tower in Arabic that we were going to land. He didn't understand, the pilot said, and told us we should ask for clearance and wait. I said, "This is my country. I do not need permission from the Zionist vultures to land."

I spoke to the tower in English, saying: "Here we come again. Shadiah Abu Ghaselah has come back to life. There are millions of Shadiahs who will be returning again and again to reclaim the land." The Israeli tower must have been terrified for a while because I said that we intended to blow up the plane right in the airport. In seconds three Israeli Mirages appeared on the horizon and tried to prevent us from landing. I turned the intercom on so that the passengers could hear the exchange.

I declared anew that the pilot and the Israelis were responsible for the safety of the passengers and the plane, and that we intended to do no harm to anyone if our orders were obeyed. The co-pilot asked if he could speak to the Israelis and I let him. He said, "Popular Front, Free Arab Palestine, Armed people have threatened to explode the plane with hand grenades if your Mirages don't clear out." Until this moment the Israeli tower was still addressing us as TWA 840. My patience ran out and I told him to shut up and turned him off, saying that there will be no further communications until he addressed us as Popular Front, Free Arab Palestine.

In seconds he did so as we swung around my beloved Haifa. The pilot asked, "What shall I do now?" I said, "Let's take a seven-minute tour of the fatherland." My father's image appeared before my eyes, and I could hear his voice saying "When will we return home?" My whole world came together. I was silent. I looked out at the greenery and mountains of Palestine. I could see Tel Aviv below. I wept out of affection and longing, and said softly, "Father, we shall return. We shall redeem your honour and restore your dignity. We shall become the sovereign of the land some day." Suddenly, I remembered that the mission preceded personal emotions. I instructed the pilot, "Go to Lebanon, where my people live as refugees." The Israeli planes continued to pursue us. At the Lebanese border, they zoomed away. I called Cyprus and sent greetings to its heroic anti-imperialist fighters, and sent messages to my people in South Lebanon. The pilot interrupted. "We must ask for clearance from Beirut." "We don't need to ask for clearance," I said. "This is an Arab country." We circled Beirut briefly before I ordered the pilot to go on to Damascus. He objected, "The airport there couldn't accommodate the Boeing 707." "Look, do you think we're so backward that we couldn't handle your damned plane?" I said strongly. He didn't respond. I took the microphone and addressed the passengers for the last time: "Evacuate immediately on landing; have a happy holiday in Syria. I trust we shall have a smooth landing."

The fuel gauge was reading empty; the pilot sought clearance and I ordered him to land immediately on the runway farthest from the air terminal. "Let's have a smooth landing," I said, "because if I fall, the hand grenade could explode and that would be a terrible anticlimax to a happy journey." He landed smoothly and in less than three minutes the plane was empty. Salim and I tried to tell the passengers to slow down and to take their personal belongings with them. Most ran out barefooted. Even the crew left their jackets behind. As Captain Carter stepped out, I saluted and thanked him for his co-operation. He looked at me in astonishment. The co-pilot said, "You're most welcome."

I checked the plane. All the passengers had left. Salim wired the cockpit and lit the fuse. I slid out on one of the torn emergency chutes and fell to the ground on my rear. Salim followed and landed on my shoulders. The plane did not explode as scheduled. Salim's personal courage made him climb back in and set everything in motion once more. When Syrian soldiers arrived on the scene, I distracted them by saying, "The Israeli officers ran in that direction. Go and get them." Salim was still in the plane. I feared for his safety, but admired his heroism and selfless devotion. I tried to leap in and couldn't. Suddenly he appeared and waved reassuringly. The Boeing still did not explode. He fired a few shots into the wing of the plane, but there was no fuel left, so it wouldn't readily ignite. When sparks finally fluttered, we took cover twenty yards away. Half a mile away, the passengers in the terminal watched the bonfire and the explosion of the Boeing. The Syrian soldiers returned, astounded. They were even more surprised when Salim and I surrendered to them and turned over our weapons. The *Al-Hadaf* photographer, who was parachuted by the Front to film our landing and the explosion, was so excited that he forgot to remove the lens cap from his camera.

Our Syrian hosts took us to the air terminal, where I delivered a brief speech to the passengers:

Confronting Fear

• • •

Ladies and gentlemen, thank you for your kind attention
and co-operation during the flight. I am captain Shadiah
Abu Ghazalah. That's not my name; my name is Khaleda.
Shadiah is an immortal woman who wrote: "Heroes are
often forgotten, but their legends and memories are the
property and heritage of the people." That is something
historians and analysts cannot understand. Shadiah will
not be forgotten by the Popular Front and by the generation of revolutionaries she helped mould in the path of
revolution. I would like you to know that Shadiah was a
Palestinian Arab woman from Nablus; that she was a
schoolteacher and a member of the Popular Front underground; that she died in an explosion at her own home at
the age of twenty-one on November 21, 1968, while manufacturing hand grenades for the Front. She was the first
woman martyr of our revolution. I assumed her name on
flight 840 to tell the world about the crimes the Israelis
inflict upon our people and to demonstrate to you that
they make no distinctions between men, women and
children. But for their own propaganda objectives they
repeatedly state in your press how we attack their "innocent" women and children and how cruel we are. I want
you to know that we love children, too, and we certainly
do not aim our guns at them. We diverted flight 840
because TWA is one of the largest American airlines that
services the Israeli air routes and, more importantly,
because it is an American plane. The American government is Israel's staunchest supporter. It supplies Israel
with weapons for our destruction. It gives the Zionists
tax-free American dollars. It supports Israel at world

conferences. It helps them in every possible way. We are against America because she is an imperialist country. And our unit is called the Che Guevara Commando Unit because we abhor America's assassination of Che and because we are a part of the Third World and the world revolution. Che was an apostle of that revolution. We took the plane to Haifa because Comrade Salim and I come from Haifa. Both of us were evicted in 1948. We took you to Tel Aviv as an act of defiance and challenge to the Israelis and to demonstrate their impotence when the Arabs embark on offensive rather then defensive strategy. We brought you to Damascus because Syria is the pulsating heart of the Arab homeland and because the Syrians are a good and generous people. We hope you will enjoy your stay in Damascus. We hope you will go home and tell your friends not to go to Israel—to the Middle East war zone. Please tell your neighbours that we are a people like you who wish to live in peace and security in our country, governing ourselves. Please tell the Americans that if they hate war and the exploitation of others, they should stop their government from making war on us and helping the Israelis to deprive us of our land. Tell your people that coming to Israel helps her to deny our rights. Revolution and peace. Greetings to all lovers of the oppressed!

In early March 1970, I left Amman for an undisclosed destination where I underwent three plastic surgery operations so that I could continue our planned military operations. It was difficult at first, to find a doctor ready to put his medicine at the service of the revolution. After extensive searches a physician was found who was anxious to help, but he couldn't understand why a prospective husband would want to see his wife's face "disfigured" before he'd marry her. "He must be nuts," the good doctor insisted. "Nuts," we agreed, but "Please operate," we said. The doctor shook his head, booked an obstetrics hospital and reached for his "syslestics". It was March 13, 1970, when the first "face-twisting" was performed. It was extremely painful. Since I refused a general anaesthetic, I could see as well as feel the thrust of the needles. I suppose people in the West will conclude that I must be a masochist, but I assure them that I am not. I have a cause higher and nobler than my own, a cause to which all private interests and concerns must be subordinated. Here then I lay on the operating table while my comrades were being tortured, my sisters being raped and my land pillaged.

For twenty days after the first operation I had to live on liquids. I felt terribly weak. Since the operation was a secret which less than a half dozen people knew about, I languished in the hospital with no visitors to break the boredom. I spent my days watching the comings and goings in the maternity ward across the hall. To complicate matters, my nurse spoke neither Arabic nor English. She was an Armenian and we could communicate only by sign language, a situation which didn't help my painful face. Happily no one in the hospital recognised me. But one day when I was calling for a nurse, a man who was visiting his wife in the room next door walked in to help. He recognised me and called me by my first name. I denied that I was Leila. He didn't believe me. When I left the hospital I gave his new daughter a necklace made of bullets and wished her a long, long revolutionary career.

Zero hour was approaching rapidly, yet more surgery was required to complete my "beauty treatment". Two more operations were performed, the last a few days before the scheduled hijacking. Most of my comrades were already in Europe waiting to meet me. Suddenly word came through that everything must be postponed to avoid confrontation with Jordan. I was a little disappointed, but not disheartened.

• • •

The Israelis and their allies however, were a vigilant and sleepless enemy. I had been released from the hospital. It was July 11, 1970, at two-fifteen a.m. and I was sitting in Dr. Wadi Haddad's apartment and we were discussing strategy. His wife and child were asleep in the next room. From out of nowhere a volley of rockets struck the bedroom. Neither of us was hurt. We reached for our guns. Then in the midst of flames his family burst out of the bedroom screaming and bleeding. The electricity failed. We panicked momentarily as we tried to extinguish the fire. I grabbed eight-year-old Hani, and ran up and down the stairs shouting "Fire, Fire". Hani was bleeding from the chest and his feet looked squashed. A neighbor invited us to take refuge in her apartment and called the fire brigade. I was anxious, but Hani was absolutely calm and silent. He forced a smile and said to me, "Leila, revolutionaries of the Front ought not to be fearful. You ought to be ashamed to be frightened." I was a little shocked by the reminder from this child revolutionary, and I pounced on him and carried him outside to take him to the hospital. I stopped a cabby, who refused to transport us, and I spat in his face. Suddenly Abu Dardock, a member of the Front, appeared on the scene and away we went to the American University hospital's emergency ward. As I rushed in with Hani in my arms, blood covering both of us, I cried, "Find me a doctor please". Within minutes a doctor was there but before he even looked at the child, he callously enquired if I had the money to pay for the treatment. I shrieked at him, "Are you a doctor or a carpet salesman?" He firmly explained that AUB was a "hospital not a charity centre". "Since you are in business, take me for ransom, but please look after the child," I begged. At that moment Dr. Haddad and his wife stormed in looking for their child. His mother was almost hysterical. The American doctor recognised Dr. Haddad, a fellow MD. He was taken aback and apologised profusely. His apologies fell on deaf ears. I voiced my threats loudly,

"Yankee doctor, the revolution will make AUB's hospital a hospital for the poor and your kind of doctor will have to be disbarred or sent back to America." He flashed a barefaced grin and said "I'm sorry."

• • •

The attack on Dr. Haddad's apartment strengthened our resolve to fight the enemy with all the power at our command. We were much more determined to die for the cause than ever before. The sight of the apartment in flames was constantly on my mind as I flew to Frankfurt in August. In Frankfurt, I stayed at a moderately-priced hotel whose owner turned out to be Jewish. He greeted me in Arabic and I hesitated momentarily before replying, then casually reciprocated his greeting, pretending that I was a non-Arab. He persisted in talking Arabic to me and boastfully announced: "I am a Jew you know." I promptly replied, "I am an Arab and I am not against the Jews; I am against the Zionists and the people who occupied Arab territory." He countered agreeable, "I am a Zionist for religious reasons, but I am not interested in politics." Our confrontation ended, I went upstairs to my room and stayed put until the following morning. Finally I became restless and hungry and decided to go out to eat and take a long walk. My Jewish friend was at the desk. He greeted me volubly and asked if I would like to go to Amsterdam on a trip he was organising for this guest. I smiled, declined the invitation and rushed out to fetch some food. On the way I purchased several English newspapers; all were filled with news from Jordan and some had editorial comments on the impact of the Rogers proposals on the Arab world, Israel, and the great power relations. Practically every paper I read speculated on forthcoming hijackings. I felt uneasy at first, but then relieved when I read that the hijackings were supposed to be taking place in Zurich and elsewhere, not in Amsterdam.

I was obsessed with the idea of my mission. I rehearsed it on the hour every hour of my waking days. I roamed the city of Frankfurt for a few days, bored with the waiting; then I went to Stuttgart briefly and on to

Amsterdam. Our rendezvous with history was approaching; all plans had to be translated into action; history was ours to write; Patrick Arguello was to write it in blood, I was not so honoured.

• • •

I met Patrick Arguello for the first time in September, 1970, in front of the air terminal at Stuttgart. We briefed each other on our mutual assignment and reviewed the plan thoroughly. The following day we flew together to Frankfurt. At Frankfurt airport, Mr. Diaz (Patrick) was inspected as I watched the passengers of a TWA Tel Aviv-bound flight being thoroughly searched. I felt very happy that we were causing the enemy so much trouble. "What fools, that's the plane we're going to hijack on its way back from Tel Aviv," I thought to myself. Patrick was cleared through customs without suspicion.

The next stop was Amsterdam. On September 6 Patrick and I met in front of the El-Al counter at ten a.m. We waited for half an hour for the El-Al Office to open. It never opened that day. We checked the flight schedule; the bulletin board still showed El-Al flight 219 as departing for New York at eleven twenty a.m. We asked the KLM ground hostess for assistance. She took our tickets and called El-Al office. There was no answer.

The KLM hostess seemed a little surprised. She asked, "Why take El-Al flight, there are others, which are better and more comfortable." We assured her that "we'd rather travel El-Al." As we waited Pan Am flight 840 arrived and I happily remembered TWA flight 840 of August 29, 1969. I was not aware at that moment that two of our comrades, having been barred in an earlier attempt by the Israelis, were on their own to seize Pan Am flight 840 a half-hour after take-off. They took the 747 to Cairo where they blew it up as a declaration of Palestinian independence. Neither Patrick nor any of the other five male hijackers knew that three planes were our target that day. Only the three female Palestinian captains and a handful of other leaders knew of the entire plan. We lingered in the waiting room until about twelve-o-five. There was still no sign of the El-Al counter-staff.

Suddenly an armed police officer in Israeli uniform emerged. "Why are you late?" he demanded. I accommodatingly explained, "We arrived at ten o'clock, officer," and suggested that he ask the KLM hostess, who vouched for us. "Your passport please," he said. Both Patrick and I showed him our passports without comment. The officer carefully examined each page. He looked at my photograph and then back at me several times. He paced back and forth as he addressed us. He asked me to empty my handbag and identify every item in it which I did. I looked completely normal. Patrick was wearing a business suit and I was dressed in a mini-skirt and jacket. I did not pretend to be other than calm Maria Sanchez from Honduras. Routine questions went on for several minutes. Suddenly I heard loud voices. I saw three Arabs walking in my direction. My heart sank. I knew and recognised one of them. What if he greeted me? We would be exposed immediately. Fortunately the Israeli officer had his back to them. Since we were already holding hands for his benefit, I quickly threw my arms around Patrick. He seemed a little surprised, but what man will rebuff a woman under such conditions? The embrace lasted until my Arab friend passed by unnoticed by the El-Al officer or anyone else. The officer seemed untroubled by us. Politely he invited us to go with him to the basement to check our baggage. "Officer, our luggage is open, you could inspect it anytime you like," I said. "Regulations state, Madam," he explained, "that owners must be present." We happily agreed. The officer was no amateur. He systematically went through every item not once, but twice. He asked informal but pertinent questions as he inspected our possessions.

Then he pointedly turned to me and asked: "Has anyone given you any gifts?" "No," I replied emphatically. "Do you have anything sharp or dangerous?" "Such as?" I said. "Such as a pistol, a knife or anything sharp?" "No Sir. What would a girl like me ever do with a pistol or knife, officer?"

He smiled apologetically and said, "You can go back to the transit hall." Then it suddenly dawned on him to ask me in English if I spoke

Spanish. "Si, senor," I blurted out boldly. "Have a good journey," he said. Patrick was a little surprised. "Why would you say to him you spoke Spanish when you don't?" "Look Patrick," I said, "if he knew how to speak Spanish he would have addressed us in Spanish from the beginning. Calm down, we're clear."

As we re-entered the hall, I saw some thirty or forty youngsters waiting to board El-Al flight 219. I was shocked and secretly lamented that once again I had to face the agonising problem of what to do to avoid hurting children. I love children and I know they are free from guilt. Although I remembered the children of Palestine napalmed by the Israelis and Dr. Haddad's child running out of his flaming room, I nevertheless vowed to do my utmost not to jeopardise the lives of the passengers need-lessly. I sat semi-paralysed for a few seconds wrestling with the moral issues of our action. Meanwhile Patrick was walking around the hall trying to spot our two comrades. As I looked at the children a beautiful little girl walked towards me, her eyes directed longingly towards the sandwich in my hand. Her mother pulled her away as I almost said to her, "*Taali ela houna.*" (Come here and take it.) No sooner did I hold my tongue, than her mother called "*Taali ela houna ya binti,*" (Come here my child). I was startled. Patrick had just joined me. I tried to dispel any sign of anxiety by whispering furtively to him "Guess what?" "Yes," said Patrick, thinking I had spotted our comrades. "The lady with the children oppo-site us is an Israeli; imagine if she were assigned to hijack this plane and she wanted to take it in one direction and we in the other. Who is likely to win the contest?" I asked. Patrick laughed and assured me "We shall win."

We waited. Minutes seemed like hours. No Israeli plane was in sight. Only the damned KLM planes were there and we had no use for them. The jumbo jet had taken off at eleven-thirty. It was now a little after twelve. The Israeli officer reappeared and we went through the same routine inspection. We were ordered to another side of the room. I tried not to show my frustration. The third inspection started and we were told to move back to our original places. By the end of this inspection, it was one-thirty. The hijack proclamations were supposed to have been simultaneously announced at twelve-twenty. I figured that either the hijackings were announced and the blasted Israelis had heard about them and decided to transfer us to KLM, or they had captured our two other comrades and were desperately looking for us. I had two hand grenades; Patrick had one hand grenade and a pistol. I said to Patrick who was aware only of our own hijack plans, "Commandos do not surrender, we have to play Samson if they discover us." Patrick resolutely agreed. We were asked to walk downstairs. The same officer was standing at the gate checking every passport and passenger. I said "Officer, we are late." "That's all right, madam, we're doing it for your own security," he declared. We marched to the plane surrounded by all kinds of armed guards. I was delighted that the resistance was causing so many difficulties and making the Zionists paranoid and jittery. I felt that Patrick and I had already conquered the enemy and accomplished half of our mission by making a fool of him and proving that his precautionary measures were not foolproof. I realised that the enemy's fortress was not impregnable as I ascended the plane with twelve guards of honour bearing sub-machine guns guaranteeing my "security". When I stepped into the El-Al plane, I felt for the first time since April 13, 1948, that I was at home again in Haifa. I was indeed in a lion's den. Never before had I felt so elated and proud of being a member of the Popular Front than at that moment.

Patrick and I searched for two empty seats. We were moved around twice until we were finally seated together in the second row of the tourist class. We heaved a sigh of relief as a hostess asked if we were comfortable. I was exhilarated and looked forward to the second half of our mission. Patrick seemed a little frightened as El-Al finally took off around one-thirty. Patrick knew me only as Shadiah. I thought if I revealed my identity his morale would be greatly boosted. I did. Patrick was heartened. He gave me a victory salute. The lady next to me fell asleep immediately. All the passengers seemed tired. At one-fifty-five, we noticed that someone was watching us from the back of the plane. I told Patrick to stay still. I turned around and looked directly at the man for a minute. He was in civilian clothes. When he saw that I was watching him he shyly looked the other way. At that moment Patrick prepared his hand grenade and pistol, and I pulled the safety pins off my two hand grenades and rushed forward through the first class section and towards the cockpit. We shouted "Don't move," as some of the passengers tried to take cover. Three stewards were in front of us wielding hand guns. In a couple of seconds I could count six guns. But we had anticipated a battle. A hostess fell to the ground crying to me in Arabic. I threatened to blow up the plane if anyone fired at us. I displayed my two grenades and dropped the safety pins on the floor hoping to convince everyone we intended business and to avert a bloody battle. Patrick held the armed stewards and the passengers at bay. "Go ahead, I'll protect your back," he instructed me. I forced the hostess to stand up and walk ahead of me. The moment she opened the door, she staggered forward in a state of panic. I couldn't see the captain or crew. Shots were fired. There was another door before we could reach the pilot's cabin. Both of us banged on the door. No one opened the door. Suddenly someone was looking at us through a spy-hole. I brandished my hand grenades and ordered him to open the door or else. I heard more shots and the plane went into a spin.

Several people attacked me at the same moment. I thought the plane was disintegrating. The firing continued and suddenly I found myself besieged by a pack of wolves, El-Al staff as well as passengers. Someone screamed "Don't shoot at her! She has two hand grenades." No one fired at me. But some people were kicking me, others hitting. A few just stepped all over me. Two were holding my hands and trying to take away the grenades. One finally succeeded in prying one grenade from me without exploding himself and the plane. I held tightly to the other until I was knocked unconscious for a second and was overpowered.

At first I didn't know what was happening to Patrick. Within a few minutes I was dragged to the first-class compartment where Patrick was lying, bleeding profusely and breathing heavily. I could see he was still alive. The Zionists were acting like mad dogs. They trampled over every part of our bodies. By that time Patrick was too weak to resist. I was fighting like a caged lion. I fought until I was completely exhausted. Then a vicious thug pounced on me, pulled my hair mercilessly, called me a wicked bitch, a malicious Arab and all sorts of obscene names. I spat contemptuously in his face. I bit his hands. He and the others around me beat me incessantly for several minutes.

The plane was travelling smoothly; the remaining passengers were staying in their seats. Suddenly an Israeli guard emerged from the cockpit area. Patrick was lying on his side. The man turned him over on his stomach and started tying him up with wires and a necktie. Someone asked "How are they?" A voice replied "We don't know. He is . . . we're not sure. She's three-quarters dead." The man stepped on Patrick's hips and Patrick looked at me in agony, his hands tied behind his back. Then the Zionist guard fired four shots into Patrick's back. Someone screamed from the back of the plane "Please stop the bloodshed. Please, Please, Please!" The four shots that were fired into Patrick's back were fired from a distance of less than one foot. Patrick looked at me, gave me a deathly smile, and bid me an eternal goodbye.

Then came my turn. I was tied up in the same fashion: hands behind my back, my feet and legs immobilised with wires. I expected to join the ranks of our martyrs as Patrick had just done. But the Zionists did not execute me. I was certain they were not moved by any humanitarian concern or by the pleading voice from the back of the cabin. They needed me for display purposes in their human zoo in Israel. I presumed they wanted a witness to testify to their "bravery"—a prisoner to torture and to extract confessions from. As they finished tying me up, the pilot announced, "We are going to Tel Aviv." Yet within minutes, I felt the plane descend and then touch down. As it hit the runway I fell off my seat and my "bodyguard" fell on top of me. He pulled me back up shouting obscenities and kicking me ruthlessly. The passengers disembarked. I could hear the sound of an ambulance outside. Two uniformed officers walked in. I didn't know where we were. Another officer walked in to the first-class compartment where I was being held. He demanded that I be turned over. An Israeli officer declared, "She is our prisoner. Get out of here. This is Israeli property." The first two men stood their ground. Then the Israeli pilot, yes the pilot, in the presence of two British officers, came out of his cockpit, lifted me off my seat and gave me a couple of vicious kicks in the bottom. The British officers screamed, "Shame," and pushed him aside. More British officers stepped into the fray, identifying themselves as members of Scotland Yard. The captain told them, "To hell with you and your government. She is my prisoner. Get out of this plane." The British officers tried to seize me. Three Israelis pulled me in one direction by my trussed up legs; the British pulled my hands in the other in a tug-of-war which the British won. A great husky English officer carried me over his shoulders and threw me down to the waiting arms of two other officers below. I was in British hands. I knew it would be safer here for me than in Tel Aviv.

excerpt from:

Abu Nidal

by Patrick Seale

Abu Nidal was the dictatorial head of the world's most notorious Leftist terrorist organization, named after its founder, that numbered at its height some one thousand members. Nidal the man was sponsored by Libya, Syria, and finally by Iraq, where he lives today. His organization attacked the El Al ticket counter at Rome's airport in 1985, killing scores of passengers. This is one of the few times Abu Nidal killed non-Arabs. Nidal himself spent most of his time assassinating moderate PLO members, and finally his own men. According to author Patrick Seale, it is generally acknowledged that Abu Nidal was either a Mossad agent himself or that the organization had been infiltrated at the highest levels. In the first excerpt we share the horrifying experience of the interrogation and training of a new recruit. Rather than simply being a test of a young man's mettle, the sadism recounted here could be borne out of a hatred for Palestinians and a way to murder potential troublemakers in the guise of rigorous indoctrination. Next, Seale recounts the mass murders by Abu Nidal of his own followers. This purge takes on a different meaning in the light of the accusations that Abu Nidal is actually an agent of Israel. Patrick Seale is one of Britain's most important Middle East experts and has written extensively on Syria and its president, Hafez al-Assad.

Jorde's Testimony

(What follows is based on one man's account of his experiences in Abu Nidal's organization, related to me in the summer of 1990.)

He was a short, stocky man in his late twenties, with a bull neck, close-cropped hair, and the round thighs and springy walk of an athlete or male dancer. His code name, he told me, was Hussein Jorde Abdallah, and for a Palestinian his background was unusual. His grandfather was a Kabyle from Algeria, one of several thousand Berbers who immigrated to Palestine from North Africa at the turn of the century. His father was born in Palestine, but when the Israelis took over in 1948, he fled with his family to Lebanon, ending up in Burj al-Shamali, a tented camp near Tyre, one of several erected by the United Nations Relief and Works Agency (UNRWA) in the immediate aftermath of the Palestine war. It was there that Jorde was born in 1961. But life for Palestinians in Lebanon was not easy. Sometime in the early seventies, once Algeria had settled down to its independence, Jorde's father decided to take his family back to their place of origin in Kabylia, the fiercely independent hill country just east of Algiers. And it was there that Jorde grew up, speaking Arabic, one or two Berber dialects, and a smattering of French. He was a restless, resourceful boy who scrounged for food, became a skilled shoplifter, and, after finishing school, joined Algeria's vast army of the unemployed. The family's main asset was Jorde's younger brother, Abdallah, who had gone to the Gulf in search of work and found a job with Kuwait Airlines.

When his father, the family breadwinner, died in 1986, Jorde was expected to provide for his mother and his two younger sisters. But he could hardly face the prospect and decided to escape. With money begged from Abdallah in Kuwait, he bought an air ticket to Barcelona and boarded an Iberia flight, with no visa for Spain and no passport save for a Lebanese laissez-passer, such as is issued to Palestinians. On arrival he had a stroke of luck. A domestic flight had landed at about the same time as his own and its passengers were filing into the arrivals hall a few feet away from those on his international flight. There was only a narrow passage between the two lines. When his fellow travelers, all of them Algerians, rushed for the immigration desk, Jorde quietly joined the other line and entered Spain unchallenged.

Jorde spent three months in Barcelona, living in cheap hotels and at night hanging about discos frequented by Arabs. He robbed those less sharp-witted than himself, stole food from supermarkets, and made friends with petty criminals, until one night he was picked up by the Spanish police in Plaza Catalonia and, after interrogation, deported to Lebanon.

In Beirut, he met a girl and started going out with her. She confided that she worked for a secret outfit that she called the Council, but she warned him not to get involved. He was intrigued. He coaxed the facts out of her. Its full name was Fatah: the Revolutionary Council, and it was run by Abu Nidal. Jorde was broke and seeking fame: With its aura of clandestinity and power, the Council seemed right for him. He heard it had an office in the Mar Elias refugee camp, and he knocked on the door and asked to volunteer.

A young man behind a desk looked him over and listened to his story. What could he do? What skills did he have? Why had he come? Jorde told him about his knowledge of languages. He said he was ready to work for a meal a day and somewhere to sleep.

"What do you think of Arafat?" the young man asked.

"Hopeless!" Jorde replied. He had an inkling this was their line. "He wants to liberate Palestine by making speeches. What was taken by force can only be recovered by force!"

Within days Jorde had signed on, been given a code name and a mattress on the first floor of the building, and written a twenty-seven-page life story in which, to make himself sound important, he told a lot of fibs. He wrote that he had murdered a Jew in Spain, that he had played football for a famous team in Algeria, that he had worked as an interpreter in a travel agency in Pamplona. He listed a score of Spanish women he claimed to have made love to. It was pure fiction.

Jorde was not well suited for the Council. He was a braggart and a compulsive talker; he did not take kindly to discipline; he showed undue curiosity in an organization where information was restricted to those with the need to know; he tried to make friends with colleagues, although friendships were discouraged as a matter of policy; he loved to show off his languages and was hopeless at self-criticism. In such a paranoid outfit, where everyone was constantly spying on everyone else and forever writing up reports, he was certain to get into trouble. But he showed a talent for martial arts and got to the top of the class. He was also good at drill and at physical exercises, and once he had been transferred down to Sidon, he was put in charge of a squad. However, the fact that he shaved every day aroused suspicion. Where had he learned such fastidious habits? Fearing that he had been planted on them, his superiors asked him once again to write his life story. He labored away, but this time around he could no longer remember the names of the girls he previously claimed to have known or the fictitious addresses he had given them.

Nevertheless, since nothing serious was found against him, he was soon flown to Libya with a batch of other recruits and bused to the desert camp. It was 1987. Billets and wash houses were still being built—by the men—and in the meantime the accommodation was in tents. The routine was punishing. Roused at dawn, the men were sent out to jog for an hour, returning to a light breakfast and a long, hard shift of building work from 7:30 a.m. to 1 p.m. This was followed by a break for a Spartan lunch and a short rest until 3 p.m., before the start of another shift of work until six o'clock. They then were allowed to wash and change for the evening's program of lectures and political films. Jorde discovered to his agony that if one was five minutes late for meals, one would not be allowed into the canteen at all. If one didn't get up on time in the morning, one's mattress would be turned over or one would be doused by a pail of cold water. If one put down tools to take a breather, reproaches and abuse came raining down. One needed permission to go to the lavatory, and one had to be very ill indeed, practically spitting blood, before the camp doctor allowed any sick leave. Complaints were utterly forbidden, on pain of being hauled away to Station 16, from which men emerged scarcely able to walk. Jorde tried to sneak away in mid-morning for a shave and a rest, but he was soon found out and threatened with a thrashing.

When they had been at the camp for about a month, Jorde's section was told that it would shortly be receiving a visit from a "comrade" to whom every man could open his heart. "Speak freely and answer any question he puts to you," their commander instructed.

"What alerted me to Abu Nidal's arrival," Jorde said, "was a driver springing to attention and saluting. I saw a man dressed in civilian clothes and accompanied by three senior camp officials in uniform. I looked at him closely. He wasn't very tall. He had a bald head with a fringe of gray hair, blue-green eyes, and a plump face. I said to myself, This must be the big chief.

"When we assembled in the sports center, he began by telling us that our six-month course was just the first step in our career with the organization. Each of us would in time get the job of his choice, the one best suited to his talents. Then, very quietly, he started to draw us out, asking us about our background, interests, and ambitions. Each man in turn had to step forward, give his code name, and tell him his problem.

"When it was my turn, I stood up and said my name, Hussein Jorde Abdallah.

" 'Where do you come from?'

" 'North Africa.'

" 'Are you a Palestinian?'

" 'Yes.'

" 'Were you born in Algeria?'

" 'No. In a refugee camp in Tyre.'

" 'But Jorde is not an Arab name.'

" 'I am not an Arab!'

"At this, everyone stared at me in surprise. My group leader tried to say it was just my code name, but Abu Nidal waved to him to keep silent.

" 'Are you a Spaniard?'

" 'No, I'm a Kabyle.' And I explained my family's travels from North Africa to Palestine and then back again, via Lebanon, to the Berber capital of Tizi-Ouzo, in Algeria. Jorde, I said, was a Catalan version of Jorge or George: It was a name I had borrowed from a Spanish acquaintance. I told him about the languages I spoke. He asked the camp commander, Husam Yusif, to make a note of what I was saying."

This exchange with Abu Nidal made Jorde a marked man, for in drawing the leadership's attention to his potential, he was also sharpening its suspicions about him. He was asked to report the next day to the camp commander.

"Do any members of your family work for an intelligence or a security organization?" he was asked.

"No." He had an aunt and uncle living in Kuwait; two uncles in America, one in Michigan and the other in Ohio, but he knew very little about them. Another aunt, his father's sister, whom he had not seen for twenty years, lived in Benghazi. It was the usual pattern of Palestinian dispersal.

"What about you? Have you ever worked in intelligence?"

"No."

"Are you quite sure?"

"Yes, I am."

"This is a matter of life and death. Don't forget that in Beirut you signed a statement saying you would accept death if you were found to have an intelligence connection. Write your life story for us again, but this time put down every single detail about yourself and about all your relatives—their names, addresses, and everything else about them."

This was the third time Jorde had been set this task. Confined to his tent with pens and a notepad, he spent the best part of two weeks writing and growing increasingly resentful and anxious. He was worried that his earlier lies would now be exposed. He stopped eating and cried a good deal. The camp commander, Husam Yusif, came to see him.

"What's the matter with you? What's wrong?"

"I want to get out of here! I can't stand it anymore."

The next morning Husam Yusif and a strongly built man called Baha, who was said to be the Palestinian karate champion, frog-marched him to the back door of the kitchen bloc and ordered him into a dark closet, cluttered with mops and dirty rags, situated just behind the kitchen's huge gas burners, whose roar could be heard through the wall.

"We haven't brought you here to imprison you but to stop you from doing anything foolish," Husam said. "Sami will want to see you when he gets back from Tripoli in a couple of days." Sami was the man in charge of Section 16, the prison and interrogation bloc.

Dirty and unshaven, Jorde was brought before Sami two days later.

"Where is your life story?"

Jorde told him he had hidden it under the mattress in his billet.

"Have you told us the whole truth?"

"Yes."

"Before we resort to other measures, let me make one thing absolutely clear. You are still our comrade! If you are in any sort of trouble, you must tell us about it. If you are in danger, so are we all. No one can fool us. God judges in heaven, we judge here on earth. Several of our comrades turned out to be agents of other intelligence services. When we caught them, they told us they had been blackmailed into it. We were able to help them. We can do the same for you. I am going to give you another week to write your life story. Forget about the earlier drafts. Just tell us whom you work for!"

"But I don't work for anyone!"

"Yes you do! We can prove it. But I want you to admit it yourself. Tell us the whole truth. Don't force us to use other methods."

So Jorde started scribbling again. He confessed that he had not played football in Algeria nor worked as an interpreter in Spain. The travel agency in Pamplona did not exist. The twenty-five girls he said he had slept with were all invented. But he really had entered Spain without a visa by jumping a queue at the Barcelona airport.

By this time he had been confined for ten days in the closet. His beard had grown. His body itched all over. When the burners were lit in the kitchen, the temperature soared. He stripped down to his underpants. One day, still scantily dressed, he was taken outside, and, wedged in the backseat of a Toyota between Sami and another man, he was driven out of the camp into the open desert. His first thought was that they were going to kill him. Behind a dune, they came on a single tent pitched directly on the sand. It was empty. There was no ground sheet or bed, nothing except for some iron pegs in the ground, to which they now tied him. There they left him for a couple of days, visiting him once a day with some bread and a cup of water.

"Have you decided to tell us the truth?"

"I've already told you the truth," he groaned.

"Listen," Sami said. "Beating is not allowed in our organization except by decision of the Central Committee. But if you don't talk, the Central Committee will have no alternative . . . "

Jorde remained silent. He was filthy and starving. He stank. He began to hope that a scorpion bite would finish him off.

The following day Sami, Baha, and three other men came to the tent. One was carrying a rope, another a length of rubber hose, the third an oxygen cylinder, a bottle of disinfectant, and some rags.

Baha came up to him. "Stand up!" he roared. "Are you going to tell us the truth?" But before Jorde could utter a word, he was struck across the face. He fell down, only to be hauled to his feet again. "Stand to attention! Don't raise your hands! Give me the hose!" And they all set to, punching and beating him.

One of his tormentors was a young thug called Mas'ud, who had been in the physical-exercise squad that Jorde had led. Jorde had pushed him hard to run and jump, and Mas'ud had hated him for it. Now he got his own back. They tied Jorde down, propped his legs up on a stone, and attacked the soles of his feet. Screaming and weeping, his mouth full of sand, he begged them to spare him.

"Stop! Stop! I'll tell you the truth. It's Algeria. I work for Algerian intelligence. They sent me here. They made me do it. I was scared for my family. Stop!"

"OK," said Sami. "That's it. Don't be afraid. We'll look after your family." They sat him down and untied his bonds.

"Is that it?" asked Jorde through his tears. "All finished?"

"Yes, that's it. We'll have a chat together over dinner. Now you are safe. You are once again our comrade. But you will have to tell us everything!" Jorde could not stand up. They carried him to Sami's tent a little way off, gave him some tea, and treated his wounds.

This is what he told them: When he was living in Algeria with his family, he used to buy small quantities of hashish from his neighbor, a petty smuggler. This man told him that they had to watch out for a certain Captain Kamal of military intelligence, whose job it was to chase the drug dealers. Jorde learned to recognize the captain's car. One day Captain Kamal visited Jorde's family at home, and soon afterward he called Jorde to his office and offered him a job as an informer. He wanted to know about smugglers, then he asked Jorde to keep an eye on student agitators in the town, and finally, when Abu Nidal opened an office in Algiers, which it was feared might be used to plan attacks on visiting Palestinians, Jorde was sent to Spain and from there to Beirut to penetrate the organization.

This was Jorde's hastily concocted story. There were elements of truth in it. Captain Kamal was a real person. But the rest was invention. Under questioning, it did not stand up. He got confused and contradicted himself. Sami was unimpressed. Later that night, Jorde was taken back to the tent and the beatings resumed. Desperate to save himself, he racked his brains for a more plausible story. He said he worked in Bilbao for the Basque nationalist movement ETA; he was a member of its military wing. It was ETA that had sent him to Beirut to join Abu Nidal, ETA that had made a soldier out of him! He had never been to Pamplona or slept with Spanish girls; that part was a lie. He was sorry, very sorry. He had only wanted to make himself interesting. The beatings went on at intervals throughout the night.

In the following days, they stopped asking him for the truth and concentrated only on breaking him. It was extremely hot inside the tent. Sami cut his water ration to three small mouthfuls a day. He was so thirsty he could hardly speak. They gave him a tin in which to do his business. Flies gathered on his back and on the filth around him. Blood dried on his wounds. His body was all pain. They forced a potato into his mouth, blindfolded him, and turned Mas'ud loose on him. To escape the blows, he feigned madness, throwing himself on the ground in spasms.

"What do you think?" he heard Sami say to Baha. "Shall we get him a doctor?" He was carried to the surgery, tied to a bed, and given an injection. He was aware that Sami and Baha came to see him several times during the night. Half-asleep, he answered their questions, and they realized he had been faking.

"Have you ever had a wire inserted in your penis?" Sami asked. "Have you been trussed up like a chicken and forced to sit on a broken bottle? We will cut out your tongue. What you've written is all untrue. Every word of it. Who recruited you? Who sent you to us? Tell us about the Syrians! Tell us about the Jordanians!"

"Have pity! Oh God, have pity! I swear I told you the whole truth in the kitchen. The more you beat me, the more I'll lie."

Mahmud, a tall, gray-haired man from the Central Committee, came to look him over. "Take him to Station 16," he said.

There, in a tiny concrete underground cell, they made him stand to attention all night facing the wall, and the next night and the whole of the next two weeks. Jorde learned to sleep standing up. In the morning the guards would crowd in and each one would slap him across the face a hundred times. He had to count the slaps silently and, when it was time, utter only the words "One hundred!" If he fell to the ground or let out so much as a moan, they would start again. His face swelled up like a football and an ugly liquid flowed from his ears. Once every two or three days he was allowed to go out to the lavatory. The stench in the cell was terrible. From time to time Sami would arrive and play a tape of Umm Kalthoum, the undisputed queen of Arabic song, whereupon the guards would rush in, throw Jorde to the ground, put a brick under his feet, bind his legs, and thrash his soles until he fainted.

A bucket of cold water would bring him half-alive again. "Where did you learn yoga? Who taught you to sleep standing up? Speak, you dog! Who but a soldier would shave every day? You're an agent. Confess it!"

"I'm not an agent! I am a poor son of the camps! Please believe me."

Jorde spent two months in prison, being beaten every day. One night, when he was still in his underground cell, a wedding was celebrated in the camp. A comrade was marrying a female member, and all the guards went to enjoy the festivities except for Mas'ud, who stayed behind.

"Tonight," he said, "I'm going to finish you off!" He unfurled a length of wire, threw a switch in the corridor, and dangled a bright electric bulb into Jorde's cell through the tiny skylight above the door. "Hold it!" he shouted. "Hold it in your hand! If you drop it, I'll break your bones." Jorde obeyed. After a few minutes, smoke rose from his fearfully blistered palm. Swooning with pain, he was saved by the guards returning from the party.

For the tenth time, Sami gave him a pad and a pen and told him to write his life story. The prescribed routine was for him to write during the day, sitting on the concrete step in his cell, and then stand to attention throughout the night.

One evening, after reading what he had written, a grim-faced Sami came down to the cellblock. "Tonight," he whispered, "you are going to die! You had better say your prayers." They brought him water for his ablutions and stood watching as he prostrated himself. Then they dressed him in military uniform, wrapped a scarf around his head, and took him out beyond the prison compound to where a deep hole, evidently part of the sewage system, had been dug. A ladder led down to the noisome depths. Below him was another hole, shaped like a grave.

"Lie down!" Sami ordered as he drew his Browning and cocked it. "Do you have anything to tell us? This is your last chance."

"I am innocent!" Jorde cried in a storm of tears. "I have told you the truth." And as the filthy water lapped about him, he closed his eyes in a last prayer.

"All right! Get him out," Sami ordered. Shivering and demented, racked by sobs, Jorde was carried back to prison, given fresh clothes, and put in a clean cell. It was warm and dark. He curled up on a blanket on the floor and fell asleep.

Sami woke him up the next morning.

"Congratulations!" he said. "You've passed!" He reached into his pocket and gave Jorde a handful of sweets. "I believe you are innocent! Have a wash and a shave and some breakfast. We'll talk later. We have to behave like this to protect ourselves. There are a lot of enemies outside . . ."

Since the 1970s, Israel has also regularly sent ground forces on punitive missions north of its self-styled security zone, established in southern Lebanon in 1978. And as we have seen, it has also sent hit teams to many countries to seek out and kill prominent Palestinians. Most of these attacks are described as preemptive, intended to keep the enemy off balance. If the Palestinians do from time to time manage to slip a punch through Israel's defenses, massive retaliation always follows: It is Israel's official policy that attacks on it must never go unpunished—and with one curious exception, they never do go unpunished.

Abu Nidal has very largely been left alone. Despite his attacks on the El Al counters at airports in Rome and Vienna, his murderous assaults on synagogues in Istanbul and several European cities, and other anti-Jewish crimes, his organization in Lebanon and Libya has never seriously been hit by the Mossad's assassination squads or by the Israeli air force, which has so extensively bombed other Palestinian positions. That Abu Nidal should be left to kill Jews with impunity is an extraordinary—indeed outrageous—departure from Israeli policy. A German expert on counterterrorism told me in London in 1990, "Those that the Israelis want to destroy, they destroy, even if it means sending in assassins. But what have they ever done to Abu Nidal in fifteen years? He seems more like a protected species that the Mossad wants to keep alive!"

Abu Nidal's large establishment near the village of Bqasta, east of Sidon, in Lebanon, known as the Cadres School, is in fact a military camp, standing alone and exposed in the mountains. It presents an unmistakable target from the air. Only once, in the summer of 1988, has the Cadres School been attacked, when an Israeli precision bomb hit a single tent, killing eight female trainees but leaving intact dozens of other buildings housing Abu Nidal's troops and staff.

Before a split within Abu Nidal's ranks that would make them fear each other, the top men in his organization moved about southern Lebanon unprotected, as if they knew they were not at risk from Israel. They slept in unguarded houses and, in spite of their rhetoric about being threatened by "hostile services," lived perfectly normal lives. This complacency reigned even though everyone knew that the organization had hit Israel's ambassador in London in June 1982, to say nothing of the Istanbul synagogue and other Jewish targets.

There have been no victims of Israeli reprisals among Abu Nidal's top leadership.

Operation in the Occupied Territories

Another aspect of Abu Nidal's activities puzzled me. Palestinian nationalists from the socialist left to the Islamic right regard the *intifada* in the occupied territories as the great national battle, a unique effort, after years of passivity, to liberate the territories. Abu Nidal has struck targets in nearly all parts of the world—Bangkok, Australia, Peru. Yet he has not thrown a stone in the occupied territories, either before or during the *intifada*. In all the years I have been talking to people from the territories, no one has ever heard of a single operation—no matter how trivial—attributed to Abu Nidal. Eight-year-old children throw stones at Israeli troops. Old women brave tear gas. Abu Nidal does nothing. Palestinians from the territories hardly know his name, because he has committed no men, donated not a penny, done nothing at all—absolutely nothing—to support their struggle against Israeli rule. When the United National Leadership of the Uprising (UNLU), the umbrella organization running the *intifada*, was set up in 1988, Abu Nidal's publications considered it an extension of Arafat's PLO and ignored it completely.

Abu Nidal's inattention to the Palestinian cause is reflected in the structure of his organization. The Intelligence Directorate's Committee for Special Missions—which mounts assassinations—employs dozens of cadres and has unlimited funds. The Organization Directorate's Palestine/Jordan Committee has almost no funds or facilities and was for a long time manned by only two persons—Samir Darwish, who was sent on a mission to Peru, where he was arrested, and Fadil al-Qaisi, who died in London after undergoing heart surgery. Throughout the entire *intifada*, Abu Nidal has given no additional resources to the Palestine/Jordan Committee and mounted no operations in southern Lebanon, like those by other Palestinian organizations, to harass the Israelis.

In 1988, Atif Abu Bakr called for a special session of the leadership to see what could be done to help the *intifada*. Abu Nidal sabotaged the meeting by discussing such trivia as whose wife had been seen at the hairdresser's? Who had lunched at a fancy restaurant in Switzerland instead of making do with a sandwich? And who had thrown away a kilo of perfectly edible tomatoes at the training camp?

Far from supporting the *intifada*, Abu Nidal has deliberately interfered with it, as, for example in the case of the mysterious Lt. Col. Ma'mun Mraish. Universally known in the Palestinian underground as Ma'mun al-Saghir, Mraish was one of Fatah's ablest and most active officers. He was based at its clandestine naval station in Greece, where, in association with Abu Jihad, he was principally concerned with moving men and weapons into the occupied territories. The Mossad had every reason to want him dead.

But there was a further dimension to Mraish. Palestinian sources say that he had excellent contacts with the Soviets and had given them information, and even sensitive technical equipment, which he was well placed to acquire. The CIA must therefore have been on his trail as well.

On August 20, 1983, a hot summer's day, in a coastal suburb of Athens, a gunman riding pillion on a motorcycle came abreast Mraish's car and killed him outright with a burst of machine-gun fire. The PLO concluded that either the Mossad or the CIA was responsible.

But the Russians did not let the matter rest. They considered Mraish their man and wanted his killer. They investigated the case for several months and concluded that Mraish had been killed by Abu Nidal. They presented their evidence to Atif Abu Bakr, then head of Abu Nidal's Political Directorate, and demanded an explanation. Was Abu Nidal aware, they asked, of the risks he was running by killing Soviet agents?

When I interviewed him in Tunis after he had defected from Abu Nidal, Atif Abu Bakr told me that he had confronted Abu Nidal with the Soviet accusation and that to his great surprise, Abu Nidal had said they were right, he had killed Mraish to get back at Fatah. But he made it clear,

Abu Bakr added, that he did not want his part in the affair to come out. Many Palestinians knew that Mraish was one of the most effective links between the PLO and the West Bank, and Abu Nidal, therefore, did not want it to be known that he had killed him.

It was not only in the occupied territories that Abu Nidal's behavior seemed to me suspect. It is well known that southern Lebanon, north of Israel's security zone, has for years been home to a number of rival parties and militias of widely differing composition and ideology—Shi'ite, Druze, Nasserist, communist, Ba'athist, pan-Syrian, as well as the various Palestinian factions—which often clash as they seek to defend their turf. Men from several of these groups have told me that whenever one Palestinian faction clashed with another, Abu Nidal's men would fire at both sides, provoking further conflict. Abu Nidal has also used similar tactics against the two Shi'ite factions, Amal and Hizballah.

Sidon is the major port of southern Lebanon. It is presided over by the "Nasserist" leader Mustafa Sa'd, whose city lives next to, and in reasonable amity with, the large PLO-dominated refugee camp of Ain al-Hilwa. Yet a defector from Abu Nidal's organization told me that Abu Nidal repeatedly sent masked men to infiltrate the refugee camp at night, to throw grenades and wreak havoc there, and at the same time plant bombs in Sidon, as if to incite hostilities between the PLO camp and Sa'd's militia. In the summer of 1990, these tactics were uncovered and several of Abu Nidal's members were expelled from both Sidon and Ain al-Hilwa.

Former officers of Abu Nidal's People's Army told me that Abu Nidal himself used to instruct his people in Lebanon to report to him on the strength, dispositions, and operations of other forces in Lebanon, and particularly the Syrian army. The Syrians once intercepted a messenger carrying reports back to Abu Nidal. Why and for whom, they wanted to know, was Abu Nidal collecting information about them?

A former member of Abu Nidal's Justice Committee told me that when Mossad agents were captured by the organization, they would usually be killed almost at once, often on the very day of their arrest. The standard practice is to keep such prisoners alive long enough to extract as much information as possible from them. If a prisoner is killed before he has talked, then the killing is usually to prevent him from talking. My informant suspected that someone had been planted in the Justice Committee to kill off captured Mossad agents before they could confess.

The Case of Ziyad Zaidan and Fathi Harzallah

In July 1989, Abu Nidal's People's Army, his militia in Lebanon, learned that a two-man Mossad cell was operating in the big Palestinian refugee camp of Ain al-Hilwa, near Sidon. One of these Mossad operatives, Ziyad Zaidan, voluntarily confessed his links with the Israelis to the head of security of the People's Army in South Lebanon, who was code-named Sufyan. He said he wanted to clear his conscience and wash away the stain on his past. He was prepared to die for the terrible wrongs he had done to the Palestinian cause.

He told Sufyan that he had been captured by the Israelis near Sidon during the 1982 war, taken to Israel, jailed, recruited, trained, and sent back to Lebanon as a spy.

Zaidan revealed that he and his colleague, Fathi Harzallah, a relative from the West Bank town of Tal, near Nablus, had worked for the Mossad in South Lebanon since 1982, interpreting aerial photographs taken by Israeli reconnaissance aircraft. They would be sent films (he had one with him at the time, which was several meters long) of the Ain al-Hilwa camp and other locations, on which individual buildings were numbered in red. His job was to identify the buildings and tell the Israelis who was living and working there and when they were most likely to be at home.

He told Sufyan that over the years, he had radioed to Israel, using a cipher he had been given, no fewer than seven thousand messages and that he had been responsible for scores of Israeli air raids on Lebanon and for hundreds of Palestinian casualties. He said he was making good money at it.

Zaidan had returned to Israel two or three times for debriefing and further training. He would be told by radio where to wait on the shore for a small boat with frogmen in it to pick him up, usually before dawn. In the case of trouble, Zaidan and his colleague Harzallah could raise a white flag on a certain rooftop and be whisked away by an Israeli helicopter or be rescued from the beach by an Israeli patrol boat.

Abu Nidal's cadre Sufyan was immensely excited by Zaidan's confession. His first thought was that the cell could be "turned" against the Mossad. At the very least, Zaidan and Harzallah could serve as bait to draw onto the shore an Israeli boat or aircraft, which could then be shot up or captured.

Immediately, he took Ziyad Zaidan to see Wasfi Hannun, head of Abu Nidal's People's Army Directorate, who referred the case to Mustafa Awad (Alaa), Abu Nidal's highest-ranking intelligence officer in Lebanon, who was in constant touch with Dr. Ghassan al-Ali and with Abu Nidal. Alaa seemed indifferent to Zaidan's story, even bored by it. He said Sufyan's suggestion of playing back the cell was foolish. It would never work. Puffing calmly on his pipe, he tried to give Sufyan the impression that uncovering a Mossad cell, complete with film and intercepted messages, was routine, unimportant. Alaa did suggest, however, that Zaidan's partner, Fathi Harzallah, be brought in and made to confess his role in the affair, on pain of imprisonment or death.

When Harzallah was confronted, he admitted he was frightened of Israeli reprisals against his two wives and children if he quit. But if he did agree to be turned, he wanted the organization to pay him the $1,500 a month he said he was getting from the Mossad. Harzallah's family and connections in the West Bank seem to have been more heavily involved as collaborators with Israeli intelligence than were Zaidan's. Some years earlier, Fathi had gone to the United Arab Emirates in search of work and had been recruited by Jordanian intelligence. Then, he said, a man from his hometown had come to see him and suggested that if he returned home, the Mossad, in view of his background in intelligence work, would give him an even better deal than Jordan had done. He complied and was recruited and was then sent to Lebanon to work with Zaidan.

Though Alaa discouraged the idea, Sufyan and Zaidan went to the trouble of convincing Fathi to let himself be played back against the Israelis. He finally agreed to cooperate.

Within a day or two of this decision, the Mossad sent Zaidan a radio message summoning him to Israel, only the third such message he had had in the seven years he had been working for the Mossad. Sufyan argued that this was a good opportunity to kill or capture whoever the Israelis sent to pick up Zaidan. He drew up a plan, which he submitted to Alaa, and proposed that if the organization did not have the military resources needed for the operation, another Palestinian group, such as Jibril's PFLP-General Command, would be glad to help.

A day later and without telling Sufyan, Alaa, on direct orders from Abu Nidal, suddenly arrested Fathi Harzallah and charged him with working for the Mossad. The local PLO, which as usual was watching Abu Nidal's operations, learned of Harzallah's arrest and what he was charged with. It immediately arrested Zaidan, the man it knew to be his colleague—even though it was Zaidan who had first confessed and had indicated his readiness to be turned.

Alerted by the arrest of their agents, the Israelis aborted their planned landing. The operation was blown. Within a month of Zaidan's original confession, any hope of exploiting the Mossad's intelligence failure had collapsed completely.

Palestinian sources with direct knowledge of the case pointed to several suspicious features:

> Alaa's skepticism and seeming lack of interest;
> the fact that, a year after Fathi Harzallah's arrest, Abu
> Nidal had still not released anything about his trial or
> punishment and had not shared with other Palestinian

organizations information it may have gathered about Mossad methods, about other links Harzallah may have had, or about the estimated damage done to Palestinian security by the cell;

when Zaidan first approached Sufyan, he remarked that he had hesitated a long time before turning himself in, because of his suspicions about Abu Nidal's organization: Its methods of work, its tradecraft, and its communications, he said, were uncomfortably similar to those of the Mossad, in which he and his fellow agent had been trained;

finally, that Alaa, on orders from Abu Nidal, had aborted the operation suggested complicity with Israeli intelligence.

Sufyan was convinced by Abu Nidal's suspect handling of the case that it was time for him to leave the organization.

The Case of Mustafa Ibrahim Sunduqa

Sanduqa, as we have seen, was in charge of the Committee for Revolutionary Justice, the body responsible for prisons, interrogation, torture, and executions. He had previously served as the minute-taker at meetings of the Political Bureau and Central Committee and was married to one of Abu Nidal's nieces.

In October 1989, a certain Yusif Zaidan (no relation to Ziyad Zaidan) emerged as yet another link to the Mossad.

Yusif Zaidan was a German-trained scientist who, on graduation, had joined the PLO's Scientific Committee, first in Beirut, then in Baghdad. When Abu Nidal split from Arafat in 1974 and took over the PLO's Iraqi-based assets, Zaidan made the switch as well and was employed in Abu Nidal's Scientific Committee—a career that, until that point, was not unlike that of Dr. Ghassan al-Ali, the British-trained chemist who was head of the Secretariat and who is widely suspected by intelligence sources throughout Europe of being the high-level link to Mossad.

In November 1989, Yusif Zaidan disappeared in Lebanon. I was told by my sources that Abu Nidal immediately suspected that he had been kidnapped by his new principal rival, the breakaway Emergency Leadership, which Atif Abu Bakr had formed that month. A man was sent from Sanduqa's Justice Committee to attempt to penetrate the Emergency Leadership and locate Zaidan.

The attempted penetration was discovered, and Sanduqa's man was arrested and interrogated in June 1990—by none other than our old friend Sufyan, the defector from Abu Nidal's organization, who was now representing the Emergency Leadership. The interrogation was done conscientiously, without torture or undue force, according to Atif Abu Bakr, and was videotaped, so that it could be shown in Palestinian camps in South Lebanon (as part of the Emergency Leadership's campaign against Abu Nidal).

Sanduqa's man confessed 1) to working for Mossad; 2) that his case officer was none other than Mustafa Ibrahim Sanduqa; and 3) that his mission had been to find Yusif Zaidan, to help him escape, and if he couldn't, to kill him.

The Emergency Leadership concluded that it had stumbled on a Mossad cell inside Abu Nidal's organization, the members of which included not just Zaidan and Sanduqa but the biggest fish of all, Sulaiman Samrin, otherwise known as Dr. Ghassan al-Ali.

Yusif Zaidan and Dr. Ghassan had been friends since the early 1970s, in the days of Fatah's Scientific Committee. PLO intelligence sources confirm that there had been security worries about both of them, because it was feared that they might have been contacted by the Mossad during their student years. They had, in fact, been transferred by the PLO from Beirut to Baghdad, to remove them from the center of PLO operations. But when Abu Nidal took them over in 1974, he instead promoted them. Dr. Ghassan, in particular, rose rapidly.

The Emergency Leadership concluded that when Yusif Zaidan disappeared and was presumed kidnapped, both Dr. Ghassan and Mustafa Ibrahim Sanduqa must have feared that they would be exposed if Zaidan talked. So Sanduqa's man was sent to find Zaidan, to free him or kill him. Atif Abu Bakr's assumption, which he put to me, was that the Israelis had in Dr. Ghassan al-Ali and Mustafa Ibrahim Sanduqa agents at the highest level in Abu Nidal's organization, well placed to carry out, as we shall see, the mass executions by Abu Nidal of his own fighting men in 1987–88.

The Emergency Leadership issued a communiqué declaring that those torturing and killing the organization's members on spying charges were themselves Mossad spies.

The Uthman Brothers

According to my sources Faruq Uthman was an actual link between the Mossad and Abu Nidal. His brother, Nabil Uthman, was for many years a member of Abu Nidal's Organization Directorate, at one time responsible for the Palestine/Jordan Committee. In the late 1980s, he became Abu Nidal's undercover representative in Kuwait. According to PLO intelligence sources, Nabil's brother, Faruq, has, since the early 1970s, been a Mossad agent, working in the occupied territories and abroad; he is said to have betrayed scores of Palestinian families to the Mossad.

Faruq Uthman's minder, according to Atif Abu Bakr, is a Mossad officer who is said to have helped plan the killing of Majid Abu Sharar, an important and influential Fatah official, in Rome in 1981; the raid on PLO headquarters in Tunisia at Hammam al-Shatt in 1985; and the killing of Abu Jihad, Arafat's deputy, in Tunis on April 16, 1988, by an Israeli assassination squad. In this last operation, the Mossad officer worked with Faruq Uthman.

According to Tunisian intelligence sources, Faruq was in Tunis between April 1 and April 17, 1988, traveling on a forged Egyptian passport. On April 17, the morning after the killing of Abu Jihad, he flew from Tunis to Malta, then from Malta to Libya (on a Jordanian passport, said to be the one he normally uses), to visit his brother, Nabil, Abu Nidal's man, and stay in one of Abu Nidal's safe houses in Tripoli.

Abu Nidal knew about Faruq Uthman's background from his cadres, but he did nothing. He said he did not want to embarrass Faruq's brother, Nabil, and told one of his members that offering hospitality to a Mossad agent might one day prove useful.*

Muhammad Khair was a Palestinian from Gaza, born in 1961, who had been a student in Turkey. Abu Nidal trusted him, and in 1986, when the organization was based in Syria, he was put in charge of the archives of the Political Directorate.

But Atif Abu Bakr, then head of this directorate, told me that he disliked Khair's dry manner and his habit of trapping his comrades in unguarded talk so that he could write reports about them. Abu Bakr transferred Khair to Beirut.

A short while later, the organization arrested a Mossad agent in Beirut. Muhammad Khair was told to interrogate him, but instead he killed him immediately, so that he had no chance to tell what he knew about the Mossad. This aroused the suspicions of Khair's colleagues. He was arrested and interrogated in turn—and confessed that as a student in Turkey, he had committed some misdemeanor and been jailed. The Mossad heard about him and, upon his release, had recruited him.

Khair surprised his interrogators by admitting that one of his tasks had been to kill Atif Abu Bakr by poisoning his coffee. When Abu Bakr was told about this, he was intrigued. Why should the Mossad want to kill

*More than two years after Abu Jihad's murder, the London journal *Middle East International* reported, on October 12, 1990, that Muhammad Ali Mahjubi, the Tunisian police commissioner at the time of the killing, had been arrested. Press reports recalled that the police patrol on permanent duty outside Abu Jihad's house was absent on the night of April 16. Mahjubi was said to have been in contact with a woman who owned a fashionable hairdressing salon, much patronized by the wives of senior Palestinian officials, who was also put under arrest at the same time as Mahjubi and for the same reason—as a suspected Mossad agent.

him? He was not a terrorist. He was against terrorism and, since 1985, had endeavored to distance the organization from criminal activities and focus it instead on political work. Spurred by the War of the Camps, he had engineered a political and military transformation in the nature of the organization, much to Abu Nidal's displeasure.

When Muhammad Khair was asked about this in Beirut, he replied:, "That was just it. The organization had been a criminal gang before Atif tried to politicize it. From Israel's point of view, he had made it far more dangerous. That is why they wanted him dead."

Abu Nidal started to kill early in his career in Baghdad—first in his struggle with Fatah, a parent he rejected and for whom he developed a lifelong hatred.

Fatah's sentence of death on him, passed in absentia in 1974, and its murder that same year of his friend Ahmad Abd al-Ghaffur, unleashed a torrent of violence in him. If Fatah could behave like this, so could he. It was Fatah that had taught him to kill, he said, and it was fear of Fatah, of its revenge, of its penetration of his organization, of its enveloping powers, that would become his obsessive preoccupation. If one of his members so much as telephoned a Fatah office, Abu Nidal considered it treachery.

Early Brutalities

From the early 1970s, Abu Nidal built his organization on brutality and fear. Scores of his members disappeared on his orders during the Baghdad years, ending up in pits at the Hit training camp or buried in cement at Center 85 in Baghdad. When the intended victim was too prominent to be murdered in Iraq, Abu Nidal would arrange to send him "traveling" on a foreign mission and have him killed abroad. Abd al-Rahman Isa, his intelligence chief at the time, recalled that Abu Nidal asked him about the location of a certain arms cache in Europe. Isa had replied that the man who knew about it was so-and-so. Pensively, Abu Nidal looked into the distance. "Wasn't he one of the members we sent traveling?" he asked. The man who had buried the weapons had himself been buried. In such cases it was usual for the organization to claim the missing man as a "martyr" and mourn his passing with an obituary notice in its magazine.

No doubt Abu Nidal was influenced by the ferocious system Saddam Hussein was then putting in place in Iraq. But his casual resort to murder owed much to his own brutal paranoia. It was also a deliberate strategy: Ruthlessness, he believed, would make his enemies fear and respect him. That the victims were often innocent did not concern him. Their deaths would keep others in line. Once he began prowling in the darkness beyond the campfire of society, legal and moral restraints had no further hold on him, nor did a sense of common humanity.

Internal Massacres

With the passage of years, the blood shed by Abu Nidal swelled into a torrent. Dozens of men were murdered in the 1970s, when the organization was based in Iraq. Twoscore and more, including women and university students, were kidnapped in Syria in the 1980s, smuggled out to Lebanon, and butchered in the Badawi refugee camp, in the north of the country. Another forty-seven prisoners being held in a jail at Aita, in the Bekaa Valley, could not be transported when the organization moved from there to South Lebanon, so they were killed en masse in 1987, without even having been interrogated. By 1986–87, beatings and torture in the organization's prisons had become routine. According to eyewitnesses, interrogators seemed hardly concerned to discover the truth about detainees or to investigate their background. Sentences were passed on the basis of confessions, and condemned men would be shot at night and buried in the woods.

These killings were merely the prelude to the orgy of murder in both Lebanon and Libya that started in November 1987 and continued more or less unabated until the end of 1988, when Abu Nidal, encountering opposition from his colleagues, found it prudent to pause. In a little over a year, it is estimated that Abu Nidal murdered some six hundred of his own people, between a third and a half of his total membership, mostly young men in their early twenties—almost as many Palestinians as Israel killed in the first three years of the *intifada*.

excerpt from:

One Day in September

by Simon Reeve

Early on the morning of September 5, 1972, a group of Palestinian terrorists snuck into the Olympic village in Munich and took eleven athletes and coaches hostage. The entire world watched on television as, over the next twenty-four hours, German authorities negotiated with the terrorists. The kidnappers and the athletes were taken by helicopter to a small airport where the police had prepared a trap that went tragically awry. All the hostages, five of the terrorists and a policeman were killed. In this excerpt, Simon Reeve provides an uncompromising analysis of the failure of the German authorities to organize and equip its security forces. Reeve is an English journalist who has also written *The New Jackals,* excerpted in this collection.

Shortly after 4 a.m. on the morning of September 5, 1972, a small gang of shadowy figures arrived on the outskirts of the Olympic Village and silently made their way to the six-foot-high perimeter fence supposed to offer protection to the thousands of athletes sleeping within.

Creeping through the darkness carrying heavy sports bags, the group made for a length of the fence near Gate 25A, which was locked at midnight but left unguarded. The thirty-five-year-old leader of the small troop, Luttif Afif, a.k.a. "Issa," had carefully chosen the point at which his men were to enter the Village. On previous nights he had seen athletes climbing the fence near Gate 25A while returning drunk from late-night parties. Security was lax and none of the athletes had been stopped. Issa dressed his seven colleagues in tracksuits, reasoning that if guards saw them they would assume they were just sportsmen returning to their quarters.

Jamal Al-Gashey, at nineteen one of the youngest members of the group, remembers the tension building as they approached the fence. As they drew closer they came across a small group of drunk American athletes returning to their beds by the same route. "They had been forced to leave the village in secret for their night out," Al-Gashey said. "We could see they were Americans . . . and they were going to go over the [fence] as well." Issa quickly decided the foreign athletes could give his group cover if they helped each other over the fence. "We got chatting," recalled Al-Gashey, "and then we helped each other over." He lifted a member of the U.S. team up onto the fence, which was topped not by barbed wire but by small round cones, and then the American turned and helped to pull him up and over.

Several officials, including six German postmen on their way to a temporary post office in the Village Plaza, saw the groups climbing the fence with their sports bags at around 4:10 a.m. But as Issa had assumed, none of the passersby challenged them because they thought the fence-climbers were just athletes returning home. "We walked for a while with the American athletes, then said goodbye," remembered Al-Gashey. The group split up and stole through the sleeping Village to a drab three-story building on Connollystrasse, one of three broad pedestrianized streets, adorned with shrubbery and fountains, snaking from east to west through the Village. Even if the unarmed Olympic guards or the Munich police had been alerted, it would probably have been too late. For the eight men were heavily armed terrorists from Black September, an extremist faction within the Palestinian Liberation Organization. The *fedayeen* ("fighters for the faith") were carrying Kalashnikov assault rifles and grenades, hidden under clothing in the sports bags, and they were fully prepared to fight their way to their target: 31 Connollystrasse, the building in the heart of the Olympic Village that housed the Israeli delegation to the Olympic Games. The new entrants were about to make their mark on the XXth Olympiad.

The Black September terrorists knew exactly where to go after scaling the perimeter fence. The attack had been weeks in the planning, and Issa and his deputy, "Tony" (real name, Yusuf Nazzal), worked undercover in the Olympic Village to familiarize themselves with its layout. Issa had lived in Germany for five years and attended university in Berlin. He took a job in the Village as a civil engineer. Tony, who is believed to have worked for a Munich oil company, went undercover as a cook.

The temporary jobs allowed both men to roam freely through the Village. As the world revelled in sporting glories, Issa and Tony sat on a bench on Connollystrasse together and played chess in the sunshine, watching athletes coming and going from No. 31. Tony proved to be a particularly good spy. Luis Friedman, an official with the Uruguayan team, which was sharing 31 Connollystrasse with the Israelis, even found him inside the building at 8:00 a.m. on September 4. Speaking in English the Palestinian shyly told Friedman that he was a worker in the Village and that someone in the building occasionally gave him a few pieces of fruit. Friedman walked over to a crate of apples and pears sitting on a table and gave him all the fruit he could carry.

The next night Issa and Tony led their squad of terrorists quickly through the Village. They paused just around the corner from the Israeli building, changed out of their athletes' tracksuits into the clothes they would wear during the attack, and then headed towards Connollystrasse (named after the American athlete James B. Connolly, a gold-medal winner at the 1896 Olympics).

There were twenty-four separate apartments in No. 31: eleven of the apartments were spread over two floors, with an entrance on the main street and a garden at the back; the rest were on the fourth floor, which was topped by two penthouses. Twenty-one members of the

Israeli delegation were housed in the duplex apartments 1–6. The block was also home to athletes and officials from Uruguay, who had the other duplex apartments, 7–10, and several more on the fourth floor, and the Hong Kong team which occupied five apartments on the fourth floor and the two penthouses. A German caretaker lived in the remaining duplex with his wife and two young children, and a steward had the remaining fourth-floor apartment.

Shortly after 4:30 a.m. the terrorists assembled at the far end of the building, opened the blue main entrance door to apartment 1, and crept into the communal foyer. Whereas the other ten duplexes opened directly onto the street, apartment 1 had a foyer with an elevator and stairs leading up to the fourth-floor and penthouse apartments and down into the lower-level streets and parking lot. The door was never locked.

"When we got to the building, the leader of the operation gave out jobs to us," Al-Gashey said. "My job was to stand guard at the entrance of the building and the others went up the steps into the building to begin the mission." With Jamal guarding the entrance, the rest of the group positioned themselves outside apartment 1, home to seven Israelis, and tried to open the door with a key they had obtained during their preparations for the attack.

Inside the apartment the Israelis were fast asleep: Amitzur Shapira, athletics coach, Kehat Shorr, marksmen coach, Andre Spitzer, fencing coach, Tuvia Sokolovsky, weightlifting trainer, Jacov Springer, weight-lifting judge, and Moshe Weinberg, wrestling coach. Yossef Gutfreund, a wrestling referee, was the only one awakened by the faint sound of scratching at the door.

Gutfreund crept out of his bedroom and into the communal lounge, not wanting to wake the others. As he stood barefoot by the door, listening for a sound, it opened just a few inches. Even in the dim light, with sleep still misting his eyes, he saw the eyes of the fedayeen and the barrels of their Kalashnikov assault rifles. Sleep turned instantly to horror.

"CHEVRETISTATRU!!" ("Take cover, boys!!"), screamed the 6-foot, 3-inch Gutfreund, thrusting his two-hundred-ninety-pound bear-like physique against the door as the terrorists abandoned their keys and began pushing from the other side.

The apartment erupted. Tuvia Sokolovsky, who shared Gutfreund's room, jumped from his bed and ran into the communal lounge. Gutfreund was wedging the front door closed with his body.

"Through the half-open door I saw a man with a black-painted face holding a weapon," said Sokolovsky. "At that moment I knew I had to escape."

Sokolovsky screamed to his friends in the other rooms, leapt back into his bedroom and sprinted towards the window. "I tried to open it but couldn't. I pushed it with all my force."

Behind him three terrorists were desperately trying to dislodge Gutfreund and shove the door open. They pushed with their hands, they braced their legs against the other side of the corridor wall, and then they stuck the barrels of two Kalashnikovs through the small opening and used them as levers in the frame. Man-mountain Gutfreund held them for at least ten seconds before they spilled into the apartment, forcing him to the ground at gunpoint.

In a blind panic Sokolovsky finally broke the window open. "It fell out and I jumped and began to run." The fedayeen ran into the bedroom behind him. "The Arab terrorists started shooting at me and I could hear the bullets flying near my ears."

Sokolovsky never looked back. He ran through the small garden barefoot in his pyjamas, rounded the corner onto an offshoot of Connollystrasse, and hid behind a raised concrete flowerbed.

Back in apartment 1 the terrorists pulled Gutfreund off the floor and began rounding up the other athletes. Shapira and Kehat Shorr, a Romanian who fought the Nazis during the Second World War, were both bundled out of bed. But one of the Israelis was awake and moving quickly.

As Issa burst into another bedroom he was confronted by Moshe Weinberg, who grabbed a fruit knife from a bedside table and slashed at the terrorist leader, slicing through the left breast pocket of his jacket but missing his body.

Issa fell to one side, and one of the other terrorists standing behind him fired a single round from his rifle directly at Weinberg's head. The bullet tore through the side of Moshe's mouth, exiting on the other side to leave a gaping wound. The force of the bullet sent him spinning, blood pouring from the side of his face.

According to Al-Gashey, Weinberg attacked Issa "and grabbed him." "At that moment, another member of the group entered the room and opened fire on the athlete who was holding the leader and had taken his weapon."

The attack was now horribly real. Blood, Jewish blood, was once again being shed on German soil.

The fedayeen pulled Weinberg off the floor and dragged him into the communal lounge. Then they pushed the other four Israelis up the stairs within apartment 1 into the bedroom of Andre Spitzer and Jacov Springer. All the Israelis were tied up tightly at their wrists and ankles with rough cord precut to the correct length.

Despite his appalling wound, Weinberg was still conscious. While Issa and the other two terrorists guarded their prisoners, Tony and the rest of the Palestinian squad dragged the injured Israeli out onto Connollystrasse and began pushing and shoving him along to the next apartment—the fedayeen wanted more hostages.

Inexplicably, however, the terrorists passed apartment 2, where the lightly built Israeli fencers Dan Alon and Moshe Yehuda Weinstain, marksmen Henry Herskowitz and Zelig Shtroch, and the walker Dr. Shaul Ladany were all sleeping. Instead the fedayeen dragged Weinberg a few more yards down the pedestrianized street until he was outside apartment 3, home to six Israeli wrestlers and weightlifters.

The Village was still deathly quiet, and sleeping quietly inside No. 3 were David Berger, an American graduate of the Columbia Law School and son of a wealthy family from Cleveland; Zeev Friedman, a 5-foot, 3-inch powerhouse born in Siberia; and Eliezer Halfin, Yossef Romano, Gad Tsabari, and Mark Slavin, perhaps the most gifted of the Israeli wrestlers. The Palestinians cocked their assault rifles, opened the door, and crept inside.

Tsabari, a 5-foot, 4-inch wrestler who had finished a highly respectable twelfth in the Olympic freestyle event, had been awakened by the shot that had ripped into Moshe Weinberg (it was "something like an explosion," he said). But like dozens of other athletes and officials in surrounding houses who heard that first shot, he thought he was dreaming and merely turned over in his sleep. Minutes later he heard voices outside his bedroom door. Curious but not particularly fearful, Tsabari clambered out of bed, careful not to wake his roommate, young David Bergen, jumped into a pair of trousers, and sleepily opened the door to see what was going on outside.

Tsabari was confronted by a terrorist in a bright yellow sweater, pointing a gun at his friends Mark Slavin and Eliezer Halfin, who had already been captured. As soon as Tsabari emerged the Palestinian turned his gun on him. "From that moment I had to stand close to the terrorist and he ordered Slavin and Halfin to stand closely behind me." Other curious members of the Israeli team heard the commotion, and a few seconds later David Berger appeared behind Tsabari. He "made the same mistake that I did," recalled Tsabari. "I came out and so did he . . . and this is how he was also trapped."

Screaming commands at the Israelis, the terrorists thrust the barrels of their Kalashnikovs into the athletes' chests. The Israelis were pushed down the stairs to join the muscular weightlifters Yossef Romano and Zeev Friedman and poor Moshe Weinberg, clutching a scarf to the side of his face. The Palestinians had their targets. Weinberg began cleaning his wound with the scarf, then squeezed the cloth until his blood dribbled onto the shiny floor.

While one of the terrorists began checking the rooms for any other members of the Israeli team hiding in cupboards or under beds, those already captured stood half naked under wavering gun barrels. Tony bounded down the stairs from the second floor, demanding to know where the rest of the team were hiding. Nobody answered.

"Let's pounce on them!" said David Berger quickly, speaking in terse Hebrew to the other Israelis. "We have nothing to lose!" But the Palestinians were too quick. "One of the terrorists understood David Berger and put the barrel of the gun against my waist and ordered me to go in the direction of the corridor, towards the exit," Tsabari recounted.

The terrorists pushed the Israelis into a line with their hands on their heads—even Yossef Romano, on crutches after tearing a ligament in his leg during competition—and motioned them out onto Connollystrasse.

Tsabari knew the situation was desperate. The Palestinians pushed them towards apartment 1, where the other Israelis were being held, but Tsabari had no idea what was happening. The Palestinians might have been about to execute all of them, for all he knew. With David Berger's cry that they had nothing to lose still running through his mind, Tsabari decided to make a break for freedom.

As they were led down Connollystrasse and back into the foyer entrance to No. 1, Tsabari darted to one side: "Instead of going toward where the trainers were I went down the stairs." "I believe it was God's hand that guided me," Tsabari has said.

Tsabari shoved a terrorist blocking his path and dived down the stairs from apartment 1 towards the underground basement and Olympic parking lot, a warren beneath the athletes' accommodations. At least one of the terrorists chased after him, but the pillars in the underground parking lot offered Tsabari protection as he sped to safety. "I felt two or three rounds being shot at me. I ran for my life, zigzagging to avoid the salvo of shots. I could not believe that none of them hit me. It only lasted a few minutes but every minute was as long as the years in my life."

Tsabari left chaos behind. As the wrestler made his break for freedom the badly injured Weinberg tackled one of the terrorists, a nineteen-year-old code-named "Badran" (actually Mohammed Safady), landing a massive punch in his face which knocked out several of Badran's teeth and fractured his jaw.

With a Kalashnikov trained on them from behind, Yossef Romano and David Berger could only watch helplessly as Weinberg made a grab for Badran's gun, which he had knocked to the floor. One of the terrorists firing at Tsabari spun round, drew a bead on the troublesome Israeli, and fired a burst of shots straight into his chest, peppering him with bullets. Weinberg collapsed on the ground in a bloody mess.

The Palestinians, of course, see events in a different light. Although they do not shy away from confirming details of the killing, they are adamant they wanted no loss of life. According to Abu Daoud, a Black September commander and one of the Palestinian militants who planned and organized the attack, the terrorists never had any specific instructions to open fire on the hostages. However, he says, "one of the athletes, a heavily built man, tried to grab one of the guns of the [group], and so he was forced to shoot him, otherwise they would all have died. It's logical to shoot someone in self-defense."

Jamal Al-Gashey appears to offer confirmation: "We never had instructions to kill anyone, either to put pressure on anyone or for any other reason." However, the Palestinians had been told to shoot if they encountered any resistance, and they must have known these strong, athletic Israelis would not submit willingly to an armed threat. Violence was a tragic inevitability.

After killing Weinberg the fedayeen knew the burst of shots had awakened

218

others sleeping nearby. Lights were flickering on in rooms along Connollystrasse; curtains rustled open. The police would surely be on the scene within minutes, and the terrorists began shouting and hustling their remaining hostages at gunpoint towards the upstairs room of 31 Connollystrasse, where Gutfreund and the other athletes were already being held.

But Yossef Romano, an interior decorator who would pump iron at home in Israel for up to four hours a day, was not prepared to go quietly. Even the sight of bullets tearing into Moshe Weinberg had not quenched his fighting spirit. As Romano was pushed into the upstairs room he threw down his crutches and lunged at a terrorist, desperately trying to grab his gun and save his friends. He had a Kalashnikov in his hands when a burst of fire from another Palestinian scythed into his body. Yossef, the beloved father of three young girls, fell to the floor. A second Israeli was dead.

"It was necessary and beyond anyone's control," Al-Gashey claimed. "They nearly caused the failure of the operation. They were strong athletes. The second one was another powerful athlete who attacked a member of our group and grabbed his gun, and had almost wrestled it from his hand, so we had to open fire on him as well."

Issa and Tony clambered up the stairs into the plane and spent a few moments checking it for police officers and hidden booby-traps. Issa guessed it was a trap. "They came back and were yelling," said Ulrich Wegener. "They were running back to the helicopters."

Georg Wolf was lying on the roof above [Ulrich] Wegener with two snipers looking down on the helicopters, their guns trained on the terrorists guarding the German chopper crews. Further to one side another sniper had his gun trained on Issa and Tony as they trotted back to the helicopter. Wolf had no idea what Snipers 1 and 2 were doing because, astonishingly, none of the snipers was given a walkie-talkie. The other two had only been told that the snipers on the tower would open fire first, and they should pick their targets immediately and start shooting at will.

Three terrorists were standing beside [a] western helicopter and another by [an] eastern chopper. Two terrorists were still inside the second helicopter, which had its sliding doors open.

As Issa and Tony reached the middle of the tarmac apron on their way back to the choppers, shouting as they jogged, the other terrorists guarding the hostages were lifting their gun barrels, wary of a trap. At this point the sniper with his gun on the two Black September leaders had to move slightly to keep the terrorists in his sights. It was a fateful moment.

Wolf, an honorable man left in an appalling position by other officials, quietly gave the order to open fire. Immediately, two shots rang out from his two snipers, and the two terrorists guarding the helicopter pilots—Ahmed Chic Thaa and Afif Ahmed Hamid—fell to the ground, although only one was killed outright. The rescue operation had begun.

There was instant chaos. The four German members of chopper crews began sprinting for safety in all directions. Issa and Tony began running back towards the helicopters, as the third sniper near Wolf opened fire on them. His first shot missed, ploughing into the tarmac near Issa, who steadied himself and then sprinted in a zigzag towards the helicopters. The sniper fired again, hitting Tony in the leg. He collapsed on the tarmac.

Jamal Al-Gashey and the other three terrorists immediately ducked into the black shadows underneath the choppers, rendering themselves invisible to the German snipers, and began returning fire with their Kalashnikovs. Battle commenced as the terrorists swept the airport buildings with bullets.

The firepower of the terrorists was awesome. They raked the airfield with fire, pumping bullets at the main building, at the lights, at the 727, and at the fleeing chopper crews.

Bullets sliced through the room where Wegener was standing with

Genscher, Zamir, and Cohen, shattering model aircraft on top of a cupboard. Genscher dived under a desk to avoid being hit.

The terrorists were shooting wildly, but their bullets began hitting targets. As the snipers had fired their first shots Anton Fliegerbauer, the young police brigadier at the base of the control tower, opened fire on Issa and Tony with his submachine gun. He had fired less than half the bullets in his magazine when a random shot from one of the fedayeen tore through a window in the control tower and hit him in the head. He died immediately.

Out on the airfield behind the choppers, Sniper 2 was still stuck in the line of fire, keeping shelter behind a low wall: "Immediately after the first shooting a hand grenade exploded near my position, only a few yards away from me." The sniper glanced over the top of the wall and could see a man standing between the two helicopters "who was shooting . . . continuously in the direction of the tower." The sniper steeled himself as bullets whizzed around his head, then raised his gun. "I was just going to shoot at that man when I suddenly saw that a second person was running in a permanent zigzag towards my location and kept crossing my line of sight."

As automatic gunfire echoed around the airport the sniper aimed his gun at the man sprinting towards him and then realized it was not a terrorist but one of the helicopter pilots desperately trying to reach safety. The pilot's life was saved because Sniper 2 had been warned the German flyers would be wearing white flight helmets. It was one of the few pieces of crucial information the authorities actually remembered to tell their gunmen. The pilot, Ganner Ebel, dived for cover by the wall, the sniper screamed across to him that he was there, and the two men sheltered together as the gunfight raged on.

By now the German snipers on the tower were starting to return fire. Jamal Al-Gashey was hit in the hand and claims "my gun flew out of my hand." It was probably a lucky shot. Ulrich Wegener said the Germans were firing wildly: "They were firing on everything . . . which was moving in front of the tower. They didn't see the targets, you know, they fired into the helicopters, and I only hoped that our people, and the Israelis, could get out of the helicopter. But they'd tied them together."

Some of the German shots hit home. Another terrorist was shot in the chest. But Heinz Hohensinn agrees the operation was chaotic: "Nobody had an overview. There were shots and nobody knew where from and towards whom." It was only at 10:50 p.m., well after battle had commenced, that one of the senior officers at the airfield decided armored support was needed, and several of the armored cars still waiting at the Olympic Village were finally ordered to race towards Fürstenfeldbruck.

Even Manfred Schreiber appears to believe the situation was out of control. He claims he had wanted the snipers to shoot Issa "in such a way that he would drop in front of his comrades." Schreiber believed that having seen their leader killed in front of their eyes the rest of the terrorists would immediately surrender: "Unfortunately, [Issa] wasn't fatally wounded and so he didn't lie there on the ground as a psychological . . . monument, thus furthering our cause. Instead of lying there . . . he crawled to the helicopters." Issa eventually reached safety and began sweeping the airfield with machine-gun fire.

Schreiber admits that the German officials watching felt "paralyzed." "We had expected a kind of steady progression, beginning with my initial 'embracing' tactic when he had considered taking Issa hostage early in the morning and culminating in the exertion of psychological pressure on the airfield. We all felt paralyzed. The only person who exploded in rage against the perpetrators was the former Minister-President Strauss. He screamed at them and cursed them. The rest of us were incapable of doing even that."

The litany of errors made by German officials at Fürstenfeldbruck is staggering. The five snipers at the airport, some of whom were approximately

100 yards away from their commander, were not issued walkie-talkies, an oversight of awesome proportions. In contrast, unarmed security guards at the Olympic Village had all been issued the devices.

Sniper 2 requested a walkie-talkie while he was still at the Olympic Village and then repeated his demand on arriving at the airfield ("I was told none [were] available."). Sniper 1 demanded a walkie-talkie at 6:00 p.m. while conducting a preliminary examination of the scene at Fürstenfeldbruck. Ludicrously, the Bavarian authorities later decided there had not been enough time to obtain the walkie-talkies.

Yet there were hundreds of walkie-talkies in the Olympic Village, and they were absolutely vital to ensure a coordinated assault by the snipers. Without them the rescue commander Georg Wolf was able to issue instructions only to the three snipers lying next to him.

The arming of the snipers with rifles with twenty-inch-long barrels must also be questioned. Some officials claim rifles should have been chosen with barrels at least twenty-seven inches long to ensure accuracy over the range the snipers were expected to shoot at Fürstenfeldbruck.

It is also alleged that several of the snipers' guns were not fitted with telescopic sights, although the order to obtain such weapons had been given as early as 5:40 a.m.," and none of the officers had infrared sights. Not one of the snipers was issued a bulletproof vest or steel helmet (a bullet actually grazed Sniper 4 on the head), yet Schreiber and Wolf had demanded the vests and helmets as early as 8:45 a.m. Bulletproof vests and helmets would have given the snipers a greater degree of self-confidence and may have encouraged them to expose themselves and secure better shots at the terrorists. German officials have never been able to explain these multiple failures.

There can be little excuse for the lack of equipment. The resources of the Munich police were vast: for example, there were twenty-four helicopters of the Bundesgrenzschutz (border patrol) and the Bavarian police at the disposal of the Munich crisis center. Yet the police were unable to provide their own snipers with adequate protection.

Tactical mistakes compounded these failures. Snipers 3, 4, and 5, who were on top of the control tower building, were not told where snipers 1 and 2 were positioned. So Sniper 2 was placed in the firing line without his colleagues even being aware of his presence.

However, the most damning complaint against the Munich police and the Bavarian government relates to the number of snipers: only five men were allocated the task of tackling a larger group of heavily armed and committed Palestinian terrorists.

Some German officials have claimed there was "not enough space" for additional snipers to hide themselves at the airfield. This is palpable non-sense. The office complex at the Furstenfeldbruck airbase consisted of three sections: the tower, measuring roughly thirteen yards on the northern front where the choppers landed, a middle section of offices (forty-four yards), and the fire station (ten yards). Three marksmen were lying on the tower platform; below them were three floors containing a total of fourteen windows facing north towards where the helicopters landed. The middle section of the building comprised two stories, a flat roof and sixteen windows, plus two entrances to a cellar on each side. The fire station was smaller, but it still had two large gates (each four yards wide) behind which snipers could have hidden and a story above the main garage with four windows facing the helicopters. Snipers should have been spread around the complex (linked, of course, by walkie-talkies), thus ensuring that they had a clear line of fire into the helicopters and the terrorists guarding the hostages within.

It now appears that three well-trained snipers from the Munich police were left behind at the Olympic Village, where two of them thought they had been forgotten and asked to be released, and a third was told he was no longer needed and drove home.

Another problem was the standard of police marksmanship among Munich officers. Even before the debacle at Furstenfeldbruck it was known to be poor, and the authorities had allocated time for extra training. Even Sniper 2 criticizes his lack of training for the task: "I am not a sharpshooter. Unlike the officers of the city police I was not asked whether I would participate in such an action or not. I was just ordered. I thought it was certainly very, very bad that we were practically cut off from the action leadership and that we had no radio."

The watching Israeli experts were astonished at the ineptitude of the German rescue operation. "There was no rescue plan, no preparations, nothing whatsoever," said Zvi Zamir contemptuously. "There [was] no light on the helicopters, there were no snipers, if there were [snipers] I don't know where they were. I mean, it was just nothing." Zamir had no doubt that a well-planned rescue operation at Fürstenfeldbruck by trained officers could have been successful: "I couldn't think of a better place anywhere, because it was an open area." While admitting "it doesn't mean that all the Israelis would have come [through] unhurt," Zamir believed a majority would have survived.

On the ground below, in the heart of the battle, two of the German helicopter crew were desperately trying to crawl to safety; another was playing dead, praying that he would not be hit by fire; and the other was pressing himself into the ground behind the low wall protecting Sniper 2. For the German officials watching it was a tragic sight; it was bad enough that Jewish foreigners were facing death, but several of their own men were under threat.

Yet there was nothing they could do. They had no adequate plan for saving the hostages or the German pilots and were unprepared to rush the terrorists from all sides. The deadlock could be resolved only by armored cars, and they were still on their way to the airfield. It turned out they were stuck in appalling traffic jams caused by the thousands of Munich sightseers trying to reach the airfield to see what was happening. Ulrich

Wegener was almost as distraught as the Israelis. He pleaded with one of the senior Munich police officers: "What are you going to do? You have to move your people there! Pull out the hostages! DO SOMETHING!" But, recalled Wegener sadly, "They didn't do anything."

"I have no orders," a senior German police officer told him meekly.

"It was a really tragic story," Wegener said. "We could only look."

excerpt from:

Fugitive Days
by Bill Ayers

Bill Ayers's autobiography recounts the rise and fall of the Weather
Underground, probably the most violent group to emerge from the
middle-class, white, student movement of the 60s. The Weather
Underground was formed out of the disintegration of the New Left,
which had splintered over sectarian issues. Born out of frustration with
this impasse, the Weather Underground announced that their goal was
"to bring the war home," not just to promote peace in Southeast Asia.
The Weathermen broke up into small cells that scattered around the
country and began bombings, all of which were of extremely limited
scope and had minimal effect, other than to mobilize various police
agencies and reporters. In 1974 they issued the Prairie Fire Manifesto
that provided an elaborate anti-imperialist justification for their acts.
Their call to war on behalf of the third world fell on deaf ears. Two
members of the group were killed in an explosion at a bomb factory in
a posh Greenwich Village townhouse in 1970. First we learn of the
wave of world events that shaped the thinking of the New Left and of
the Weather Underground; then we read of Ayers in action at the
Pentagon. Today he is a professor of education and has written several
books on teaching. He is married to Bernadine Dohrn who was a fiery
orator and member of the group's leadership. She currently practices
law in Chicago.

In January Benjamin Spock, baby doctor to our generation, was arrested and charged with federal conspiracy to help young men resist the draft.

Khe Sanh, once a modest American military observation outpost in the Central Highlands of Viet Nam, was beefed up with thousands of GIs, and U.S. airpower soon turned the area into the most heavily bombed target in the history of warfare.

On January 30, the Tet Offensive exploded across South Viet Nam, punctuated by uprisings in thirty-six provincial capitals including Hue. In Sai Gon, U.S. forces battled to retake their own embassy, briefly under Viet Cong control. I was riveted to our little black and white television as CIA operatives in business suits crouched behind walls, rose and fired machine guns—rat-tat-tat—into their own windows, and then ducked back down again. I thought, this is here, this is now.

When South Viet Nam's wiry chief of national police, Nguyen Ngoc Loan, bareheaded, strode purposefully up to a skinny unnamed boy of maybe twenty—torn shirt, hands cuffed behind his back, face misshapen from a recent smacking around in interrogation—and without a word or a pause raised his sinewy arm and popped a round from a silver pistol into the boy's temple, even those of us with no illusions gasped. The whole thing was captured on throbbing newsreel tape—the young man pulling his face away, eyes forced shut, like holding his breath before going off the high dive, falling to the street as a steady stream of blood pulsed rhythmically from a neat hole onto the pavement, and—BAM!—into every TV in America.

In March, a presidential commission announced in a long-awaited report concerning last year's urban uprisings—including the deadly flare-up I'd lived through in Cleveland—that "Our nation is moving toward two societies, one Black and one white, separate and unequal." Moving toward? I thought, remembering the fire and the fury. Where have they been?

In Orangeburg, South Carolina, police fired on student protesters whose demonstrations had grown in anger and intensity. Thirty-four Black students were injured, and five were murdered.

On the Ides of March, American casualties surpassed those of the Korean War. Keeping with the cynical fiction, Vietnamese casualties were always reported meticulously in a daily body count and these were always in the zillions; U.S. casualties were always vaguely "light" or "moderate" and we would soon win the war. There was an official and oft-repeated light at the end of the tunnel.

Senator Eugene McCarthy launched a "Children's Crusade" against LBJ and nearly won the New Hampshire primary. Bobby Kennedy quickly entered the presidential race then, and although we didn't know it yet, on the day he announced his candidacy, U.S. troops rampaged through the hamlet of My Lai, slaughtering women and children and throwing their bodies into a ditch, later reporting to headquarters that they had killed 128 Viet Cong troops. Those 128 were added to the official body count. Rat-tat-tat.

And then without warning, LBJ went on live national television to announce that he was suspending the bombing of North Viet Nam and added, seemingly out of nowhere: "I shall not seek, and will not accept, the nomination of my party for another term as your president . . ."

I almost fell over. I didn't know how to feel. Relieved? Victorious? Cynical? Vindicated? Happy?

I thought of LBJ just four years before, running for president and painting the Republican candidate Barry Goldwater as the loose cannon not to be trusted with his itchy finger on the big bomb—Goldwater's answer to the persistent charge of right-wing nuttiness had been that extremism in defense of liberty is no vice—and promising that we were not about to send American boys 10,000 miles away to do what Asian boys ought to be doing for themselves. I'd rallied for Johnson, marched in his campaign, and two years later was leading the chants: Hey, hey LBJ, how many kids did you kill today? It drove him nuts and maybe now it even drove him from office. He looked sad and spent that night, but I felt not an ounce of sympathy.

A spontaneous celebration broke out, then, and people poured from their houses to dance in the streets and sing at the tops of their voices "I Believe the War Is Over." There was a sense of unreality, none of us quite believing we'd at last reached the end. It was the eve of April Fool's Day, anyway, and Ron St. Ron said it was more than likely just a big joke. But for this night I wanted nothing more than to revel and rejoice.

We weren't happy long.

On April 4 on a motel balcony in Memphis, as his body slumped and a crowd of comrades rushed to his side, looking up and toward the path of that fateful bullet, pointing in desperation and disbelief, Martin Luther King Jr. was assassinated, that certain dream once again deferred.

Dark smoke smudged American skylines as 125 cities exploded simultaneously in response. Fifty-five thousand troops were called out to quell the riots, and by week's end twenty thousand people had been arrested, forty-six killed. Mayor Daley, quivering and stumbling with rage, famously ordered Chicago cops to shoot to kill all arsonists, to shoot to maim all looters. To me the rising smoke indicted the country, and the spontaneous rebellions were a small part of the dues for broken promises and dashed dreams.

At Columbia University students were agitated by the trustees' plan to build a new gym in Harlem—a massive temple to jocks where only the golden youth of the Ivy League would splash in privileged splendor in their Olympic-size pool—and then incensed when they unearthed clear and graphic evidence that their citadel of freedom and intellectual inquiry had become a whore to war with lucrative research contracts flowing from the ivyed walls straight to the Pentagon. Buildings were seized, and it took a thousand New York City cops to clear the campus. One hundred and twenty charges of police brutality were filed.

Political Terrorism

The whole world was spinning wildly now, and the escalating upheaval sent an urgent jolt of energy through me. In Paris, 367 were injured in rioting as a worker-student strike toppled the government, while in Czechoslovakia Soviet troops overran the country, ending the nonviolent resistance of "Prague Spring." University protests were huge, police responses violent in Bonn and Frankfurt, Rome and Zagreb, Tokyo and Turin.

Mexico City convulsed as police and army troops fired on student demonstrators on the eve of the Olympic Games—10,000 rallied in Tlateloco Square, and 500 were killed. The Mexican government admitted to 32. U.S. athletes set world records in the long jump, the 100, 200, and 400 meters, and the 4 x 400 relays, but on the victory stand Tommie Smith and John Carlos bowed their heads and raised their fists in a Black Power salute as the national war anthem groaned over the stadium. The U.S. Olympic Committee stripped them of their medals and sent them home. When Tommie Smith spoke in Oakland he looked triumphant, not disgraced, and the crowd serenaded him with freedom songs. It would be a glorious day indeed when "We Shall Overcome" replaced "The Star-Spangled Banner," and I thought it likely it would happen in a year or two, three at the outside.

In Atlantic City Ruthie Stein and a small group of other feminists burned bras to protest the Miss America pageant. Women are not meat, they chanted.

Robert Kennedy was shot in L.A., and I watched the image on TV over and over, the repeating chaos stretching for days and weeks. Robert Kennedy dying again and again, just like his brother.

When JFK was killed, Malcolm X said it was a case of the chickens coming home to roost, the mighty U.S. so vehement to have its way everywhere, exporting murder and assassination, scorching the earth and then forced to face itself.

Everything seemed urgent now, everything was accelerating—the pace, to be sure, but also the stakes, the sense of consequences. Madmen were at the controls, several compartments were already in flames and our future existence hung in the balance. It fell to us—and we were just kids—to save the world. Don't trust anyone over thirty, we said to one another in solidarity and in warning, the slogan of a conspiracy so deep and so wide that no one outside of it could quite imagine its furthest dimension. Stay young. Stay beautiful. Youth will make the revolution. But ours was becoming an exacting idealism, and I hurled myself forward, racing toward the edges, stumbling over things trying just to keep step.

Day to day the air itself glowed and shimmered, intoxicated me, seared my lungs, crackled, exploded, and made me high. I'd been beaten and hurt and arrested and jailed. Undeterred I became euphoric, feeling everyday blessed to be alive and aware at this most excellent moment. I was on a freedom high, and all I needed to feed my habit was one more hit of the action. I couldn't remember a world without war or a day without resistance. The war and the idea of freedom defined me, propelled me out of bed every morning, powered my hopes and my fears, troubled my sleep, and, for better and for worse, consumed me. I would, I was sure, be a casualty or a hero of war, or both.

I felt myself hanging on a hinge in history, suspended in midair, one hand gripping familiar ground—our intimate existence, our awakening into a moving world, our growing awareness of the corruption and evil woven into the fabric of our favored little nests—the other hand stretching toward a distant highland barely visible through the cottony clouds. We were, all of us, on the hook: utopian dreams and wild visions beckoned from the distant shore, and yet, as everyone but us seemed to know, hinges swing both ways.

"Where have you gone, Joe DiMaggio?" sang Simon and Garfunkel, the nation turning lonely eyes to him. There were no American heroes left for us, even as *Apollo 8* circled the moon. We were bent on revolution right here on earth, right here in America.

Political Terrorism

. . .

We geared up for survival and fanned out across the country in search of lost comrades, autonomous fighters, militant youth who, strong-willed and lighthearted, were, we knew, on the loose in the world. Our hope was to build some unity of purpose, to prevent further disasters like the Townhouse, to talk politics, argue strategy and tactics, and to disarm the crazies.

We had claimed half a dozen bombings, each one hugely magnified because of the symbolic nature of the target, the deliberate and judicious nature of the blow, and the synchronized public announcements suggesting the dreadful or exhilarating news that a homegrown guerrilla movement was afoot in America. A positive wave of violence and despair blew up, but we had few illusions now about our own real capacity, and we could see what was happening in the wider world. Bombings of ROTC buildings, Selective Service offices, and induction centers had been escalating for at least two years, and targets of political violence now included corporate giants most clearly identified with U.S. aggression and expansion: Bank of America, United Fruit, Chase Manhattan Bank, IBM, Standard Oil, Anaconda, GM. From early 1969 until the spring of 1970 there were over 40,000 threats or attempts and 5,000 actual bombings against government and corporate targets in the U.S., an average of six bombings a day. All but two or three of this orgy of explosions were aimed at property not people; to me they were entirely restrained. Five thousand bombings, about six a day, and the Weather Underground had claimed six, total. It makes you wonder.

Still, we dreaded the possibility of two, three, many Townhouses, and we hoped to use our celebrity in the lunatic left as well as the gathering Weathermyth in the larger world to persuade others to pull back. We knew where to find a few organized groups—the Red Family and the Proud Eagle Tribe, for example, the Motherfuckers and the White Panthers—and we held several secret summits where we had the traditional frank exchange of

233

views and hammered out some kind of new formal understanding. Only once, in a dingy basement hideout near Houston, were guns drawn, but it was based on a misunderstanding—the crazies thought Jeff had said, "We can turn you shits in in D.C." when he had actually said, "We can turn you into fish in the sea"—and we laughed about it later as we passed a joint.

Why did you bomb the Pentagon?

My dad wants to know. He was once offered a cabinet position and was once considered for Secretary of the Army. He knows that I bombed a lot of things—Those were crazy times, he says, better forgotten—and he knows, too, that Diana, whom he liked, is dead—She was older, he says now, and she led you astray. He's stuck in other patterns as well—You need a haircut, he says automatically, and, You'd better cover that tattoo in front of Mother—and now he wants to know why I bombed the Pentagon.

I didn't really think that three pounds of dynamite would knock it down or even do much damage—although it turns out that we blew up a bathroom and, quite by accident, water plunged below and knocked out their computers for a time, disrupting the air war and sending me into deepening shades of delight. I didn't think that our entire arsenal, 125 pounds of dynamite, would actually count for much in a contest with the U.S. military, but I was never good at math, and I did think that every bomb we set off invoked the possibility of more bombs, that the message—sometimes loud and clear—was that if you bastards continue to wage war, we'll go into places you don't want us to go, places like the Pentagon, and we'll retaliate, and soon—who knows?—you might completely lose control.

It was a story we told ourselves, and a story we spun out into the world. Armed anecdotes. Explosive narrations.

RELIGIOUS TERRORISM

Religious Terrorism

The central questions raised by the World Trade Center and 'Pentagon attacks of September 11 are these: Why were so many men willing to give up their lives to make such a violent assault on the United States, and why do some people overseas appear to support such an action? Al Qaeda's strength rests almost entirely on the unshakable faith of its core members and on their willingness to undertake actions based on that faith. The suicides were made all the more troubling by the knowledge that those who hijacked the four planes seemed to be educated, middle-class young men who could have been part of the mainstream, yet rejected the lives offered to them.

The answers lie in events that occurred as far back as the Crusades and in the antagonism between the great warrior religions of the Mediterranean region, Christianity and Islam. Since 1979, everything begins with Afghanistan and ultimately returns there, as we are now discovering.

The ten-year battle to defeat the Russian military gave the Mujahadeen the opportunity to arm and organize a jihad machine prepared to do global battle with any force opposed to creating a worldwide Muslim nation (see *Taliban*, page 345, and *Unholy Wars*, page 363). The real threat to the ascetic religious-political vision of the Muslims was, in fact, never the Russians, who had failed to permanently install their system anywhere except Cuba, but rather the free-market system spearheaded by the United States (see *Jihad vs. McWorld,* page 275). Here was a powerful and seductive alternative to the notion that all power comes from Allah, that the Muslim faith is an all-encompassing worldview and code of daily behavior governing every aspect of existence. The markets pay lip service to religion, but they define wealth as material and social relations in purely utalitarian terms. For some fervent Muslims who see social and religious activity as stemming from one spiritual power based on faith in God and total subservience to him, the United States and its global network of products and services can be seen as a fundamental threat.

Bin Laden and his followers now insist that their immediate goals are pragmatic and political: to end the United States' presence in Palestine and Saudi Arabia. But when Bin Laden calls for a jihad against the United States and asks for a boycott of all U.S.-made goods, he is really advocating a boycott on the American way of life in its entirety (see *Declaration of War Against the Americans Occupying the Land of the Two Holy Places,* page 402). This war is not only a political conflict, but also a social one in the broadest sense of the word.

Defining the struggle in this way, one can at least begin to grasp the vehemence of the proponents of jihad. But there is another factor that may help explain the intensity of the attack by Muslim extremists. While they publicly assert that provoking the United States into a major military response marks the beginning of a new era of global war, they may also recognize that on other fronts of this battle of diametrically opposed cultures, the Muslims are suffering irreversible defeats. If the recent feeble response to the extremist call for general strikes in Pakistan is any indication, this pivotal country of 140 million Muslims is already largely in the camp of commerce. From this perspective, a bold surprise attack may also be a desperate one.

There is a great deal to learn about our vulnerabilities from the events of September 11, and not just on the military and political fronts. What gave the Muslim terrorists room to operate so successfully is not only the openness of American life, but also its anonymity. They counted on the wall of silence that surrounds us in our hurried, tightly organized daily routines. In a suburban housing development, urban apartment complex, or large office building, people generally don't know who their next-door neighbors are, let alone what they are doing or thinking. The oft-repeated line describing the terrorist or the madman next door, "He was well-behaved, quiet, polite, kept to himself . . . " is not a unique portrait of the undercover terrorist as much it is a general description of an ordinary person whom one does not know. It is interesting to note that after September 11 a number of airline pilots suggested to their passengers that they introduce themselves to the people seated next to them as a way of establishing a rapport.

The recent war to root out terrorism will accomplish certain limited objectives. But this is not only a military confrontation over specific territory based on material superiority. Nor is it simply an encounter between good and evil. It is a battle between fanatical faith and global commerce, a battle of rival visions. It may be fought with bombs, but it ends with minds.

excerpt from The Introduction to:

Social Justice in Islam
by Hamid Algar

Sayyid Qutb was the leading theorist of Egypt's Muslim Brotherhood.
This is his most important work and one that is still key for understanding the fundamentalist approach to social activism. Published in
1953, it lays out the fundamentals of jihad: the necessity of viewing all
aspects of Islamic life—political, social, economic, religious—as an
indivisible totality; the depictions of the West as neo-Crusaders; and the
importance of addressing social inequality. Qutb's life was one of continuous agitation against the Egyptian state before he was executed by
Nasser's regime in 1966. This selection from the biographical introduction by U.C. Berkeley professor of Islamic Studies Hamid Algar draws
strong parallels with today's extremists who forge a good portion of
their ideas and their passion in prison. The Brotherhood is still alive in
Egypt and other countries. In Palestine it has effectively merged into
Hamas. The introduction to the English language translation of Qutb's
work excerpted here depicts the depth of his commitment and prefig-
ures the fervor of many current Muslim extremist leaders.

Sayyid Qutb, who some twenty-eight years after his death is still the most influential ideologue of the Islamic movement in the contemporary Arab world, began life in the obscurity of the village of Musha (or Qaha) near Asyut in Upper Egypt. He was born there in 1906 to a father who was well regarded in the village for piety and learning, despite the hard times on which he had fallen. Sayyid Qutb was the eldest of five children. He was followed by a brother, Muhammad Qutb, also destined to gain fame as an Islamic writer and activist, and three sisters, two of whom, Amina and Hamida, came to attain some prominence in the ranks of the Muslim Brethren. Encouraged by both his parents, Sayyid Qutb swiftly developed a love for learning, and by the age of ten he had completed memorization of the Qur'an at the local primary school. Three years later, the family moved to Helwan, enabling him to enter the preparatory school for the Dar al-'Ulum in Cairo, a prestigious teachers' training college which he joined in 1929. This marked the beginning of his long and fruitful involvement in education and its problems. On graduating in 1933, he was himself appointed to teach at the Dar al-'Ulum, and a few years later entered the service of the Egyptian Ministry of Education.

The year 1933 also saw the beginning of Sayyid Qutb's extraordinarily varied and prolific literary career. His first book was *Muhimmat al-Sha'ir fi 'l-Hayah (The Task of the Poet in Life)*, and for more than a decade literature remained—together with education—his principal preoccupation. He wrote poetry, autobiographical sketches, works of literary criticism, and novels and short stories dealing with the problems of love and marriage. After embracing Islam as an all-inclusive ideology, he came to repudiate much of this early work. At the time, however, it served to elevate him to the proximity of leading figures on the Egyptian literary scene, such as 'Abbas Mahmud al-'Aqqad (d. 1964) and Taha Husain (d. 1973), whose Western-tinged outlook on cultural and literary questions he initially shared. For example, there are traces of individualism and existentialism in some of Sayyid Qutb's novels, above all *Ashwak (Thorns)*.

Like his mentor al-'Aqqad, Sayyid Qutb was an active member of the oppositional Wafd party, and he became a prominent critic of the Egyptian monarchy. This brought him into inevitable conflict with his superiors at the Ministry of Education, and it took the strenuous efforts of Taha Husayn to dissuade him from resigning. Sayyid Qutb sought anew, in 1947, to emancipate himself from government employ by becoming editor-in-chief of two journals, *al-'Alam al-'Arabi (The Arab World)* and *al-Fikr al-Jadid (New Thought)*. He lost his position with the former as a result of editorial disagreements, and the latter, which sought in a hesitant way to present the model of an Islamic society free of corruption, tyranny, and foreign domination, was proscribed after only six issues. While continuing to write for a wide range of literary and political periodicals, Sayyid Qutb was thus compelled to continue working for the Ministry of Education.

In 1948, the ministry sent him on a study mission to the United States, doubtless with the assumption that direct acquaintance with America would incline him more favorably to official policies and induce him to abandon the oppositional activities that were increasingly taking on an Islamic aspect. Sayyid Qutb's impressions of America were, however, largely negative, and may even have been decisive in turning him fully to Islam as a total civilizational alternative. While noting American achievements in production and social organization, Sayyid Qutb laid heavy emphasis on materialism, racism, and sexual permissiveness as dominant features of American life. His sojourn in the United States coincided, moreover, with the first Palestine war, and he noted with dismay the uncritical acceptance of Zionist theses by American public opinion and the ubiquity of anti-Arab and anti-Muslim prejudice. After completing a master's degree in education at the University of Northern Colorado in Greeley, Sayyid Qutb decided to forego the possibility of staying in America to earn a doctorate and returned to Egypt in 1951.

One of the most widely read of all Sayyid Qutb's books, *al-'Adalat al-Ijtima' iyyah fi 'l-Islam (Social Justice in Islam)* had been published during his absence in America, and with its attacks on feudalism and emphasis on social justice as an Islamic imperative, it earned the approbation of leading figures in the Muslim Brethren. His critical response to Taha Husain's *Mustaqbal al-Thaqafah fi Misr (The Future of Culture in Egypt)*, a work which sought to present Egypt as an essentially Mediterranean society—i.e., as an appendage of Europe—was also highly appreciated in the same circles. For his part, Sayyid Qutb had been increasingly well disposed to the Muslim Brethren ever since he witnessed the ecstatic reception given in America to the news of the assassination, on February 12, 1949, of Hasan al-Banna, founder of the organization. His perception of the Brethren as defenders of Islam was further strengthened after his return to Egypt when a British official, James Heyworth-Dunne, told him that the Brethren represented the only barrier to the establishment of "Western civilization" in the Middle East.

Sayyid Qutb's cooperation with the Muslim Brethren began almost immediately after his return from America, although his formal membership in the organization may not have begun until 1953. This new allegiance marked a turning point in his political and intellectual life. He had quit the Wafd on the death of its founder, Sa'd Zaghlul, and joined the breakaway Sa'dist Party in 1938, which claimed a greater degree of fidelity to the original ideals of the Wafd. He was also involved in the activities of *al-Hizb al-Watani (The Patriotic Party)* and *Hizb Misr al-Fatah (The Young Egypt Party)*. However, none of these groups engaged his energies and devotions as fully as did the Muslim Brethren, which was, after all, far more than a political party, having aimed since its foundation in 1928 at establishing the hegemony of Islam in all areas of Egyptian life. Conversely, Sayyid Qutb's entry into the ranks of the Brethren provided the organization with its first true ideologue and led ultimately to a radicalization of the whole Islamic movement in Egypt.

In 1951, Sayyid Qutb began writing for periodicals of the Muslim

Brethren such as *al-Risala (The Message)*, *al-Da'wa (The Summons)*, and *al-Liwa' al-Jadid (The New Banner)*, and finally realized his ambition of resigning from the Ministry of Education, ignoring the last-minute allurement of an appointment as special adviser to the minister. He then joined the Brethren formally, and in recognition of his talents was made editor-in-chief of *al-Ikhwan al-Muslimun*, the official journal of the organization. In January 1954 the journal was banned, and Sayyid Qutb embarked on the long ordeal of imprisonment and persecution that was to end in his martyrdom some twelve years later.

On July 23, 1952, the Egyptian monarchy had been overthrown in a coup d'etat mounted by a group of soldiers who styled themselves the Free Officers; they were formally led by General Muhammad Najib (aka Naguib), but it soon became apparent that Jamal 'Abd al-Nasir (aka Nasser) was the driving force behind the group. Although the coup was widely popular and its authors grandiloquently dubbed it a revolution despite the absence of mass participation, the Free Officers lacked any organized political base of their own. They therefore turned to the Muslim Brethren, with whom some of their number had already been in contact, for the effective mobilization of popular support. The political counsels of the Brethren were divided, and Hasan Hudaybi, who had succeeded al-Banna as leader, was in addition woefully lacking in political acumen; what is certain is that the idea of taking power at this crucial juncture in Egyptian history did not occur to those who determined the policies of the Brethren. There thus ensued a period of collaboration between the Muslim Brethren and the new regime.

Sayyid Qutb was prominent among the members and associates of the Brethren who collaborated with the Free Officers. According to reliable testimony, leaders of the coup including 'Abd al-Nasir, visited Sayyid Qutb in his home a mere four days before the coup, (Khalidi, 1981, pp. 37–39). About one month after the coup, Sayyid Qutb delivered a lecture on "Intellectual and Spiritual Liberation in Islam" at the Officers' Club in

Cairo, and 'Abd al-Nasir was in attendance. More significantly, Sayyid Qutb was appointed cultural advisor to the Revolutionary Council, established by the Free Officers, and was the only civilian to attend its meetings.

Before long, however, differences arose between the Muslim brethren and the military rulers of Egypt. As a prelude to eliminating the Brethren as an autonomous force capable of challenging him, 'Abd al-Nasir sought first to coopt the organization by offering cabinet posts to some of its leading members. It was thus intimated to Sayyid Qutb that the Ministry of Education was his for the asking. He was also invited to become director of the *Hay'at al-Tahrir* (Liberation Rally), the newly established government party, and to draw up its program and statutes. Qutb refused all such offers, and most of his colleagues in the Brethren also had the good sense to resist full-scale absorption into the emerging structures of the Nasserist state.

At the same time, it became increasingly apparent that the Revolutionary Council intended to perpetuate its rule indefinitely and was in no mind to listen to the exhortations of the Brethren, either to return to civilian rule based on elections or to call a constitutional referendum. Likewise, it paid no heed to the demand of the Brethren that it should ban alcohol as a first step toward the implementation of the *shari'ah*. Gravest of all was the intention of the Revolutionary Council—carried out in July, 1954—to conclude a new treaty with Britain providing for the retention of a British garrison in the Suez Canal zone and the posting of British troops elsewhere in Egypt whenever Britain deemed its interests in the Middle East to be under attack. This early indication that the nationalist credentials of the Free Officers were not as strong as they proclaimed them to be was profoundly shocking to the Brethren, many of whose members had fought and died in the struggle to evict the British from the Suez Canal zone. The criticisms of the treaty made by the Brethren, and their demand that it be subjected to a referendum, fell on deaf ears.

On January 12, 1954, the Revolutionary Council decreed the dissolution of the Muslim Brethren, and Sayyid Qutb entered jail for the first time. A temporary change in fortune came on March 28 when, thanks to the efforts of Najib, the ban on the Brethren was rescinded and Qutb, together with other leaders of the Brethren, was released. He was now appointed to the Guidance Council of the Brethren, the governing body of the organization, with overall responsibility for its publications.

Soon, however, 'Abd al-Nasir struck back. Having removed Najib from the Revolutionary Council and gained control of the army and police, he reinstated the January decree proscribing the Brethren and moved toward an attempted destruction of the entire organization.

On October 23, 1954, there took place in Alexandria what appeared to be an unsuccessful attempt on the life of 'Abd al-Nasir. There is reason to think that the affair was stage-managed by 'Abd al-Nasir himself. The man said to have fired the shots, Mahmud 'Abd al-Latif, a member of the Brethren, was personally known to 'Abd al-Nasir as an excellent marksman; it is therefore conceivable that 'Abd al-Nasir should have hired him to attempt an "assassination," trusting him deliberately to fire somewhat askew, and then doublecrossed him by executing him to ensure his silence. Significant, too, is the fact that the incident enabled 'Abd al-Nasir to start posing before the Egyptian masses as their embattled hero and thus to inaugurate the adulatory cult surrounding him that continued to infect much of Arab public opinion, even after the disastrous defeat of June 1967. Most compelling of all is the fact that the incident provided 'Abd al-Nasir with a pretext to round up members of the Brethren on a then unprecedented scale. More than one thousand people were swiftly arrested, and show trials got underway with suspicious promptness. On December 4, 1954, seven leading figures, including Hudaybi, were sentenced to death. Hudaybi's sentence was commuted to life imprisonment, but the remaining six were hung.

Predictably enough, Sayyid Qutb was rearrested on this occasion. He was ill at the time of his arrest, but this did not in any way dissuade his jailers from torturing him, in accordance with the still-observed norms of Egyptian justice. Because of extreme physical weakness, Sayyid Qutb was not present in the court in July 1955 when he was sentenced to fifteen years' imprisonment. He was now destined to spend the rest of his life in prison, with the exception of eight short months of relative liberty in 1965.

The ordeal of imprisonment has been a common, almost universal experience for Muslim thinkers and activists in the modern world. For many of them, it has meant not only suffering, but also the opportunity to reflect on past struggles, to review theories and strategies, to deepen and sharpen their insight, to plan and reorganize. It was for this reason that Said Nursi (d. 1960) described prison as the "Josephian School" *(medrese-i yusufiye)*, alluding both to his own experience of jail in Kemalist Turkey and the imprisonment of the Prophet Joseph by the Pharaoh.

While in jail, Sayyid Qutb was able to complete a number of his most important writings, including above all the Qur'anic commentary *Fi Zilal al-Qur'an* (In the Shade of the Qur'an) he had begun in 1962. Clearly inspired by the circumstances of daily struggle and confrontation in which he lived, this commentary is radically different from traditional exegeses, with their verse-by-verse attention to philological and historical detail and their extensive citation of previous authorities and variant opinions. Emphasizing guidance to correct action as the pre-eminent function of the Qur'an, Sayyid Qutb's concern is to draw out the practical commands and instructions contained in each group of verses of the Qur'an and, beyond that, to demonstrate the coherent structure interrelating the variegated topics found in each section of the Qur'an, an aim inspired, perhaps, by his earlier literary interest. *Fi Zilal al-Qur'an* has been translated in part or in whole into a number of languages, and it is probably true to say that it has been more widely read than any other modern commentary on the Qur'an.

Reflected in several passages of this commentary are the radical theoretical insights which the experience of prison inspired in him. The savagery he and his fellow inmates suffered over the years—including the massacre of twenty-one members of the Brethren at the Liman Tura military jail in June 1957—forced him to conclude that a regime unprecedented in its ruthlessness had come to power in Egypt, and that the primary problem was no longer overt foreign rule or the absense of social justice. It was rather the total usurpation of power by forces intensely hostile to Islam, with the result that the entire life of society was fixed in the non-Islamic patterns into which it had gradually fallen as a result of decay and neglect. Drawing on the terminology and theories of Abu 'l-A'la Maududi and Abu 'l-Hasan Nadwi (although ultimately of course on the Qur'an itself), Sayyid Qutb decided that Egypt, together with the rest of the contemporary Islamic world, was strictly comparable to pre-Islamic Arabia in its disregard for divine precepts, and that its state could therefore rightly be designated by the same term—*jahiliyyah*. Occurring only four times in the Qur'an, the term *jahiliyyah* assumed central significance for Sayyid Qutb, encapsulating the utter bleakness of the Muslim predicament and serving as an epistemological device for rejecting all allegiances other than Islam.

According to Sayyid Qutb, this new *jahiliyyah* had deep historical roots, and it was moreover fostered and protected by all the coercive apparatus of a modern, authoritarian state; it could not, therefore, be easily remedied in the short term. What was needed was a long-term program of ideological and organizational work, coupled with the training of a dedicated vanguard of believers who would protect the cause in times of extreme danger (if necessary by recource to force) and preside over the replacement of *jahiliyyah* by the Islamic order once circumstances had matured.

Sayyid Qutb first developed these ideas in dialogue with a small number of his fellow inmates, and then included them in notes that were smuggled out of jail to be read by members of his family and others close to them. Many other members of the Brethren, dissatisfied with the uncertain leadership provided by Hudaybi, became aware of the existence of the letters, and, at their request, Sayyid Qutb consented to have the letters made more widely available. Thus there came into being a group of about 250 people who were all affiliated with the Muslim Brethren but were bound together primarily by their devotion to the ideas of Sayyid Qutb.

In December 1964, Sayyid Qutb was released from jail. It is said that his release was due in part to continuing ill health and in part to the intercession of 'Abd al-Salam 'Arif, the president of Iraq, who invited him to settle in his country. Given the tragic denouement to this last period of relative freedom in the life of Sayyid Qutb, it is however possible that the Egyptian government set him free in order to create the conditions for his rearrest, trial, and final elimination; although accused of a conspiracy, he was in fact the victim of one.

In 1964, before Sayyid Qutb's release from jail, a slim volume entitled *Ma'alim fi 'l-Tariq (Milestones)* had been published and met with instant success; during the first six months of 1965, it went through five further editions. *Ma'alim fi 'l-Tariq* consisted of some of the letters Sayyid Qutb had sent from prison and key sections of *Fi Zilal al-Qur'an,* and represented a concise and forceful summary of the main ideas Sayyid Qutb had developed: the *jahili* nature of existing society, government, and culture, and the longterm program needed for the establishment of an Islamic order. Continuously read and reprinted down to the present, and translated into most Muslim languages, *Ma'alim fi 'l-Tariq* must definitely count among the historic documents of the contemporary Islamic movement.

On August 5, 1965, Sayyid Qutb was rearrested; two weeks later, his sisters Amina and Hamida were also arrested, together with Zaynab al-Ghazali, the leading female member of the Brethren. Sayyid Qutb was accused of subversion and terrorism and the encouragement of sedition. The first charge rested only on the fact that in 1959 he had been entrusted by

Hudaybi with responsibility for organizing the Brethren in the jails and prison camps of Egypt. This organization, known as the *Tanzim,* was supposedly linked to the circles studying his prison letters and dedicated to the immediate and violent overthrow of the Egyptian government. No evidence was presented in court to show that Sayyid Qutb or any group linked to him was plotting armed insurrection, and Sayyid Qutb was even able to establish that on two occasions he had dissuaded members of the Brethren from attempting such activity, not least because the needed change, by its very nature, had to be brought about by popular action. In support of the second charge, the encouragement of sedition, the prosecution placed great emphasis on *Ma'alim fi 'l-Tariq,* and it became apparent that this book, with its proven widespread appeal and long-term revolutionary implications, represented the nub of the Egyptian government's concern. In no way deterred by its inability to find in the text of the book any call for the immediate seizure of power, on May 17, 1966, the court condemned Sayyid Qutb to death, together with six other prominent members of the Brethren, including Hudaybi. Four of the sentences were commuted to life imprisonment, but Sayyid Qutb was hanged in Cairo, on August 29, 1966, together with two of his companions, Muhammad Yusuf 'Awash and 'Abd al-Fattah Isma'il.

The trial had been essentially of a book and the ideas it contained. However, certain political circumstances may also have influenced the fate of Sayyid Qutb. In 1965, the principal superpower patron of 'Abd al-Nasir was the Soviet Union, and it may be significant that the execution of Sayyid Qutb took place shortly after 'Abd al-Nasir had returned from a trip to Moscow; the influence of the Brethren in general and Sayyid Qutb in particular had, after all, served to block the spread of Marxism in Egypt. Moreover, facts came to light in 1976 suggesting that the affair was in part the result of rivalry between two centers of power within the Egyptian regime: the *Mukhabarat,* the military intelligence, and the *Mabahith,* the intelligence arm of the Ministry of the Interior. Anxious to prove its vigilance in protecting 'Abd al-Nasir and at the same time to discredit the *Mabahith,* leading officials in the *Mukhabarat* manufactured the story of a Qutbist plot against the regime. This, at least, is what can be deduced from the memoirs of Shams Badran, the number-two figure in the *Mukhabarat,* who also took responsibility, without any shade of embarrassment, for having prisoners tortured in preparation for the trial.

It is axiomatic that ideas are more difficult to eradicate than those who formulate and expound them, particularly when the passage of time demonstrates ever more persuasively the congruence of those ideas with reality; the intellectual legacy of Sayyid Qutb is thus very much alive.

It is true that several leading figures of the Brethren distanced themselves from Sayyid Qutb's identification of Egyptian society (and by extension Arab and Muslim society in general) as *jahili.* Notwithstanding his own experiences in jail, Hudaybi wrote what was in essence a refutation of *Ma'alim fi 'l-Tariq,* under the title *Du'at la Qudat (Summoners, Not Judges).* He insisted that the *jahiliyyah* was exclusively a historical phenomenon, not a recurrent state, and that it was therefore inadmissible to designate contemporary Muslim society as *jahili.* Muhammad Qutb, brother of Sayyid Qutb, came to endorse this implicitly non-judgmental position, despite having himself published in 1964 a book entitled *Jahiliyyat al-Qarn al-'Ishrin (The Jahiliyyah of the Twentieth Century).* Other Brethren intellectuals who discovered a congenial environment in Saudi Arabia and other Gulf states also foreswore Sayyid Outb's radicalism.

By contrast, leaders and sympathizers of the Brethren outside Egypt, such as Sa'id Hawwa and Marwan Hadid in Syria, Fathi Yakan in Lebanon, Rashid al-Ghannushi in Tunisia, and Hasan Turabi in Sudan, all assimilated Sayyid Qutb's analysis of the Muslim predicament to one degree or another, and oriented their movements accordingly. Within Egypt itself, the legacy of Sayyid Qutb has helped give rise to a new generation of radical activists no longer affiliated to the Brethren: 'Abd al-Salam Faraj,

author of *al-Faridat al-Gha'ibah (The Neglected Duty)*, a text that supposedly inspired the assassins of Anwar Sadat to act; the group labeled by the
Egyptian authorities *al-Takfir wa 'l-Hijrah (Identifying Society as Dominated
by Unbelief and Migrating front It)*; the amorphous but evidently powerful
groupings known as *al-Jama'at al-Islamiyyah (The Islamic Societies)*; and
their supposed mentor, Shaykh 'Umar 'Abd al-Rahman, now incarcerated
in the United States.

From one point of view, *Social Justice in Islam* is therefore to be evaluated
as a document of the first postwar decades in which Islamic movements
and personalities were striving to demonstrate the imperative relevance of
Islam to concrete socioeconomic problems. This task gained particular
urgency from the relative appeal and vitality of Marxism in a number of
Muslim countries at the time, not least in Egypt. This helps to explain the
frequency of references to Communism and the Soviet Union. Sayyid
Qutb's refutation of Marxism often goes together with a critical evaluation of Christianity, presented as essentially an asceticism with no positive
implications for worldly life and historically unable to modify Europe's
determining legacy of pagan materialism inherited from Rome. In this
comparative context, Islam becomes the ideal mean, avoiding both the unre-
lieved materialism of Marxism and the otherworldliness of Christianity,
and balancing the needs of the individual against those of society. Such a
comparison was no doubt inevitable, given the (legitimately) polemical
and exhortatory nature of Sayyid Qutb's work; it nonetheless contradicts
his own warning against describing Islam in terms other than itself,
whether by way of similarity or dissimilarity.

Many other insights of Sayyid Qutb have, however, stood the test of time.
His assertion that a virulent crusading spirit remains at the core of Western
culture, despite a relative decline in active adherence to Christianity, has
been tragically vindicated by the genocidal assaults on the Muslims of

Bosnia, that were spearheaded by Croats and Serbs but enjoy the complicity of the entire Western world. Similarly, the support instinctively rendered by this crusading spirit to Zionism continues unabated. More importantly, Sayyid Qutb's insistence on the comprehensiveness of Islam as worldview, civilization, and socioeconomic order; his summons to cultural and educational reform; and the moral urgency underlying the whole of his book retain all their validity today, some fifty years after its first publication. For despite all the ink that has been spilled by Muslims and others concerning the "Islamic resurgence," it can hardly be claimed that the Muslim world as a whole is substantially better situated than it was in 1949.

excerpt from:

The New Terrorism
by Walter Laqueur

State-sponsored terrorism—the use of surrogates to achieve what may
be politically disadvantageous for a government to accomplish on its
own behalf—has a long history going back to Rome and Byzantium.
This approach could be offensive, preparing the way for an invasion or
other form of expansion, or defensive, attacking potential enemies. As
military technology has become more sophisticated in the modern era,
aid to terrorist groups has taken the form of weaponry as well as
money. In the 60s and 70s the Soviet Union funded numerous groups
including the PLO and, through the Cuban Secret Service, various Latin
American guerrilla bands. The Czechs helped the Italian Red Brigade,
the East Germans aided the Baader-Meinhof group and Carlos the
Jackal. In the U.S., state-sponsored terrorism is equated mainly with the
support given to various fundamentalist extremists in Libya, Iraq, Syria,
Somalia, Yemen, Iran, etc. But there are many on the Left who consider
that U.S. aid to the Contras in Nicaragua, to the anti-Castro Cubans,
and to other "freedom fighters" in Latin America and elsewhere constitutes the same strategy. For a discussion of this policy in Europe see *On
Terrorism and the State* (page 75). Laqueur is America's foremost terrorism expert (see note on page 4). In this excerpt he describes the
extensive and interlocking network of terrorism funded by the Arab
states. Laqueur believes that Khadafi and the Iranians were among the
most active sponsors.

State-sponsored terrorism, warfare by proxy, is as old as the history of military conflict. It was an established practice in ancient times in the Oriental empires, in Rome and Byzantium, in Asia and Europe. No empire, however powerful, could afford to live in a state of perpetual war with its neighbors. There was a cheaper and less risky alternative: to support dissenters, separatists, ambitious politicians, or simply malcontents inside a rival state. Sometimes this strategy was defensive, meant to forestall aggressive designs on the part of a potential enemy. At other times it was part of an offensive strategy, intended to weaken the neighbor and perhaps even to prepare the ground for invasion.

Since military technology was then primitive, such support for rebellious tribes manifested itself not in the supply of arms, as in modern times, but mainly by way of financial help and, of course, political promises. The Roman maxim *Divide et Impera* was applied not only to relations between other states but also to minorities and dissident tribes.

There are countless examples of state-sponsored terrorism in modern history. For instance, Britain used it against the French in the Indian wars in America, and vice versa. The rebellious Irish received help from Paris during the age of the French Revolution, and the British helped forces opposed to Napoleon in Spain and elsewhere. This tactic was widely employed in Central Asia in the nineteenth century in the various Afghan wars. The Russians supported their fellow Slavs in the Balkans. In his novel *Greenmantle*, John Buchan described the attempt by the Central Powers in World War I to unleash a jihad, a Muslim holy war, from Turkey to India through a mixture of propaganda, political promises, and financial support. Though political science fiction, it is in many ways not that far from reality. Bulgaria used the Macedonian revolutionary terrorists against Yugoslavia after World War I, and the Croat extremists offered their services to Mussolini, who also employed the French Cagoule to liquidate political enemies in exile. The Western powers supported all kinds of nationalist and anti-Communist rebels, without much success, against the Soviet Union during the early years of its existence. And the Soviets made collaboration with national liberation fighters, mainly in Asia, its declared policy at the Baku congress in 1921. Warfare by substitutes has been common practice in the struggle for Kashmir between India and Pakistan. Terrorism was involved in one way or another in all these instances.

Khadafi's Adventures

In the 1970s and 1980s, Libya was one of the foremost sponsors of international terrorism. Its involvement was almost as pervasive as that of Iran, a much larger and more populous country. Libya's sponsorship of terrorism predates that of Iran, dating back almost to the coup in 1969 that brought Colonel Khadafi to power. Khadafi's ambition was to spearhead an Arab-Islamic revolution in which lie saw himself not only as the chief ideologist (by virtue of his little "Green Book") but also as chief strategist. Libya's income from the sale of oil provided the wherewithal to finance a variety of terrorist activities, but in subsequent years it became apparent that the country was too small and backward to sustain any major political and military initiatives. Furthermore, Khadafi's erratic behavior (to put the best possible gloss on it), his inordinate ambitions, and his rapidly changing alignments antagonized virtually everyone in the Arab world and isolated him from all but his most needy clients. Doubts were expressed concerning his mental state, not only in the West but also in the Arab and Third World capitals. Was he a madman in the clinical sense, or just highly emotional, unbalanced, and unpredictable? Khadafi even became an embarrassment to those closest to him in outlook.

Though Libya experienced strong economic growth in the early years of the Khadafi regime because of massive oil exports, its growth stalled after 1985 and eventually declined by 1995. Nevertheless, the Libyan regime was still able to spend considerable sums sponsoring terrorist activities abroad and on the construction of factories to produce poison gas and other chemical weapons. Support was given primarily to Arab terrorist groups, but also to a variety of Central and West African groups, and eventually to terrorists from Ireland to the Philippines. Among the recipients of Libyan help were the German RAF as well as the so-called Black September. According to unconfirmed reports, about eight thousand foreign terrorists, most of them Arabs, were trained each year in Libyan camps in the 1980s, and those select Palestinian groups favored by Khadafi received an annual subsidy of $100 million. Among the most famous terrorists on the Libyan payroll was Carlos the Jackal, who had been enlisted by the Popular Front for the Liberation of Palestine.

However, the list of recipients of Libyan money changed quickly, sometimes overnight. While relations with Fatah and Arafat had been close at one time, they deteriorated later, and the PLO (and many thousands of Palestinian guest workers) were expelled from Libya as Khadafi shifted his support to the most extreme Palestinian factions, such as the one headed by Abu Nidal. Even Carlos, who had been of so much use to the Libyans, was ultimately refused entry to Libya.

Libyan-sponsored terrorism manifested itself in a variety of other activities, including attacks against Libyan political émigrés. In 1984, some twenty-five such attacks were counted in Europe and the Middle East, and the assassinations continued in later years, albeit on a reduced scale. In one famous instance, Khadafi personally gave orders to his agents in London to open fire on the British police in front of the Libyan legation, an action that annoyed even the Soviets. Khadafi, they, felt, was giving international terrorism a bad name. Attacks were carried out by Libyan agents against American and European targets but also against moderate Arab countries. To give a few examples, mines were laid in the Red Sea near the entrance to the Suez Canal after plots to kill President Mubarak of Egypt failed. The bombing of the Berlin nightclub La Belle Discothèque in April 1986 killed three American soldiers, wounded eighty, and claimed some two hundred German civilian victims. Six years later a German court established that while the attack had been carried out by a Palestinian, two officials of the Libyan legation in East Berlin had provided the explosives and logistic support and cover, and that East German espionage services had also been indirectly involved. In Africa, Libyan agents tried to destabilize and overthrow the then moderate government of Sudan, as well as those of the Central African countries of Chad, the Central African Republic, and Zaire.

By 1985, Khadafi's prestige was high among the terrorists, even though they were aware that the Libyan dictator tended to promise more than he delivered. But he certainly seemed more willing to accept the risks of provoking major powers than any other country. The more extreme the group, the more likely it was to find help and, if need be, a refuge in Tripoli. At the same time Khadafi's active and seemingly successful opposition to Islamic fundamentalism made some of Libya's unfriendly neighbors hesitate to take drastic action against Khadafi. Those who did not admire him seemed to fear him, at least in the Arab world. Khadafi's successes made him lose whatever remnants of a sense of reality he still possessed. He overstepped the limits of what was internationally acceptable, and invited a reaction that led to a drastic decline in his standing and a reduction of Libyan-sponsored terrorist operations.

Following Libyan terrorist attacks in Vienna and Rome airports, the Belle Discothèque bombing in West Berlin, and an attempt to bring down a TWA plane over Greece, the United States launched an air strike called El Dorado Canyon in April 1986 against selected targets in Libya. El Dorado Canyon was a one-time strike, not all targets were hit, and the damage caused was not very great. Nevertheless, to the surprise of most of America's European allies, the attack had an immediate effect. The Libyans showed much greater caution afterward, whereas earlier they had boasted of not being afraid to tackle a superpower.

America's European allies assumed that the American attack would have the opposite effect. France and Spain banned the F-111 aircraft engaged in the operation from flying over their territory. However, their fears were misplaced. During 1986–89, there was a decline in terrorist operations all over the Arab world, not just on the part of Libya. The fear that once America lost patience and felt that its vital interests were involved it might react violently and indiscriminately on a massive scale had been planted. While this might not have frightened small extremist groups, it certainly frightened their sponsors.

It was clear that the effect of a limited operation such as El Dorado Canyon would wear off, and after a number of years the bombing of Pan Am flight 103 over Lockerbie, Scotland, and the French airliner UTA flight 722 over Chad took place. (Khadafi apparently wanted to humiliate the French for having ousted the Libyan armed units from Chad, which Tripoli thought part of its sphere of influence.) In both cases, no one claimed credit for the operations, and traces of Libyan involvement were well hidden. Indeed, it seems likely that in the case of the Lockerbie disaster Iran and Syria might also have been involved. However, only Libyan involvement could eventually be proven with reasonable certainty. The matter was taken to the United Nations, where the Security Council unanimously adopted resolution 731, according to which the Libyan government was requested to hand over two of their agents who had been indicted in the United States and in Britain for their part in the Lockerbie disaster. The Security Council resolution also stipulated that Libya accept responsibility for the downing of the French airliner, disclose all evidence, and pay appropriate compensation. The Libyans refused to do so and brought upon themselves a series of sanctions, including an aviation embargo, limitations on the Libyan diplomatic presence in foreign capitals, drastic reductions in oil sales, and other measures that did considerable harm to the Libyan economy and to Libya's international standing. It was a humiliation for Khadafi, and for once he had no response.

The Libyan refusal to comply had no immediate dramatic consequences inasmuch as Khadafi remained in power. But it soon appeared that he had underrated the long-term consequences of being branded an outcast. While the Tripoli government continued to harass exiles from Libya (there were reports of the abduction of a human rights activist in Cairo and a murder in London), these occurred on a much smaller scale than before. Tripoli continued to give some help and shelter to the most extreme Arab terrorist groups, particularly those unwilling to contemplate peace with Israel under any conditions, but reduced its support of non-Arab terrorism. Libyan propaganda was almost as violent as before, but there was one considerable difference: hardly anyone in the outside world paid it any attention. Prior to 1985, Khadafi seemed to have almost gained the stature of a world leader. By the 1990s he was virtually ignored, not just by the outside world but even by his fellow Arabs. He had started his career with far-flung schemes to promote Arab unity, and terrorism had been one of the main means to that end. By the 1990s he had reached the conclusion that Libyan expansion to the south, toward Africa, was more promising and certainly less risky. The Khadafi saga demonstrates what should have been clear from the beginning: that an unscrupulous and relatively unimportant government could buy influence by investing heavily in international terrorism, but once it became more than a mere irritant, a backlash was inevitable and its power would wane.

Iranian Foreign Terrorism

In the 1980s, Iran became the world's chief sponsor of international terrorism and maintained this dubious distinction throughout the subsequent decade. Terrorist operations had been launched by the Iranian government under the Shah. The ruthless Iranian secret police, Savak, had stalked exiled opponents of the regime and had given occasional support to separatist groups outside its borders, such as the Kurds in Iraq. However, while émigrés hostile to the Shah's regime had been harassed, they were not killed. Compared to the scale and deadliness of the activities of the clerico-fascist regime that succeeded the monarchy, Savak operations had been child's play. Furthermore, the Shah had conducted his operations in secret, whereas under Ayatollah Khomeini publicity was part of Teheran's terrorist campaign.

Iran was in a considerably stronger position than Libya to engage in state-sponsored terrorism. It is a much bigger country, and Persian nationals could be found in many parts of the world. Teheran could spend larger sums on its ventures, and it had a more inspiring message, that of radical Islam, which proved incomparably more powerful than Colonel Khadafi's "Green Book." While Khadafi's message was mainly nationalist and pan-Arab, the message sent by Teheran was not just anti-Western but pan-Islamic and populist. Iranian clerics appeared as the advocates of the downtrodden and oppressed. In contrast to Tripoli, Teheran hardly ever supported non-Islamic terrorists. On the other hand, the orthodox Shiite character of the regime did not preclude financial and military aid for radical Sunni groups in countries such as the Sudan, Egypt, Algeria, Israel, Lebanon, and elsewhere, despite their theological and ideological differences. Iran used terrorism for ideological reasons and to extend its influence in the Persian Gulf area, as well as to weaken Saudi Arabia and to undermine small states such as Kuwait and particularly Bahrain. It supported, as did other countries, certain factions in the civil war in Afghanistan, despite being on bad terms almost from the beginning with the most radical faction, the Taliban, and directly or indirectly assisted the Kurds in Iraq and Turkey. Iran had no direct interests in Israel, but the destruction of the Jewish state was identified by the Teheran clerics as a religious duty of the highest order, and Iran heavily supported Hizbullah, Hamas, and like groups. The Iranians also wanted to strengthen the Shiite element in the multi-ethnic, multi-religious, secular Lebanese state. Appearing as a leading sponsor of the anti-Israeli crusade and a bitter enemy of the peace process, Iran intended to score political points in the Arab world. No one knows to what extent deep religious conviction and true fanaticism were involved in Iran's policy vis-à-vis Israel or to what degree political calculation played a role, but it would be safe to say that both did. Furthermore, it must have appeared as an almost risk-free strategy, because Teheran was far from Tel Aviv and any Israeli retaliation was bound to affect its immediate neighbors.

Iran carried its terrorist war against its enemies, primarily émigrés, to virtually all parts of the globe, engaging in a systematic campaign of elimination of those considered most threatening. In one essential respect this campaign was unprecedented, because the Iranians claimed that their enemies were the enemies of God and divine right overruled the secular norms of the international right. The reward announced for the killing of Salman Rushdie, author of *The Satanic Verses* and an Indian by nationality, was almost unprecedented in the annals of international affairs. The *fatwa*, or religious injunction, issued by Khomeini was not withdrawn by his successors.

Shifts in the intensity of Teheran's terrorist campaign reflected the international situation as well as power struggles inside Iran, with some leaders taking a more aggressive line than others. But terrorism did not cease; it was considered by the Iranian rulers a legitimate—indeed, a vital—instrument of domestic and foreign policy.

Iranian terrorist operations in the Middle East were usually carried out by local Shiite militants such as Dawa in Iraq and Hizbullah in Lebanon, opponents to the regimes in the Gulf area, and Palestinian Sunni groups such as Hamas. Iranian nationals were only indirectly involved in these operations, mainly providing weapons and training, although some eight hundred Iranian "volunteers" were stationed for years in the Baqa Valley in Lebanon. In terrorist operations outside the Middle East, on the other hand, Iranians participated at every level. On the basis of a meticulous reconstruction of the assassination of activists of the Kurdish Democratic Party in a restaurant in West Berlin, a Berlin court issued a warrant in March 1996 for the arrest of Ali Fallahian, Iranian minister of security and information. It had been known for some time that assassinations were carried out by VEVAK, the Iranian secret police, with the help of Iranian military intelligence and other government agencies, but this was the first time that a Western court had documented the line of command. This decision by an independent German court caused no little embarrassment to the German Foreign Ministry, for Fallahian had once been the official guest of the German government and he had been active in negotiations for the release of German and other Western hostages kept in Lebanon and Iran. Fallahian was not, of course, the head of terrorist operations; the orders came from Khomeini and his successors, such as Ali Khameini. These spiritual and political leaders never made a secret of their great appreciation for their underlings who were "combating and uprooting" the enemies of Islam inside and outside Iran.

The enemies targeted by Iran were first and foremost political dissidents, including some very prominent figures, such as Shapour Bakhtiar, the last prime minister under the Shah, who was murdered in Paris in August 1991 at the age of seventy-six. This was not the first attempt on his life in Paris: in an earlier attempt a Frenchwoman and a police officer were killed. The terrorists were apprehended and given life sentences but released after a short time and returned to Teheran. European governments knew from bitter experience that the Iranian authorities would retaliate against the arrest of their agents, and the French had a tradition of caving in more quickly than other European governments. If Iranian diplomats involved in blatant terrorist activities were asked by the host government to leave, the Iranians would retaliate by expelling Western (or Turkish or Arab) diplomats. Occasionally, the Iranians would withdraw their diplomats before an official demand was made; this happened, for instance, in Buenos Aires, where Iranian terrorists had attacked Jewish schools and other organizations.

Among Iranian targets was the leadership of the left-wing Mojahedin, the main émigrés opposition group, but monarchists, Communists, and members of the Flag of Freedom group were also singled out for assassination, as well as Kurdish activists and some individuals who had no known political ties to Iran. In a variety of cases, Iranian agents attempted to abduct political émigrés in foreign countries even though such operations were always more complicated and the risk of failure or discovery greater. Altogether, Iranian terrorists assassinated more than sixty émigrés, although the number of attempted assassinations may have been closer to two hundred. These operations took place in Turkey, Iraq, and Pakistan, as well as in France, Germany, Switzerland, Austria, Italy, and other European countries, and even as far away as Venezuela.

While the risks involved from the Iranian point of view were not enormous, there was still the danger that, like Libya, Iran would be isolated as the result of blatant and frequent terrorist actions. Iran certainly suffered economically from retaliatory measures taken by the United States and other countries.

Why, then, did Iran continue to sponsor terrorism? It could be that the rulers in Teheran felt insecure even though open opposition had been suppressed inside Iran. It could also be that they were pessimistic about their long-term political future and thought that unless they crushed the émigré opposition their position inside Iran would weaken.

The Iranian leadership all agreed in principle on the use of terrorism outside the country, but there were differences of opinion as to how many abductions and assassinations could be safely carried out. The hard-line Montazeri faction seems to have advocated an aggressive policy in the early years of the regime, whereas president Ali Rafsanjani, who had recently prevailed in the struggle for power, advocated a more cautious approach. In any case terrorism, albeit on a somewhat reduced scale, has continued under his rule as before.

There was a decline in the number of political assassinations in foreign countries carried out by Iranian agents after 1992. That year there had been twenty such cases, whereas in the four years after there were only six, four, seven, and eight, respectively. The Iranians had to some extent achieved their aims, inasmuch as the French had expelled the Mojahedin from Paris, where they constituted a graver danger to the Iranian regime than in Baghdad, where they settled down next. Ironically, Khomeini, when exiled because of pressure from the Shah's government, had settled in France for many years. Thirty years later, the French no longer had the stomach for extending asylum to political refugees, as they were more afraid of the wrath of the clerics in Teheran than they had been of the displeasure of the Shah. However, the Iranian terrorist apparatus must have been given orders to slow down, because the continuing assassinations were causing more harm than good to the clerical regime; it made it more difficult, for instance, to acquire and develop weapons of mass destruction, which was an important long-term aim of Teheran.

By 1997, Iranian political ambitions had increased. They wanted to play host to a big Islamic conference in Teheran and to show that they were not only a militant but also a responsible power that abided by most of the norms of international relations. A new president, Khatemi, had been elected with a substantial moderate majority, and even though most of the key positions in the country were still in the hands of the diehards headed by Ali Khameini, the internal balance of power had changed somewhat. Terrorist operations directed against Western countries and the Arab Gulf states declined. Operations did not cease altogether, but they were camouflaged far better than in the past. When, for instance, terrorists attacked an American base in Saudi Arabia or Jewish institutions in Argentina, Iranian involvement seemed certain. There was insufficient legal proof, however, and other sponsors may have participated as well, so retaliation against Iran alone was difficult to justify. In various major terrorist attacks, a group that called itself Islamic Jihad took the credit. But there was no independent organization named Islamic Jihad; it was part of the military wing of Hamas. To hide their tracks, the Iranians had used the surrogate of a surrogate.

The high tide of Iranian anti-Western terrorism occurred in the

1980s, and the main scene was Lebanon. These operations, carried out by surrogates, included the bombing of the U.S. embassy in Beirut and the American and French military barracks in 1983–84, which cost many lives; the bombing of a variety of embassies and Saudi travel agencies from Vienna to New Delhi; the taking of hostages, first in Teheran and later in Beirut; and the hijacking of planes. The hostage saga lasted for eight years (1984–92), and the Iranians played this game with consummate skill. They were instrumental in inspiring and guiding the kidnappers, and helping them to keep the hostages—altogether about one hundred over the years—in Lebanon and Iran. At the same time, they presented themselves as honest brokers eager to resolve the crisis between the kidnappers, with whom they pretended to have no connection, and the Western countries, which were trying to secure the release of their nationals. In this way they obtained from America all kinds of concessions, including economic help and even an official expression of thanks on the part of then President Bush.

But those who had hoped that moderation had prevailed in Teheran were disappointed when, in 1989, Ayatollah Khomeini, in the last months of his life, published his famous *fatwa* against Salman Rushdie. The Indian author's *Satanic Verses* was thought to be blasphemous, and every good Muslim was called upon to kill Rushdie as well as those instrumental in publishing it. To reinforce this appeal, an obscure foundation in Teheran announced an award of $2 million (plus expenses) for killing Rushdie. The Iranians dispatched a suicide bomber who accidentally blew himself up in a London hotel room. The book's Japanese translator was stabbed to death, and there were attempts on the lives of the Italian and Norwegian publishers. The *fatwa* was not withdrawn after Khomeini's death, despite strong diplomatic pressure and abject apologies by the author.

The Rushdie affair had many curious aspects. While the intention of the work was satirical, there have been many more outspoken attacks in Western literature against Islam and the prophet Muhammad, just as in

Muslim countries there have been scurrilous attacks against Judaism and Christianity. The Teheran government could have demanded with greater justification, for instance, the ban and destruction of the works of Voltaire, who wrote in a truly outrageous manner about the prophet. Why single out Rushdie? And why promise a substantial monetary award for what was proclaimed to be no more than the holy duty of every Muslim believer? Did the Ayatollahs trust so little the religious fervor of their core-ligionists as to bring in a demeaning material incentive? The affair attracted enormous attention, and it revealed an inconsistent component in the thinking of the Teheran rulers.

If there was a decline in Iranian-sponsored terrorist operations against the West and in the Gulf, there was an upsurge in such attacks against Israel and Jewish communities elsewhere, mainly in the form of arms support given to Hizbullah in Lebanon and also to Sunni anti-Israeli militants such as Hamas (groups named Hizbullah or Hamas also exist in other countries). Although, according to some reports, the annual subsidy to Hizbullah of about $150 million was subsequently halved, the supply of arms was not reduced. The monetary cuts might have been inevitable in light of Iran's strained economic circumstances and its need to fund other terrorists in the Middle East and Afghanistan.

What benefits did the Iranian rulers derive from their massive invest-ment in international terrorism? The Ayatollahs may have believed during Iran's war against Iraq that, because they were not strong enough to achieve decisive victory, they had to turn to terrorism, which was infinitely cheaper. But Iran's involvement with terrorism did not begin with the war against Iraq, nor did it end with it. Up to a point the Iranian sponsorship of terrorist groups was successful: the fact that its substitutes had com-pelled the United States to flee Lebanon certainly added to Iran's image as the fearless champion of Arab extremism. But it did not enhance Iran's military and political standing in the long term. Though Iran was feared by its neighbors, such fear did not make them bow to Iranian demands, but rather induced closer collaboration against Teheran.

Investment in terrorism certainly did not help export the Iranian revolution. This would have been difficult in any case because of the traditional tension between Shiites and Sunni. Even Sunni fundamentalists of the Muslim Brotherhood variety, who accepted Iranian help, declared on every occasion that they were no admirers of the kind of government established in Iran, and that they aimed at a different kind of society.

Support for anti-Israeli terrorism was also problematic from an Iranian point of view. The intent was to be recognized as the staunchest and most radical champion of the Palestinian cause and as the opponent of any peace process. But since the now cautious Iranians seldom acknowledged openly their terrorist operations (they never claimed credit, for instance, for the two bombings in Buenos Aires in 1992 and 1994), their support must have appeared halfhearted to radical Palestinian militants, who always expected more assistance than they got. At the same time, the Iranian rulers exposed themselves to considerable risk. There was always the danger that if the terrorist threat became unacceptable, the Israelis, less inhibited than the Western countries, would strike back at Iran rather than the surrogates. Having never recovered from the war with Iraq, the Iranian military would be unable to effectively respond.

Seen from this perspective, massive Iranian involvement in terrorism was a double-edged sword. It undoubtedly reaped benefits for Iran at a relatively cheap price. On the other hand, it was a dangerous gamble, for even if Iranian leaders acted entirely rationally in weighing possible gains and risks, which they did not always do, there was the danger that their operations might get out of hand and backfire. The surrogates Teheran used had their own agenda and priorities, and it was impossible to control them fully.

excerpt from:

The Diversity of Bio-Weapons
by Joshua Lederberg

A great deal has been written recently on the real and imagined threat of these weapons of mass destruction. A kind of mass hysteria bubbles just below the surface, ready to attach itself to any event. In this atmosphere, solid information is the best defense. Dr. Joshua Lederberg is the recipient of the 1958 Nobel Prize in Medicine. His to approach to biological threats is aggressive and programmatic. In this article he delineates the difference between infectious and viral agents and discusses the ways to contain each disease. He outlines likely future countermeasures currently being researched. Though Saddam Hussein is considered to be the most likely potential source of future biological attacks, Muslim extremists groups such as Al Qaeda have been actively seeking weapons of mass destruction. Lederberg holds out hope that DNA-based solutions may eventually outflank this threat.

I will pursue how we might be dealing with present and future technologies for bio attack and defense. Very innovative approaches are being developed (a good part in the national laboratories) for the rapid sensing and diagnosis of infectious agents in the environment and from tissue and blood samples from exposed individuals. That's absolutely critical to recognizing that an attack has happened, that it might be going on, and as well as for the care and treatment of those at risk.

Even so, for the next few years, we would be very lucky to be able to detect a clandestine anthrax or smallpox attack before a substantial number of people have started showing symptoms. That would be squandering two or three days of very precious time that is absolutely crucial to the management of the consequences.

We perhaps put too much stress on an acute incident, an explosion, a compelling notice that something really awful has happened. That would entail the involvement of emergency responders. But no shrewd user of a BW weapon is going to give you that opportunity. The "incident" will be people accumulating illness, disease, death. Finally, then the evidence may become overwhelming that this is out of the ordinary, and the public health system will begin to take hold.

So a very important aspect for defense against BW is to adopt the correct level of paranoia, when possibly random fluctuations of the incidence of disease, an epidemic of a mild, or not so mild, influenza starts bringing people to the hospitals. Or even speculating that a new disease like West Nile now transmitted by mosquitoes in New York and the crows falling at our feet might that be a BW attack or not.

Advances in diagnosis will march on, depending on specific diseases. I think we will beat the bacterial infections, and we'll recover our overwhelming defense capability even in the face of the waves of antibiotic resistance that bacteria have generated out of careless use of antibiotics. Diagnosis will be important in order to know which agents to use.

I wish I could be quite that optimistic about viral infections for which therapeutic measures are few and far between. Our frustration in dealing with AIDS is an example of that, which has had the most concentrated effort in history at the development of therapeutics. Perhaps there will be some improvement if there is renewed investment in dealing with other virus diseases. That is the only approach that I can see as being feasible on a strategic level in dealing with smallpox. Are we going to persuade ourselves or others that we ought to revaccinate the entire world's population? Once you stop and think about the implications on doing this on a merely regional or national level without the world being involved, you'll

see why it is an "all or none" global decision. But if we could have therapeutics that could deal with a smallpox attack once it had started, so that
it is not so inevitably lethal as it offers to be at the present time, that would
greatly alter the picture.

The same might apply for preparedness for a broad range of other
viral attacks. So it's a little bit chancy but one could be moderately optimistic about the pace of development of therapeutic management measures coming from the technologies of the next five to 10 years.
Nevertheless, the offense will be preponderant as we understand infectious disease in greater and greater depth: our ability to conduct DNA
analysis sequencing, moving bits of DNA from one organism to another,
and genetic engineering as it is applied to very beneficent purposes. It's
just built in that the knowledge that is being accumulated in the basic bio-
chemistry of infection is going to make it a lot easier to perfect biological
weapons than to build defenses against them.

One way of expressing my level of concern is that the technologies are
so accessible. Growing anthrax is as easy as baking a pie; finding anthrax
seed is not that tough. Outbreaks of it occur in cattle from time to time.
Any large farm community will know some field where some cow has died
of it and where you could recover anthrax from the soil with a little dig-
ging around. High school students are going to have to be added to our
roster of potential sources of threat. Thousands of high school kids are
doing biotechnology as part of their high school research projects, at a
level that is quite sophisticated enough for devising brand new agents.
They have laboratory facilities to do it and you buy kits over the counter.
When you're a young high school student nothing looks as tough as it may
appear to a 30 or 50 year old. It's mostly a metaphor, but something to be
taken somewhat seriously about where technology is heading us.

Now, why is high tech microbiology even more dangerous than natural disease? I used to teach that it would not be. I taught that the evolution of disease agent was very complicated. That putting together all the

things needed for a bug to adapt itself to the environment of a host, defeat its defense systems and so forth would make it unlikely that you could synthesize a brand new pathogen, even with quite deep bio-technical knowledge. And that is still true. But I've had further reflection.

Consider the business of our natural infecting agents, the influenza that you'll get, the common cold, your boils, your gut infections, your staph on your skin and so on and so forth. Their economy is not to kill their host. But things happen. They happen as a byproduct of the skirmishing between them and host defenses. If you look around the world of infectious disease, in fact you find that with rare exceptions, our most lethal diseases are almost accidental byproducts of a bug moving away from its natural host. That's outstandingly true of HIV-AIDS which is in equilibrium with its primate hosts and does not cause an enormous amount of mischief there. It has jumped into humans just as plague has jumped into humans, just as Avian flu has jumped into humans, and there can have devastating results. In their natural historical environment, most bugs are selected for moderated virulence, because they will survive better in that natural world if they do not kill the host.

That is where technology would override that natural restraint. If we were to see the importation of, say, botulinum toxin, to a wide variety of other existing pathogens, we might find they would be far more lethal in a way that would be self-destructive to them (and to us) in their natural environment. But these would make even more horrendous kinds of weapons in the artificial circumstance of technical use. There have been two or three published experiments down that line in which anthrax has been used as a vehicle for importing still other toxins. Anthrax is a well-adapted pathogen. Usually there's a local lesion; in cattle it's rarely that fatal. Even in humans you typically have a skin lesion from contact with an infected animal. In its natural mode of transmission, it has a moderately low lethality. Only when it is artificially disseminated by aerosols and by an inhalation portal of entry does it have the features we now recognize for BW. But by putting other toxins into anthrax, this stands a very good chance of defeating the vaccine that we have developed, and we are going to need a very different approach in vaccine design when it is not the natural anthrax toxin but the imported one.

On the other hand, in nature, where do we find botulinum toxin? It's the most potent toxin around by a factor of 100 or so compared to even other bacterial toxins. You do not see it in the ordinary pathogens that cause systemic disease. You see it in the bottom feeders: in the anaerobic bacteria that live in the bottom of lakes, or in sealed cans of food. The human body is a very unnatural part of its life cycle. The bottom of a lake is an anaerobic, non-air environment. We do not find the toxin in other pathogens, not because it couldn't migrate from species to species. We know very well that it could, and there are biological mechanisms for it. But it is too hot to handle. It would be selected against very rapidly as a natural entity because of its high lethality—a rule that would be abrogated in intentional use. So there is a lot to worry about in the future.

But let me turn from that to where solutions might come from. Basically, we have to look at intentions as well as capabilities in this sphere. The capability of doing mischief, for a very long time, has greatly exceeded what has actually been done. BW has not in modern times reached the currency in formal warfare that chemical weapons did, as they did in WWI with a vengeance. BW has been subject to restraints at various times. We do not understand them very well. We experience a very deep sense of moral revulsion and outright fear. Some of this comes from our understanding: you let that tiger loose, he's going to come back and eat you up as well. There is no limit as to what the eventual spread of BW will be. You know, let smallpox loose, you've made war against the world.

We have made some very serious mistakes in the past. Above all, during the Cold War we continued our own offensive BW program for decades during a time when nobody in his right mind really believed we would ever use biological weapons. We never needed them. We had weapons perfectly capable of providing whatever level of deterrence or compellence we needed, and in a far more precisely targeted way than with BW. I do not know what our own doctrine was for the conditions under which they would be applied. I half suggest it was a never very serious one.

Overall, as President Nixon eventually recognized, it was very much against the national interest of this country to continue to fund major offensive programs over the years that we had them. They left a cache of secrets that can't be kept silent that long, that deeply. Not 20, 30, 40 years: the promulgation of the core knowledge of what happened in the offensive program is part of what we are worrying about at this very moment with the prospects that they will be used against us. I was greatly in favor of the BW disarmament convention because we have at least de-legitimated biological weapons. BW programs, if they continue on the plan of others, will have to be done under some cloak of secrecy and evasion, and we then have a lot of leverage about our own enforcement measures, about how we can mobilize world opinion and mobilize our own resolve in terms of responding to them.

Essentially on political grounds, I do not worry that Russia is going to use BW against the United States. I do worry that there may be leakage from their programs to other countries. Either at official levels, or much more likely at unofficial ones of private individuals who otherwise do not know how to feed their families, going to sell themselves to the devil and provide material and some degree of insight and so on. That's a matter that's been widely discussed. We would be in a very poor position to take measures against that roguery if we did not have the treaty framework as a basis for de-legitimization of these kinds of weapons.

There is one program of a very positive kind that would reinforce it all, and would be a very great benefit to us directly as well. That is to be, even more than we are, a major partner in our global attacks against infectious disease. In this world today 700 to 800 million people are considerably damaged by malaria infection, 200 or 300 million with tuberculosis, and several million a year die from avoidable diseases. Even deployment of our existing technology could go a long way to alleviating that kind of distress. There is a very direct connection between cooperation with other populations anywhere around the globe and our own survivability as we sit very comfortably behind our borders. These bugs do not recognize those borders. And it would be a very important part of the bargain that we are tacitly making with underdeveloped countries, who can't afford our sophisticated weapons. The nonproliferation regime says "look, if we're in this game together, you forego the biological weapons that might even the playing field from your point of view and we will continue to be part of that global effort to fight infectious disease as an enemy of all humankind."

Now I will also submit that there would be nothing more devastating to our security than a successful demonstration of the power of an attack with weapons of mass destruction. I do not in any way want to minimize the efforts at organization, at preparedness, at coordination, at anticipation, at intelligence, at warning. The first successful attack will not be the last one. And to the extent that the culprits can get away with it and demonstrate its power, they will be setting an example that will be ever more difficult to avert later on. So there's much, much more at stake than the casualties that might be involved in any single incident. We're really at a turning point in what the future history of biological weapons might be.

excerpt from:

Jihad vs. McWorld
by Benjamin R. Barber

Benjamin Barber's thesis is that with the end of the Cold War the major conflict that engulfs the world is between modern consumer capitalism and religious and tribal fundamentalism. These two forces both oppose and feed off each other, uniting us at the expense of the traditional nation-state and political democracy and thereby creating a global society of fragmented specificities. Barber posits that our future lies in the ways these two perspectives will interact. This book, first published in 1995, has become a key text in understanding the deep ideological motives of fundamentalist extremists. This excerpt lays out the key similarities and differences between capitalism and fundamentalism. Barber, the author of numerous books on power, teaches political science at Rutgers University, where he heads the Walt Whitman Center for the Culture and Politics of Democracy.

T he language most commonly used to address the ends of the reinvented and self-described tribes waging Jihad—whether they call themselves Christian fundamentalists or Rwandan rebels or Islamic holy warriors—remains the language of nationalism. Religion may represent a more profound force in the human psyche, but as politics it finds its vessel in nationalism. Yet nationalism can be elusive and its many usages are so variously inflected that it is not clear if a common language is actually being spoken. If, as Michael Ignatieff suggests, "the key narrative of the new world order is the disintegration of states" and the "key language" of that dissolution is ethnic nationalism, are we to assume that this is the nationalism of Mazzini and Yael Tamir? Or the nationalism of the Nazis and Vladimir Zhirinovsky? Ignatieff speaks cautiously of a "new" nationalism, but strictly speaking, the sundry opponents of McWorld appear to be neither nationalists nor religious zealots. Their rhetoric is too worldly for true religion and far too sectarian and exclusive to be nationalist. The Crusades were murderous in their fanaticism but universalist and expansionist in aspiration—more imperialist than reactionary—which indeed accounts for their bloodiness. Universal ideals can create universal mayhem while the effects of parochial ardor are often far more modest. Our new tribes are murderous and fanatical but small-minded and defensive: trying to secure islands of parochial brotherhood in a sea that relentlessly leaches away essence and washes away fraternal bonds.

The critical question is whether postmodern "new" nationalism, with the nation-state as its target, is assimilable to traditional nationalism, on which the nation-state was founded. Rather than offer either a phenomenological answer (*both* varieties count as nationalism) or an essentialist answer (only *this* one or only *that* one counts as nationalism), I want to suggest here a more dialectical response. Nationalism clearly has now and has perhaps always had two moments: one of group identity and exclusion but another, equally important, of integration and inclusion. Today's "nationalists" boast about their deconstructive potential and revel in hostility to the state and other constituencies that make up the state. In its early modern manifestation, however, nationalism permitted Europe to emerge from feudalism and facilitated the architecture of the nation-state. Early European atlases like the sixteenth-century *Cosmography* show Macedonians and Bulgarians, Danes and Vandals, Sicilians and Hungarians, both as constituent pieces of a larger body (a feudal empire) and inclusionary national wholes that assembled parochial tribes into national entities like Italia and Germania.

• • •

Nowhere is the tension between democracy and Jihad more evident than in the Islamic world, where the idea of Jihad has a home of birth but certainly not an exclusive patent. For, although it is clear that Islam is a complex religion that by no means is synonymous with Jihad, it is relatively inhospitable to democracy and that inhospitality in turn nurtures conditions favorable to parochialism, antimodernism, exclusiveness, and hostility to "others"—the characteristics that constitute what I have called Jihad.

While *Jihad* is a term associated with the moral (and sometimes armed) struggle of believers against faithlessness and the faithless, I have used it here to speak to a generic form of fundamentalist opposition to modernity that can be found in most world religions. In their massive five-volume study of fundamentalisms, Martin E. Marty and R. Scott Appleby treat Sunni and Shiite Islam but pay equal attention to Protestantism and Catholicism in a variety of European, and North and South American forms, to Hinduism, to the Sikhs, to Theravada Buddhism, to Confucianist Revivalism, and to Zionism. Marty and Appleby take fundamentalist religions to be engaged in militancy, in a kind of permanent *fighting*: they are "militant, whether in the use of words and ideas or ballots or, in extreme cases, bullets." They fight back, struggling reactively against the present in the name of the past; they fight for their religious conception of the world against secularism and relativism; they fight with weapons of every kind, sometimes borrowed from the enemy, carefully chosen to secure their identity; they fight against others who are agents of corruption; and they fight under God for a cause that, because it is holy, cannot be lost even when it is not yet won. The struggle that is Jihad is not then just a feature of Islam but a characteristic of all fundamentalisms. Nevertheless, *Jihad* is an Islamic term and is given its animating power by its association not just with fundamentalism in general but with Islamic fundamentalism in particular and with the armed struggles groups like Hamas and Islamic Jihad have engaged in. There are moderate and liberal strands in Islam, but they are less prominent at present than the militant strand.

The Moroccan sociologist Fatima Mernissi insists that "throughout its history Islam has been marked by two trends: an intellectual trend that speculated on the philosophical foundations of the world and humanity, and another trend that turned political challenge violent by resort to force." The first trend offered a meditation on reason akin to Western humanism; the second "simply thought that by rebelling against the imam and sometimes killing him they could change things." Both traditions "raise the same issues that we are today told are imports from the West," issues of resistance and accountability—that is to say, of democracy.

There is thus a sense in which Islamic fundamentalists are genuine resisters against corrupt worldly political authority, much as the early Christians were. The zealots who assassinated Anwar Sadat in 1981 were members of a group called literally "Jihad" and when, their bloody deed done, they shouted, "I have killed Pharaoh, and I do not fear death," they were speaking the language of martyrs of liberation. In Algeria, fundamentalists came to power by the ballot in 1991 and it was the secular party of national liberation under the tutelage of the army that shut down democratic institutions rather than turn them over to its adversaries, who had vanquished them in the polls. Observers thus continue to believe that Islam and democracy have a future together. At a 1992 conference held by the United States Institute on Peace, conferees spoke of a "new synthesis" in which the "clash of opinions on the relationship between Islam and democracy could yield a new synthesis view in which Islamic notions enhance and give new meaning to democratic concepts beyond their current western-dominated usages."

How real is this promise? Is democracy in Islamic countries more a victim of colonial repression and postcolonial exploitation than of indigenous Islamic forces, as critics like Edward W. Said contend? Or is Islam an "exception" that rules out a free civil society and thus precludes real democracy? If democracy means Western democracy and modernization means Westernization, there would seem to be little hope for reconciliation since Islam regards Western secular culture and its attending values as corrupting to and morally incompatible with its own. But if democracy takes many forms, and is an ancient as well as a modern manifestation of the quest for self-governing communities, then perhaps it can be adapted to notions found in the Koran such as *umma* (community), *shura* (mutual consultation), and *al maslaha* (public interest). As other Islamic scholars have argued, understood this way, Islam may not be "antithetical to the telos of democratic values." Islamic fundamentalists may insist that since Allah's will is sovereign, the people's will cannot be, but moderates point out that this still leaves ample room for the majority to exercise political authority as long as it does so within a framework that acknowledges the ultimate hegemony of divine power. Neither France nor Italy has a formal constitutional separation of church and state and both have constructed relatively viable democracies. Ultimate obedience to God can act as a brake on authoritarian and licentious worldly government, while affording a moderate people, constrained by faith, room to govern themselves democratically in the manner of Calvinist Geneva or Puritan Massachusetts before the Revolution.

Nevertheless, democracy has always found a way to accommodate religion, and Jihad's war has been less with democracy than with McWorld. In the 1920s, Hasan al-Banna, founder of the Muslim Brotherhood, was railing against "the wave of atheism and lewdness" engulfing Egypt, a wave that "started the devastation of religion and morality on the pretext of individual and intellectual freedom." Al-Banna could be reproaching

Rupert Murdoch or Barry Diller when he assailed Westerners for importing "their half-naked women into these regions, together with their liquors, their theaters, their dance halls, their amusements, their stories, their newspapers, their novels, their whims, their silly games, and their vices." He had taken the measure of McWorld long before McWorld had jelled sufficiently to take the measure of itself. Grasping the superior corrosiveness of knowledge over arms and of communications over armies, he warned in the 1920s that the culture of the West "was more dangerous than the political and military campaigns by far." Where colonial empires failed, he seemed to prophesy, McWorld would succeed.

Al-Banna's indignation goes to the very heart of Jihad's campaign against the modern, the secular, and the cosmopolitan. It captures the essence of fundamentalism as it has existed since the seventeenth century, growing up alongside the devil modernity to which it has played angel's advocate for Puritans and Muslims, Buddhists and born-again Baptists alike.

If McWorld in its most elemental negative form is a kind of animal greed—one that is achieved by an aggressive and irresistible energy, Jihad in its most elemental negative form is a kind of animal fear propelled by anxiety in the face of uncertainty and relieved by self-sacrificing zealotry—an escape out of history. Because history has been a history of individuation, acquisitiveness, secularization, aggressiveness, atomization, and immoralism it becomes in the eyes of Jihad's disciples the temporal chariot of wickedness, a carrier of corruption that, along with time itself, must he rejected. Moral preservationists, whether in America, Israel, Iran, or India, have no choice but to make war on the present to secure a future more like the past: depluralized, monocultured, unskepticized, reenchanted. Homogenous values by which women and men live orderly and simple lives were once nurtured under such conditions. Today, our lives have become pulp fiction and *Pulp*

Fiction as novel, as movie, or as life promises no miracles. McWorld is meager fare for hungry moralists and shows only passing interest in the spirit. However outrageous the deeds associated with Jihad, the revolt the deeds manifest is reactive to changes that are themselves outrageous.

This survey of the moral topography of Jihad suggests that McWorld—the spiritual poverty of markets—may bear a portion of the blame for the excesses of the holy war against the modern; and that Jihad as a form of negation reveals Jihad as a form of affirmation. Jihad tends the soul that McWorld abjures and strives for the moral well-being that McWorld, busy with the consumer choices it mistakes for freedom, disdains. Jihad thus goes to war with McWorld and, because each worries the other will obstruct and ultimately thwart the realization of its ends, the war between them becomes a holy war. The lines here are drawn not in sand but in stone. The language of hate is not easily subjected to compromise; the "other" as enemy cannot easily be turned into an interlocutor. But as McWorld is "other" to Jihad, so Jihad is "other" to McWorld. Reasoned communication between the two is problematic when for the partisans of Jihad both reason and communication appear as seductive instrumentalities of the devil, while for the partisans of McWorld both are seductive instrumentalities of consumerism. For all their dialectical interplay with respect to democracy, Jihad and McWorld are moral antinomies. There is no room in the mosque for Nintendo, no place on the Internet for Jesus—however rapidly "religious" channels are multiplying. Life cannot be both play and in earnest, cannot stand for the lesser gratification of a needy body and simultaneously for the greater glory of a selfless soul. Either the Qur'an speaks the Truth, or Truth is a television quiz show. History has given us Jihad as a counterpoint to McWorld and made them inextricable; but individuals cannot live in both domains at once and are compelled to choose. Sadly, it is not obvious that the choice, whatever it is, holds out much promise to democrats in search of a free civil society.

The Moral Logic of Hizballah

by Martin Kramer

Hezbollah, the Party of God, was born in the poverty of the Bekaa Valley in Lebanon. Its members are Shiite Muslims who look to Iran for guidance and financial support. Hezbollah came to international prominence after the suicide bombing of the U.S. Marine barracks in Beirut killed two hundred forty one soldiers in 1983, and considers the United States to be its main enemy, principally for its support of Israel in the 1982 assault on Lebanon. Allied to such shadow groups as the Islamic Jihad (who committed more than eighty kidnappings of foreigners, ten of whom died in captivity), the group also administered a number of social welfare programs in Lebanon funded mainly by the Iranian government. They ran numerous businesses including fisheries, factories, bookshops and bakeries. Hezbollah has built a number of low-cost housing facilities and medical clinics. In fact they had taken over these functions from the paralyzed Lebanese government who took several years to address the concerns of Shiites.

One of the major obstacles to suicidal terrorism is the Koran which strictly prohibits self-destruction. In this excerpt we see the Hezbollah (also spelled Hizballah) leadership grappling with this restriction, aware that it was nullifying a potentially terrifying weapon. Rejected by one cleric, they turned to Sayad Fadlallah, a powerful imam, who initially responded with ambivalence. But the pressure did not let up and the rest is deadly history. Martin Kramer is the Associate Director for Middle Eastern and African Studies at Tel Aviv University.

Suicide and martyrdom

Hizballah owes much of its reputation in the wider world to the unprecedented wave of suicidal bombings carried out by Lebanese Shi'ites from the spring of 1983 to the summer of 1985. These attacks were directed against U.S., French, and Israeli targets in Lebanon, and they met with astonishing success in bringing about policy reassessments by all these extraneous powers. In the best-planned of these operations, individual suicide bombers caused tens and even hundreds of casualties. Responsibility for most of the bombings was claimed by Islamic Jihad, and prominent figures affiliated with Hizballah were careful to disavow any involvement in the attacks. Nonetheless, it was Hizballah that most directly benefited from the suicide operations. The movement's own military capabilities were still very limited, and its militia had yet to take effective form. Yet the spectacular bombings suggested that religious fervor could compensate for small numbers and that Hizballah commanded a kind of devotion from its adherents that no other militia could claim. Hizballah could no longer be ignored. Its leading figures sought to assure this recognition even as they distanced themselves personally from the attacks, by justifying the operations as though they were Hizballah's own.

In one sense, it was an uncomplicated moral logic that justified the highly effective October 1983 suicide attacks against the U.S. and French contingents of the Multinational Force (MNF) in Beirut. Although he invariably denied any personal involvement in the attacks, Islamic Amal's Husayn al-Musawi saw the attacks as defensive acts against foreign occupation. "Even if we, the people of Islamic Amal, do not have relations with those who committed these attacks, we are nevertheless on the side of those who defend themselves, by whatever means they have chosen."[1] In

[1] Interview with Husayn al-Musawi, *Le Monde*, 2 November 1983.

his view, the MNF was a military force committed to armed struggle against Lebanon's Muslims, a view held widely in Beirut's southern suburbs and widely preached by Shi'ite clerics in mosque sermons throughout the country. "I accept these attacks," declared Musawi. "The French and Americans came to Beirut to help the Phalangists and Israelis—our enemies—against the Muslims. They evacuated the Palestinians to enable the Israelis to enter Beirut."[2] Musawi denied knowing any members of Islamic Jihad, which claimed credit for the attacks. But he would later declare, "I supported their glorious attacks against the U.S. and French forces in Lebanon. I have said repeatedly that I have no connection with them, but we respect them and we support them fully and we bow our heads to the greatness of their work."[3]

The Hizballah leader in the Biqa Valley, Sayyid Abbas al-Musawi, felt justified in declaring that the attacks "represented the opinion of all Muslims. The MNF should not have acted the way it did. When you knock on someone's door, you must wait for an answer before entering."[4] For Sayyid Ibrahim al-Amin, spokesman of Hizballah in Beirut, this aggressive intrusion was part of a "war" with the United States, which had "transformed Lebanon into a military test laboratory for their advanced weapons." It was "our right to rise up against our enemies," and the October 1983 attacks "deserve proper recognition, homage, and deference," for they were "unprecedented in the history of mankind."[5] Hizballah's leaders deemed the MNF a hostile force in time of war, not a neutral force dispatched to preserve peace. Therefore, attacks against the MNF were military operations against an enemy, not acts of terrorism against political neutrals. And as spectacularly successful military operations, the attacks were widely applauded, not only by Hizballah but by

[2] Interview with Husayn al-Musawi, *Le Figaro*, 12 September 1986.
[3] Interview with Husayn al-Musawi, *Kayhan*, 29 July 1986.
[4] Interview with Abbas al-Musawi, *La Revue du Liban*, 27 July 1985.
[5] Interview with Ibrahim al-Amin, *Kayhan*, 19 October 1985.

other Lebanese factions as well as by Iran and Syria. When attacks launched against Israeli forces in Lebanon enjoyed comparable success, they met with similar accolades.

The more complicated moral issue from Hizballah's point of view concerned the method of the attacks, which depended on the premeditated sacrifice by Muslims of their own lives. The frequency with which this issue was addressed by Shi'ite clerics following the attacks suggests that resort to this method did not meet with universal approbation within Hizballah, because of the strong Islamic prohibition against suicide.[6] Some activists were also distressed that the method tended to obscure the message, because the many psychologists called upon to interpret the attacks suggested clinical rather than political interpretations for the motives of the perpetrators. These interpretations had some effect in the Shi'ite street, where it was rumored that the terrorists who had carried out the operations were possibly disturbed, making it necessary for Islamic Jihad to conceal their identities even after the attacks. If this had been the case, Islamic Jihad's operational planners had exploited the psychological distress of unbalanced youngsters, who had acted without the full possession of their faculties.

Sayyid Muhammad Husayn Fadlallah gave this issue the most systematic exposition in his interviews, speeches, and sermons. It was a subject he could not avoid, yet one that had to be addressed in cautious terms. Reports by the intelligence branches of the Lebanese army and the Lebanese Forces (Phalanges), which were leaked to the American press, had Fadlallah granting religious dispensation to the attackers on the eve of their mission.[7] He denied this accusation immediately and consistently, as the inevitable preface to his analysis of the moral implications of the

---

[6] The accepted theological view is that suicide is a grave sin, and the person who commits suicide is doomed to continual repetition in Hell of the action by which he killed himself. Franz Rosenthal, "On Suicide in Islam," *Journal of the American Oriental Society* 66 (1946): 243, 245.

[7] The original story appeared in the *Washington Post*, 28, 30 October 1983.

attacks. This he made from the point of view of an interpreter of religious law, to whom persons both within and beyond Hizballah turned for judgment on the moral admissibility of the method employed in the operations.

Fadlallah's initial declaratory position was one of ambivalence toward the attacks. One of his professed doubts was strictly situational. In the immediate aftermath of the attacks, he expressed concern about possible retaliation against the southern suburbs and about the likelihood that the bombings might drive the United States to adopt a still more aggressive posture. The attacks were liable to create "a climate that makes it easier for imperialism to implement its plans. This is what happened with the two explosions. The United States benefited from them in invading Grenada and in exerting political pressure in Lebanon to further its interests."[8] But Fadlallah's concerns about the effect of the attacks on the resolve of the United States were soon dissipated; it rapidly became clear that the attacks had shattered that resolve and hastened the withdrawal of the MNF. Yet Fadlallah was still left with the complex moral and legal issue of the method employed in the attacks, especially because he and other Shi'ite clerics who looked to him for guidance were besieged by believers' questions. Some of these wanted an explicit judgment based on religious law— a *fatwa*—sanctioning the method of suicidal attack.

Fadlallah knew the nuances of the law: He did not hesitate to declare that, "based on my individual interpretation of Islamic law, I have reservations about resorting to suicidal tactics in political action."[9] And so Fadlallah resisted all pressures to rule decisively on the matter. Although he publicly commented on the merit of individual operations, he generally avoided any blanket endorsement of the method, which remained highly problematic from the point of view of religious law. "In many cases,

[8] "Interview with Fadlallah, *al-Khalij* (Sharjah), 14 November 1983.
[9] Interview with Fadlallah, *al-Khalij*, 14 November 1983.

I stated that these martyrdom operations are not justified, except in very difficult cases. I can say that I have not issued any *fatwa* since the beginning of these operations and up to now. On the contrary, I am one of those who stood against all this commotion for *fatwas*. Despite the positive points which come out of this action, I believe that there are many negative points."[10] But this went without saying; it was his own philosophical assumption that "naturally, there is a positive aspect and a negative aspect to every event in the world,"[11] and "there is evil in everything good and something good in every evil."[12] No act of violence could be justified or condemned without knowledge of specific context. Having considered the specific circumstances of the operations, Fadlallah eventually gave them the fullest possible endorsement short of an explicit *fatwa*.

First, he said, no other means remained to the Muslims to confront the massive power commanded by the United States and Israel. In the absence of any other alternative, unconventional methods became admissible and perhaps even necessary. "If an oppressed people does not have the means to confront the United States and Israel with the weapons in which they are superior, then they possess unfamiliar weapons. . . . Oppression makes the oppressed discover new weapons and new strength every day."[13] The method itself redressed a gross imbalance in the capabilities of the competing forces. "When a conflict breaks out between oppressed nations and imperialism, or between two hostile governments, the parties to the conflict seek ways to complete the elements of their power and to neutralize the weapons used by the other side. For example, the oppressed nations do not have the technology and destructive weapons America and Europe have. They must thus fight with special means of their own. [We] recognize the right of nations to use every unconventional method to fight these

[10] Interview with Fadlallah, *al-Mustaqbal* (Paris), 6 July 1985.
[11] Interview with Fadlallah, *al-Nahar al-arabi wal-duwali*, 21 July 1986.
[12] Fadlallah Friday sermon, *al-Ahd*, 6 December 1985.
[13] Interview with Fadlallah, *at-Ittihad* (Abu Dhabi), 7 June 1985.

aggressor nations, and do not regard what oppressed Muslims of the world do with primitive and unconventional means to confront aggressor powers as terrorism. We view this as religiously lawful warfare against the world's imperialist and domineering powers."[14] The imbalance of power, coupled with the obligation of self-defense, therefore necessitated extraordinary and unconventional methods of waging war, because the oppressed stood at a distinct disadvantage in any face-to-face confrontation with the formidable forces of imperialism.

But although Fadlallah had established the need for unconventional methods, this did not constitute a clear endorsement of those unconventional methods that might also be in conflict with Islamic law, such as the self-destructive attack. One could not simply argue extenuating circumstances to a constituency devoted to the implementation of Islamic law. Here Fadlallah's argumentation became subtle. "These initiatives," he insisted, "must be placed in their context." If the aim of such a combatant "is to have a political impact on an enemy whom it is impossible to fight by conventional means, then his sacrifice can be part of a jihad, a religious war. Such an undertaking differs little from that of a soldier who fights and knows that in the end he will be killed. The two situations lead to death; except that one fits in with the conventional procedures of war, and the other does not."[15] Fadlallah, denying he had told anyone to "blow yourself up," did affirm that "the Muslims believe that you struggle by transforming yourself into a living bomb like you struggle with a gun in your hand. There is no difference between dying with a gun in your hand or exploding yourself."[16]

---

[14] Interview with Fadlallah, *Kayhan*, 14 November 1985; oppressed peoples "do not consider anything forbidden in the pursuit of these objectives. The legitimacy of every means stems from the legitimacy of the end sought"; interview with Fadlallah, *al-Majallah* (London), 1 October 1986.

[15] Interview with Fadlallah *Politique internationale* (Paris) 29 (Autumn 1985): 268.

[16] Interview with Fadlallah, *Middle East Insight* (Washington, D.C.) 4, no. 2 (June-July 1985): 10–11.

This point would ultimately constitute the crux of Fadlallah's argument: Deaths in suicide bombings are no different from more commonplace deaths of soldiers who enter battle knowing that some of them will not return but confident that their sacrifice will advance the common cause. "What is the difference between setting out for battle knowing you will die *after* killing ten [of the enemy], and setting out to the field to kill ten and knowing you will die *while* killing them?" Fadlallah argued that there was no difference. This the psychologists failed to understand. They had explained the operations as the necessary result of the "brainwashing" of the bombers, who had been "suspended in air in a magical paradise." But the psychologists knew nothing of oppression and how it moved men, for "he who has never known hunger in his life cannot understand the cries of hunger." There are Muslims who have set the aim of changing a certain political situation, and even if they die in doing so, their cause is advanced. The death of such persons is not a tragedy, nor does it indicate an "agitated mental state." Such a death is calculated; far from being a death of despair, it is a purposeful death in the service of a living cause. The suicide drivers who reportedly went "grinning" to their deaths were not contemplating paradise, as the media imagined, but were rejoicing in their hearts that they were able to advance their cause one step forward.[17]

Fadlallah thus retrospectively sanctioned operations that he believed had served the interests of Islam and had been carried out with full awareness of their purpose and consequences. But he himself would not issue a *fatwa*; nor would he acknowledge having sanctioned any operation in advance. He simply indicated that he had been approached by those

---

[17] Fadlallah's lecture was delivered on 18 July 1984 and published in pamphlet form under the title *al-Muqawama al-Islamiyya fil-Junub wal-Biqa al-gharbi wa-Rashaya* (n.p., n.d.), 16–19; it was also reproduced in the collection of Fadlallah's sermons and lectures entitled *al-Muqawama al-Islamiyya: afaq wa-tatallu'at* (Beirut: 1986), 48–51.

willing to make such a sacrifice out of a full awareness and that these sup-
plicants had been difficult to dissuade.[18]

Fadlallah's moral logic thus rested on two opposite but complemen-
tary assertions. The Muslims had just cause and need to resort to extraordinary means; yet the suicide bombings were not that extraordinary after
all, and his closer analysis revealed that those Muslims who perished in
such attacks died deaths that did not differ from battlefield deaths. These
were the complex mechanisms of moral disengagement that permitted
Islamic Jihad, in good conscience, to recruit and deploy young men in
suicidal missions. Unlike simple mechanisms of disengagement, which
culminate in dehumanization of "the other,"[19] these complex mechanisms allowed Hizballah's clerics to sanction the sacrifice of indisputably
human—Muslim—lives. It was the specificity of those lives that posed
the moral dilemma. Whereas a commander may know for certain that
some of the soldiers in his charge may die in a conventional operation, he
cannot know who among them will perish. It is God's will, or fate, or
random luck that determines who will die, relieving the commander of
direct and personal responsibility. But in the operations conceived by the
commanders of Islamic Jihad, it was impossible to displace responsibility
by the same simple process of dissociation. The clerics of Hizballah thus
fashioned the necessarily complex logic that reached its highest refine-
ment in the intellectualized reflections of Fadlallah.

Indeed, the moral logic of Fadlallah may have been too refined for
Hizballah's rank and file, for his ideas were often simplified in the pro-
nouncements of lesser clerics. A lesser cleric in Hizballah explained that
suicide operations could neither be sanctioned nor banned absolutely,

[18] Interview with Fadlallah, *al-Majallah*, 1 October 1986. Here, too, Fadlallah criticized the
American use of "psychologists and sociologists to come up with sensational phrases
that will be popular with world public opinion."
[19] For the crucial role of moral disengagement in terrorism, see Albert Bandura's article
in this volume (Chapter 9).

because their admissibility depended on circumstances and every Muslim was under a religious obligation to preserve his own life if possible. But those who carried out attacks for the good of Islam would go to paradise, and "we believe that those who carried out suicide operations against the enemy are indeed in paradise."[20] In contrast, Fadlallah never made explicit reference to the fate of the souls of those Muslims who died in the attacks. And others did not believe, as Fadlallah did, that his intellectual justifications were an adequate substitute for a formal legal ruling by a Muslim religious authority. According to one lesser cleric in Hizballah, acts of "self-martyrdom" (*istishhad*, as opposed to suicide, *intihar*) "were carried out by our youth under our inspiration. Some came to consult me about acts of self-martyrdom. I explained to them that this requires a *fatwa* from one of the highest authorities, that is, the Imams Kho'i or Khomeini, for a believer will do nothing without giving consideration to the principles of law." Three known men who carried out suicide operations against Israeli forces in South Lebanon were named as having "martyred themselves in accord with a *fatwa*."[21] For these acts to be accepted as legitimate, many in Hizballah found intellectual justifications necessary but not sufficient; hence the popular clamor for formal *fatwas*, to which Fadlallah himself alluded. Still, the logic of such *fatwas* would not have differed in kind from the public statements by Fadlallah and Hizballah's other leaders justifying the suicide operations.

Following the withdrawal of the MNF and successive Israeli redeployments southward, the options for operations that would produce a high number of enemy casualties diminished. As time passed, similar operations were undertaken by groups that were not aligned ideologically with Hizballah. And because of various countermeasures, potential targets of

[20] Interview with Shaykh Ali Yasin, *al-Liwa* (Beirut), 9 July 1984. This person, originally from Majdal Silm, directs an Islamic institute in Tyre.
[21] Interview with Shaykh Yusuf Da'mush, *al-Safir* (Beirut), 14 August 1986. This person is the prayer leader of the village of al-Saksakiyya.

such attacks became more difficult to reach and destroy, and some attempts took a significant toll in innocent Lebanese lives. At the same time, the fighters of Hizballah began to benefit from improved Iranian training in the Biqa Valley and were able to launch effective conventional operations against the South Lebanon Army.[22]

Under these altered circumstances, the method of the suicidal bombing attack was set aside. By late 1985, Fadlallah confirmed the change in approach: "We believe that suicide operations should only be carried out if they can bring about a political or military change in proportion to the passions that incite a person to make of his body an explosive bomb." Fadlallah deemed past operations against Israeli forces "successful in that they significantly harmed the Israelis. But the present circumstances do not favor such operations anymore, and attacks that only inflict limited casualties (on the enemy) and destroy one building should not be encouraged, if the price is the death of the person who carries them out."[23] Fadlallah, in essence, admitted that the legitimacy of this extraordinary method rested ultimately on its extraordinary success. When such success could no longer be assured, the many reservations that had been submerged beneath his moral logic reasserted themselves. Fadlallah and the Shi'ite clerics of Hizballah, men conscious of the dictates of Islamic law, could never allow that the mere success of these operations was their own justification. But once spectacular success began to prove elusive, all other arguments collapsed. Such attacks, done on what Fadlallah once described as "the Islamic pattern,"[24] were discontinued, and the issue ceased to figure in the running public commentary by the

---

[22] For Hizballah's own assessment of its military capabilities in the South (where it had about 500 men under arms), see *al-Ahd*, 12 December 1986.

[23] Interview with Fadlallah, *Monday Morning*, 16 December 1985. The Tyre and Metulla operations were those regarded as "successful."

[24] Interview with Fadlallah, *Kayhan*, 14 November 1985. Fadlallah specifically mentions the attacks on the MNF and the bombing of the "two Israeli spy centers."

leaders of Hizballah. Nevertheless, Sayyid Ibrahim al-Amin warned in 1986 that "suicidal operations may be used again" if opportunities presented themselves.[25] Hizballah's organization of a successful suicide bombing against Israeli forces in South Lebanon in October 1988 signalled that the method had been abandoned for tactical rather than moral reasons, and that it might be revived in changing circumstances.

[25] Interview with Amin, *Kayhan*, 9 February 1986.

Hamas Website

This text is from the Hamas English-language website www.palestine-info.com/hamas. The website gives us an unfiltered and revealing presentation of what Hamas is and what it believes.

HAMAS—IN THEIR OWN WORDS

Sheikh Ahmad Yasin
Founder of Hamas

Ahmad Ismael Yasin, born in 1938 in Al Joura village of Al Majdal District south of the Gaza Strip, took refuge in the Gaza Strip with his family after the 1948 war.

He was injured in an accident in his early youth while he was practicing exercises resulting in complete paralysis of all of his limbs.

He worked as a teacher of Arabic and Islamic education. Then he worked as a "Khatib" and a teacher in Gaza mosques. He became the most popular Khatib in Gaza in the years of occupation because of being a competent authority.

Chairman of the Islamic Complex in Gaza.

He was arrested in 1983 on charges of possessing weapons, forming a military organization and inciting others to remove the Zionist State. Sheikh Yasin was tried before a Zionist military court and sentenced to 13 years imprisonment.

Released in 1985 in a prisoners swap deal between the Occupation authorities and the Popular Front for the Liberation of Palestine—General Command—after having spent 11 months in jail.

Established the Islamic Resistance Movement, Hamas, in Gaza Strip in 1987 with a number of other Islamic activists.

The Occupation forces raided his house in late August 1988, searched the house and threatened to deport him to Lebanon.

On 18 May 1989, the Occupation authorities arrested him along with hundreds of Hamas supporters in an attempt to stop the armed resistance which took the form of "knives war" against the Occupation soldiers, settlers and collaborators.

On 16 October 1991, a Zionist military court sentenced him to life imprisonment plus 15 years. Sheikh Yasin was accused of 9 crimes, including inciting others to kidnap and murder Zionist soldiers and the establishment of Hamas and its military and security apparatus.

In addition to being completely paralyzed, Sheikh Yasin suffers from several diseases, including lost vision in his right eye as a result of injuries to it sustained at the hands of interrogators, weakness of sight of his left eye, chronic inflammation in his ear, bronchitis and some other diseases and inflammation of the stomach. His health had deteriorated because of detention circumstances that led to his being moved to hospital several times.

On 13 December 1992, a commandos group of Ezzul Deen Al Qassam Brigades kidnapped a Zionist soldier. The group offered to release the soldier for the release of Sheikh Yasin and a number of Palestinian and Arab prisoners in the Zionist jails. The Zionist government refused the offer and broke into the place where the soldier was hidden. The kidnapped soldier and the commander of the attacking unit were killed along with the members of the commando group in a house at Ber Nibala near Jerusalem.

Released on 1 October 1997 in a deal between Jordan and Israel against the extradition of two Zionist agents arrested in Jordan following the bungled assassination attempt in Amman on Mr. Khalid Misha'al, Chairman of Hamas Political Bureau.

• • •

Khalid Misha'al
President of Hamas Political Bureau

Born in Silwad of Ramallah (Palestine) in 1956.

Displaced to Kuwait in 1967 and lived there until the 1990 Gulf crisis.

Studied his primary schooling in Silwad and completed the intermediate, secondary and university studies in Kuwait.

Led the Palestinian Islamic group at Kuwait University and participated in the foundation of the Islamic Haqq Bloc, which competed with Fateh's blocs on leading the General Union for the Palestinian Students in Kuwait.

Holder of a Bachelor of Science degree in Physics from Kuwait University.

Married in 1981 and has seven children: three girls and four boys.

Served as a teacher of physics in Kuwaiti schools besides his engagements in serving the Palestinian Question.

Devoted himself to political work since his arrival in Jordan.

One of the founders of the Islamic Resistance Movement (Hamas).

Member of Hamas Political Bureau since it was established, then was elected as Chairman of the Bureau in 1996.

He escaped an assassination attempt on his life on 25 September 1997 in Jordan's capital, Amman, by Mossad agents. The assassination attempt failed when Mr. Misha'al's bodyguards chased and arrested the Mossad agents. Sheikh Ahmad Yasin, Hamas spiritual leader, was released from an Israeli jail as a result of this bungled attempt.

Martyr Yahya Ayyash
Leader of Ezzul Deen Al Qassam Brigades
The Engineer

Born on 6 March 1966 in Rafat near Nablus, north of the Occupied West Bank.

Completed his secondary school education in Rafat with an excellent grade that qualified him to study engineering at Beir Zeit University.

Received a Bachelor's degree of electrical engineering in 1988.

Married with two boys (Bara' and Abdel Latif).

Became active in the ranks of Ezzul Deen Al Qassam Brigades from the beginning of 1992. He specialized in making explosives from raw materials available in the Palestinian territories. Later he developed the martyrdom (suicide) bombings following the massacre of Al Ibrahimi Mosque in Hebron in February 1994. He was considered responsible for the martyrdom bombings, which made him a major target for the Zionists.

He was pursued for three years. The Zionists assassinated him after recruiting hundreds of collaborators to trail him.

He was killed in Bet Lahia, north of the Gaza Strip, on 5 January 1996 by a small explosive planted in a mobile phone he used occasionally.

About half a million Palestinians attended in his funeral.

Al Qassam Brigades carried out a series of martyrdom bombings to retaliate the assassination of Martyr Yahya Ayyash killing more than 70 Zionists and injuring hundreds.

Martyr Emad Aqel
Leader of Ezzul Deen Al Qassam Brigades in Gaza

Born in Jabalia camp of the Gaza Strip on 10 July 1971. His family was displaced from Bar'er village near Majdal in 1948.

He completed his secondary school education in 1988 and excelled the students in the camp.

He applied for admission to Al Amal Institute in Gaza to study pharmacology but soon was arrested by the Israeli authorities on 23 September 1988. He was tried on charges of affiliation with Hamas and participation in the intifadah activities. He spent 18 months in jail and was released in March 1990.

In the academic year 1991/1992, he was admitted in Hitteen College in Amman to study Islamic Sharia, but the Occupation authorities did not allow him to cross the bridge to Jordan.

In the beginning of 1991 he was nominated as a liaison officer between the "Martyrs group", the first militant group of Al Qassam Brigades, and the Brigades command. The Martyrs group basically specialized in killing the collaborators with the Zionists and collecting their weapons that were later used in military attacks against the Occupation patrols and soldiers.

Since 26 December 1991, the Zionists pursued him after some Hamas members under torture made forced admissions against him.

On 22 May 1992, he moved to the West Bank and formed several military cells there.

On 13 November 1992, he returned to Gaza after establishing the military work in the West Bank and after scores of Al Qassam militants in the West Bank were arrested.

He refused to leave the Gaza Strip in December 1992 and insisted to stay in Palestine.

On 24 November 1993, after two years of pursuit by the Zionists, the Zionist forces surrounded Shaja'eya quarter in Gaza and he exchanged fire with them. A number of Israeli soldiers were killed and Emad was attacked with an anti-armour shell in his face, killing him instantly.

Hamas is an acronym that stands for the Islamic Resistance Movement, a popular national resistance movement which is working to create conditions conducive to emancipating the Palestinian people, delivering them from tyranny, liberating their land from the occupying usurper, and to stand up to the Zionist scheme which is supported by neo-colonist forces.

Hamas is a Jihadi (fighting for a holy purpose) movement in the broad sense of the word Jihad. It is part of the Islamic awakening movement and upholds that this awakening is the road which will lead to the liberation of Palestine from the river to the sea. It is also a popular movement in the sense that it is a practical manifestation of a wide popular current that is deeply rooted in the ranks of the Palestinian people and the Islamic nation. It is a current which sees in the Islamic faith and doctrines a firm base in which to work against an enemy which endorses religious ideologies and plots which counter act all plans to lift up the Palestinian nation. The Hamas movement groups in its ranks all those who believe in its ideology and principles and all who are prepared to endure the consequences of the conflict and to confront the Zionist scheme.

In February of 1994, a Jewish terrorist settler called Barraugh Goldstein committed a crime against Palestinians who were praying in Al Ibrahimi Mosque in Hebron when 30 Palestinians fell martyrs and 100 others were wounded.

The conflict with Zionism in Hamas ideology

The Hamas movement believes that the conflict with the Zionists in Palestine is a conflict of survival. It is a conflict of civilization and determination that can not be brought to an end unless its cause—the Zionist settlement in Palestine, usurpation of its land, and the displacement of its people—is removed.

Hamas sees in the Hebraic state an antagonistic totalitarian regime, not just an entity with territorial ambitions, a regime that complements the forces of modern colonialism which aim to take hold of the nation's riches and resources and to prevent the rise of any grouping that works to unify the nation's ranks. It seeks to achieve this objective by promoting provincialism, alienating the nation from its cultural roots and clamping down on its economic, political, military and even intellectual hegemony.

The Hebraic state forms an instrument that breaks the geographic continuity of the central Arab countries, and it is a device to deplete the nation's resources. It is also a spearhead which is ready to strike at any project that aims to raise the nation up.

The main confrontations with the Zionist entity is taking place in Palestine where the enemy has established its base and stronghold. But the threats and challenges posed by the Zionists run deeper and so threaten all Islamic countries. Hamas believes that the Zionist entity, since its inception, has constituted a threat to the Arab countries and also in their strategic depth, the Islamic countries. The 90s witnessed huge transformations that highlighted this danger which knows no limits.

Hamas believes that the best way to handle the conflict with the Zionist enemy is to mobilize the potentialities of the Palestinian people in the struggle against the Zionist presence in Palestine and to keep the firebrand burning until the time when the conditions to win the battle have been realized, and wait until all the potentialities and resources of the Arab and Islamic nation are mobilized under a common political will and purpose. Until that happens and there is belief in the sanctity of the Palestinian cause and its Islamic importance and an awareness of the ultimate goals and dangers of the Zionist project in Palestine, Hamas believes that no part of Palestine should be compromised, that the Zionist occupation of Palestine should not be recognized and that it is imperative for the people of Palestine, as well as all Arabs and Muslims, to prepare themselves to fight the Zionists until they leave Palestine the way they migrated to it.

Military action in Hamas program
The Hebraic state represents an entity which is antagonistic to all aims of Arab and Islamic awakening, for it is known that had it not been for the state of deterioration and decadence through which the nation was passing, the Zionists would not have realized their dream of establishing their state in Palestine.

Recognizing this fact, the Zionists work against any program which they think would add to the Arab and Islamic capabilities. They believe that any attempts aiming at achieving an Arab and Islamic awakening constitute a strategic threat to Israel. The Zionists also believe that if Arab power was unified under a comprehensive program of awakening, it would pose a major threat to the Hebraic state. This conviction has prompted the Zionist leaders to transform their state from an alien entity in the Arab and Islamic surrounding to become part of it under the influence of economy. This explains why they support the (peace) settlement and promote projects with an economic orientation. It is within this context that the military action in the Hamas program should be viewed. Military action is the movement's strategic instrument for combating the Zionist element. In the absence of a comprehensive Arab and Islamic plan for liberation, military action will remain the only guarantee that would keep the conflict going and that would make it difficult for the enemy to expand outside Palestine.

Hamas believes that Israel's integration into the Arab and Islamic region would hamper every plan that seeks to uplift the nation.

Hamas resistance against the occupation is not directed against the Jews as followers of a religion, but rather against the occupation, its existence and oppressive practices. This resistance is not associated with the peace process in the region as alleged by the Hebraic state and the supporters of the current settlement. The resistance was there before the convening of the Madrid Conference; and the movement has no hostilities or battles with any international party, nor does it target the interests of the properties of the various countries. This is because it considers that the scene of its battle against the Zionist occupation is limited to the Occupied Palestinian Territories. When the Zionist officials threatened to transfer the battle with Hamas to areas outside the Occupied Territories, Hamas warned the Zionist authorities against the serious dangers of such a step. This testifies to the fact that Hamas does not wish to enlarge the circle of the conflict.

External Relations

1. Hamas believes that the difference in opinions over developments does not prevent it from contacting and

cooperating with amiable parties that are prepared to support the steadfastness of the Palestinian people.

2. Hamas is not interested in the internal affairs of countries and does not interfere in any government's domestic affairs.

3. Hamas seeks to encourage Arab and Islamic countries to resolve their differences and to unify their attitudes towards national issues. However, it does not side with one party against the other, nor does it accept joining one political axis against another.

4. Hamas believes in Arab and Islamic unity and blesses any effort made in this respect.

5. Hamas asks all Arab and Islamic governments and parties to assume their responsibilities to endorse the cause of our people and support its steadfastness against the Zionist occupation and to facilitate the work of our movement towards achieving its mission.

6. Hamas believes in the importance of dialogue with all governments and world parties and forces irrespective of faith, race or political orientation. It remains ready to cooperate with any side for the sake of the just cause of our people and for informing the public about the inhuman practices of the Zionist occupation against the Palestine people.

7. Hamas does not seek enmity with anyone on the basis of religious convictions or race. It does not antagonize any country or organization unless they stand against our people or support the aggressive practices of the Zionist occupation against our people.

8. Hamas is keen on limiting the theater of confrontation

with the Zionist occupation to Palestine, and not to transfer it to any arena outside Palestine.

9. Hamas expects the world's countries, organizations and liberty movements to stand by the just cause of our people; to denounce the repressive practices of the occupation authorities which violate international law and human rights; and to create a public opinion pressurizing the Zionist entity to end its occupation of our land and holy shrines.

Hamas' position towards other liberation movements

As a resistance movement that confronts the occupation and Israeli racism, Hamas sympathizes with the world's liberation causes and supports the legitimate aspirations of people that struggle to get rid of occupation and the policy of racial discrimination. Hamas stood with the South African people in their struggle against apartheid and welcomed the change that put an end to the apartheid policy that was prevailing there.

excerpt from:

The Hunt for the Engineer
by Samuel M. Katz

Yehiya Ayyash was the master Hamas bombmaker known as the
Engineer. Until his death in 1996 he was the most feared terrorist operating in the Occupied Territories. Ayyash produced dozens of explosive
devices that killed hundreds of Israelis, mainly bus and car bombs. The
opening excerpt describes the mass shooting at the Hebron mosque by
Baruch Goldstein in February of 1994 in which fifty worshippers were
killed. This attack immediately escalated the conflict. After a series of
successful bombings, we learn that the Engineer was elevated to a
hero's status to most Palestinians. We read of the destructive power of
one of Ayyash's bombs in a Tel Aviv bus. We see the Israeli police
threatening the Engineer's mother and learn about an Arab informant
who agrees to help set him up. Ayyash is given a cell phone containing
a small amount of plastic explosive. He receives a phone call and the
mini-bomb detonates, killing him instantly. Samuel Katz is a journalist
and author who has written about terrorism, special military operations
and law enforcement.

t had been a cool winter by Middle Eastern standards, and rainfall had been plentiful. The hills around Hebron, usually barren for eleven months of the year, had begun to blossom in a miraculous explosion of green surrounded by oceans of white and purple wildflowers. The promise of the Oslo Accords had provided many with the hope that spring would bring about an end to the killing. Israeli forces were to begin withdrawing from Jericho and Gaza shortly. For the first time in recent memory, the Moslem holy month of Ramadan was a festive one.

Early on the morning of February 25, 1994, some seven hundred children and adults had gathered inside Hebron's Ibrahim Mosque at the Cave of the Patriarchs. The sun had yet to rise over the jagged peaks across the Jordan River to the east, and a slight drizzle had begun. At 5:20 a.m. a man wearing olive-drab fatigues and sporting captain bars on his epaulets and a purple sports bag over his shoulder approached the northeast entrance of the mosque. He calmly walked up to the guard on duty and demanded to be let into the usually off-limits prayer area. He had already passed through an Israeli Army checkpoint where four soldiers, pulling the last hours of night duty, waved him in. The Arab guard on duty knew the man was a resident of Kiryat Arba. He had seen him before around the no-man's-land that separated Muslim and Jewish worshippers at the shared holy site. He knew the man was a fervent supporter of the militant Kach movement.

Mohammed Suleiman Abu Sarah made every attempt to keep the officer out of the building, but there was little he could do. "It is forbidden," Abu Sarah told the captain. But in a city run by the IDF, there was little the unarmed Arab could do. As he tried to resist the captain, a man wearing a yarmulke hit him with the metal stock of his Galil assault rifle, knocking him to the ground. Abu Sarah was lucky. His life was spared.

That man from Kiryat Arba was Dr. Baruch Goldstein, a Brooklyn-born native and a physician who, one Friday morning during the month of Ramadan and the Jewish festival of Purim, simply snapped. Throughout history, men seeking spiritual salvation had traveled to the Holy Land only to succumb to passion and insanity. But Goldstein had crossed the invisible line of mental health armed with an assault rifle capable of firing 550 rounds per minute.

The mosque was packed to capacity. Cradling his weapon, Goldstein watched as the prayer services commenced. Worshippers knelt on plastic mats, eyes closed, as they offered their devotion to God, foreheads touching the ground in respect. Without warning, the physician peered through the sights of his IDF assault rifle, squinted his left eye to lock down on his targets, and, with the fire-selector switched to semiautomatic, he began to squeeze the trigger. Goldstein's barrage was not indiscriminate—he was taking aim for head shots. Blood sprayed on walls and on prayer carpets. Pandemonium ensued. Those attempting to flee stepped over the dead and the dying. Children screaming in anguish sought their fathers who, covered in blood and paralyzed by fear and disbelief, watched their sons killed before their eyes. According to survivors, it was impossible to tell who was hit and who wasn't because everyone was covered in blood.

Goldstein's murderous spree was methodical. When one thirty–round magazine of ammunition was spent, he inserted a fresh clip into his assault rifle and continued firing in deliberate bursts. Goldstein took great care not to waste ammunition. He had brought seven magazines with him that fateful Friday morning—210 lethal 5.56 mm bullets—and in 10 minutes of incessant gunfire he managed to squeeze off 110 rounds. As Goldstein removed a spent clip from the red-hot barrel of the Galil, a mob that had taken cover behind a wall rushed him in one desperate attempt to end the madness. Before he could insert a fresh magazine in his assault rifle, Dr. Baruch Goldstein was cornered by the mob and bludgeoned to death with a fire extinguisher. Goldstein's end was brutal. The angry mob ripped the Brooklyn-born physician's body to shreds.

Just as chaotic was the attempt to rush the wounded to local hospitals. The sound of gunfire and the screams of the victims alerted Israeli forces, who, faced with a human stampede of some seven hundred frantic souls, panicked; some of the soldiers posted at the Tomb, fearing that they were the targets, fired at the crowds. There was a mad scramble to ferry those suffering from horrendous gunshot wounds to the emergency room. Parking lots turned into triage centers. Dr. Goldstein's one-man crusade had been an efficient one. Some fifty Palestinians had been killed that Friday morning and more than seventy had been seriously wounded.

As a high-ranking battalion commander in the Izzedine al-Qassam Brigade, Yehiya Ayyash knew that some sort of military response to the Hebron massacre would be forthcoming. This was a crime that demanded swift and unforgiving punishment. But Ayyash was not allowed to commence an offensive on his own. He could select targets, pinpoint times and locations, and determine the means, but, according to a Jordanian intelligence official, "He was permanently at a traffic stop waiting for either the red or green light. When he had a red light, he did what all law-abiding citizens do. He stopped. When the green light was issued, though, it meant free reign and great liberty to inflict as much damage as humanly possible."

The orders to mobilize Ayyash's cell came via fax, from either Teheran or Damascus, Shin Bet officials believe, disseminated through a third country with direct phone links to Israel and the Territories and then handed down to its final recipient via a long list of messengers. One would receive the message from a political director and leave it in a dead drop, somewhere public, where another operative would retrieve it and deliver it to a third dead drop, who would then pick up the note and deliver it personally to Ayyash. The last link in the chain was the most trusted member of the cell—usually the second in command, for he was, in reality, the only person who knew where Ayyash would be at any given time. It was a highly circuitous method for transmitting operational directives, but it was secure, and security was sacrosanct to Hamas.

To avenge the Hebron massacre Hamas would enact suicide bombings against the very lifeline of Israeli society: its ability to move from point A to point B. The attacks would be indiscriminate and unforgiving. When the order was received to avenge Hebron, Ayyash went into action. There were devices to design and construct, and martyrs to recruit who would bring the war directly to the enemy.

Yehiya Ayyash had managed to insulate himself from the inner workings of Izzedine al-Qassam operations, commanders, and cell leaders. Only a handful of men whose dedication and loyalty were unyielding—even inside the bunker of a Shin Bet holding cell—knew where he was at any one given time. Hamas operators lucky enough to receive a one-day seminar in the art of explosives from Ayyash had no idea, up until the start of class, who they'd be meeting or what they'd be studying. Since no one willing to talk knew his whereabouts, he was impossible to pinpoint or trap. And since he had become a master of disguises in what was closing in on his third year on the run, fewer still knew what he looked like. His narrow face, spectacles, and intelligent grin had by the spring of 1995 become front-page imagery in newspapers throughout Israel and the Middle East, though he could have been any one of the million or so people milling about in the West Bank at any given time. He had mastered camouflaging himself as an old man and even an old Arab woman. His small library of Majd-supplied identity papers, passports, drivers licenses and even gun permits was dazzling. Indeed, according to legend and intelligence reports, Ayyash's favorite disguise was that of an Orthodox Jewish settler or even an Israeli Army reservist. At least dressed as one of the enemy he'd be allowed to carry a weapon and, if everything looked alright at first glance, be permitted to drive through checkpoints unhindered and armed to the teeth.

Following the Beit Lid bombing, Ayyash's legendary stature throughout the Territories grew by leaps and bounds; many Palestinians understood the necessary evil of bombing civilians, though killing soldiers, the dreaded tools of the Intifadah, was cherished, even by those not toeing the Hamas line, as holy work. Shin Bet agents pursuing leads to Ayyash's whereabouts were stymied by the legend. According to one popular story that had become folklore in the Territories, Ayyash was cornered in a safe house near Rafatt by the Shin Bet and the undercover squads. After holding off the advancing Israeli teams for hours in pitched battles, angels descended from heaven to pluck Ayyash to safety as bewildered Israeli commandos and agents looked on. Children in village elementary schools swore that they saw Ayyash personally kill Shin Bet agents with his trusted assault rifle. According to one law enforcement official working in the American embassy in Tel Aviv, "To the Palestinians in the territories, Ayyash was like Babe Ruth, Jackie Robinson, Audie Murphy, and Santa Claus wrapped up into one terrifying package!"

The legend of the Engineer grew each day he wasn't killed or caught. "I see him with Israeli soldiers surrounding him," Muyasser Ayyash, Yehiya's sister-in-law, told reporters. "They are about to kill him but he turns invisible and walks right by them." The more Shin Bet agents pressed the family members in Rafatt about his whereabouts; the more anonymous tips turned out to be dead ends; the more men and women who ended up in Shin Bet interrogation rooms; the grander the legend became. When Shin Bet agents drove through certain West Bank towns and villages en route to a meet, or to simply reconnoiter the terrain, they were met with verbal fusillades, some tossed by kids, promising that no one will ever be able to find the Engineer because he is a ghost and a hero. But what angered many in the Shin Bet, and indeed the Israeli special operations community was the fact that by having such little success in the pursuit they had helped contribute to the Engineer becoming a cult figure.

Yehiya Ayyash wasn't just a fugitive, he was a national hero. Folk songs were written about him, parents began naming their first-borns Yehiya, and women embroidered tablecloths with his image. Yehiya Ayyash had become the Palestinian version of a rock star, a sports hero, and a national leader. He was seen as an elusive enigma that was larger than life and more powerful than the region's most acclaimed intelligence service. Worse, the myth of one man humbling the vaunted Shin Bet and Mossad was a word-of-mouth recruiting poster for those wanting to martyr themselves.

The soldiers, spies, and policemen who hunted Yehiya Ayyash were angered by the legend and the taunts they received from the locals but not humbled. They were battling the clock. "We all knew that if we get him, perhaps even as he was building a device, it would mean one less massacre," claimed a former Ya'ma'm team leader. "We knew that each day that went by that we didn't get the SOB, the odds that a bus would blow up or a group of shoppers would be incinerated by a blast became more likely." Many of the soldiers and spies on the trail of Ayyash were on the verge of burnout, an operational hazard rarely talked about in Shin Bet circles. Following pointless leads took its toll on men who were nurtured by determination and caffeine. Agents, especially seasoned veterans of the hunt, were frustrated beyond words by their complete lack of success in getting to Ayyash. Many began to take the hunt personally. "Anger could never become a part of the equation, nor could vengeance," according to Ya'akov Perry. "The agents in the service need to remain focused on being professional, otherwise their effectiveness is compromised."

Many agents believed that Ayyash had long since fled the West Bank and had found safe haven in Gaza, where getting to the wily bomb maker would be difficult but not impossible.

• • •

On the hot and muggy morning of July 24, 1995, the No. 20 bus was making its way south on Jabotinsky Street, past the Ramat Gan Diamond Exchange, to the entrance of the Tel Aviv city limits. The Monday morning rush hour was typical Tel Aviv—a slow crawl through choke points jam-packed with vehicles. Passengers on board the bus contemplated yet another day when they'd be late for work. Bus driver Moshe Ilan, a fifty-five-year-old veteran of the frustrating reality of Israeli gridlock, carefully maneuvered the rectangular box of a bus through the narrow lanes and packed thoroughfares.

The passengers that morning had little time to notice a young man with a dark complexion attentively gazing out the window as he read-justed his yarmulke over his close-cropped spikes of black hair. He carried a knapsack and a blank and vacant stare. At precisely 8:40 a.m., he pressed a small button affixed to the strap of his pack. A blinding flash of light was followed by the complete blackness of heat, smoke, and death. Seats melted in the fiery gush, windows were blown fifty feet, and anyone in the path of the shrapnel and fire was killed instantly. Hands and legs, blown from their bodies, were strewn about the bus and on the street below. Motorists and pedestrians around the bus hit the pavement for cover and then raced to the bus to pull victims out of the wreckage. Five people died that morning, and an additional thirty were seriously wounded.

There had always been certain unwritten rules etched in the Shin Bet's playbook as to what they could or wouldn't do in counterterrorist opera-tions. Suspects, informants, or any of the other characters that came across their path could be manipulated, threatened, roughed up, and, in some cases, tortured; but a different set of rules had always applied to women, especially Muslim women. In a region of the world where butchery was an accepted practice of settling disputes, sexual respect had remarkably been maintained. Israeli troops and Shin Bet agents were always taught to never touch an Arab woman, and never question her alone, without a chaperone nearby. The rulebook was not always adhered to, but the Shin Bet had a markedly superior record to their Palestinian counterparts who, according to claims made by Amnesty International, had routinely threatened male prisoners that their wives, mothers, and sisters would be raped before their eyes if they did not cooperate, confess or compromise fellow operatives.

Political correctness and cultural sensitivities had not brought the Shin Bet any closer to getting its hands on Yehiya Ayyash, however, and, three years into the chase and some seventy bodies later, it was time for the rules to change.

Aisha Ayyash was dragged out of her house just before 4:00 amid the cries of her family; it was just early enough to avoid a large-scale riot by villagers and the handful of armed Hamas men who lived in Rafatt. The Shin Bet raced the Engineer's mother to its holding facility inside the Russian compound in Jerusalem, where the local police maintained a sprawling headquarters. Investigators interrogated the sickly woman without respite about her son's whereabouts, though they all knew he was, in the best-case scenario, in Gaza, and in the worst-case scenario teaching new pupils in a classroom in Khartoum in Qom. But Aisha's arrest was a maternal pressure point designed to cause Ayyash's insides to buckle. Shin Bet agents wanted Yehiya to think about his mother inside the grueling and inescapable box of a Shin Bet interrogation room, and they wanted him to think about the hands of the filthy and hated Shabakniks touching the matriarch of a family at the center of the Jihad. According to Hamas folklore, Aisha managed to smuggle a note from prison to her son, pleading for justice. "Oh my beloved son," the note elaborated, "they arrested me because I delivered you. They tied me up, burned me, and much, much more!"

On October 29, 1995, the Ramallah Military Court issued an indictment against the mother of the Engineer. The official charge was "utilizing
forged documentation to enter the Gaza Strip;" the military prosecutor
contended that Aisha had illegally crossed into the Palestinian Authority to
meet with her son, and to cooperate with a "hostile terrorist organization."
The legal action was designed to elicit a response. Sons have done remarkable things to keep their mothers from harm's way. Shin Bet agents were
hoping that Ayyash was man enough to expose himself to the crosshairs.

In the operational scheme of things, the fact that Ayyash was inside the
confines of Gaza was a source of comfort to the Shin Bet agents hunting
the Engineer. Unlike the West Bank, with its vast stretches of terrain and
endless caves, wadis, and groves, Gaza was basically an imprisoned slum-
state without the expanses of forests, mountains, plains, or lowlands.
Gaza's one window to the sea, its Mediterranean shoreline, was constantly
watched by the vigilant eyes, and 20 mm cannons, of Israeli Navy patrol
boats. It was doubtful that the Egyptians would allow Ayyash to cross the
Rafath checkpoints into Sinai; Mubarak, after all, had learned his lesson in
providing safe passage to terrorists who had killed Americans following
the bungled Achille Lauro seajacking. And, even if he made it to the West
Bank, it would be doubtful if the Jordanians would not arrest him on
sight. Ayyash was trapped. He was hiding inside a city of squalor and
prying eyes. He had been swallowed up by the mysterious depths of an
angry and volatile human sea. But that human sea was desperately poor,
and it routinely gave up its most valued resources if the price was right, or
if the pressure points were squeezed just tight enough.

The Palestinians had turned a blind eye to Ayyash's presence in Gaza,
as well as to much of the Hamas infrastructure that openly strutted its
power and potential inside the Strip's myriad refugee camps. Blindness

had been prudent. Ayyash was merely a nuisance to be tolerated in Gaza. But November 4, 1995, changed everything. Rabin's death made Ayyash expendable. Suddenly, counterterrorist cooperation between the Palestinians and Israelis, sometimes at the behest of the CIA station chief in Tel Aviv, began to flourish.

In an interview with the daily newspaper *Ma'ariv*, former deputy director of the Shin Bet Gideon Ezra described the hunt for Ayyash as more of a challenge than an obsession. One of the most beguiling aspects of the challenge was the search for the one Achilles' heel that would betray Ayyash and provide the Israeli hunters with an "in." Once an "in" had been established, the remaining aspects of any operation, whether it be an arrest, a kidnapping, or an assassination, were merely technical in nature and limited to the scope and flair of the case agent's imagination. Finding an "in" with Ayyash was incredibly difficult. "He was one of the most paranoid individuals I had ever come across," claimed an Israeli police special operations officer who hunted Ayyash, "and paranoia sparked intuition, and that intuition drove him to be incredibly careful." Yet paranoia is a pitfall for life ruled by fear—especially for someone who was determined to live for his wife, son, and future-born. Ayyash's life on the run turned him cold, bitter, sad, and tired. His life on the run became a jog instead of a dash. He stopped sleeping in a different bed every night. He began to trust confidants and school chums. He provided the Israelis with the "in."

Yehiya Ayyash had, as a result of his "larger-than-life" reputation inside the West Bank and Gaza Strip, enjoyed the hospitality of a good many anonymous strangers eager to do their part in the struggle by hiding him for a night, providing him with identity papers, or trekking to Rafatt with gifts and notes for his family. The help provided by the owners of the safe houses was greatly appreciated, but it could not be trusted. Noble gestures are, after all, often suspect in a guerrilla war. In Beit Lahiya, in Gaza, Ayyash came across Osama Hamad, a Hamas operative and close friend from his days at Bir Zeit University who offered him a place to stay, apartment 4 in one of his uncle's houses, a two-story building at No. 2 Shaheed al-Khaluti Street. The shelter wasn't luxurious, but it was far from prying eyes.

Ironically, Hamad's house was located only fifteen hundred yards from the Israeli frontier at the Erez checkpoint. It must have given Ayyash considerable satisfaction to be able to wake up in the morning and look directly into Israel and realize he was untouchable. The house on Shaheed al-Khaluti Street was also only fifty yards from one of the largest Palestinian police stations in Gaza. He assumed the name of Abdullah Abu Ahmed and communicated with his Hamas commanders through messenger—and with his parents, courtesy of cellular phone.

When news of Ayyash's new identity and new landlord reached Shin Bet HQ, through a surreptitious route of information that remains classified, the name "Hamad" set off alarms. Searching through the massive Shin Bet computer database, agents came across Osama's uncle, Kamil Hamad, a forty-three-year-old real estate broker, car salesman, and jack-of-all-trades who had managed, quite miraculously, to build a small fortune in one of the poorest spots in the world. Hamad was also a merchant in that always-valuable Gaza commodity known as information—he had been a low-level Shin Bet informer for nearly twenty years.

In exchange for information and other amenities, the Israeli authorities, at the Shin Bet's request, had helped Hamad grow wealthy in Gaza, often excusing him from paying taxes, duties, and other forms of required levies that broke the back of many an honest businessman. It was a lucrative relationship for Hamad, and he became a useful asset for the Shin Bet. But the Palestinian Authority was clamping down on tax dodges and demanding exorbitant sums from Gaza's richest citizens. Hamad's profits decreased and the riches were dwindling. Only those in the Arafat inner circle had any hope for riches in the new and autonomous Strip.

Hamad had attempted to court key individuals in the security services, and he was seen at lavish dinners with General Musa Arafat as well as the offices of military intelligence officials. Hamad had, through his contacts with General Arafat, arranged the release of Osama after he was arrested in the Strip following the summer bombing wave in Ramat Gan and Jerusalem. Izzedine al-Qassam commanders were intrigued by his connections and wary of his clout. Hamad became a VIP in Hamas circles. He was a man to be trusted—and protected.

Kamal Hamad was a character straight out of an espionage film. He was, claims a former A'man officer, "worthy of a John Le Carré novel." Rich enough to maintain two armed and well-dressed bodyguards and three wives ranging in age from forty-two to twenty, Kamal Hamad had fathered eighteen children and, reportedly, was involved in raising fifteen "luxurious" apartment blocks in the sands of Gaza. But instead of investing in real estate, where the savvy made a killing in Arafat's Gaza, Hamad invested heavily in building on other people's properties. His expenses skyrocketed. His line of credit with banks in Israel, and the Cairo-Palestine Bank in Gaza, diminished. His building projects were stopped cold in their tracks—often incomplete and with a trail of investors demanding their money back; the flats he was building, which he often sold to the well-connected and powerful in Gaza, ended up as nothing more than drywall cubes without running water or electricity. Hamad was in trouble. Former Shin Bet informants with a fondness for Mercedes sedans, English-tailored suits, and trips to Europe with pretty young women walked a tightrope when they teetered on financial ruin. He would be lucky to survive, let alone keep any sliver of his empire.

To the majors, colonels, and generals of the Palestinian intelligence services, Hamad was a cash cow who would secure them fancy homes and penthouse apartments at a fraction of the going price. To the Israelis, he was an asset, a screw to be turned. He was the "in."

One sunny and unseasonably warm afternoon, Kamal Hamad ventured into Israel to retrieve two Mercedes sedans he had purchased and was waiting to clear through customs at an Ashdod dockyard; one car was to be a bribe to General Musa Arafat, and the second was to serve as a "family" car. As he dealt with the bureaucracy of his customs paperwork in a secluded port office, Hamad was approached by several Shin Bet agents. The contact was reestablished—an old working relationship rekindled. Before Hamad left Ashdod, he found an envelope with several thousand dollars in the glove compartment of his car and a bill for one shekel—less than thirty cents—that he owed customs for the two cars. Business was back to normal.

According to reports, the Shin Bet had been slowly turning the screws on Kamal Hamad as far back as early 1995 when they learned that he had, through his real-estate holdings, been helping Hamas fugitives in Gaza find shelter and work. In October 1995, Hamad met with a high-ranking Shin Bet official responsible for the southern command known only by his nom de guerre of Abu Nabil. Abu Nabil, a veteran of the counter-espionage games in Gaza, was after information—detailed information. Hamad wasn't opposed to becoming a shill in the Israeli hunt for Ayyash, although he wanted a contract with the Shin Bet in which the General Security Service would guarantee Hamad's safety and, most important, his fortune. He also wanted Israeli identity cards for himself and his wives. The Shin Bet didn't cut contracts with informers, even invaluable ones, and Abu Nabil bargained hard with the Palestinian developer, realizing that Hamad had little choice and few options. If he refused to help the Shin Bet, all it took was an anonymous tip to Hamas, the jihad, or even the Palestinian Authority, that Hamad was a long-standing helper of the dreaded Shabak and he was as good as finished; all the gold in Gaza didn't protect a traitor from a horrid death. The Shin Bet was not in the mood for demands and requests. The agents wanted information and access.

With the "in" in their hands, the agents on the trail of the Engineer needed to assemble an accurate dossier on Ayyash and a plan on what to do with him. Kamal Hamad was asked to provide his handlers with an incredibly intimate portrait of Ayyash. Where did he sleep? When did he wake up? When did he shower? When did he go to the bathroom? Who visited him? How did he communicate with the outside world? The Shin Bet was looking for the one chink in the Ayyash armor that could technically be exploited.

Ayyash had, true to form, lived the life of a pious fugitive. Most of his days were spent in prayer, or at work, teaching the basics of improvised bomb-making to classes of new cell commanders being prepared for the continuation of the struggle. Life on the run must have been lonely and boring for Ayyash. Separated from his wife, his son, and his parents, telephone conversations with his family at Rafatt were his only contacts. Because land-line communications were most certainly monitored by the Shin Bet, as well as the Palestinians, the Ayyash family maintained a link by cellular phones.

Israelis called them *Pelephones*; the Arabs, unable to pronounce the letter *P*, called them *"Bilephones."* With more than two million cellular telephones in use inside Israel and the West Bank, it is an obsession that Jew and Arab shared equally. The addiction to the small phones originated with the old socialist monopoly that once controlled phone service in Israel. Israelis often had to wait a dozen years for a phone line—service was erratic, expensive, and light years behind the United States and Western Europe. In the Territories, phone service was a hundred times worse. When cellular phone service came to Israel, anyone could finally have a phone—no waiting list and no payoffs. In fact, cellular phone rates were sometimes cheaper than land-line charges, and the connection was far clearer. Cellular phones became an Israeli obsession. Bathers in the Mediterranean carried phones with them into the chest-high surf, and couples on double dates often communicated with one another, at opposite ends of a cinema, by a cellular phone. In the West Bank, cellular phones were often the sole means of communication between villages left without phone service by the Israeli authorities. Ironically, Ya'akov Perry, following his retirement from the Shin Bet, became CEO of Cellcom, Israel's most successful cellular carrier.

The cellular phone was the one means by which Ayyash could be monitored, tracked, and, if possible, eliminated. If he carried the phone with him at all times, the Israelis could electronically track and trace his movements; knowing the phone's number, the Israelis could monitor his conversations and, perhaps, be waiting for him in a dark alley one night instead of a Majd team transferring him to another safe house. It was even possible to booby-trap a cellular phone with a small explosive charge that, when placed to the head, would shoot fire and shrapnel into the target's brain.

Rigging a phone with explosives was nothing new—in fact, it was a Mossad innovation that had been used with lethal results. On January 9, 1973, Dr. Mahmoud Hamshari, the Black September commander in France, answered the telephone inside his second-story apartment in a middle-class Paris neighborhood. "May I please speak with Dr. Hamshari?" the voice asked with a distinctively native Parisian accent. "This is Dr. Hamshari" was the firm reply. A switch igniting a high-frequency signal connected to a detonator and a hundred grams of Grade A plastique put an end to the call. The explosion was a relatively small one, but the results were major. Hamshari, one of the architects of Black September's 1972 Munich Olympics massacre, died hours after much of his face had been blown off.

The prospects of rigging a cellular phone were intriguing—and challenging. The explosive charge would have to be very small. It would also need to be a shaped charge, concentrating the maximum destructive force into one intended area. The device would also have to be small enough in order not to interfere with the day-to-day functions of the phone, and it needed to be light enough so that the person clutching the deadly device to his ear would not be suspicious. For the planners of the operation, there was also a significant—and all-important—consideration. Only the target was to be harmed—innocent civilians killed or wounded in the collateral blast would not be acceptable. The device would be outfitted with a safety to ensure that a radio signal from a walkie-talkie or a kid's remote-control toy did not detonate it. The planners needed to be absolutely certain that it was the target placing the phone to his head seconds before the explosion. The phone that Dr. Hamshari was holding when it exploded was rigged with a safety device which was disabled only after the assassin had made absolute voice confirmation of the target's identity. Hamshari lived with his wife and small child and it was imperative that they were to be spared from harm.

In getting to Ayyash through a cellular phone, the operational challenge was not what to do with the phone: that was technical. The main obstacle was getting their hands on his phone.

For the operation to succeed, it was crucial for Hamad to believe that the cellular phone ruse would be used only for eavesdropping purposes. "Listen," Abu Nabil Hamad is reported to have told Hamad, "we know he sometimes spends time in your house and we know that he communicates with other Hamas big-shots from your property. All we want to do is for you to help us eavesdrop on Ayyash. That's it. This way we can intercept the bombers before they kill lots of women and children. You don't want to see more innocent people die, do you? We know that every few weeks he changes his cellular phone number. Just let us know the next time it happens, and we'll take care of the rest."

According to former Shin Bet deputy director Gideon Ezra in an interview with Israeli television, operations targeting an individual aren't openly sanctioned—or ordered—by the higher political authorities, but rather handled at the operational level and approved by management. Approval usually required a foolproof plan as well as an opportunity. January 1996 was seen as the ideal time to handle this lingering matter. Elections in the Palestinian Authority were scheduled for January 20, and many in Hamas would be more occupied with the political campaign waged against Arafat for the ballot box, than in the security of a man who, though teaching a future generation of craftsmen and martyrs, had outlived his operational usefulness.

Paranoia had been the staple that kept Yehiya Ayyash alive for a remarkable three years on the run. Paranoia had made him savvy, smart, and successful. Ayyash knew the Shin Bet was still gunning for him, no matter how demoralized the service might have been over the Rabin assassination. Yet there were reasons for concern, even from within the ranks of Hamas. Political infighting had turned ugly inside the political hierarchy, inside the al-Qassam cells, and inside the Majd. The detention of Musa Abu Marzouk and the continued Israeli adherence to Oslo II, even in the aftermath of the Rabin assassination, persuaded many of the Young Turks that the time was ripe for an all-out suicide campaign to settle the score once and for all. The politicians in Damascus and Teheran, however, opposed wanton bloodshed. Assets had to be deployed as needed, not in one massive show of bloodshed that was bound to backfire politically. Hamas, for the first time in its successful terrorist campaign, had begun to splinter, and there was even talk of an armed conflict between opposing camps. Ayyash now had to watch his back from the men he had so faithfully served, while also guarding against Arafat's men and, of course, the Shin Bet and Mossad.

By January 1996, with his wife and son safely smuggled into Gaza and living in a safe house a kilometer away, Yehiya Ayyash began to settle into a routine existence, although he was still suspicious and extremely careful. When he would visit Heyam, he never came at the same time or announced his visits; according to his wife, he often came to the door in costume, dressed as a woman. If there was one weakness he displayed that winter, even after his wife and son were safe and sound in the Strip, it was his longing for Rafatt and his parents. He phoned them regularly and at regularly scheduled times. "You can take the bomber out of the village," commented a Jordanian intelligence officer, "but you can't take the village out of the bomber." Ayyash was a prisoner of his longing for his mother and father—and he was concerned about the incessant Shin Bet attention the family received.

The phone calls home lasted longer and longer. Even men responsible for the deaths of nearly ninety women and children get homesick. The calls were made about once every two weeks. Ayyash had spent a long time on the phone with his father on December 25, after Heyam had given birth to a bouncing baby boy. Ayyash was proud and happy; he wanted his father to see the newest addition to the family. The next conversation was scheduled for the morning of January 5.

Ayyash had always suspected that the Shin Bet was listening in to his phone conversations, and he would change the phone he was using once every few weeks. From time to time the clarity of the calls would go from okay to terrible. Static would fill the lines, as would weird high-frequency sounds.

At the same time, Kamal Hamad had purchased a cellular phone for Osama at the Nabil's electronics store in Gaza City—the phones came from Israeli dealers who marketed them through local agents. Hamad's phone, ostensibly, was to be used for the nephew to communicate with his uncle when working at one of the family's properties, or when Hamad traveled on business to Israel or the West Bank. Osama routinely allowed his friend in college to use the phone; in fact, Ayyash used the phone with such frequency that he passed the number, 050-507497, to his father, Abdel-Latif Ayyash, as *the* number by which he could be reached. Yet before handing off the Motorola telephone to his nephew, Hamad brought it to his Shin Bet handlers. It is widely believed that Hamad Kamal had no clue what the handlers would do with the phone. He probably thought they'd plant a microchip eavesdropping device somewhere in the circuitry that would enable men with earphones on their heads to pick up, with great clarity, everything that Ayyash told his parents and his comrades in the Izzedine al-Qassam Brigade. When Hamad received the phone back, it looked exactly as it had before. It was still in off-the-shelf, out-of-the-box condition: it didn't smell any different or weigh any more and, most important, it worked well.

By January 1996 the Shin Bet had suggested to Hamad that he take a brief leave of absence from the Gaza Strip. There was nothing suspicious about Hamad leaving the beauty and splendor of the strip on a dark and cold winter's night. He had managed to get through the frontiers during closures and during firefights before. Business was business, and in the gray no-man's-land between Israel and the Palestinians, money talked louder than gunshots.

On January 5, Yehiya Ayyash returned home at 4:30 in the morning. Darting down the alleys of Beit Lahiya to shake any Israeli—or Palestinian—surveillance, Ayyash passed garbage cans and stray cats. He was dressed as a woman, cradling his Glilon assault rifle under his gown. Once home, Ayyash prayed, then munched on a light snack at a table adorned with a map of Tel Aviv next to a smaller table topped with electrical tape, wires, pipes, and circuits. Before laying his head on a plush mattress adorned with three large pillows, he checked the table to see if Osama Hamad's Motorola phone was on.

Wearing nothing but a pair of purple briefs, Ayyash slept for a few hours, the way he had slept for the past three years: with one eye open and one ear listening for the ominous sound of footsteps. A small transistor radio had been turned on, the volume knob angled as low as it would go so the news broadcasts were still audible. The first rays of daylight had yet to emerge from the dark purple-and-orange skies that foretold of an impending rainstorm. Rain did not mix well with the Gazan landscape. Unpaved roads turned to mud, poorly constructed roofs leaked, and the stench of uncollected trash and open sewage lines were stirred up in the cruel harsh rains of January. Winter in Gaza made any West Bank native long for the open splendor of plush green hills and the smell of olive trees and citrus groves.

At a command post just outside the barbed wire forest that separated Gaza from the rest of the world, near the Erez checkpoint some fifteen hundred yards from the house at No. 2 Shaheed al-Khaluti Street, a group of men wearing blue-and-green winter parkas juggled field radios, cellular phones, black boxes, and field glasses. The men were impatient. The sound of a small-engine prop-driven plane flying was heard overhead. Eyes scanned the frontier into Gaza through field glasses that had been carried on endless stakeouts in front of the house in Rafatt and the safe house in Nablus.

At 8:40 a.m., Osama Hamad's Motorola cellular phone rang. Rushing to his worktable, Ayyash rubbed his eyes and grabbed the ringing phone with his right hand. Majd officers had warned Yehiya that cellular communications were easier to monitor. Ayyash's father had tried to reach his son on the regular phone in the Hamad house, but mysteriously the line had not been working properly all week—most people trying to reach the residence heard a busy signal. So, with a backup number at his disposal, he tried the cellular phone.

Abdel-Latif Ayyash had told his son that he had been trying, since 8:00 a.m., to call on the land line but it had been busy. As the two men spoke, the low-flying plane that had been buzzing Beit Lahiya leveled at a cruising altitude. The plane was nondescript, a trainer it appeared, and bore no markings linking it to any nation. The passenger, cradling a black box with a switch, a red light, and a green light, listened attentively to his headset as it relayed a link to the command post down below.

Father and son spoke in brief and affectionate sentences. "How are you father?" was the last words heard at the end of telephone number 050-507-497. When Abdel-Latif Ayyash tried the number again, all he received was a recording from the connecting service informing him that the line was unavailable.

The Engineer would have appreciated the technical mastery involved in the construction of the bomb that killed him: its light weight simplicity, its miniaturized might. Fifty grams of RDX explosives molded into the battery compartment of a telephone had been designed to kill only the man cradling the phone to his ear. The force of the concentrated blast caused most of the right side of Ayyash's face to implode around his jaw and skull; shrapnel and energy raced into his brain. A slab of flesh hung over his premolars; a burnt and smoldering nub of flesh had replaced his ear. The booby-trapped cellular phone had been so ingeniously built, and so target specific, that the left side of Ayyash's face had remained whole. The right hand which held the telephone was neither burnt or damaged.

Yehiya Ayyash, "The Engineer," the most wanted man in modern Israeli history, was dead.

excerpt from:

Dollars for Terror

by Richard Labeviere

The political and social forces at work in the Middle East and Asia are complex and often contradictory. Richard Labeviere, a Swiss journalist, analyzes this world with great clarity. He presents the interests of the major national powers in the region: Egypt, Saudi Arabia, Iran and Pakistan. He places a good deal of blame squarely on the shoulders of the U.S. government for its unquestioning support of the Afghan rebels. He relates U.S. oil politics in Central Asia to our tolerance for the dictatorial policies of the Taliban government, a government that was in negotiations with American companies to build energy pipelines across the country until bin Laden bombed the U.S. embassies in Africa in 1998. He ties bin Laden's success closely to his shadowy relationship with the Saudi power structure and shows how the Saudis aggressive advocacy of Wahhabi extremism in Afghanistan and Pakistan is essentially indistinguishable from extremist jihad. He demonstrates how the exporting of jihad is the best guarantee that the Saudi's have for preserving domestic peace. Ultimately Labeviere believes that the lack of any consistent U.S. policy in the region encouraged fundamentalists to believe that they could conduct jihad without serious consequences. In this excerpt Labeviere details the slick maneuvers of the Saudi regime as it finds various ways to hide support of the radical brand of Islam it ultimately favors.

n the Pantheon of those who "made America," President Roosevelt occupies a unique position, since he played the role of the father of the great oil adventure. A few weeks before the Yalta Conference, the president read with the greatest attention Senator Landis's report on American interests in the Middle East. Fundamentally, this text (which became the White House bible on Arab affairs) predicted the imminent break-up of the "sterling zone" and the establishment of direct relations between Washington and the Arab countries. On his way back from Yalta, Roosevelt—who made a stopover in Egypt—asked the American consul in Jeddah to organize a meeting with the King of Saudi Arabia. The meeting took place on February 14, 1945, on board the *Quincy*, a cruiser anchored in the great lake Amer between Port-Saïd and the mouth of the Suez Canal. We owe the most detailed account of this interview to an expert on the Arab-Muslim and Turkish worlds, Jacques Benoist-Méchin. The meeting put an end to what had been, for a century and a half, a private hunting preserve for His British Majesty. With all the honors due to the head of an important state, Ibn Sa'ud boarded the cruiser. A shade of fine white muslin was stretched across the bridge to allow the king to sleep in the open air during the crossing of the Red Sea. Very sure that this hospitality would not fail to have its effect on the old Bedouin, Roosevelt extended both his hands and exclaimed,

"So glad to meet you . . . What can I do for you?"

"But it is you who asked to see me," retorted the old warrior, adding, "I suppose that it is you who have something to ask of me!"

After this rather rough start, the two men talked for several hours in the shade of the artillery on the upper bridge. King Ibn Sa'ud remained inflexible on the future fate of the Jews of Palestine. Roosevelt asked him to accept this infusion of population while pointing out to him that it would constitute only a very small percentage of the total population of the Arab world. The president returned two or three times to the subject by different routes, but each time encountered a total and absolute rejection.

Attempting to relax the atmosphere, Roosevelt tackled a second subject, the American high command's need for harbor infrastructures in the Arab-Persian Gulf. The king was more conciliatory, although he asked for much in return. Lastly, the president broached the most important question, which he had kept for the end: oil. He wanted the kingdom to grant the United States a monopoly on the exploitation of all the oil-bearing layers discovered in Saudi Arabia.

Ibn Sa'ud, who had carefully prepared for the interview, negotiated hard on each American request. Finally, the discussion would lead to an agreement that has been baptized the "*Quincy* Pact." It is articulated around five sets of themes that still apply:

1) The stability of the kingdom is in the "vital interests" of the United States. In and of itself, the kingdom holds 26% of the world's proven oil reserves. Its importance as an essential supplier became clear to the Americans during the Second World War, when other sources of supply were cut off by the Japanese occupation. Traditionally choosing a policy of moderate prices, the kingdom guarantees that the bulk of America's fuel need will be met. In return, the United States ensures unconditional protection against any possible external threat. In 1991, American engagement in the second Gulf War constituted a spectacular illustration of "*Quincy* Pact." Ibn Sa'ud did not lose an inch of territory. The concessionary companies are to be tenants only. The duration of the concessions is to be sixty years. "Upon the expiry of the contracts, i.e. in the year 2005, the wells, the installations and the material are to return entirely to the monarchy's possession. The premium paid to the king is to go from 18 cents to 21 cents for every oil barrel exported from Arabia. The Aramco concession is to be extended to a territory covering 930,000 square miles."

2) By extension, the stability of the Arabian Peninsula is also in the "vital interests" of the United States. Indeed, American support of the

kingdom is based not only on its capacity as oil supplier at moderate prices, but also on hegemonic power over the Arabian Peninsula. The United States thus jointly controls the priority task of the House of Sauds' "Arab diplomacy": to guarantee the stability of the Peninsula and more generally of the entire area of the Gulf. "Since the first wells were beginning to be exploited," one oil expert specifies, "Aramco, the American governmental oil company, ensured the kingdom all kinds of legal, even military, aid in the dispute between the Sauds and the other emirates of the Peninsula." While it now takes other forms, this assistance is still topical.

3) An almost exclusive economic, commercial and financial partnership continues to link the two countries since the adoption of "*Quincy* Pact." The United States increases its oil purchases in exchange for more and more substantial deliveries of American weapons. Shortly after the Gulf War, the United States signed the largest contracts (and on exclusively political criteria) to the detriment, of course, of other members of the anti-Iraqi coalition. This preferential treatment of American contractors does not apply to the weapons sector alone. One may cite the example of the contract for modernizing the Saudi telephone network, allotted to an American firm in 1994, on the basis of a simple phone call from President Clinton, whereas other partners were objectively much better positioned. Because of pressures from the American government, the contract for refurbishing Saudia Airlines airliners in 1995 was given to Boeing and McDonnell Douglas, a preference that was both technologically and economically unfounded. In return, experts estimate that some $350 billion (public and private) in Saudi funds are directly invested in the United States, especially in Treasury bills. One might easily think that the kingdom is maintaining this "American preference" as an insurance policy.

4) American non-interference in questions of Saudi domestic politics is the flip side of the American preference in economic, financial and commercial matters. Usually so prolix any time the question of human rights

comes up anywhere in the world, the American government here observes a muteness that is both constrained and absolute. "The most powerful liberal democracy in the world is indeed allied with an absolute monarchy by divine right," comments a European diplomat, "a monarchy that is, on social and political matters, one of the most obscurantist regimes on earth." The United States government is unable to close this question, which constantly threatens to put it in an embarrassing position vis-à-vis the public opinion that is so quick to flare up over whatever indignities the media selects. "Indeed, the Saud monarchy is, today, hardly more justifiable than the Pahlavi one was in Iran, just before the Islamic revolution," adds the diplomat. Being unable to provide an adequate justification on this significant subject, the American government tries to minimize, if not to deny, the question that regularly comes up in "confidential proceedings" at the U.N. Commission on Human Rights. In addition, one is obliged to note that the American mass media, usually so attentive to these problems, do not get particularly agitated over these cases.

5) The only dark area in the "*Quincy* Pact" is the Palestinian question. This marks the limit of the American-Saudi partnership. Indeed, whereas President Roosevelt was not able to extract from King Ibn Sa'ud any agreement on the increase in Jewish immigration to Palestine, the kingdom never could obtain from Washington the least flexibility with regard to its policy of unconditional support for the State of Israel. While the American administration completely supports the House of Saud in its hegemonic rule over the Arabian Peninsula, it leaves it very little room for maneuver in the Israeli-Palestinian process. It is, however, within the narrow confines of this corridor that the Islamist movements are financed.

The discussion then turned to the construction of a Trans-Arabian pipeline, a tube some 1240 miles long, intended to connect the oil-producing region of Hasa to a port on the eastern Mediterranean. And Jacques Benoist-Méchin concludes that "In spite of the slightly rough turn that the conversation had taken at its beginnings, Roosevelt and Ibn Sa'ud were left enchanted with each other. They both had the impression that they had made an excellent deal."

An excellent deal, an unfailing alliance and an "old story," the pact sealed on board the *Quincy* marked a decisive break in the history of the international relations of the post-war period. Nothing would be the same any more. By evicting the British influence, this pact establishes the United States as the dominant partner in the Middle East game, to the detriment of the European states. Lastly, it ratifies a bargaining method that persists and continues to be used as the model for other agreements of the same type, especially in Central Asia.

This historical bargain would prove to have many consequences: black gold for the security, survival and continuity of what is one of the most reactionary religious dynasties in the world and, moreover, guardian of the holy places of Islam.

This last reason, too, is strategic on two accounts. By circumscribing the emergence of lay Arab nationalism, this protection also makes it possible to ensure the security of the state of Israel. These two requirements may, however, seem contradictory. We will see, on the contrary, how they connect the two sides of the same process whereby Islamism constitutes a common thread. On board the *Quincy*, the American president and the king of Saudi Arabia not only concluded an "excellent deal." They also secured an unfailing alliance that would lead them, one and the other, and their successors as well, to becoming the godfathers of Islamism.

Saudi Arabia plays the lead role in financing contemporary Islamist movements, within the Arab-Muslim world but also in Africa, Asia and Europe. In August 1996, an "influence" meeting was held in Madrid during which Riyadh endeavored to get a grip on the "Islamic centers" that were the beneficiaries of its largesse. Saudi Arabia finances this "checkbook diplomacy" to buy legitimacy and peace while exerting its hegemony over Sunni Islam; only Shiite Iran seeks to dispute its control. Obsessed with this goal, upon which the survival of their dynasty depends, the Sauds have created a whole battery of powerful financial tools. Dar al-Mal al-Islami (DMI), the "Islamic financial house," is a kind of model. Other banks, innumerable foundations and "humanitarian organizations" ensure continuity between the checkbook and policy decisions, the most visible of which is Riyadh's unfailing support for the totalitarian regime of the Taleban. The Sauds' "Arab diplomacy" focuses on three areas: the Arabian Peninsula; the Middle East; and the Western world. The "American insurance policy" guarantees this diplomacy in exchange for direct access to the greatest oil reserves in the world. The security of the kingdom of Saud is thus part of the "vital interests" of the United States.

The cradle of Arab identity and of Islam, Saudi Arabia asserts these two claims with pride. It seeks to foster a double network of influence and solidarity—one that considers the Muslim world as a whole, and the other targeting the Arab world, starting with the Peninsula and, to a degree that declines over the distance, extending to the gates of the Near East. Consequently, the House of Saud invests a great deal of money in "Muslim" and "Arabic" diplomacy, two different concepts, the stakes and the developments of which do not, in the long-term, coincide. Islamism and its factions are influenced by both these spheres of influence, which are themselves dependent on the special relationship entertained with the United States since the kingdom was founded.

Islam and "Arabity" are not one and the same thing. Even if most Arabs are of Muslim faith (Arabic being the sacred language of the youngest monotheist religion), most Muslims are not Arab. Indonesia, with its 220 million inhabitants, is the most populous Muslim country, ahead of even the Muslim communities of India and Pakistan. Thus the Muslim world is far greater than the Arab world, in terms of both quantitative and qualitative stakes. Its demographic weight and its geopolitical importance open opportunities upon which the Saud dynasty, obsessed with security and survival, wants to be able to rely if necessary. Indeed, the fact that Saudi Arabia is one of the richest countries of the world makes it extremely fragile and vulnerable.

Occupying most of the Arabian Peninsula and covering some 1.4 million square miles, its population hardly exceeds 12 million, including 4 million immigrants. By way of comparison, its turbulent neighbor Yemeni claims 15 million inhabitants on a territory smaller than France (330,000 square miles). This disproportion is even more salient when measuring wealth. In Saudi Arabia, the GNP per capita is thirty times superior to that of Yemen, ten times greater than that of Egypt and five times greater than what Syria claims. In such a context, one can easily understand that the House of Saud, managing the country like its own property, seeks to contain its neighbors' envy and prefers influence over confrontation.

Looking for "diplomatic" ways to secure a position of central influence within the Muslim world as well as in the Arab world is one of the country's major concerns. This partially explains the constant aid that Saudi Arabia has rendered to Islamist movements since the foundation of the kingdom. "The Saud family," wrote Alain Chouet, "pays particular attention to all those in the Sunni world and in Arabia proper who, like the Muslim Brothers, could elevate the debate over who holds the reins of power to the plane of religion; for that reason, Riyadh strives to fill the role of religious leadership to the greatest possible extent." To fill the religious space completely, to preserve the peace and maintain its monopoly over the political arena, those are the main objectives of the Saudi Club.

Beyond this intangible geometry, Saudi Arabia has woven a network of international, governmental and nongovernmental forces, secular, religious, economic, humanitarian and political organizations, to relay its influence throughout the Arab-Muslim world. Superimposed on this cartography of interlocking apparatuses, the private initiatives of the House of Saud and the Princes form only the most visible layer of the complex construction of the kingdom's "Muslim diplomacy," a discreet diplomacy that advances under cloak and mask. It is imperative that we examine this cartography if we wish to comprehend the "masked strategy," which is the main beneficiary of contemporary Islamist movements.

Within this nebula, the Organization of the Islamic Conference (OCI) plays a central role, since it represents a kind of U.N. of the Muslim world. Created after the Islamic Summit of Rabat (1969) to divide and the unmanageable and "too socialist" Arab League, the OCI is the kingdom's latest tool for imposing its diplomatic priorities. Thus, from the very start of the Soviet intervention in Afghanistan, the OCI launched a call to "holy war" against the infidel invader. Some time later, it condemned "Khomeinism and Shiite activism," before passing along the kingdom's views favoring the Muslims of Bosnia, Chechnya and more recently Kosovo. With some fifty member countries, its permanent secretariat is in Jeddah.

Equipped with considerable financial clout, the Conference controls several "technical agencies;" the main one is the Islamic Development Bank, created in 1973 to finance infrastructure and development plans in Islamic countries. It is a semi-secular, semi-religious institution. 25% of the bank's capital is held by the State, and its financial strategy is aligned with the kingdom's political-religious decisions. Lately, the BID raised the ceiling on its loans to Pakistan from $150 to $400 million to help it handle the sanctions imposed following its nuclear tests.

There are other instruments in this Islamic financial toolbox. "Development funds from OPEC for international businesses, with 30% Saudi capital; the Arab Bank for Economic Development in Africa (24.4% Saudi capital); "Arab Funds for Economic and Social Development;" and, with a capital of $21 million, the "Saudi Development Fund," which is fully funded by the kingdom. Until now, the principal recipients have been Pakistan, Tunisia, Algeria, Syria and Lebanon.

Let us add the specific or regular granting of direct budgetary aid that is a means of influence on recipients like Egypt, Syria (especially after the Israeli-Arabic war of 1973) and Yemen. Obviously, the amount of these donations is a "state secret." Generally, Saudi Arabia uses its own financial instruments and its investments in international organizations to encourage "brother countries" and its own objectives.

Copied on the system of the United Nations, the other major "agencies" of the OCI are the Academy of Muslim Law and Isesco, the Islamic Organization for Education, Science and Culture, created in Islamabad in 1981 as a kind of Islamic UNESCO. Its sponsorship of the Madrid conference is perfectly in line with its areas of concern, which relate to the protection of Muslims living in non-Muslim countries. In opposition to UNESCO, it formulates its interventions in terms of clashes and confrontations; in spite of its calls for a "dialogue of cultures and civilizations," its creators have very well grasped the geopolitical impact of cultural activity.

In order to create a shadow of the U.N.'s system of international organizations with Islamic equivalents, Saudi Arabia sponsored the drafting of "an Islamic Declaration of Human Rights," opposing the "Universal Declaration of Human Rights" of 1948. Although it was a founding member of the U.N. in 1945, Saudi Arabia did not ratify this declaration and has no intention of recognizing it. Examining the kingdom's tools of "Muslim diplomacy" in this way illustrates one of the major principles of the House of Saud. "The dynasty and the great families," explains a European military attaché, "share the conviction that the universality of Western culture is factitious and that to escape its influence it is necessary to promote a Muslim counter-culture that will redeem all of humanity."

The World Islamic League is one of the principal tools by which they exploit Islam at the international level. Created in December 1962, as an outgrowth of the "Islamic summit" convened that year in Mecca by King

Fayçal Bin Abdelaziz, its statutes provide that its General Secretary must be of Saudi nationality and have a diplomatic passport. In 1995, King Fahd himself nominated Abdullah Bin Saleh al-Obaid. One of his predecessors became the vice-president of the Majlis al-Choura (the Consultative Assembly); the grand mufti of the kingdom, Abdulaziz Bin Baz, is president of its legal committee. Represented in 120 countries, it remains an essential foreign policy tool of the Saudis.

"The League, or the organizations that depend on it, has to its credit several spectacular constructions in Europe: the Islamic Center of Brussels and the mosques of Madrid, Rome, Kensington and Copenhagen," writes the journalist Antoine Sfeir, editor of *Books of the East.* "In France, the League does not directly intervene in financial arrangements. It is used as an intermediary for advising and directing possible investors. It thus lent a hand to the National Federation of Muslims of France (FNMF) when it needed it. It helps projects that are on the verge of bankruptcy: the mosque of Mantes-la-Jolie, launched with the joint generosity of Morocco and Libya, was finished thanks to that of the Saudis. Similarly, the mosque in Evry proved to be a financial black hole and cost the League nearly $5 million."

A small part of the oil revenue is thus devoted to the construction of mosques and Islamic centers everywhere in the world: Ottawa, Quebec, Toronto, Brasilia, Lisbon, Gibraltar and Zanzibar . . . the mosque of the Islamic Center of Rome caused a great fuss because the plan for its minaret was higher than the dome of Saint-Peter (as well as the giant mosque of Bethlehem). Indonesia, Japan, South Korea, New Zealand, the Fiji Islands, Argentina, Mauritania and Djibouti have also benefited from Saudi generosity. Today, the kingdom finances 875 Islamic societies and centers in the world.

The Sauds' "Muslim diplomacy" is also expressed through the financing of charitable societies and other charitable institutions whose activities always fall somewhere between the religious, the political and the humanitarian. It would be tiresome as well as useless to enumerate an exhaustive list. Let us cite only the World Association of Muslim Youth, and the Organization of the International Islamic Relief Organization— IIRO, whose publications are particularly aggressive with respect to other religions, especially Christianity.

This last organization, which funds many "missionaries" abroad, uses them as the intermediary in maintaining relationships with most, if not all, of the known Islamist groups. A subsidiary organization of the World Islamic League, the IIRO was deeply involved in Bosnia, and President Izetbegovic regularly traveled to Riyadh to request financial aid from his co-religionists. The material and financial support available to these "missionaries" makes one wonder whether one of their roles, and perhaps their primary objective, is to acquire the favor or the neutrality of the impoverished countries toward which they are directed, toward the Iranian intrigues and competition from Shiite expansionism.

"In the same way, Saudi 'charity' with regard to 'minority or oppressed Muslim populations' in Palestine, Afghanistan, Somalia, in Bosnia at one time, in Chechnya and Kosovo today, is hard to see as being disinterested," explains an expert in Islamic finances. He adds: "Nevermind what all the official statements claim, it is not Islam but money that is at the heart of the Saudi system." In addition to the State apparatuses and the official foundations, these "diplomatic funds" require such fluidity and such silence in the face of any probing that it became necessary to create banking fronts as discreet as they are effective.

In 1981, in the backrooms during the Islamic summit in Taëf, Mohammed Bin Fayçal al-Saud, brother of Prince Turki's brother, brought together major investors from Saudi Arabia and the United Arab Emirates to create a private Islamic bank, Dar al-Mal al-Islami. DMI, the "Islamic financial house," shares a headquarters in the Bahamas with the bank of the Muslim Brothers. The Sudanese Islamist leader Hassan el-Tourabi took part in setting it up. One year later, King Fahd charged his brother-in-law, Sheik Saleh Kamel, with launching another private Islamic bank, Dallah al-Baraka ("the blessing").

Thus opened a new axis of Saudi financing for Islamism. Via these two banks the innumerable Islamic nongovernmental organizations, the Saudi agencies of influence for "Muslim diplomacy" would be funded.

In terms of traditional foreign policy, Saudi Arabia's ambitions are shaped according to the impact they can have on the Peninsula and the Gulf region. They thus delimit a strictly finite arena centered on the geographical cradle of the dynasty. This area opens three angles whose amplitude increases as one moves away from the center from gravity.

The first angle is formed by the Peninsula, baptized the island of the Arabs, "Jazirat al-Arab". For most Saudis this constitutes the true center of the world, because it is the home of the Arab people chosen by God to disseminate the revelation of his beneficence. "This 'insular' conscience should not be underestimated," explains a European diplomat stationed in Riyadh. "It adds to the meaningfulness of the vision according to which the Arabs (in particular) and the Muslims (in general) are surrounded by a hostile world against which they must defend themselves." The political, economic and cultural independence of the Arabic peninsula, backdrop of Islam's two holy places, is clearly the primary objective of the Saudis' "Arab diplomacy". And to demonstrate that he is still on his own territory, the King does not delegate to his powers to the Crown Prince when he visits a country on the Peninsula, whereas he usually does so whenever he travels abroad.

This "sovereignty by proximity" rests on making the small Emirates into satellites and dividing or isolating Yemen, which is too large and too populous to be neutralized in the same way. The "satellization" of the smallest neighbors, in particular Bahrain, Qatar and Kuwait, has not encountered any major difficulty up until now; but the same cannot be said for the United Arab Emirates (UAE) and Oman, which have the means to assert an economic and political autonomy. Since the discovery of the first oil reserves, the Saudis have sought to create more than a simple union of oil-producing nations, a sort of oil patriotism. "The expression 'Arab oil' has quite a precise meaning, both political and economic. It is the sense of jointly sharing a resource, and a wealth that gives the Arabs strength vis-à-vis the Western powers that dictated their law to them for centuries."

This "oil patriotism" benefited from the Iran-Iraq war (1981) by being formalized, through the creation of the "Council of Cooperation of the Arab States of the Gulf" (CCG), from which Yemen is naturally excluded. Financed mainly by Saudi Arabia, the CCG (whose headquarters is in Riyadh), actually functions like a sound booth to record and broadcast the decisions of the House of Saud, which is thus ensured of maintaining its undivided supremacy over its "private preserve," whose only unknown factor resides at Sanaâ. "The good fortune of Arabia depends on the misfortune of Yemen, as light is dependent on the sun;" the Princes heard this historical pronouncement from King Abdulaziz on his deathbed. It is true that since this last word, Riyadh has not spared any effort in seeking to divide Yemen into two mutually hostile States. Therefore the reunification of July 1994 is seen in Riyadh as a policy failure.

The Saud continue, in any case, to talk tough in Sanaâ, on the frontier dispute that opposes the two countries as well as on the million Yemeni immigrant workers expelled from Saudi Arabia during the Gulf War. Having taken sides with Saddam Hussein, Sanaâ lost a major source of foreign currency. Hostile on principle to international arbitration, Saudi Arabia wants to treat these questions as a "package," and in a strictly bilateral way. Thus it is ensured of being able to take advantage of the Yemenis' unfavorable financial situation while "buying," here again, security, allegiance and peace from neighbors who are proud, savage, and unpredictable, and who regularly hold—horror of horrors—legislative elections.

The second angle delineates the "Near Middle East." Here too, "Arab diplomacy" can be summarized as "buying and dividing, to rule." Pan-Arabism was never very much favored in Riyadh, which remains indifferent if not frankly hostile to the Arab League which it suspects of latent laicism. The Nasser version of Arab nationalism is seen as the devil incarnate by the kingdom, which was always hostile to the United Arab Republic (Egypt-Syria), playing a subtle balancing game between the two ba'as-ist enemy brothers, Iraq and Syria.

Today, the Sauds entertain good relations with Syria, which preserves a traditional reverse alliance against Israel, and against Iraq since 1990. If necessary, this could prove useful against the Hashemites of Jordan, historical enemies whom the Sauds dispossessed of Hedjaz and the holy places at the beginning of the century. Everything augurs well for future relations with Damascus, since one of the designated Crown Prince's wives—Hassa al-Chaalane—is Syrian and, what is more, sister of the wife of Rifaat el-Assad, the brother of the Syrian president, who is thus the brother-in-law of the next King of Arabia. These family and tribal relations can only consolidate a Riyadh-Damascus axis.

Relations with Egypt are currently characterized by nonaggression and by economic cooperation; more than a million Egyptian nationals work in the kingdom. Over time, this work could be threatened with "Saudization" in order to give jobs to the kingdom's youth: more than half the population of Saudi nationality, today, is under the age of 30. The kingdom would compensate for this loss by increasing its direct subsidies of the Egyptian budget. Indeed, several foreign ministries acknowledge that Cairo is already given substantial Saudi aid, although no numbers are given.

"In fact," a former French ambassador to Riyadh summarizes, "Saudi Arabia forms (with Egypt and Syria) a self-sufficient 'decision-making triangle' for everything that generally relates to shaping the Arab attitude with respect to the Palestinian question. It is an undeniable success of the Sauds' 'Arab diplomacy'." Indeed, it is traditionally admitted that no war against Israel is possible without Egypt, and no peace without Syria. In spite of its significant funding capacities, Saudi Arabia—a giant banker, but a dwarf soldier—is in no position to be a major actor in the Israeli-Palestinian process. But, in this "decision-making triangle" with Egypt and Syria, it is placed on an equal footing with two Arab partners that are strategically much greater than itself.

Lebanon is emblematic of the immense Saudi capacities of financing, and is a tactically key for Saudi sponsorship of Islamist movements. Having little strategic importance—even though it is on the front line vis-à-vis Israel—Lebanon indeed arouses Riyadh's interest completely out of proportion to its weight on the regional scene. All the great Saudi families are economically omnipresent in Beirut, and Riyadh regularly supports the exchange rate of the Lebanese currency. The principal pan-Arab newspapers, initially Lebanese, are controlled today by Saudi finance; the Lebanese former Prime Minister Rafic Hariri himself owes a good share of his personal fortune to the royal family, which conceded to him a quasi-monopoly over the construction and maintenance of innumerable Princely palaces, as well as major public works projects. Furthermore, he holds a Saudi passport, thus making an exception to the rule that formally precludes dual citizenship with Saudi Arabia.

Having become one of the principal financial outposts of the kingdom, Lebanon is located at the crossroads of the Sauds' Arab and Muslim diplomacies. In Lebanon, a Saudi "financial protectorate", all the underwriters and the beneficiaries of Saudi "generosity" meet. To counter the pro-Iranian Hezbollah engaged against Israel in southern Lebanon, but now represented in the Lebanese parliament, the Saudis employ the same "recipe" they apply everywhere: they use money. This is a perilous approach, because the benefit is not always proportional to the cost. Thus it sometimes happens that Islamist factions financed by the Saudis turn against their benefactors.

Here we are touching on a major difference between the Iranian school and the "Saudi" approach. Until the end of the war in Lebanon, Iran's approach guaranteed it complete control of the distribution channels, from the origin of the funds to the execution of the operations, even the material organization of influence and its political dividends. The Sauds too often consider, even today, that giving money is enough to control the whole process. In short, "checkbook diplomacy" à la Saud does not provide for after-sales service.

The last angle embraces the Western world. Most of the countries comprising this area remain little known, or unknown, to most Saudis (including members of the royal family) except as seen through the American prism. Saudi diplomacy does not follow any particular principle vis-à-vis the West; rather it displays a thorough sense of pragmatism in defending its interests, particularly through very large investments. Indeed, money from the State and from Saudi private individuals is heavily invested in various sectors of the developed economies.

It is not the least paradox that Wahhabi money thus participates in the prosperity of a Western world that is not only laic but is regarded as diabolical; the royal family and the Princes encourage the development of this "antimonde" that is decadent, even dangerous for the future of the Arab world and the religion of the prophet. "Islam does not have an evangelical contempt of wealth," write Simonne, Jean Lacouture and Gabriel Dardaud. "The prophet was an active and prosperous merchant. The Koran, which does not include any 'sermon on the mount'" and which takes care not to praise the state of poverty, does not place any man above the honest tradesman."

According to several financial experts, the amount of money the Sauds have invested in the West is incomparably greater than the amount devoted to the propagation of Islam. More awkward for the Saudi dynasty, the monarchy's detractors use this "blasphemous" imbalance as a basis for their argument.

In fact, it is precisely to seek to exonerate themselves of this charge that Saudi Arabia continues to finance the most radical Islamist movements. The monarchy hopes thus to bring into better balance its commercial activities and its religious investments. The "profane part" of a system based on money, made up of unverifiable gifts and return gifts, the financing of Islamism ends up melding into a swirl of interconnected financial and commercial activities.

This system that the Saudis ended up generating was built for more than fifty years under the eaves of American protection. The United States has pursued this policy since it first began to exploit the Saudi oil concessions. Unconditional protectors of the House of Saud, they take care of any internal and external problems. While seeing the kingdom's stability as part of its "vital interests," the United States endeavors not to interfere in the monarchy's Arabic policy. The CIA is, however, omnipresent inside the kingdom, and in the external operations of the Saudi secret service.

In spring 1998, according to various reliable sources, the palace gave a $25 million check to Sheik Yassin, the chief of the Palestinian Hamas. Although they were perfectly well aware of what was happening, the U.S. agencies strangely did not do anything to prevent this payment being made, even though anything that strengthens the hand of Hamas weakens the Palestinian authority of Yasser Arafat. In spite of the U.S. State Department's appeals and efforts to reinforce the economic aid to the Palestinian Authority, the CIA continues to preserve, if not to promote, the interests of Hamas. In this sense, the U.S. agency plays the same role as its Israeli homologue, going along with an approach that was largely favored by Netanyahu's entourage which, in the long term, was counting on an intra-Palestinian war.

In this respect, the Israeli secret services also remained passive in the face of major weapons deliveries to the armed branch of Hamas during

1998. A military attaché stationed in Tel-Aviv explains that "Shin Beth (Israeli internal security and counter-espionage) is persuaded that the death of Arafat will inevitably start a Palestinian civil war that will blow the Palestinian Liberation Organization apart, as well as the political and military leadership of the Islamists."

You would scarcely be able to detect this convergence of views with the United States and Israel if you looked only at the official positions taken by the monarchy. And yet, pragmatism and respect for power, which are the two invariables of Saudi diplomacy, always lead the palace to tacitly maintain its alliance with Washington as the intangible guarantor of the kingdom's independence. "The only ambition of the Sauds is to remain master at home. To do that, no matter what happens, they need the United States," adds our military attaché, "while internal stability is, for the moment, maintained through a flawless ballet between the religious and police authorities." The alliance with the United States is as much in place now as it ever has been. Year by year, the alliance is renewed, with Washington guaranteeing Riyadh absolute immunity to any external threat, while Riyadh guarantees Washington a sure and tightly controlled source of energy for the Western world.

Taliban

by Ahmed Rashid

The Taliban and Osama bin Laden have a symbiotic relationship that
grew out of the defeat of the Russian occupation in Afghanistan. Their
brand of Muslim extremism enjoyed strategic support from Pakistan,
Saudi Arabia and the United States until very recently. As soon as they
came to power in 1996, they gave Al Qaeda a base in exchange for
financial and logistical support. Ahmed Rashid is a journalist focusing
on South and Central Asia.

A t Torkham—the border post at the head of the Khyber Pass
between Afghanistan and Pakistan, a single chain barrier separates
the two countries. On the Pakistani side stand the smartly turned
out Frontier Scouts—paramilitaries in their grey shalwar kameezes and
turbans. It was April 1989, and the Soviet withdrawal from Afghanistan
had just been completed. I was returning to Pakistan by road from Kabul,
but the barrier was closed. Exhausted from my journey I lay down on a
grass verge on the Afghan side of the border and waited.

Suddenly, along the road behind me, a truck full of Mujaheddin
roared up and stopped. But those on board were no Afghans. Light-
coloured Arabs, blue-eyed Central Asians and swarthy Chinese-looking
faces peered out from roughly wound turbans and ill-fitting shalwar
kameezes. Except for one Afghan, who was acting as interpreter and guide,
not a single one of the 30 foreigners spoke Pushto, Dari or even Urdu. As
we waited for the border to open we got talking.

The group was made up of Filipino Moros, Uzbeks from Soviet
Central Asia, Arabs from Algeria, Egypt, Saudi Arabia and Kuwait and

Uighurs from Xinjiang in China. Their escort was a member of Gulbuddin Hikmetyar's Hizb-e-Islami. Under training at a camp near the border they were going on weekend leave to Peshawar and were looking forward to getting mail from home, changing their clothes and having a good meal. They had come to fight the jihad with the Mujaheddin and to train in weapons, bomb-making and military tactics so they could take the jihad back home.

That evening, Prime Minister Benazir Bhutto had hosted a dinner for journalists in Islamabad. Among the guests was Lieutenant General Hameed Gul, the head of the ISI and the most fervent Islamic ideologue in the army after Zia's death. General Gul was triumphant about the Soviet withdrawal. I asked him if he was not playing with fire by inviting Muslim radicals from Islamic countries, who were ostensibly allies of Pakistan. Would these radicals not create dissension in their own countries, endangering Pakistan's foreign policy? 'We are fighting a jihad and this is the first Islamic international brigade in the modern era. The communists have their international brigades, the West has NATO, why can't the Muslims unite and form a common front?' the General replied. It was the first and only justification I was ever given for what were already called the Arab-Afghans, even though none were Afghans and many were not Arabs.

Three years earlier in 1986, CIA chief William Casey had stepped up the war against the Soviet Union by taking three significant, but at that time highly secret, measures. He had persuaded the US Congress to provide the Mujaheddin with American-made Stinger anti-aircraft missiles to shoot down Soviet planes and provide US advisers to train the guerrillas. Until then no US-made weapons or personnel had been used directly in the war effort. The CIA, Britain's MI6 and the ISI also agreed on a provocative plan to launch guerrilla attacks into the Soviet Socialist Republics of Tajikistan and Uzbekistan, the soft Muslim underbelly of the Soviet state from where Soviet troops in Afghanistan received their supplies.

The task was given to the ISI's favourite Mujaheddin leader Gulbuddin Hikmetyar. In March 1987, small units crossed the Amu Darya river from bases in northern Afghanistan and launched their first rocket attacks against villages in Tajikistan. Casey was delighted with the news and on his next secret trip to Pakistan he crossed the border into Afghanistan with President Zia to review the Mujaheddin groups.

Thirdly, Casey committed CIA support to a long-standing ISI initiative to recruit radical Muslims from around the world to come to Pakistan and fight with the Afghan Mujaheddin. The ISI had encouraged this since 1982 and by now all the other players had their reasons for supporting the idea. President Zia aimed to cement Islamic unity, turn Pakistan into the leader of the Muslim world and foster an Islamic opposition in central Asia. Washington wanted to demonstrate that the entire Muslim world was fighting the Soviet Union alongside the Afghans and their American benefactors. And the Saudis saw an opportunity both to promote Wahabbism and get rid of its disgruntled radicals. None of the players reckoned on these volunteers having their own agendas, which would eventually turn their hatred against the Soviets on their own regimes and the Americans.

Pakistan already had standing instructions to all its embassies abroad to give visas, with no questions asked, to anyone wanting to come and fight with the Mujaheddin. In the Middle East, the Muslim Brotherhood, the Saudi-based World Muslim League and Palestinian Islamic radicals organized the recruits and put them into contact with the Pakistanis. The ISI and Pakistan's Jamaat-e-Islami set up reception committees to welcome, house and train the arriving militants and then encouraged them to join the Mujaheddin groups, usually the Hizb-e-Islami. The funds for this enterprise came directly from Saudi Intelligence. French scholar Olivier Roy describes it as 'a joint venture between the Saudis, the Muslim Brotherhood and the Jamaat-e-Islami, put together by the ISI'.

Between 1982 and 1992 some 35,000 Muslim radicals from 43 Islamic countries in the Middle East, North and East Africa, Central Asia and the Far East would pass their baptism under fire with the Afghan Mujaheddin. Tens of thousands more foreign Muslim radicals came to study in the hundreds of new *madrassas* that Zia's military government began to fund in Pakistan and along the Afghan border. Eventually more than 100,000 Muslim radicals were to have direct contact with Pakistan and Afghanistan and be influenced by the jihad.

In camps near Peshawar and in Afghanistan, these radicals met each other for the first time and studied, trained and fought together. It was the first opportunity for most of them to team about Islamic movements in other countries and they forged tactical and ideological links that would serve them well in the future. The camps became virtual universities for future Islamic radicalism. None of the intelligence agencies involved wanted to consider the consequences of bringing together thousands of Islamic radicals from all over the world. 'What was more important in the world view of history? The Taliban or the fall of the Soviet Empire? A few stirred-up Muslims or the liberation of Central Europe and the end of the Cold War?' said Zbigniew Brzezinski, a former US National Security Adviser. American citizens only woke up to the consequences when Afghanistan-trained Islamic militants blew up the World Trade Centre in New York in 1993, killing six people and injuring 1,000.

'The war,' wrote Samuel Huntington, 'left behind an uneasy coalition of Islamist organizations intent on promoting Islam against all non-Muslim forces. It also left a legacy of expert and experienced fighters, training camps and logistical facilities, elaborate trans-Islam networks of personal and organization relationships, a substantial amount of military equipment including 300 to 500 unaccounted-for Stinger missiles, and, most important, a heady sense of power and self-confidence over what had been achieved and a driving desire to move on to other victories.'

Most of these radicals speculated that if the Afghan jihad had defeated one superpower, the Soviet Union, could they not also defeat the other superpower, the US and their own regimes? The logic of this argument was based on the simple premise that the Afghan jihad alone had brought the Soviet state to its knees. The multiple internal reasons which led to the collapse of the Soviet system, of which the jihad was only one, were conveniently ignored. So while the USA saw the collapse of the Soviet state as the failure of the communist system, many Muslims saw it solely as a victory for Islam. For militants this belief was inspiring and deeply evocative of the Muslim sweep across the world in the seventh and eighth centuries. A new Islamic *Ummah*, they argued, could be forged by the sacrifices and blood of a new generation of martyrs and more such victories.

Amongst these thousands of foreign recruits was a young Saudi student Osama Bin Laden, the son of a Yemeni construction magnate Mohammed Bin Laden who was a close friend of the late King Faisal and whose company had become fabulously wealthy on the contracts to renovate and expand the Holy Mosques of Mecca and Medina. The ISI had long wanted Prince Turki Bin Faisal, the head of *Istakhbarat*, the Saudi Intelligence Service, to provide a Royal Prince to lead the Saudi contingent in order to show Muslims the commitment of the Royal Family to the jihad. Only poorer Saudis, students, taxi-drivers and Bedouin tribesmen had so far arrived to fight. But no pampered Saudi Prince was ready to rough it out in the Afghan mountains. Bin Laden, although not a royal, was close enough to the royals and certainly wealthy enough to lead the Saudi contingent. Bin Laden, Prince Turki and General Gul were to become firm friends and allies in a common cause.

The centre for the Arab-Afghans was the offices of the World Muslim League and the Muslim Brotherhood in Peshawar which was run by Abdullah Azam, a Jordanian Palestinian whom Bin Laden had first met at university in Jeddah and revered as his leader. Azam and his two sons were assassinated by a bomb blast in Peshawar in 1989. During the 1980s Azam had forged close links with Hikmetyar and Abdul Rasul Sayyaf, the Afghan Islamic scholar, whom the Saudis had sent to Peshawar to promote

Wahabbism. Saudi funds flowed to Azam and the Makhtab al Khidmat or Services Centre which he created in 1984 to service the new recruits and receive donations from Islamic charities. Donations from Saudi Intelligence, the Saudi Red Crescent, the World Muslim League and private donations from Saudi princes and mosques were channelled through the Makhtab. A decade later the Makhtab would emerge at the centre of a web of radical organizations that helped carry out the World Trade Centre bombing and the bombings of US Embassies in Africa in 1998.

Until he arrived in Afghanistan, Bin Laden's life had hardly been marked by anything extraordinary. He was born around 1957, the 17th of 57 children sired by his Yemeni father and a Saudi mother, one of Mohammed Bin Laden's many wives. Bin Laden studied for a Masters degree in business administration at King Abdul Aziz University in Jeddah but soon switched to Islamic studies. Thin and tall, he is six feet five inches, with long limbs and a flowing beard, he towered above his contemporaries who remember him as a quiet and pious individual but hardly marked out for greater things.

His father backed the Afghan struggle and helped fund it, so when Bin Laden decided to join up, his family responded enthusiastically. He first travelled to Peshawar in 1980 and met the Mujaheddin leaders, returning frequently with Saudi donations for the cause until 1982 when he decided to settle in Peshawar. He brought in his company engineers and heavy construction equipment to help build roads and depots for the Mujaheddin. In 1986 he helped build the Khost tunnel complex, which the CIA was funding as a major arms storage depot, training facility and medical centre for the Mujaheddin, deep under the mountains close to the Pakistan border. For the first time in Khost he set up his own training camp for Arab Afghans, who now increasingly saw this lanky, wealthy and charismatic Saudi as their leader.

'To counter these atheist Russians, the Saudis chose me as their representative in Afghanistan,' Bin Laden said later. 'I settled in Pakistan in the

Afghan border region. There I received volunteers who came from the Saudi Kingdom and from all over the Arab and Muslim countries. I set up my first camp where these volunteers were trained by Pakistani and American officers. The weapons were supplied by the Americans, the money by the Saudis. I discovered that it was not enough to fight in Afghanistan, but that we had to fight on all fronts, communist or Western oppression,' he added.

Bin Laden later claimed to have taken part in ambushes against Soviet troops, but he mainly used his wealth and Saudi donations to build Mujaheddin projects and spread Wahabbism amongst the Afghans. After the death of Azam in 1989, he look over Azam's organization and set up Al Qaeda or Military Base as a service centre for Arab-Afghans and their familes and to forge a broad-based alliance amongst them. With the help of Bin Laden, several thousand Arab militants had established bases in the provinces of Kunar, Nuristan and Badakhshan, but their extreme Wahabbi practices made them intensely disliked by the majority of Afghans. Moreover by allying themselves with the most extreme pro-Wahabbi Pashtun Mujaheddin, the Arab-Afghans alienated the non-Pashtuns and the Shia Muslims.

Ahmed Shah Masud later criticized the Arab-Afghans. 'My jihad faction did not have good relations with the Arab-Afghans during the years of jihad. In contrast they had very good relations with the factions of Abdul Rasul Sayyaf and Gulbuddin Hikmetyar. When my faction entered Kabul in 1992, the Arab-Afghans fought in the ranks of Hikmetyar's forces against us. We will ask them (Arabs) to leave our country. Bin Laden does more harm than good,' Masud said in 1997 after he had been ousted from Kabul by the Taliban.

By 1990 Bin Laden was disillusioned by the internal bickering of the Mujaheddin and he returned to Saudi Arabia to work in the family business. He founded a welfare organization for Arab-Afghan veterans, some 4,000 of whom had settled in Mecca and Medina alone, and gave money to the families of those killed. After Iraq's invasion of Kuwait he lobbied the Royal Family to organize a popular defence of the Kingdom and raise a force from the Afghan war veterans to fight Iraq. Instead King Fahd invited in the Americans. This came as an enormous shock to Bin Laden. As the 540,000 US troops began to arrive, Bin Laden openly criticized the Royal Family, lobbying the Saudi *ulema* to issue fatwas, religious rulings, against non-Muslims being based in the country.

Bin Laden's criticism escalated after some 20,000 US troops continued to be based in Saudi Arabia after Kuwait's liberation. In 1992 he had a fiery meeting with Interior Minister Prince Naif whom he called a traitor to Islam. Naif complained to King Fahd and Bin Laden was declared persona non grata. Nevertheless he still had allies in the Royal Family, who also disliked Naif while he maintained his links with both Saudi Intelligence and the ISI.

In 1992 Bin Laden left for Sudan to take part in the Islamic revolution underway there under the charismatic Sudanese leader Hassan Turabi. Bin Laden's continued criticism of the Saudi Royal Family eventually annoyed them so much that they took the unprecedented step of revoking his citizenship in 1994. It was in Sudan, with his wealth and contacts that Bin Laden gathered around him more veterans of the Afghan war, who were all disgusted by the American victory over Iraq and the attitude of the Arab ruling elites who allowed the US military to remain in the Gulf. As US and Saudi pressure mounted against Sudan for harbouring Bin Laden, the Sudanese authorities asked him to leave.

In May 1996 Bin Laden travelled back to Afghanistan, arriving in Jalalabad in a chartered jet with an entourage of dozens of Arab militants, bodyguards and family members including three wives and 13 children. Here he lived under the protection of the Jalalabad Shura until the conquest of Kabul and Jalalabad by the Taliban in September 1996. In August 1996 he had issued his first declaration of jihad against the Americans whom he said were occupying Saudi Arabia. 'The walls of oppression and humiliation cannot be demolished except in a rain of bullets,' the declaration read. Striking up a friendship with Mullah Omar, in 1997 he moved to Kandahar and came under the protection of the Taliban.

By now the CIA had set up a special cell to monitor his activities and his links with other Islamic militants. A US State Department report in August 1996 noted that Bin Laden was 'one of the most significant financial sponsors of Islamic extremist activities in the world'. The report said that Bin Laden was financing terrorist camps in Somalia, Egypt, Sudan, Yemen, Egypt and Afghanistan. In April 1996, President Clinton signed the Anti-Terrorism Act which allowed the US to block assets of terrorist organizations. It was first used to block Bin Laden's access to his fortune of an estimated US$250–300 million. A few months later Egyptian intelligence declared that Bin Laden was training 1,000 militants, a second generation of Arab-Afghans, to bring about an Islamic revolution in Arab countries.

In early 1997 the CIA constituted a squad which arrived in Peshawar to try and carry out a snatch operation to get Bin Laden out of Afghanistan. The Americans enlisted Afghans and Pakistanis to help them but aborted the operation. The US activity in Peshawar helped persuade Bin Laden to move to the safer confines of Kandahar. On 23 February 1998, at a meeting in the original Khost camp, all the groups associated with Al Qaeda issued a manifesto under the aegis of 'The International Islamic Front for jihad against Jews and Crusaders'. The manifesto stated 'for more than seven years the US has been occupying the lands of Islam in the holiest of places, the Arabian peninsular, plundering its riches, dictating to its rulers, humiliating its people, terrorizing its neighbours, and turning its bases in the peninsular into a spearhead through which to fight the neighbouring Muslim peoples'.

The meeting issued a fatwa. 'The ruling to kill the Americans and their allies—civilians and military—is an individual duty for every Muslim who can do it in any country in which it is possible to.' Bin

Laden had now formulated a policy that was not just aimed at the Saudi Royal Family or the Americans but called for the liberation of the entire Muslim Middle East. As the American air war against Iraq escalated in 1998, Bin Laden called on all Muslims to 'confront, fight and kill' Americans and Britons.

However, it was the bombings in August 1998 of the US Embassies in Kenya and Tanzania that killed 220 people which made Bin Laden a household name in the Muslim world and the West. Just 13 days later, after accusing Bin Laden of perpetrating the attack, the USA retaliated by firing 70 cruise missiles against Bin Laden's camps around Khost and Jalalabad. Several camps which had been handed over by the Taliban to the Arab-Afghans and Pakistani radical groups were hit. The Al Badr camp controlled by Bin Laden and the Khalid bin Walid and Muawia camps run by the Pakistani Harakat ul Ansar were the main targets. Harakat used their camps to train militants for fighting Indian troops in Kashmir. Seven outsiders were killed in the strike—three Yemenis, two Egyptians, one Saudi and one Turk. Also killed were seven Pakistanis and 20 Afghans.

In November 1998 the USA offered a US$5-million reward for Bin Laden's capture. The Americans were further galvanized when Bin Laden claimed that it was his Islamic duty to acquire chemical and nuclear weapons to use against the USA. 'It would be a sin for Muslims not to try to possess the weapons that would prevent infidels from inflicting harm on Muslims. Hostility towards America is a religious duty and we hope to be rewarded for it by God,' he said.

Within a few weeks of the Africa bombings, the Clinton administration had demonized Bin Laden to the point of blaming him for every atrocity committed against the USA in the Muslim world in recent times. In the subsequent indictment against him by a New York court, Bin Laden was blamed for the 18 American soldiers killed in Mogadishu, Somalia in 1993; the deaths of five servicemen in a bomb attack in Riyadh in 1995 and the deaths of another 19 US soldiers in Dhahran in 1996. He was also suspected of having a hand in bombings in Aden in 1992, the World Trade Center bombing in 1993, a 1994 plot to kill President Clinton in the Philippines and a plan to blow up a dozen US civilian aircraft in 1995. There was a great deal of scepticism, even amongst US experts that he was involved in many of these latter operations.

But the Clinton administration was desperately looking for a diversion as it wallowed through the mire of the Monica Lewinsky affair and also needed an all-purpose, simple explanation for unexplained terrorist acts. Bin Laden became the centre of what was promulgated by Washington as a global conspiracy against the USA. What Washington was not prepared to admit was that the Afghan jihad, with the support of the CIA, had spawned dozens of fundamentalist movements across the Muslim world which were led by militants who had grievances, not so much against the Americans, but their own corrupt, incompetent regimes. As early as 1992–93 Egyptian and Algerian leaders at the highest level had advised Washington to re-engage diplomatically in Afghanistan in order to bring about peace so as to end the presence of the Arab-Afghans. Washington ignored the warnings and continued to ignore Afghanistan even as the civil war there escalated.

The Algerians were justified in their fears, for the first major eruption from the ranks of the Arab-Afghans came in Algeria. In 1991 the Islamic Salvation Front (FIS) won the first round of parliamentary elections taking some 60 per cent of the seats countrywide. The Algerian army cancelled the results, declared Presidential rule in January 1992 and within two months a vicious civil war began which had claimed some 70,000 lives by 1999. FIS itself was outmanoeuvered by the more extreme Islamic Jihad, which in 1995 changed its name to the Armed Islamic Group (GIA). GIA was led by Algerian Afghans—Algerian veterans from the Afghan war—who were neo-Wahabbis and set an agenda that was to plunge Algeria into a bloodbath, destabilize North Africa and lead to the growth of Islamic extremism in France. Algeria was only a foretaste of what was to come later. Bombings carried out in Egypt by Islamic groups were also traced back to Egyptian veterans trained in Afghanistan.

Bin Laden knew many of the perpetrators of these violent acts across the Muslim world, because they had lived and fought together in Afghanistan. His organization, focused around supporting veterans of the Afghan war and their families, maintained contacts with them. He may well have funded some of their operations, but he was unlikely to know what they were all up to or what their domestic agendas were. Bin Laden has always been insecure within the architecture of Islam. He is neither an Islamic scholar nor a teacher and thus cannot legally issue fatwas—although he does so. In the West his 'Death to America' appeals have been read as fatwas, even though they do not carry moral weight in the Muslim world.

Arab-Afghans who knew him during the jihad say he was neither intellectual nor articulate about what needed to be done in the Muslim world. In that sense he was neither the Lenin of the Islamic revolution, nor was he the internationalist ideologue of the Islamic revolution such as Che Guevera was to revolution in the third world.

Bin Laden's former associates describe him as deeply impressionable, always in the need for mentors—men who knew more about both Islam and the modern world than he did. To the long list of mentors during his youth were later added Dr. Aiman al-Zawahiri, the head of the banned Islamic Jihad in Egypt and the two sons of Shaikh Omar Abdel Rehman, the blind Egyptian preacher now in a US jail for the World Trade Centre bombing and who had led the banned El Gamaa Islamiyya in Egypt. Through the Afghan jihad, he also knew senior figures in the National Islamic Front in the Sudan, Hezbollah in Lebanon and Hamas, the radical Islamic Palestinian movement in Gaza and the West Bank. In Kandahar he had Chechens, Bangladeshis, Filipinos, Algerians, Kenyans, Pakistanis and African-American Muslims with him—many of whom were widely read and better informed than Bin Laden, but could not travel outside Afghanistan because they were on US wanted lists. What they needed was financial support and a sanctuary which Bin Laden gave them.

After the Africa bombings the US launched a truly global operation. More than 80 Islamic militants were arrested in a dozen different countries. Militants were picked up in a crescent running from Tanzania, Kenya, Sudan, Yemen, to Pakistan, Bangladesh, Malaysia and the Philippines. In December 1998, Indian authorities detained Bangladeshi militants for plotting to bomb the US Consulate in Calcutta. Seven Afghan nationals using false Italian passports were arrested in Malaysia and accused of trying to start a bombing campaign. According to the FBI, militants in Yemen who kidnapped 16 Western tourists in December 1998 were funded by Bin Laden. In February 1999, Bangladeshi authorities said Bin Laden had sent US$1 million to the Harkat-ul-Jihad (HJ) in Dhaka, some of whose members had trained and fought in Afghanistan. HJ leaders said they wanted to turn Bangladesh into a Taliban-style Islamic state.

Thousands of miles away in Nouakchott, the capital of Mauritania in West Africa, several militants were arrested who had also trained under Bin Laden in Afghanistan and were suspected of plotting bomb explosions. Meanwhile during the trial of 107 Al-Jihad members at a military court in Cairo, Egyptian intelligence officers testified that Bin Laden had bankrolled Al-Jihad. In February 1999 the CIA claimed that through monitoring Bin Laden's communication network by satellite, they had prevented his supporters from carrying out seven bomb attacks against US overseas facilities in Saudi Arabia, Albania, Azerbaijan, Tajikistan, Uganda, Uruguay and the Ivory Coast—emphasizing the reach of the Afghan veterans. The Clinton administration sanctioned US$6.7 billion to fight terrorism in 1999, while the FBI's counter-terrorism budget grew from US$118 million to US$286 million and the agency allocated 2,650 agents to the task, twice the number in 1998.

But it was Pakistan and Saudi Arabia, the original sponsors of the Arab-Afghans, who suffered the most as their activities rebounded. In March 1997, three Arab and two Tajik militants were shot dead after a 36-hour gun battle between them and the police in an Afghan refugee camp near Peshawar. Belonging to the Wahabbi radical Tafkir group, they were planning to bomb an Islamic heads of state meeting in Islamabad.

With the encouragement of Pakistan, the Taliban and Bin Laden, Arab-Afghans had enlisted in the Pakistani party Harkat-ul-Ansar to fight in Kashmir against Indian troops. By inducting Arabs who introduced Wahabbi-style rules in the Kashmir valley, genuine Kashmiri militants felt insulted. The US government had declared Ansar a terrorist organization in 1996 and it had subsequently changed its name to Harkat-ul-Mujaheddin. All the Pakistani victims of the US missile strikes on Khost belonged to Ansar. In 1999, Ansar said it would impose a strict Wahabbi-style dress code in the Kashmir valley and banned jeans and jackets. On 15 February 1999, they shot and wounded three Kashmiri cable television operators for relaying Western satellite broadcasts. Ansar had previously respected the liberal traditions of Kashmiri Muslims but the activites of the Arab-Afghans hurt the legitimacy of the Kashmiri movement and gave India a propaganda coup.

Pakistan faced a problem when Washington urged Prime Minister Nawaz Sharif to help arrest Bin Laden. The ISI's close contacts with Bin Laden and the fact that he was helping fund and train Kashmiri militants who were using the Khost camps, created a dilemma for Sharif when he visited Washington in December 1998. Sharif side-stepped the issue but other Pakistani officials were more brazen, reminding their American counterparts how they had both helped midwife Bin Laden in the 1980s and the Taliban in the 1990s. Bin Laden himself pointed to continued support from some elements in the Pakistani intelligence services in an interview. 'As for Pakistan there are some governmental departments, which, by the Grace of God, respond to the Islamic sentiments of the masses in

Pakistan. This is reflected in sympathy and co-operation. However, some other governmental departments fell into the trap of the infidels. We pray to God to return them to the right path,' said Bin Laden.

Support for Bin Laden by elements within the Pakistani establishment was another contradiction in Pakistan's Afghan policy. . . . The US was Pakistan's closest ally with deep links to the military and the ISI. But both the Taliban and Bin Laden provided sanctuary and training facilities for Kashmiri militants who were backed by Pakistan, and Islamabad had little interest in drying up that support. Even though the Americans repeatedly tried to persuade the ISI to co-operate in delivering Bin Laden, the ISI declined, although it did help the US arrest several of Bin Laden's supporters. Without Pakistan's support the USA could not hope to launch a snatch by US commandos or more accurate bombing strikes because it needed Pakistani territory to launch such raids. At the same time the USA dared not expose Pakistan's support for the Taliban, because it still hoped for ISI co-operation in catching Bin Laden.

The Saudi conundrum was even worse. In July 1998 Prince Turki had visited Kandahar and a few weeks later 400 new pick-up trucks arrived in Kandahar for the Taliban, still bearing their Dubai license plates. The Saudis also gave cash for the Taliban's cheque book conquest of the north in the autumn. Until the Africa bombings and despite US pressure to end their support for the Taliban, the Saudis continued funding the Taliban and were silent on the need to extradite Bin Laden. The truth about the Saudi silence was even more complicated. The Saudis preferred to leave Bin Laden alone in Afghanistan because his arrest and trial by the Americans could expose the deep relationship that Bin Laden continued to have with sympathetic members of the Royal Family and elements within Saudi intelligence, which could prove deeply embarrassing. The Saudis wanted Bin Laden either dead or a captive of the Taliban—they did not want him captured by the Americans.

After the August 1998 Africa bombings, US pressure on the Saudis increased. Prince Turki visited Kandahar again, this time to persuade the Taliban to hand over Bin Laden. In their meeting, Mullah Omar refused to do so and then insulted Prince Turki by abusing the Saudi Royal Family. Bin Laden himself described what took place: 'He [Prince Turki] asked Mullah Omar to surrender us home or to expel us from Afghanistan. It is none of the business of the Saudi regime to come and ask for the handing over of Osama Bin Laden. It was as if Turki came as an envoy of the American government.' Furious about the Taliban insults, the Saudis suspended diplomatic relations with the Taliban and ostensibly ceased all aid to them, although they did not withdraw recognition of the Taliban government.

By now Bin Laden had developed considerable influence with the Taliban, but that had not always been the case. The Taliban's contact with the Arab-Afghans and their Pan-Islamic ideology was non-existent until the Taliban captured Kabul in 1996. Pakistan was closely involved in introducing Bin Laden to the Taliban leaders in Kandahar, because it wanted to retain the Khost training camps for Kashmiri militants, which were now in Taliban hands. Persuasion by Pakistan, the Taliban's better-educated cadres who also had Pan-Islamic ideas, and the lure of financial benefits from Bin Laden, encouraged the Taliban leaders to meet with Bin Laden and hand him back the Khost camps.

Partly for his own safety and partly to keep control over him, the Taliban shifted Bin Laden to Kandahar in 1997. At first he lived as a paying guest. He built a house for Mullah Omar's family and provided funds to other Taliban leaders. He promised to pave the road from Kandahar airport to the city and build mosques, schools and dams but his civic works never got started as his funds were frozen. While Bin Laden lived in enormous style in a huge mansion in Kandahar with his family, servants and fellow militants, the arrogant behaviour of the Arab-Afghans who arrived with him and their failure to fulfil any of their civic projects, antagonized the local population. The Kandaharis saw the Taliban leaders as beneficiaries of Arab largesse rather than the people.

Bin Laden endeared himself further to the leadership by sending several hundred Arab-Afghans to participate in the 1997 and 1998 Taliban offensives in the north. These Wahabbi fighters helped the Taliban carry out the massacres of the Shia Hazaras in the north. Several hundred Arab-Afghans, based in the Rishkor army garrison outside Kabul, fought on the Kabul front against Masud. Increasingly, Bin Laden's world view appeared to dominate the thinking of senior Taliban leaders. All-night conversations between Bin Laden and the Taliban leaders paid off. Until his arrival the Taliban leadership had not been particularly antagonistic to the USA or the West but demanded recognition for their government.

However, after the Africa bombings the Taliban became increasingly vociferous against the Americans, the UN, the Saudis and Muslim regimes around the world. Their statements increasingly reflected the language of defiance Bin Laden had adopted and which was not an original Taliban trait. As US pressure on the Taliban to expel Bin Laden intensified, the Taliban said he was a guest and it was against Afghan tradition to expel guests. When it appeared that Washington was planning another military strike against Bin Laden, the Taliban tried to cut a deal with Washington— to allow him to leave the country in exchange for US recognition. Thus until the winter of 1998 the Taliban saw Bin Laden as an asset, a bargaining chip over whom they could negotiate with the Americans.

The US State Department opened a satellite telephone connection to speak to Mullah Omar directly. The Afghanistan desk officers, helped by a Pushto translator, held lengthy conversations with Omar in which both sides explored various options, but to no avail. By early 1999 it began to dawn on the Taliban that no compromise with the US was possible and they began to see Bin Laden as a liability. A US deadline in February 1999 to the Taliban to either hand over Bin Laden or face the consequences forced the Taliban to make him disappear discreetly from Kandahar. The move bought the Taliban some time, but the issue was still nowhere near being resolved.

The Arab-Afghans had come full circle. From being mere appendages to the Afghan jihad and the Cold War in the 1980s they had taken centre stage for the Afghans, neighbouring countries and the West in the 1990s. The USA was now paying the price for ignoring Afghanistan between 1992 and 1996, while the Taliban were providing sanctuary to the most hostile and militant Islamic fundamentalist movement the world faced in the post-Cold War era. Afghanistan was now truly a haven for Islamic internationalism and terrorism and the Americans and the West were at a loss as to how to handle it.

excerpt from:

Unholy Wars

by John K. Cooley

John K. Cooley is an ABC news correspondent based in Cyprus. He covered the Algerian revolution for UPI, NBC News and the London *Observer,* and in 1965 was appointed Middle East correspondent for the *Christian Science Monitor* in Beirut. The extent to which Afghanistan, from 1979 until today, was a tabula rasa upon which the Americans, the Saudis, the Pakistanis, the Russians, the Chinese, the Iranians and the freelance jihadists wrote—thereby creating an encyclopedia of the worst aspects of narrowly defined, national-interest-based geopolitics— is painfully clear in this critical narrative of recent Afghan history.

Afghanistan had largely escaped the impact of World War II. What it did not escape were the after-effects of the partition and independence of British India in 1947. Once the British had withdrawn, the claim was revived of Afghan governments in Kabul to the lands peopled by the Pushtun (called by Rudyard Kipling and many other writers Pathan) and Baluchi ethno-tribal groups, across the border in what now became Pakistan. "Pushtunistan," as it came to be called, became an inflammatory issue between Kabul and Islamabad. Pakistan's rejection of the Afghan monarchy's revanchist claims meant that landlocked Afghanistan was prevented from gaining a port on the Indian Ocean; also a traditional goal of Russian foreign policy through long generations of Czarist rule before 1917.

King Zahir Shah, who had reigned since 1933, had chosen as prime minister a member of his own family, Prince Muhammad Daoud Khan, whose devotion to the cause of Pushtunistan was one of the factors which drew him somewhat closer to the Soviet Union, after a long post-World War II balance between Soviet and American influence. Each pursued aid projects and sought in this way and others to purchase more influence. From 1956 and 1961 onward, Moscow agreed to equip and train the Afghan army and air force respectively, after the US refused to sell to Kabul or provide it with loans on favorable terms. Soon, the Soviet Union began to build huge infrastructure projects of strategic importance, effectively seeking to incorporate the ancient monarchy into the power system of the Soviet borderlands: a highway from the border of Soviet Tajikistan to Kabul; port facilities along the Amu Darya river (where during the Afghan war of the 1980s, CIA-backed incursions of Afghan guerrillas and saboteurs into Soviet territory nearly provoked a major Soviet–Pakistani, if not Soviet–American war).

A giant new military air base was built at Bagram. In Afghanistan's north, development projects flourished, stimulated partly by discovery of huge reserves of natural gas in Jowzjan Province, close to the Soviet frontier. By 1968 Soviet engineers had completed a gas pipeline to pump low-priced Afghan gas to Soviet Central Asian industrial centers; a flow rarely interrupted even during the 1979–89 war, despite sabotage training given to prospective Afghan saboteurs by the CIA and Pakistan's Inter-Services Intelligence Directorate (ISI). The gas line was one of the few enduring Russian successes of the period. By 1985, Moscow was claiming annual gas production of 2400 million cubic meters ($m\ m^3$). Only three percent was used for Afghan needs; all the rest went to the Soviet economy.

Despite competition from US aid and that from West Germany, France, Russia, China and India, the USSR had loaned Afghanistan so much money, much of it at heavy interest charges, that by 1972 the Soviets were Afghanistan's biggest creditor. They had committed close to a billion dollars between 1957 and 1973. This was about 60 percent of all the civilian foreign aid reaching the country. A liberal constitution which King Zahir Shah initiated in 1964 brought in parliamentary democracy. Political parties, mainly small ones, flourished for a time: the Leftist one increasingly under Communist influence; the others growingly under the sway of Islamist ideology. Both the Communists and the Islamists militated most effectively in the high schools and Kabul's university, and among junior officers of the armed forces. The Leftists and Communists founded the People's Democratic Party of Afghanistan (PDPA). Its two wings were called Parcham (Banner) and Khalq (The People). Parcham recruited adherents chiefly from Persian-speaking, young urban elites; Khalq from mainly Pushtuns (Pathans) from a more humble rural background. On the fringe were a few small extremist groups, such as the "Maoist" and definitely non-religious group called *Sholah-e-Javed* (Eternal Flame), attracting non-Pushtuns, Shi'a Muslims (as opposed to the Sunni majority of about two-thirds of the population), and others discontented with the functioning of the Left-leaning constitutional monarchy of Zahir Shah.

Progressively, the King's indecisiveness and, some said, weakness, failed to prevent erosion of the democratic principles he had helped to launch with the new constitution of 1964. He was, his critics remarked, too spineless to support the more honest and capable prime ministers, five of whom tried successively to rule until 1973. Much of the blame for the mishandling of affairs, including foreign relief help at the time of the drought and famine which in 1972 killed up to 100,000 Afghans, fell on the King's son-in-law, General Abdul Wali. Then, in 1973, while the King was abroad, a junta of armed forces officers staged a sudden military coup, proclaiming a Republic and the monarchy's end. Their figurehead and in some senses their real leader, was one of Zahir Shah's cousins, Muhammad Daoud, who had functioned as an effective foreign minister from 1953 to 1963, but who was banned from power during the period of Zahir's democratic experience. Daoud tried to rule with an iron fist. He largely neglected social and economic problems. Western commentators—few of whom really understood Afghan politics or society then, nor understood their complexities later on, when the West became embroiled in its proxy war with the Russians—wrongly called Daoud "the Red Prince." They believed, though the Soviets themselves did not, that the support of Leftist

PDPA elements in his successful bid for power made him automatically a tool or a satellite of Moscow.

The events which would provoke the fateful Soviet military intervention of December 1979 could be said to begin with the reunion of the two rival PDPA factions, Parcham and Khalq, in 1977. It was fragile and temporary, but it helped to make possible another military coup, this time fatal to Daoud who with most of his family was killed resisting it. Their murders happened on April 27, 1978. They brought the PDPA, now identified by the US Central Intelligence Agency (CIA) and other Western agencies as Communist and pro-Soviet, to power at last. The winning faction in his "Saur" or April Revolution, as it was called, was the Khalq, numerically superior to the less radical and more cautious Parcham. From April 1978, the new president, Nur Muhammad Taraki, was a sort of hack Marxist writer, and a front man for the much more able politician, Hafizullah Amin.

From the beginning of Taraki's rule, the Kremlin of President Leonid Brezhnev carefully watched every development in Afghanistan. It suspected that Amin was pro-American, and possibly an agent of the CIA. In March 1979, there was a major revolt in Herat province against Taraki's government. Soviet intelligence noted that it was supported from abroad, mostly by the Iran of Ayatollah Khomeiny, the fiery cleric who had returned to Tehran from exile to become Iran's supreme religious and political chief following the Shah's departure in February 1979. Several Soviet advisory personnel were killed in suppressing the Herat uprising. To keep an eye on Amin, now prime minister, and other members of Taraki's clique who might have pro-Western leanings or worse, the Kremlin sent Vassily Safronchuk, a competent senior diplomat fluent in English, the foreign language in which Amin was most at home, to keep an eye on things in Kabul, as counselor to the Soviet Ambassador in Kabul, A.M. Puzanov.

Safronchuk found Amin to be "of middle height and solid build, with well-pronounced Pushtu features, a vigorous and polite man [who] if he wanted to, could charm any visitor from the very first." After hearing Amin's initial protestations of loyalty and friendship to Soviet Communist principles and people, Safronchuk found him actually to be "a commonplace petty bourgeois and an extreme Pushtu nationalist," both traits which Moscow considered dangerous. Amin, Safronchuk reported, was a political schemer with "boundless political ambitions and a craving for power" which he would "stoop to anything and commit any crimes" to fulfill.

Because of Amin's "suspicious" contacts with the Americans and persistent signs that the CIA, Iran and Pakistan had all begun to encourage agitation and ferment among the Islamist-minded tribal leaders (especially after the Herat uprising in March 1979), Taraki and Amin both began urging Moscow of the need for a "limited contingent"—soon to become the favorite phrase of Kremlin bureaucrats seeking to justify their military intervention—of Soviet troops. In June 1979, says Safronchuk, Amin at one of their first meetings asked him to inform the Soviet leadership of his and Taraki's request for sending "two or three battalions" of Red Army troops "to protect certain military communication lines and the Baghram airfield." Safronchuk says he told Amin he doubted there would be a positive response. Moscow, he said, feared the arrival of Soviet troops on Afghanistan's territory could be used by the West, Pakistan, Iran and China, all viewed as adversaries, to "discredit the Afghan revolution," and would be viewed in the Kremlin as an admission that the Taraki-Amin regime was weak.

During the summer of 1979, during which the principal anti-Soviet "hawk" in President Jimmy Carter's administration, National Security Advisor Zbigniew Brzezinski, got Carter to sign a secret directive for covert aid to the nascent moujahidin, or anti-Russian resistance fighters, more trouble developed for Taraki, Amin and the Soviets. On June 23, an army mutiny erupted in the heart of Kabul, close to the central Chandaval bazaar. On August 6, carefully monitored by the CIA and Pakistani observers, if not directly encouraged by them, an Afghan army unit mutinied and tried to seize the ancient fortress of Balahisar, on the southeastern slope of the hill called Shir-Darviz, inside Kabul. From this fortress, guns could be trained on all the capital's main streets and neighborhoods. The Soviet diplomats and military advisors in Kabul, as well as the KGB station, suspected that Amin had provoked these rebellions, or had known about them in advance. In any case, these events consolidated Amin's power over the Afghan armed services. The Soviets judged that Amin, long on friendly terms with the US Embassy in Kabul, was aiming for a personal dictatorship, possibly in collusion with the Americans.

Selig Harrison, former *Washington Post* correspondent whose writings on South Asian events are authoritative, describes the setting for "Moscow's monumental blunder" in invading Afghanistan. He depicts a "Byzantine sequence of murderous Afghan intrigue complicated by turf wars between rival Soviet intelligence agencies and the undercover manipulations of agents for seven contending foreign powers" (presumably the US, the USSR, Iran, Pakistan, India and Britain). The Kremlin's fatal blunder, taken by a small coterie of President Leonid Brezhnev's advisors, and imposed when Brezhnev himself, "ailing and alcoholic," imposed the secret decision without calling a full Politburo meeting, "disregarding the opposition of three key generals in his Army General Staff."

Added to this, the CIA "old boys' club," as some members of Archie Roosevelt's generation called it, felt strongly that the Soviet invasion of Afghanistan gave them a unique opportunity to challenge an enemy which had sought the West's downfall ever since the Russian revolution in 1917; a visceral as well as intellectual sense of historical revenge. It meant, in Archie Roosevelt's words, confronting "that [Russian] bear" which "has not changed since [Rudyard] Kipling's time—indeed we now see him in Afghanistan on the northern rim of the Khyber Pass." Roosevelt, like Zbigniev Brzezinski and other Carter advisors, felt the historic Khyber crossing between Afghanistan and Pakistan was the "true front line" where they felt

"the chill winds of the Cold War blowing over those forbidding mountains." Beyond those mountains, to the north, lay the vast reaches of Soviet
Central Asia. There, along the roads to the ancient Muslim cities of
Bokhara, Samarkand and Tashkent, lay the lands of Muslim Central Asia,
restless under Russian and Communist rule; perhaps ripe for a "liberation"
process which would end in independence.

"A man," wrote the American author Mark Twain in an essay on patriotism,
"can seldom—very, very seldom—fight a winning fight against his training:
the odds are too heavy." The truth of this in our time is borne out by the post-
Afghan war adventures of the Afghan holy warriors, imbued by their trainers
with martial and murderous skills they have been exercising in many parts of
the world, from the late 1980s onward.

The training process could be compared to an inverted pyramid. Nearest
to its tip were the cadremen and leaders; mainly Pakistani officers who would
themselves become trainers, but also some Afghanis and other personnel.
In the United States, they experienced tough courses in endurance, weapons
use, sabotage and killing techniques, communications and other skills. They
were required to impart these skills to the scores of thousands of fighters who
formed the center and the base of the pyramid of holy war.

As seen from CIA headquarters in Langley, the training program followed Archie Roosevelt's principles, mentioned earlier. The CIA would be the
overall manager. US Special Forces and a coalition of assorted allied specialists
would train the trainers. Pakistan's ISI, in its schools and camps, would train
the bulk of the moujahidin and send them into battle; often though not
always under the same kind of ISI supervision applied to the distribution of
weapons. A few British and American Special Forces veterans, men of the
American Green Berets and the British Special Air Service (SAS), elected to go
beyond the role of trainers chosen for them by the jihad's managers. They

volunteered for scouting and back-up roles with the Muslim mercenaries trained by themselves, their colleagues and Pakistan's ISI.

The recruiting and training processes all left indelible marks on the destinies of several nations. Equally, they have been influencing the future of American and European relations with the Muslim world.

The deadly skills which trainers of the Afghan holy warriors passed on numbered over 60. They included the use of sophisticated fuses, timers and explosives; automatic weapons with armor-piercing ammunition, remote-control devices for triggering mines and bombs (used later in the volunteers' home countries, and against the Israelis in occupied Arab territory such as southern Lebanon). The more successful aspiring guerrillas were inculcated with the Cold War principle that "brainpower replaces firepower" as the foremost fighting implement. They were also taught the tenet of Sun Tzu, the classical Chinese theoretician of the art of war: "to subdue the enemy without fighting is the acme of skill." In other words, use deception, ruse and evasion as much as possible to defeat him, rather than conventional, frontal-style warfare. Both the moujahidin and their mentors, Western and Pakistani, appeared to forget this in the latter stages of the war, when they adopted conventional warfare tactics. Although the Soviets were by then already retreating, senior moujahidin commanders were pushed by the Americans and Pakistanis to lay costly and often futile siege to fixed, fortified positions like those at Herat, which the Russian and Afghan Communist forces defended successfully, although they would have eventually yielded them without a fight when the general Russian withdrawal began.

1980–85 discovered that a full-time fighter's pay, depending in part on where he served and how much fighting he saw—there was sometimes incentive pay for those engaged in especially hazardous sabotage or other covert operations behind Soviet or Communist lines—could range from $100 to as much as $300 a month; sometimes considerably more for commanders and their deputies. For the majority of the young Afghanis, Pakistanis, Algerians, Egyptians, Filipinos and others, these were huge sums. After the war, when private Arab funds paid the new international guerrillas, both the old veterans of the Afghan jihad, and the new recruits for the unholy wars to be fought, in Afghanistan and abroad, took high salaries and fringe benefits, such as travel documents and ID papers provided by their commanders, as a matter of course.

How the refined heroin reaches Europe and the United States used to, and still does, involve elaborate webs of deception, networks of transport, ruses and variable routes, couriers and payoffs. By the time the Afghan fighters got into the business, sometimes with the established Pakistani traffickers, some of the usual routes ran through Baluchistan's bare deserts into Iran, Turkey, Syria, Egypt, Greece, Nigeria, Italy, France, England, Ireland, Germany, Belgium and the Netherlands—to say nothing of Denmark, Norway, Sweden and Finland. Since the Afghan and post-Afghan war profits began to flood into the pockets of the South Asian druglords and the mafias which work with them in the West, many new routes have been added to the old ones. These run through Eastern Europe, especially the former Yugoslavia since the Balkan wars which began there in the early 1990s; and the Muslim republics of former Soviet Central Asia. The results of these multiple new laboratories, smuggling routes and trafficking centers are dramatic and tragic for the West. From slight production before the Russians and the CIA began the war in 1979, the so-called Golden Crescent countries of Pakistan and Afghanistan have grown into the largest center of heroin production, consumed elsewhere as well as locally, in the world. By UN and other estimates, this amounted by 1997 to around 500 tons of pure white heroin powder. Its wholesale value in the United States alone was about $50 billion. US State Department narcotics reports point to a glut in supply, with world production in the late 1990s *ten times* its level in the pre-war years of the 1970s. This, despite huge expenditures on interdiction and other means of control. In both the United States and Europe, notably in the United Kingdom, heroin has made a spectacular comeback in the latter half of the 1990s. Formerly, most heroin was sold at only four percent purity. By 1998, the average purity of street heroin was 65 percent. Smoking and injecting this purer product is catching on among middle-class users. The British Home Office warned on August 3, 1998, that schoolchildren in smaller English towns, as well as London, Liverpool and other big cities, were being supplied with heroin at or near their schools and homes. Heroin deaths, in the time lapse since the Afghan war ended, are up 100 percent in most of North America. The story is similar for Pakistan, the host country of the jihad: a disastrous 1.7 million addicts estimated in 1997, up from virtually none before the 1979–89 war. The UN Drug Control Program (UNDCP), according to its December 30, 1999 news release, found that Afghanistan had become the world's top opium producer. By February 2000, new UN figures estimated that the shattered country was producing 70 percent of the world's opium crop. The UN estimated the 1999 production at 4,600 tons, over 3,000 tons in 1998. Although Pakistan's own production of opium for export of 800 tons in 1979 had fallen to only 25 tons in 1998 and was forecast to drop to 5 tons in 1999, addicts in Pakistan by the year 2000 consumed 130 tons of drugs, mostly imported from Afghanistan. Social workers found around 200,000 *child* heroin addicts in Pakistan. By January 2000, more than one million addicts, including 80,000 children, lived in Karachi alone.

Our story, almost unknown except to two or three enterprising European investigative authors who have literally risked their lives in its pursuit, involves one central character, Hadji Ayoub Afridi. He is a dark, mustachioed chief of the Pushtun clan of the Afridis. They have lived for the past 2,000 years along the Khyber mountains, connecting Pakistan and Afghanistan to Central Asia. This route has seen the passage of the armies of Alexander the Great, Byzantine kings, Mongol Khans and Queen Victoria's regiments. Most recently it is the scene of the twentieth century's unholy wars between Soviet and Russian armies, and those of the anti-Communist West, allied with militant Islamist mercenaries.

Hadji Ayoub Afridi, in his mid-sixties by 1995, had become the monarch of all he surveyed in Pakistan's Khyber Pass area. His clan or nuclear "family" (in the Sicilian sense), the Zakhakel, controls the region of the Khyber Pass and the crucial frontier post of Torkham, on the Khyber road between Pakistan and Afghanistan. When the Russians arrived in Afghanistan in December 1979, he began to do business with them. Then Pakistan's ISI, needing him for the transport of arms and all manner of supplies to the moujahidin, soon won his full cooperation. Although proof in the public domain is lacking, close observers concluded that much of Afridi's fortune came from moving opium or even heroin from Afghan laboratories back down into Pakistan in the same trucks or caravans which had carried the arms northward. Another important product which the Pakistani drug clans move southward from production laboratories in Central Asia is acetic anhydride, the "precursor" chemical essential for conversion of opium and morphine base into heroin. French investigative author Stephane Allix, a leading European expert on drugs, was told that the ISI used proceeds of its narcotics transactions to finance anti-India guerrilla operations in Kashmir and Pakistani nuclear weapons programs, as well as the jihad in Afghanistan.

$$\bullet \bullet \bullet$$

Throughout the second half of the 1990s, the single most crucial factor in the flow of drugs out of the Golden Crescent countries of Afghanistan, Pakistan and Iran has been the conquest of most of Afghanistan by the extreme Islamist movement, the Taliban. Their ambiguous attitude towards narcotics—proscribing their trafficking, sale and use on religious grounds, while tolerating and even profiting from their export—has, on balance, kept the narcotics flowing from Southwest Asia to all parts of the globe, especially the West.

To understand how the Taliban influence the Asian drug scene, one has to first try to understand the Taliban themselves, and the circumstances of their birth. The civil war that followed the 1989 Russian withdrawal from Afghanistan of the defeated Russians saw a constant struggle for control of the capital, Kabul. It was fought for three years between the two strongest parties to emerge from the war. One was the moderate Islamist faction, led by Burhaneddin Rabbani, who headed several postwar Afghan governments and his military chief, Ahmed Shah Massoud, the very successful field commander of the moujahidin. The other party was the Islamist alliance headed by Gulbuddin Hekmatyar.

While these two main groups fought over Kabul, Afghanistan's hinterlands were run largely by their parties and partly by outsiders; warlords and druglords who belonged to none of the original seven parties which had fought the CIA's jihad against the Russians. However, local control was largely held by local commanders. They levied and collected "taxes," sometimes simply exacting road tolls from travelers and on goods shipments passing through their fiefs. They punished violators and adversaries; sometimes with a kind of rough justice; often with refinements of cruelty and corruption. One abuse which weighed most heavily on people all over Afghanistan had begun during the jihad—roadblocks where gunmen stopped travelers and shook them down for money every few miles. One journalist from Peshawar, Pakistan, Rahimullah Yusufsai, as reported in *The Economist* in October 1996, counted 24 "checkpoints" where money was extorted on a three-hour drive from Spin Bodek, in the Khyber region, to Kandahar. All this made normal travel and commerce more difficult, drove up prices of everything from onions to opium, and angered ordinary people.

In summer 1994, road bandit halted a convoy on the road north of Kandahar. The convoy's owners happened to be top-drawer, influential Pakistanis who demanded that their government do something. It couldn't intervene directly. Instead officials—unclear whether they were ISI officials from the outset, or whether the ISI's control came only later—encouraged a group of Afghan students in the *madrassa* or religious schools to organize for militant action against the bandits. The guiding organization was the Islamist Jamiat-i-Ulema Islam, with outposts along the Afghan border.

About 2,000 of the students, who soon came to call themselves Taliban (which can mean simply "students" but is sometimes translated by the more romantic term, "the Seekers"), went to Kandahar and freed the convoy from the bandits. A legend sympathetic to the Taliban, and possibly true, recounts that two girl refugees, prisoners of a local commander and ill-treated by him, were freed by the Taliban. They then went on to capture Kandahar, the second largest Afghan city. There they were welcomed by most Kandaharis. This was because this original group of Taliban were Kandaharis themselves. The local strongman, a follower of Ahmed Shah Massoud, happened to be corrupt and thoroughly hated. Compared with past armed bands the Kandahar population had known, the young students behaved in exemplary fashion. When they cleared the gunmen from the roads, they merely disarmed them instead of killing them. They then sent them on their way, saying, in effect, go and sin no more. Through this, the pristine Taliban movement became associated with peace, order and Islamic law; at first without the excesses and distortions in the abuse of women and use of cruel punishments which marked their later "enforcement" of Muslim law codes.

• • •

In late summer of 1996, the Taliban moved decisively on Kabul, capturing Jalalabad on September 12. On September 26, 1996 they captured the capital and swiftly realigned all of the political forces in Afghanistan and in the entire region. Their repressive, even sadistic policies, to deny women the right to work, attend school or even go out of their homes uncovered or without the escort of a male relative; their eventual banning of television, music, enforcement of public prayer and obligatory beards for men; forbidding the playing of football in shorts and a huge list of further proscriptions, had already antagonized large segments of people, under their control, who began to realize the price they had to pay for the peace and order they had welcomed so much. However, it was the public castration and execution of Afghanistan's last Communist, President Najibullah after they had entered Kabul, which especially repelled the international community, and made it difficult for them to win recognition, except from their mentors in Pakistan, Saudi Arabia and later, the United Arab Emirates.

A further objective of both Taliban and Pakistan is the recovery of natural gas from northern Afghanistan's Shibergan province, pumped northward to Russia through Uzbekistan. This resulted from a deal signed between Moscow and the preinvasion Afghan secular government in 1977. Afghan estimates of the resources in the Shibergan gas fields run to 1,100 billion cubic meters. Export of the gas continued throughout most of the 1979–89 war, despite periodic sabotage orchestrated by the CIA and Pakistan's ISI, and carried out by specially-trained moujahidin groups. Under the contract, which continued in force between Afghanistan's government in Kabul (under Taliban control since 1996) and the Russian government in Moscow, Russia imported two billion cubic meters of gas each year. Some of the gas, but only minimal quantities, was sold locally in Shibergan and also in Mazar-i-Sharif, which the Taliban captured from its opponents on August 9, 1998. The overwhelming bulk of gas was pumped northward for Russian use. When they captured Mazar-i-Sharif, the Taliban accused General Dostom, chief of the anti-Taliban coalition, of "squandering" the Russian revenues for the gas for his own personal use. In exchange for keeping the gas flowing to Russia, a Taliban newspaper charged, "Dostum received weapons and military supplies from Russia in order to retain his hold over the northern areas, and fight against the Taliban." It remained to be seen whether in the course of consolidating their control over all of Afghanistan, the Taliban would retain the old contract with Russia, summon it to pay arrears from all the years Moscow was paying Dostum, and ask what rates, if any, it would pay in the future.

Questions about Taliban narcotics policies and practices were uppermost in his mind when he met Mullah Muhammad Omar Akhunzadeh, the nearly "invisible" leader, as Allix calls him, of the movement. Mullah Omar was born in country where the peasants cultivate opium, the Maywand district of Kandahar province of Afghanistan. Allix found him to be a tall, thin man of rather elegant appearance, with an "almost inaudible voice, broad beard and a turban." The Taliban leader had been injured three times in battles of Afghanistan's unholy wars. Allix found him to be suffering from what Allix called the "Ignatius de Loyala Syndrome," because that early Jesuit ideologue, like Mullah Omar, was "using his injuries as a means of access to God," a kind of self-righteous martyrdom while still alive and leading his soldiers. Mullah Omar offered Allix no more enlightenment on drugs than he had to other Western visitors who very rarely had access to him.

excerpt from:

The New Jackals

by Simon Reeve

Ramzi Yousef, a "new jackal," is not unlike his namesake Carlos. Both
are professional terrorists whose ideologies become murky on closer
examination and who in fact mask their mercenary tendencies with
religious beliefs. (Yousef is purported to have asked the court artist for
a date during a World Trade Center trial and is not at all religious.)
Both are cold-blooded, arrogant killers. Both are cosmopolitan and
sophisticated, operating efficiently across national borders. And both
are charismatic, able to recruit followers to execute murderous plots.
Yousef, who planned the 1993 World Trade Center bombing, was finally
captured in Islamabad, Pakistan, after a two-year global manhunt. He
is currently serving a life sentence without the possibility of parole in
the same federal prison in Colorado that houses Theodore Kaczynski.
The first selection details the moments leading up to the Trade Center
bombing. Following excerpts discuss his lack of religious conviction
and his detailed plans to blow up eleven airliners simultaneously, a
plot that was nearly ready to be staged when he was arrested in 1995.

just before 4 a.m. on 26 February 1993, a yellow Ford Econoline van bearing the markings of the Ryder hire company emerged from a driveway beside a scruffy apartment block at 40 Pamrapo Avenue, New Jersey, and turned slowly on to the deserted streets of Jersey City, just across the Hudson River from the bright lights of Manhattan. With a dark blue Lincoln and a red Chevrolet following closely behind, the three vehicles drove the short distance down J. F. Kennedy Boulevard to the Shell petrol station at the junction with Route 440 and pulled up by the pumps.

From the passenger seat of the Ford van, a dark-haired man called Ramzi Yousef watched as Willie Hernandez Moosh, the forecourt attendant working the graveyard shift, left his small booth between the pumps. Yousef lowered his window as Moosh approached.

'What do you want?' asked Moosh.

'Fill it up,' replied Yousef.

As Moosh began filling the tank, the passenger door opened, and Yousef slid out on to the forecourt, bracing himself against the cold. Yousef was a tall, wiry man with large ears and a bulbous nose. His eyes flicked over the cars behind and then swept up and down the street. Then, as if a nagging thought was preying on his mind, he began inspecting the yellow van. Moosh removed the petrol cap and watched idly as Yousef began checking the sides and glancing underneath.

Yousef knew the van was designed to hold 2,000lbs in its 295 cubic feet of space. It had been carefully selected as the perfect size for carrying a massive terrorist bomb to attack a target on American soil. Yousef had travelled thousands of miles and spent six months in America plotting and then building a 1,200lb bomb, which was resting in the back of the van with several heavy tanks of hydrogen. But was the cargo pushing the van low on its springs? Nothing could be left to chance.

Moosh was too busy watching Yousef to notice anything suspicious about the van. He had a long, pointy face, thought Moosh. The face of a horse surrounded by a beard.

The 22-gallon tank on a yellow Ford Econoline van takes a few moments to fill, and Moosh left the nozzle in the tank and walked back to the Lincoln. 'Fill it up,' said Mahmud Abouhalima from the warmth of the driving seat. A tall, stocky, red-headed man, Abouhalima had no desire to brave the bitter cold. Ramzi could handle any final inspection—after all, he was in charge.

Moosh pumped petrol into the vehicle, then walked back to the van to ask who was paying. Mohammad Salameh, a lean young man with a straggly beard, turned to Moosh from the driving seat and motioned to the Lincoln behind.

'He will pay,' said Salameh.

The Lincoln's window lowered again to let in the icy air, and Abouhalima handed Moosh a $50 note—$18 worth of petrol for the van and around $13 for the car. Abouhalima took the change, gave Moosh a $2 tip, then Yousef jumped back into the van and the drivers of all three vehicles gunned their engines.

There were few cars on the streets that night, and Moosh watched the convoy as it pulled slowly out of the forecourt. Suddenly the lead van jerked to a halt. A white Jersey City police car was coming into view, driving slowly along J. F. Kennedy Boulevard. The van quickly swung round into a parking space behind the petrol station's office, with the two cars close behind, and Yousef and Salameh jumped out and opened the bonnet.

'Can you bring us some water?' Yousef shouted to Moosh, pretending there was a problem with the van. Moosh grabbed a jug of water and walked over to the two men. Yousef and Salameh were peering into the engine bay and shooting glances at the police car cruising slowly along the street. It must have been a nerve-racking few moments for the men.

Earlier that night Salameh had calmly rung the police from near the

Pathmark supermarket at the Route 440 shopping plaza and told them the Ryder van had been stolen from the car park. It was a clever ruse to avert suspicion: Yousef was planning a heinous act of terrorism—he did not want detectives investigating his handiwork to trawl around rental centres and discover a group of Arabs had failed to return a large van. Yousef decided they would report it as stolen and give police a false licence-plate number. But even without a stolen vehicle report, many police officers might consider a three-vehicle convoy driving slowly around Jersey City before dawn vaguely suspicious.

Yousef and Salameh held their breath, but the car cruised by. Perhaps the officers did not see the small convoy. Perhaps they had not been given the report of a stolen yellow Ryder van. Moosh noticed a man in the red car motioning to the others and pointing at the road. Yousef and Salameh left the water untouched, slammed the bonnet shut, climbed back into the van, and the convoy turned back on to the streets of Jersey City.

By 8 a.m. the van was nosing through the New York rush-hour towards Manhattan. With Yousef giving directions the van arrived at a hotel in midtown Manhattan where an old friend of his called Eyad Ismoil, a baby-faced Jordanian college student, was staying for a few days. 'They were knocking on the door at 9 a.m. and saying "Hurry up, we are going to be late",' said Ismoil. 'I took a bath and went with them and he [Yousef] asked me [to] drive; he said, "You are a taxi driver and a driving expert in the street." I laughed and told them I was willing to drive.' Ismoil climbed behind the wheel of the van, and the group drove towards southern Manhattan. 'In the middle of a major street we stopped at a traffic light; he [Yousef] said "Go to the right from here" in the direction of an underground tunnel,' said Ismoil. 'I did and we went down under-ground. I was surprised . . . He said "Park here" . . .'

At the southern tip of Manhattan island, dominating the New York sky-line, the twin towers of the World Trade Center stand proud, symbolizing commercial power and the core American values of hard work and success. New Yorkers are rightly proud of the vast buildings, which rise 107 storeys or a third of a mile into the sky and are served by 250 different lifts. Tower One hosts a huge antenna which pushes the total height to 1,710 feet above sea level. The entire World Trade Center complex comprises seven huge buildings, and even the underground basement boasts impressive statistics: a subterranean world of cooling pipes, parking garages and offices, bigger than the Empire State Building, it houses a small army of 300 mechanics, electricians, engineers and cleaners who keep the towers alive for the daily working and visiting population of nearly 150,000.

On 26 February 1993, Monica Smith was one of those working in a small office on level B-2 in the town under the ground. Monica was a pretty, dark-haired, 35-year-old woman from Ecuador, a secretary whose main responsibility was scrutinizing time-sheets submitted by cleaning contractors. She had met her husband Eddie in the World Trade Center when he had gone to the building for a sales meeting, and now she was seven months pregnant with little Eddie, their first child. Her colleagues adored Smith, fussing around her attentively from the moment she announced her pregnancy. Just a few days previously Stephen Knapp, a 48-year-old maintenance supervisor, had even asked his wife Louise to bake Monica a special dish of aubergine parmigiana.

At noon the room next to Smith's office was being taken over for lunch. A meeting about maintenance services had finished with the arrival of Robert Kirkpatrick, the 61-year-old bespectacled chief locksmith for the towers, closely followed by Bill Macko, a 47-year-old maintenance worker. Kirkpatrick always sat in the same large oak chair for lunch and no meeting would get in his way. Macko unfolded a newspaper, pulled out a knife from his pocket and slowly began peeling an orange. Stephen Knapp, the next to join the group, cracked open an illicit beer from a refrigerator in the corner of the room and flopped wearily into a chair.

Bill Lavin, who worked for the chief maintenance contractor for the

Trade Center, eyed his friends, then decided he wanted to see daylight, and perhaps catch a glimpse of the snow forecast on the television that morning. It was falling lightly outside, dusting Manhattan in white. Lavin told the others he would be back in a few minutes and walked down the corridor towards the elevators.

A solid concrete wall separated the lunchroom from a ramp to the public car park. It was supposed to be a no-parking zone, with signs warning off anyone tempted to stop, but it was so close to the offices that nobody took any notice of the rules. As Knapp, Macko and Kirkpatrick ate their lunch, a yellow Port Authority van was parked in the zone. One of the basement army, a purchasing agent leaving the maintenance meeting, grabbed a set of keys to the van and drove off to buy some lunch. There were no windows through which the three workers could see another yellow van glide slowly down the ramp and into the same space. Nobody saw the driver and passenger slide out a few minutes later and disappear. There was no one to stop them, no one to question them, and certainly no one to tell them they were illegally parked. Even if a guard had seen them, he would have assumed the van was owned by a maintenance company. Yellow vans were often left on the ramp while heavy boxes were loaded or unloaded.

Nobody was planning to unload the contents of this yellow Ford Econoline bearing the markings of the Ryder hire company. In the back, Ramzi Yousef used a cheap cigarette lighter to ignite four 20ft-long fuses. They would take just 12 minutes to burn down to his massive bomb. Yousef clambered out of the van, jumped into the red car that had followed him into the garage, and then drove carefully out towards West Street. Then he had a shock: another van was blocking the exit, barring his escape from the car park. Yousef must have felt like a character in a Hollywood disaster movie, with the seconds ticking down to oblivion. The van driver shouted to Yousef he would move in a few moments, and within two minutes Yousef was out of the Trade Center and back on the crowded streets of southern Manhattan.

In her office Monica Smith was carefully checking time-sheets. Next door the lunching workers were indulging in a little verbal sparring, joking and gently teasing each other. In the back of the Ryder van the fuses, encased in surgical tubing to limit smoke, were burning down at the rate of an inch every two and a half seconds. The critical moment came at 12.17 and 37 seconds. One of the fuses burnt to its end and ignited the gunpowder in an Atlas Rockmaster blasting cap. In a split second the cap exploded with a pressure of around 15,000lbs per square inch, igniting in turn the first vitro-glycerine container of the bomb, which erupted with a pressure of about 150,000lbs per square inch—the equivalent of about 10,000 atmospheres. In turn, the nitro-glycerine ignited cardboard boxes containing a witches' brew of urea pellets and sulphuric acid.

In the split second that followed the huge explosion blasted in all directions, tearing the van to shreds and ripping through the nearest office, stamping the patterned imprint of Monica Smith's green sweater into her shoulder. It killed little Eddie, tore apart her lungs, arteries and internal organs, fractured her pelvis and broke her leg. Concrete blocks pummelled her head. She died instantly, 'blunt impact trauma' extinguishing her life.

Bob Kirkpatrick was the next to die. A veteran of the Korean war, just six months from retirement, he was hurled across the room, his skull rent apart by a piece of piping; the left side of his body flattened on impact.

Bill Macko, another ex-military man, was sitting next to Kirkpatrick: small chunks of concrete, moving faster than speeding bullets, ravaged the left side of his face. The blast ripped apart his vertebrae, tore his intestines from the side of his abdomen, and ruptured his arteries, spleen and kidneys. Before Stephen Knapp had time to close his eyelids tiny particles of concrete peppered his eyes, then his body was thrown backwards.

One floor above, Wilfredo Mercado, the 37-year-old receiving agent for the Windows on the World restaurant (that sits a quarter of a mile above the basement at the top of One World Trade Center), had been having a quiet snooze. Mercado studied engineering in his native Peru before moving to New York, and his short nap was a daily ritual, a brief moment of rest in a busy day. For most of the week Mercado worked in the twin towers checking that all the fruit and vegetables for the restaurant were delivered correctly. The other two days he returned to the building to work as a security guard. His wife Olga and two young daughters were his life. Mercado probably never woke from his brief slumber. Like a giant hand rising from below, the explosion plucked the Peruvian out of his room and sucked him down five floors. He landed head first, still in his chair, and his body was crushed under tonnes of concrete.

Back in the car park 45-year-old John DiGiovanni, a dark-haired, olive-skinned dental products salesman from Valley Stream, New York, had just parked near an underground ramp when the bomb went off. He was thrown around 30 feet, his body crumpled and bloodied. Paramedics eventually reached him and took him to St Vincent's Hospital, but it was already too late. John DiGiovanni died of traumatic cardiac arrest, caused by the extreme nature of his injuries and deep smoke inhalation.

Timothy Lang had been waiting to get into the car park behind DiGiovanni. A successful young stock-trader, Lang parked his car underground just moments before the explosion. Now he found himself dazed and barely conscious. He crawled through piles of rubble, his neck bleeding profusely, his lungs hacking from the smoke, and collapsed. Such are the vagaries of life. DiGiovanni had cut in front of Lang as their cars entered the building. Lang survived; DiGiovanni died.

The blast-wave roared upwards, passing through five reinforced concrete floors and severing all power. For a brief moment the buildings were plunged into darkness. In an underground station below the twin towers commuters screamed as the blast blew out a hole 180ft by 12ft in the side of the wall on level 2. Concrete and twisted metal flew through the air, ripping through legs and arms, and lacerating spines.

Outside on the street, several hundred feet from 'ground zero', the centre of the blast, the back window of a car waiting at traffic lights on West Street blew out. The shockwave spread out from its source, and within seconds tourists one mile away on Liberty and Ellis Islands in New York harbour felt the ground shudder gently. Many New Yorkers thought there had been an earthquake.

'There was a big boom, the building shook and I looked out of the window across the Hudson River to see if New Jersey had disappeared,' said Lisa Hoffman, a worker in the nearby World Financial Center.

There were two main elements to the Bojinka Plot, both designed to spread panic and revulsion around the entire globe. The first was to use the tiny nitro-glycerine bombs to destroy several jumbo jets and massacre thousands of men, women and children. Yousef had no qualms about mass murder, indeed he wanted to be sure everyone on the planes would die, so after fine-tuning the device he had tested in Cebu, he decided it was time to test it again—underneath public seating to simulate the conditions aboard a passenger plane.

Yousef had brought his friend Wali Khan Amin Shah, a stocky terrorist with two fingers missing on his left hand, over from Pakistan to help with preparations for the bombing campaign. On 1 December 1994, at 4.26 p.m., Shah rang Yousef on a mobile phone he had rented to use during his time in the Philippines, apparently to receive final instructions from Yousef on where he should place one of the small 'Mark II' bombs. Yousef gave his instructions and later that evening Shah allegedly left one of the bombs under a seat at the Greenbelt Theatre in Manila.

Thankfully, nobody sat in the seat, and when the bomb exploded at 10.30 p.m. there were only a few light injuries to an amorous couple sitting near by and several other locals. Twenty minutes after the explosion Shah rang Yousef again to brief him on what had happened. Yousef was pleased: the bomb had exploded precisely on time, and caused the level of destruction he had expected, but again he tinkered with the design increasing the bomb's destructive force still further. As he worked a small quantity of acid splashed on to his face, scarring his skin. He promptly flew back to Pakistan, perhaps for medical help, perhaps just to meet members of his gang, but he stayed no more than a few days and then went back to Manila.

On 8 December he set in motion the second element of the Bojinka plot, appearing at the reception desk of the Dona Josefa Apartment Building, an anonymous six-storey, 60-room block at 711 President Quirino Boulevard, where he asked if a room was available at the front of the building. Followed by a female member of staff, he climbed the stairs and cast an imperious eye over room 603, which was lying vacant. It was small, slightly dank, with just one bedroom and a little kitchenette in the corner. At first glance the room appeared to have little to offer a young terrorist growing used to a life of jetset travel and adventure.

Yousef sauntered over to the windows. The block is just a short distance from Manila Bay, and the cacophony of noise outside from the main road could wake the dead. The member of staff standing with him must have thought he would dislike the room, because she told him there were several other apartments available at the side of the block with spectacular views of the bay. Yousef just looked out of the window, gave one last glance around the room, and smiled. 'This is perfect,' he said. 'I'll take it.'

Downstairs he went through the paperwork with reception staff. 'My name is Naji Owaida Haddad,' he said, claiming to be a mechanical engineer from Morocco. 'I would like to take out a lease on the room for one month.' Yousef told the staff he was working in Manila for just a few weeks, and paid 11,880 Philippine pesos for the room (around £290 or $480). He gave the receptionist a Moroccan passport number, a home address in Rabat, Morocco, and a business address in Casablanca. The lease started that day, and Yousef retired to his room for a rest.

Yousef had something of a penchant for first-class travel, American Express Travellers' Cheques, and the luxuries of life: he was not staying at the humble Dona Josefa Apartment Building for the good of his health. The young mastermind was planning an attack designed to provoke howls of outrage and anger in the Christian world, an act of terrorism that would reverberate around the world for decades to come, with his name as an echo. This was to be the second part of his plan. Deterred from his mission to kill President Clinton by the US leader's security precautions, Ramzi Yousef decided he would instead assassinate Pope John Paul II.

His nondescript apartment block would be crucial. The Pontiff was due to visit Manila in mid-January 1995 and the Dona Josefa Apartment Building sits on President Quirino Boulevard, a major road in Manila that the Pope would use regularly during his five-day visit. The block is also roughly 500ft from Taft Avenue and the Manila home of the Vatican's Ambassador to the Philippines, which would be the Pope's official residence during his stay in the country. But Yousef still needed to do one more test to ensure the first part of the Bojinka Plot would work.

On 9 December, the day after moving into the Dona Josefa Apartment Building, Yousef walked into a travel agency at the Century Park Hotel in the Malate district of Manila. Using an Italian passport identifying him as Armaldo Forlani, Yousef bought a one-way ticket for a Philippines Airline flight to Cebu. He was, he told the travel agent with a sweep of his hand, an Italian member of parliament visiting the country. The man certainly could not be accused of lacking gall.

Two days later Yousef walked through the X-ray machines at Manila airport, a nine-volt battery hidden in each of his shoes, boarded flight 434 to Cebu and sat near the back in seat 35F. The flight took off and Yousef asked a stewardess if he could move forward to seat 26K in the economy-class section of the Boeing 747-200. 'Do you mind?' he asked. 'I can have a better view from up there.'

Air stewardess Maria Delacruz, glancing at each passenger as she made her way down the aisles, noticed the solitary Arab. His prominent nose stuck in her mind. Halfway through the short flight Yousef disappeared into the toilet, took off his shoes and assembled a bomb in a few minutes. Yousef returned to his seat, sat down and waited until Delacruz was serving snacks to the passengers. Then he leant forward and quickly tucked the tiny bomb into the life-vest under his seat. The plane flew on to Mactan Airport, Cebu, where Yousef disembarked before the final onward leg of the flight to Narita airport, Tokyo. Haruki Ikegami, a gentle 24-year-old engineer returning home to Japan from Cebu, where he had been adjusting industrial machinery for his employers, took Yousef's former seat on the right side of the fuselage, near the third door from the front.

Two hours later, after the plane had climbed to 10,000 metres and was flying over Minami Daito Island in Okinawa Prefecture, a flight attendant showing passengers a selection of duty-free goods spotted small traces of smoke rising from under Ikegami's seat. A fraction of a second later, at precisely 11.43 a.m. local time, Ramzi Yousef's tiny device exploded, mutilating the bottom half of Ikegami's body and nearly tearing him in two. The blast blew a small hole in the floor and severed the aileron cables that controlled the plane's flaps.

In the seat behind Ikegami another Japanese passenger called Yukihiko Usui had been asleep when the bomb went off. At first Usui thought the plane had blown apart or crashed, but in the split second as his eyes opened he glanced out of the window and saw clouds. Usui's oxygen mask dangled down in front of him, burnt and useless. 'I looked at the person in front of me . . . the person was trying to ask for help,' said Usui. Ikegami raised a solitary index finger in an agonizing last movement, then slumped back in his seat. Usui tried to move and reach Ikegami, but his legs were suddenly racked by excruciating pain. The bomb had burnt his legs and blasted small pieces of shrapnel into his lower body. It would take four months of hospital treatment and countless operations to repair Usui's damaged limbs.

Nothing could be done to help Ikegami: the horrific nature of his wounds meant that Ikegami could never have survived—his pulse stopped in less than a minute. Ignoring the blood, torn flesh, smoke, and the screams of other passengers, PAL air steward Fernando Bayot bravely struggled to fasten an oxygen mask on to Ikegami's mouth and cover his body with a blanket, to make it look as if he was alive so other passengers would not be scared'. He then went to brief Captain Ed Reyes on the chaos. Four other Japanese passengers and a Korean man were also badly injured in the explosion. The jet's steering was crippled and Captain Reyes was unsure whether he could turn the plane.

'I'm going to force it,' Reyes told First Officer Jaime Herrera. 'Let's see if it will turn.' The Captain dumped fuel over the sea and by brute force managed to put the plane into a wide turn. The plane limped on to make an emergency landing at Naha airport in Okinawa, on the southern tip of the Japanese archipelago, at 12.45 p.m. Only the skill of Reyes, Herrera and Flight Engineer Dexter Comendador prevented a greater disaster and the deaths of all 272 passengers and 20 crew.

Chief Inspector Taas of the Philippines National Police (PNP) had a quick look at the machine inside room 603, then took it back to his office, turned it on and had a browse through its directories. Then he contacted the PNP's Presidential Security Group, and sent it over to them in a police car for examination. A computer expert working for the PNP as a consultant and another technical investigator both examined the machine and began to find snippets of information that hinted at a massive terrorist attack.

In a file Yousef had created on his laptop under the heading 'Bojinka' he detailed how five of his men would plant bombs timed to explode simultaneously on 11 US airliners over the Pacific. If successful the operation would have caused the deaths of up to 4,000 people flying from Asia to the United States and almost certainly shut down the entire airline industry. It was an astonishing plot hallmarked by Yousef's meticulous planning. Each of the five terrorists was given a code-name:

> 1. 'Mirqas' was to plant a bomb on a United Airlines flight from Manila to Seoul and leave the flight in South Korea. The plane would then continue towards San Francisco from Seoul and explode over the Pacific. Mirqas would also plant another bomb on a Delta flight from Seoul to Taipei. That would explode on the next leg of the flight to Bangkok, but Mirqas would have left the plane in Taipei and flown to Singapore, then home to Karachi.
> 2. 'Markoa' would place a bomb on a Northwest Airlines flight from Manila to Tokyo, then disembark. The plane would blow up en route to Chicago, by which time Markoa would have already boarded a Northwest flight from Tokyo to Hong Kong and planted a bomb timed to explode over the Pacific, as the plane was on its way to New York. Markoa would get off in Hong Kong, fly to Singapore and then on to Pakistan.
> 3. 'Obaid' was to plant a bomb on the United flight from Singapore to Hong Kong: it would then detonate in the middle of the flight's continuation to Los Angeles. Obaid, meanwhile, would board the United flight from Hong Kong to Singapore, plant a bomb set to explode on the return leg to Hong Kong, and then fly directly from Singapore home to Pakistan.
> 4. 'Majbos' would fly from Taipei to Tokyo on United and leave a bomb set to go off as the jet headed on to Los Angeles. He would then fly from Tokyo to Hong Kong

and place a bomb aboard another United flight set to go off as the jet flew from Tokyo to New York.

5. 'Zyed' would have the most difficult task: he was supposed to fly Northwest to Seoul, hide a bomb under his seat and get off. The bomb would then explode on the next leg of the flight to Los Angeles. Zyed, probably the codename for Yousef, would by then have flown on to Taipei on United, left a bomb to explode on the Taipei–Honolulu leg of the flight and disembarked. He would then fly to Bangkok on United and leave the plane, having hidden a bomb under the seat timed to explode as the plane flew towards San Francisco, and leaving the terrorist plenty of time to fly to Karachi from Bangkok.

Investigators now believe that Yousef, Murad and Shah were three of the terrorists. Filipino officers and the FBI claim one of Yousef's brothers was to have been the fourth terrorist, and the fifth is alleged to have been a man called Khalid Al-Shaikh (*aka* Khalid Sheikh Mohammad) who Pakistani intelligence sources claim is Ramzi Yousef's other uncle. Mohammad allegedly arrived in Manila . . . but then disappeared; he is now a fugitive, with a $5 million reward on his head. According to Pakistani intelligence sources he is now living in Qatar.

Many reporters and analysts have applied the blanket label of 'Islamic fundamentalist' to Ramzi Yousef, suggesting—largely on the basis that he claims to be a Muslim—that his motivation is religious ideology and a wish to fight a holy war against the Christian West. It is a false assumption: there is scant evidence to support any description of Yousef as a religious warrior. 'He's not someone you would ever describe, in any shape or form, as being religious,' said Neil Herman. 'He hid behind a cloak of Islam.'

Despite the best efforts of some politicians and elements of the Western media to portray Islam as something akin to religious Communism, as a virulent and contagious disease threatening good Christian families, Islam is not and has never been a religion that espouses violence, the murder of children or the indiscriminate killing of innocent men and women. Islam is a creed of peace and veneration, but one that has in recent decades become inextricably linked with a struggle between the Western, broadly Christian democracies of Europe and North America, and the Muslim nations of the Middle East and their battle against the perceived oppressive policies of the state of Israel. Obscene crimes have certainly been committed in the name of Islam, but centuries of evil have been perpetuated by zealous Christians massacring, enslaving, torturing and destroying civilizations and races they arrogantly deemed heathen and ungodly. Identifying Yousef simply as an Islamic terrorist is not only inaccurate, it also does an injustice to one of the world's great religions.

Yousef may claim to be a religious man and a good Muslim, but while he was a student in Wales, when he was a wanted terrorist on the run in the Philippines, and even when he was on trial in New York, many aspects of his behaviour would have been frowned upon even by liberal Islamic leaders.

Good pious Muslims, for example, do not beat their young defence-less wives, as Yousef did (one of his relatives even complained about his marital violence during an interview with Pakistani investigators).

Good Muslims also do not flirt with married women or view themselves as international playboys. During a brief lull in proceedings several weeks into one of Yousef's trials his attorney approached Christine Cornell, the blonde, attractive 42-year-old married courtroom sketch artist, and told her Yousef would like to go on a date with her if he was acquitted. Was she interested, he wondered? Cornell had already realized she was becoming a target for Yousef's affections when he had turned to her during a pre-trial hearing and gave her what she later described as 'one of those up-and-under smiles'. Cornell might have liked sketching Yousef, apparently because of his 'intense eyes', but she sensibly declined his offer with a gracious 'thank you'.

After his arrest Yousef gave just one serious interview before stringent restrictions were imposed on his communications with the media: to Raghida Dergham, a senior correspondent from the London-based *Al-Hayat* newspaper, which is circulated widely within the Middle East. When asked whether he considers himself an Islamic fundamentalist, Yousef himself merely answered with another question: 'First, Israel itself was established on an extremist fundamentalist thinking, why is this not mentioned about Israel while it is said about the Muslims in every case they are accused of?'

Unlike most fundamentalist terrorists, Yousef raised no objections to being interviewed by a woman—indeed he actually tried to flirt with Dergham. He also failed to fast during the Muslim holy month of Ramadan while in jail, an event observed with pride by millions of liberal Muslims living in the West.

So Yousef did not start his bombing campaign because of simple Muslim zealotry. Although he is certainly a complex character, the prevailing view of intelligence agents and investigators who have studied Yousef closely is that he cannot be labelled simply as an 'Islamic fundamentalist'. Investigators have considered other more direct political motivations for his crimes which can be found elsewhere in his background and upbringing.

Ramzi Yousef, the investigators and agents conclude, is the first of a new breed of terrorist, one with no clear or definable political goals. His motivation was not wholly religious or wholly political, but a combination of the two which manifested itself in a desire to inflict pain and suffering on his enemies, mainly the West for its political arrogance and support for Israel, but also on those Shiite Muslims who oppose his own Sunni Muslim views.

In his eyes it is guilt by association: the West supports Israel, and the Israelis oppress the Palestinians. So the West must suffer for its crimes. Raghida Dergham from *Al-Hayat* recalls that when Yousef arrived for their interview in New York's Metropolitan Correctional Center he brought with him a whole stack of papers to prove his claim that the Israeli occupation of Arab lands was illegal.

Dergham does not believe Yousef is particularly religious. 'In fact, he did not come across as a fundamentalist as such,' she said. 'He would fit more as a freedom fighter for the liberation of Palestine than the description of an Islamic fundamentalist driven by religion. He is very convinced there is something unjust in the actions of Israel and there has to be a way to bring attention to it. By that he justifies "terror for terror". '

Although he has a Pakistani father and was born in Kuwait, Yousef identifies with two cultural groups: the Baluchi people of his father's homeland, and the Palestinians. He describes himself as 'Pakistani by birth, Palestinian by choice'. The genesis of Yousef's aggression against the West is two central beliefs. The first is that Israel is an illegitimate state, and its existence is 'void morally and legally'. The second is an almost natural conclusion of his first: because of their suffering the Palestinians have the right to attack Israeli targets and any other organization or country that interferes in support of Israel.

Yousef invokes the law of collective responsibility to justify acts that kill and maim innocent civilians. The Israelis were the first to 'kill the civilians', he says, and Israel 'has invented its own way of collective punishment'. What the Israeli authorities do when a Palestinian is suspected of a terrorist act, according to Yousef, 'is they would go inside the house, would take the whole family out and they would blow up the house. They would punish the whole members of the family because one person was charged with [terrorism]. It was only last year when more than 200 houses were blown up . . . to get a so-called terrorist.'

In his mind Yousef then makes a direct connection between the Israeli military, which have indeed been criticized by dozens of international human rights groups, and individual American taxpayers, who, he says, 'have been supporting Israel throughout all the years in killing and torturing peoples'.

'Anyone that commits a killing crime or helps the killer with money or weapon[s], legally he is considered a participant in the crime and in the punishment,' said Yousef, who believes that terrorist attacks that kill civilians are a result of the 'collective punishment' inflicted on Iraq and Libya, where 'the United States punishes the entire population for the mistakes of the government'.

Thus, according to his logic, Americans and Israelis are equally responsible for crimes committed in Palestine. America 'finances these crimes [in Israel]' and supports Israel with weapons, he says. 'These funds are taken from the taxes which the Americans pay,' so this makes the American people, 'logically and legally', 'responsible for all the killing crimes and the settlements and the torture and the imprisonment which the Palestinian people are exposed to. And it doesn't help them that they do not know the area where the money from their taxes which they pay to the government goes.'

Yousef claims he is an avenging warrior, but despite his hatred of Americans and the Israeli state, he does not appear to have an all-consuming hatred of Jews *per se*. One Jew who has met and talked with Yousef is Avraham Moskowitz, a court-appointed New York lawyer initially picked at random to represent him after his arrest in Pakistan. Moskowitz, then 38-years-old, is an Orthodox Jew who wears a yarmulke almost everywhere. 'My Jewishness is obvious from my name and from the minute you meet me,' said Moskowitz, a partner at the law firm of Anderson Kill Olick & Oshinsky. 'People tell me that it's something that I can't and I don't hide.'

With Yousef, however, a man portrayed by elements of the media as the world's most dangerous Islamic fundamentalist, Moskowitz's religion, and his 'obvious Jewishness' was not an issue. 'He didn't say, "No, I don't want you, you're a Jewish lawyer." Nor did he ever question the validity of the advice or the motivation behind what I was telling him because of the fact that I was Jewish,' said Moskowitz. 'To his credit, the issue of my being Jewish did not affect his ability to take advice from me or to relate to me.' Moskowitz admits that he was 'mildly surprised' Yousef had no objections to having a Jewish lawyer. 'There was reason to suspect that I was the last person he would want to represent him,' he said.

It is Yousef's anger at the interminable suffering of the Palestinian people that has been the central anger driving him to terrorism, and he will happily produce evidence to back his claim that crimes have been committed against 'his people'. 'The numbers of Palestinians in 1917 according to United Nations publications was about 1.1 million,' he said. 'And now after more than 80 years there are less than 700,000 and the rest of them were either killed, deported, or living now in temporary shelters and camps in overseas countries as foreigners, and you [America] have been supporting all of this killing and deportation throughout the 80 years.'

There is a distinction, says Yousef, between Israel, which he believes is fighting to expand its borders, and the Palestinians, who 'are not fighting to steal a land which does not belong to them or to confiscate properties or to steal properties which don't belong to them.' What they are fighting for, says Yousef, 'is to get their lands and confiscated properties and historic properties back while those who are killing and stealing and torturing, you are supporting them'.

Ramzi Yousef is the archetypal angry young man. Like an incandescent student radical from the 1960s, his anger crosses continents as he rails at the world's inequities. He rants against Israeli kibbutzim to which only Jews have access, and claims that such practices in America would be called racism. But America supports Israel because the US 'was based on racism and founded on racism on the slavery of black people and confiscation of land and properties of indigenous people, Indians in this country'.

In Northern Ireland, Yousef is furious that Sinn Fein, the political wing of the IRA, has engaged in talks with the British and Irish governments without guarantees that would 'bring those responsible for the occupation of Northern Ireland before a War Crimes court'. Even China has not escaped his attention. He expresses outrage at the apparent hypocrisy of the West, which keeps talking 'about human rights in China and the Chinese prisoners' when, according to him, the only reason the West is concerned is because Chinese prison inmates are forced to work for free making products that are flooding the West.

The West, says Yousef, was the first to kill innocent people and introduce terrorism into human history when America dropped an atomic bomb 'which killed tens of thousands of women and children in Japan and when you killed over 100,000 people, most of them civilians, in Tokyo with fire bombings', he said. Civilians in Vietnam, he adds, were massacred with chemicals such as Agent Orange. 'You went to wars more than any other country in this century and then you have the nerve to talk about killing innocent people. And then you have invented new ways to kill innocent people. You have [the] so-called economic embargo which kills nobody other than children and elderly people, and which other than Iraq you have been placing the economic embargo on Cuba and other countries for over 35 years.'

According to Yousef he has simply used the same tactics against America. 'Since this is the way you invented and since this is the means you have been using against other people which you continue until this day to use in killing innocent people, innocent people just to force countries to change their policies, it was necessary to use the same means against you because this is the only language which you understand. This is the only language which . . . someone can deal with you and talk with you.'

So does Yousef consider himself to be a terrorist? 'If the terrorist means to retrieve my land and to fight everyone who has attacked me and my relatives, I have no objection to being called a terrorist,' said Yousef, 'it is the right of all the Muslims, in addition to the Palestinians, to fight the Zionists'. If Jews were exposed to oppression at the hands of the Nazis, says Yousef, 'why do the Palestinians pay the price for this? And also the Blacks were exposed to slavery and oppression in [the United States], so why are they not given a state such as the Jews?'

Yousef is too arrogant to apologize for the appalling crimes he has committed, but he offers a pathetic justification. 'Although it is very painful to innocent people and very painful for anyone to lose a close relative or a friend, but it was necessary. This is what it takes to make you feel the pain which you are causing to other people and this is what it takes to make you understand what you are causing and doing to other people and the pain which you are causing.'

Although Ramzi Yousef likes to portray himself as a sophisticated polyglot, most of his knowledge is second-hand, passed on by his father, friends, family, and taken from books and pamphlets. His hatred has been imbued rather than learnt from bitter personal experience. Ramzi Yousef has never been shot at or tear-gassed by Israeli soldiers on the West Bank: he has never even visited Palestine. Yet the battle for the creation of an independent Palestinian state became a powerful romantic lure for the young radical. Born and brought up in Kuwait, Yousef does not consider himself a Kuwaiti. Despite a Pakistani father and a Pakistani passport; despite a secure upbringing, and several years of education in the West, Yousef chose to affiliate himself with the Palestinians and launch a devastating terrorist war against America on their behalf—one that could have led to terrible repercussions against the Palestinian people. Only an arrogant man could have such total belief in his own righteousness, but arrogance is a personality flaw that Yousef enjoys to excess.

When a questioner asked Yousef if he considers himself to be a genius, he thought for a brief moment, then smiled shyly and answered with conviction: 'Yes.' When he was asked to describe the type of personality that he most admires, Yousef could well have been talking about himself when he replied: 'The personality of the messenger on whom God has prayed and greeted.' Yousef sees himself as an emissary, one sent by a higher power to deliver unpalatable news to the world. His message, put simply, is that those responsible for the ill-treatment of the Palestinians, a people whose suffering he has adopted as his own, must face the wrath of God, administered by God's self-appointed representative: Ramzi Yousef.

Such is the importance of Yousef's 'mission' against the West that even his own death is little more than an occupational hazard. 'If it was true that I made the bomb which was used in the [bombing of the] World Trade Center, if this was true, then the person who manufactures the explosives, and transfers them and uses them, accepts all the risks which result from this . . . ' he said.

Within this answer perhaps lies evidence of the psychological strength necessary to survive the intense mental pressure of spending two years on the run from the determined agents of the only surviving superpower. Vanity and belief in his 'mission' has blocked any innate sense of self-preservation—even the lives of his two young daughters are expendable in pursuit of his wider objectives: 'If the case is more important than my own self, no doubt it will be more important than any other thing, we [he uses the plural to identify with the Palestinian people] haven't chosen this path voluntarily but we were forced to go through it as a result of the killing and the occupation which we are living through. He who accepts the work of manufacturing explosives accepts what is less than that of dangers . . . And if God wills they [his daughters] are in safety.'

Perhaps this supreme self-confidence makes Yousef a more seductive character. Physically, he has large flapping ears, a bulbous nose, a wiry, lean shape, dark hair and brown eyes. He also bears the scars of his trade. One of his eyes is unstable, roaming around slightly out of sync with the other. There are faint burn marks on his face, and several of his nails are cracked and broken right up to the flesh of his fingers. Yet he still retains rugged good looks which have helped to attract a wife and several girlfriends. His radical beliefs, meanwhile, won him a gang of followers in the United States, Pakistan and the Philippines, all within the space of a few years.

Yousef specialized in recruiting simpletons to act as his expendable soldiers. Several of his supporters, including Mohammad Salameh and Eyad Ismoil, are of below average intelligence. However Yousef also persuaded intelligent university graduates such as Nidal Ayyad, a conspirator in the World Trade Center bombing, to risk his life and comfortable career in grand terrorist plots, while Abdul Hakim Murad seems to have been willing to take his own life in one of Yousef's plans for a suicide attack. His talent for manipulating those around him, and his strength of personality, was even noted by the judge who presided over his later trials. 'I watched you closely during two long trials,' Judge Kevin Duffy told Yousef. 'I have observed you during your many appearances in court. You tried to charm the jury, and, I will admit, you are not without charm. So I can well understand how you were successful in charming others to join in your cause.' And, Judge Duffy added: 'You are smart.'

A senior Pakistani intelligence officer gives a similar summary: 'Everywhere Yousef went he was able to convert religious young men to his terrorist cause. His power was based partly on fear and partly on persuasion—he convinced some of these youngsters that what they were doing was in the name of Allah. He knew exactly what to say and what to do to win them over. Ramzi Yousef is an evil genius.'

Declaration of War Against the Americans Occupying the Land of the Two Holy Places

by Osama bin Laden

Osama bin Laden was a man known mainly by his violent deeds until recent events encouraged the global broadcast of several taped statements smuggled out of Afghanistan. In this written statement from 1996 he issued a *fatwa* against the U.S. Leaving aside the historical religious issue (only Mullahs have the right to issue religious decrees such as fatwas) this speech demonstrates the two aspects of bin Laden's campaign against the U.S. On the one hand he is a pragmatic politician, a kind of global spokesman for the Arab street, affirming traditional demands that require a response: the U.S. must leave Saudi Arabia and Israel. On the other he is evoking an ultimate jihad, a clash of civilizations that can only end in the triumph of one of the two parties and the destruction of the other. When one fails to convince, the other is evoked in a never-ending pirouette. It is the combination of earthly politics and messianic fervor as embodied by the Taliban regime—called by bin Laden the truest vision of Islam on earth—that has shown the deeply cynical nature of his realpolitik. Among a myriad of other details in a lengthy text filled with obscure religious references, bin Laden proposes raising the price of oil to $120 a barrel ("its true value") and boycotting all U.S. goods. Like a true political office-seeker he never says anything that would offend his potential constituency. There are pages of criticism of decadent Arab regimes, but not a word of criticism of ordinary Arabs for submitting to this tyranny. This is all the more noteworthy because bin Laden holds the American people directly responsible for their alleged complicity with their government, thus attempting to justify the killing of thousands.

P raise be to Allah, we seek His help and ask for his pardon. We take refuge in Allah from our wrongs and bad deeds. Who ever been guided by Allah will not be misled, and who ever has been misled, he will never be guided. I bear witness that there is no God except Allah, no associates with Him and I bear witness that Muhammad is His slave and messenger.

It should not be hidden from you that the people of Islam had suffered from aggression, iniquity and injustice imposed on them by the Zionist-Crusaders alliance and their collaborators; to the extent that the Muslims blood became the cheapest and their wealth as loot in the hands of the enemies. Their blood was spilled in Palestine and Iraq. The horrifying pictures of the massacre of Qana, in Lebanon are still fresh in our memory. Massacres in Tajikistan, Burma, Cashmere, Assam, Philippine, Fatani, Ogadin, Somalia, Eritrea, Chechnya and in Bosnia Herzegovina took place, massacres that send shivers in the body and shake the conscience. All of this and the world watch and hear, and not only didn't respond to these atrocities, but also with a clear conspiracy between the USA and its allies and under the cover of the iniquitous United Nations, the dispossessed people were even prevented from obtaining arms to defend themselves.

The people of Islam awakened and realized that they are the main target for the aggression of the Zionist-Crusaders alliance. All false claims and propaganda about "Human Rights" were hammered down and exposed by the massacres that took place against the Muslims in every part of the world. The latest and the greatest of these aggressions, incurred by the Muslims since the death of the Prophet (ALLAH'S BLESSING AND SALUTATIONS ON HIM) is the occupation of the land of the two

Holy Places the foundation of the house of Islam, the place of the revelation, the source of the message and the place of the noble Ka'ba, the Qiblah of all Muslims by the armies of the American Crusaders and their allies. (We bemoan this and can only say: "No power and power acquiring except through Allah").

My Muslim Brothers (particularly those of the Arab Peninsula):

The money you pay to buy American goods will be transformed into bullets and used against our brothers in Palestine and tomorrow (future) against our sons in the land of the two Holy places. By buying these goods we are strengthening their economy while our dispossession and poverty increases.

Muslims Brothers of land of the two Holy Places:

It is incredible that our country is the world largest buyer of arms from the USA and the area biggest commercial partners of the Americans who are assisting their Zionist brothers in occupying Palestine and in evicting and killing the Muslims there, by providing arms, men and financial supports. To deny these occupiers from the enormous revenues of their trading with our country is a very important help for our Jihad against them. To express our anger and hate to them is a very important moral gesture. By doing so we would have taken part in (the process of) cleansing our sanctities from the crusaders and the Zionists and forcing them, by the Permission of Allah, to leave disappointed and defeated.

We expect the woman of the land of the two Holy Places and other countries to carry out their role in boycotting the American goods. If economical boycotting is intertwined with the military operations of the Mujahideen, then defeating the enemy will be even nearer, by the Permission of Allah. However if Muslims don't cooperate and support their Mujahideen brothers then, in effect, they are supplying the army of the enemy with financial help and extending the war and increasing the suffering of the Muslims.

The ruling to kill the Americans and their allies—civilians and military— is an individual duty for every Muslim who can do it in any country in which it is possible to do it, in order to liberate the al-Aqsa Mosque and the holy mosque [Mecca] from their grip, and in order for their armies to move out of all the lands of Islam, defeated and unable to threaten any Muslim. This is in accordance with the words of Almighty God, "and fight the pagans all together as they fight you all together," and "fight them until there is no more tumult or oppression, and there prevail justice and faith in God."

This is in addition to the words of Almighty God: "And why should ye not fight in the cause of God and of those who, being weak, are ill-treated (and oppressed)?—women and children, whose cry is: 'Our Lord, rescue us from this town, whose people are oppressors; and raise for us from thee one who will help!' "

We—with God's help—call on every Muslim who believes in God and wishes to be rewarded to comply with God's order to kill the Americans and plunder their money wherever and whenever they find it. We also call on Muslim ulema, leaders, youths, and people. An injustice that had affected every section and group of the people; the civilians, military and security men, government officials and merchants, the young and the old people as well as schools and university students. Hundred of thousands of the unemployed graduates, who became the widest section of the society, were also affected.

A Portrait of the Terrorist from Shy Child to Singleminded Killer

by Jim Yardley

This article on the life of Mohamed Atta that appeared in the *New York Times* one month after the September 11th attacks puts a face on the suicide hijacker. From the inability to find social acceptance to a father who saw him as girlish and to whom he needed to prove something, Atta has updated the "psychological profile" of a suicide bomber. Even more disturbing, what emerges is a bright young man who consciously chose to become a terrorist with a suicidal mission rather than the career in urban planning or architecture for which he was being prepared. The shock and surprise of September 11 led his father to deny first that his son was dead, then that he was on the plane, and finally that he was responsible for a terrorist act.

This article is based on reporting by Neil MacFarquhar, Jim Yardley and Paul Zielbauer and was written by Mr. Yardley.

P recisely two years ago, not long before he traveled to the United States to coordinate the worst terrorist attacks in history, Mohamed Atta attended a wedding. The event was held in the German port city of Hamburg, where Mr. Atta had recently earned a university degree, but this was not the marriage of a college friend.

The groom was Said Bahaji, now the focus of an international manhunt for his suspected role in the Sept. 11 attacks. Prominent among the guests was Mamoun Darkazanli, a Syrian businessman suspected of being a financial conduit for Osama bin Laden's Al Qaeda organization. Another guest was Mr. Atta's friend, Marwan al-Shehhi, whom authorities say crashed the second hijacked airliner into the World Trade Center.

This was not what Mr. Atta's father in Egypt had imagined when he sent his son abroad to earn the sort of academic degree that would bring him prestige and success at home. Instead of becoming an architect or an urban planner, Mr. Atta had become an Islamic terrorist.

Mr. Atta's path to Sept. 11, pieced together from interviews with people who knew him across 33 years and three continents, was a quiet and methodical evolution of resentment that somehow—and that how remains the essential imponderable—took a leap to mass-murderous fury.

The youngest child of a pampering mother and an ambitious father, Mr. Atta was a polite, shy boy who came of age in an Egypt torn between growing Western influence and the religious fundamentalism that gathered force in reaction. But it was not until he was on his own, in the West, that his religious faith deepened and his resentments hardened. The focus of his disappointment became the Egyptian government; the target of his blame became the West, and especially America.

In Hamburg, his life divided into before and after. He would disappear more than once, and officials say they have strong evidence that he trained at Mr. bin Laden's terrorist camps in Afghanistan during the late 1990's. It was also in those years, German investigators say, that Mr. Atta became part of the Hamburg cell that became a key planning point for the Sept. 11 attacks.

"I remember that he changed somewhat," said Dittmar Machule, his academic supervisor at Hamburg Technical University. "He looked more serious, and he didn't smile as much."

His acquaintances from that time still cannot reconcile him as a killer, but in hindsight the raw ingredients of his personality suggest some clues. He was meticulous, disciplined and highly intelligent.

His vision of Islam embraced resolute precepts of fate and destiny and purity, and, ultimately, tolerated no compromise. He ate no pork and scraped the frosting off cakes, in case it contained lard. He threatened to leave the university unless he was given a room for a prayer group. He spoke of a desire to marry, but was remote to the point of rudeness with women, considering most insufficiently devout.

Those who had known him as a quiet student say his demeanor became more brooding, more troubled. The most obvious change was both cosmetic and spiritual: he had grown the beard of an Islamic fundamentalist.

A Shy and Sheltered Boy

The genteel gloss of the Abdein neighborhood of Cairo had dulled to shabby disrepair by the early 1980's when Mohamed al-Amir Atta entered his teenage years. The government workers who had once lived well on $100 a month found themselves in a vortex of downward mobility, working second and third jobs to survive.

Mr. Atta's father, a lawyer, considered his neighbors inferior, even if he, too, feared the economic undertow. Neighbors recalled an arrogant man who often passed without a word or a glance.

The family was viewed as thoroughly modern, the two daughters headed for careers as a professor and a doctor. The father was the disciplinarian, grumbling that his wife spoiled their bright, if timid, son, who continued to sit on her lap until enrolling at Cairo University.

"I used to tell her that she is raising him as a girl, and that I have three girls, but she never stopped pampering him," Mohamed al-Amir Atta Sr. recalled in a recent interview at his apartment.

In a high school classroom of 26 students grouped by their shared given name, Mohammed Hassan Attiya recalled that Mr. Atta focused solely on becoming an engineer—and following his father's bidding.

"I never saw him playing," Mr. Attiya said. "We did not like him very much, and I think he wanted to play with the rest of the boys, but his family, and I think his father, wanted him to always perform in school in an excellent way."

The social, political and religious pressures roiling Egypt exploded in 1981 with the assassination of President Anwar el-Sadat, the first Arab leader to make peace with Israel. Fundamentalists decried him as a puppet of the West, a traitor to Islam.

Even for a boy as sheltered as Mr. Atta, the disillusionment on the streets would have been difficult to ignore. His father, without explanation, says his son began to pray in earnest at 12 or 13, an awakening that coincided closely with Sadat's slaying. But the elder Mr. Atta said his son's religious inclination did not extend to politics.

"I advised him, like my father advised me, that politics equals hypocrisy," his father said.

The boy refused to join a basketball league because it was organized by the Muslim Brotherhood, Egypt's most established religious political organization, which also recruited from Cairo University's engineering department but not, apparently, Mr. Atta, who graduated from there in 1990.

His degree meant little in a country where thousands of college graduates were unable to find good jobs. Though Mr. Atta found work with a German company in Cairo and was reluctant to leave his mother and sisters, his father convinced him that only an advanced degree from abroad would allow him to prosper in Egypt. Soon he was headed to Hamburg Technical University on scholarship.

"I told him I needed to hear the word 'doctor' in front of his name," his father recalled. "We told him your sisters are doctors and their husbands are doctors and you are the man of the family."

From initial appearances, the slender young Mr. Atta remained the same person in Hamburg that he had been in Egypt—polite, distant and neatly dressed. He answered a classified ad and was hired part-time at an urban planning firm, plankontor. He impressed his co-workers with his diligence and the careful elegance of his drafting.

Yet he must have felt unmoored, on his own in a strange land. He took refuge in the substantial population of Turkish, African and Arab immigrants living in the blue-collar Harburg section surrounding the university. There, his religious faith, still tentative in Egypt, took deeper hold.

He brought a prayer carpet to his job and carefully adhered to Islamic dietary restrictions, shunning alcohol and checking the ingredients of everything, even medicine. He had his choice of three mosques, but the two closest to campus were dominated by Turks, whom many local Arabs disdained as less devout and too sympathetic to America.

Instead, Mr. Atta often prayed at the Arabic-language Al-Tauhid mosque, a bleak back room of a small shop where the imam, Ahmed Emam, preached that America was an enemy of Islam and a country "unloved in our world."

Mr. Atta's academic focus was Arab cities, specifically preserving them in the face of Western-style development. He returned to Cairo for three months in 1995 to observe a renovation project around the old city gates, Bab Al-Nasr and Bab Al-Futuh. The project, he came to believe, involved little more than knocking down a poor neighborhood to improve the views for tourists.

"It made him angry," recalled Ralph Bodenstein, one of two German students in the program. "He said it was a completely absurd way to develop the city, to make a Disneyworld out of it."

Over meals with Mr. Bodenstein and the other German student, Volker Hauth, Mr. Atta spoke bitterly about the government's suppression of Islamic fundamentalist groups and the clinics and day care centers they had built in ignored neighborhoods.

His sympathy for their cause, Mr. Atta feared, would doom his own future at home. His only hope for a good urban-planning job in Egypt was to be hired by an international organization. He tried but never was. The young man sent West to better his future at home now worried that he had no future in Egypt at all.

He returned to Hamburg in 1996, and investigators say he eventually moved into an apartment at 54 Marienstrasse with two other suspected hijackers, Mr. al-Shehhi and Ziad Jarrah.

In November 1997 he paid an unexpected visit to his academic supervisor, Professor Machule, to discuss his thesis, then disappeared again for about a year. Federal officials say they have strong evidence that he trained at an Al Qaeda camp in Afghanistan during the late 1990's, which could explain his whereabouts in 1998.

He reappeared in Hamburg in early 1999, the period that German investigators connect him with the cell of about 20 other suspected terrorists. At the university, he insisted on a room for an Islamic prayer group. A student council representative demurred, suspicious that such organizations were cover for terrorist recruitment.

"He said, 'This is about my life. If I cannot pray here, I cannot study here, at this university,'" said the council representative, Marcus Meyer.

Mr. Atta's degree had been on hold; suddenly, finishing it became imperative. He submitted his thesis in August 1999. When he successfully defended his thesis, graduating with high honors, Mr. Atta refused to shake hands with one of the two judges, a woman.

His father has told reporters that his son earned a masters degree in Germany, but in fact, Mr. Atta received only an undergraduate degree. But his attentions were already elsewhere. He began preparing to go to America.

A Disciplined Perfectionist

With few exceptions, Mohamed Atta regarded the Americans who crossed his path with the same contempt his father once reserved for his Cairo neighbors. He was polite when he had to be—to rent a car or an airplane—but the mildness recalled by his friends in Egypt and Germany was gone, as was his beard.

He arrived in June at Newark International Airport and would spend the next 15 months in near perpetual motion, earning a pilot's license in

Florida during the last six months of 2000, then spending the first nine months of 2001 traveling across the country and at least twice to Europe.

The awful efficiency of the attack demanded a leader with a precise and disciplined temperament, and Mr. Atta apparently filled that role. Federal investigators have told a House committee that in the fall of 2000, as he was in the middle of flight training in Venice, Fla., Mr. Atta received a wire transfer of more than $100,000 from a source in the United Arab Emirates. Investigators believe the source was Mustafa Ahmad, thought to be an alias for Shaykh Said, a finance chief for Mr. bin Laden.

For much of 2001, Mr. Atta appeared to make important contacts with other hijackers or conspirators. He traveled twice to Spain, in January and July, and officials are investigating whether he met with Al Qaeda contacts. He also used Florida as a base to move around the United States, including trips to Atlanta, where he rented a plane, to New Jersey, where he may have met with other hijackers, and at least two trips to Las Vegas. Everywhere he went, he made hundreds of cell phone calls and made a point to rent computers for e-mails, including at a Las Vegas computer store, Cyberzone, where customers can play a video game about terrorists with a voice that declares "terrorists win."

While Mr. Atta was considered a perfectionist, he was not infallible. Brad Warrick, owner of a rental agency in South Florida where Mr. Atta returned a car two days before the attack, found an ATM receipt and a white Post-it note that became key evidence. Mr. Atta's decision to wire $4,000 overseas shortly before the attacks left an electronic trail that investigators believe is leading back to Al Qaeda. Finally, authorities found his luggage at Logan Airport in Boston, containing, among other things, his will. It remains unclear if the bag simply missed the connection to his flight.

Or perhaps the introvert, the meticulous planner, the man who believed he was doing God's will, wanted to make certain the world knew his name.

FRINGE TERRORISM

Fringe Terrorism

U nlike the political and religious radicals who supposedly seek to completely transform society, the fringe elements represented in this section have specific, narrowly defined issues around which they are mobilized. It is their choice of terrorism, not the inherent threat posed by their views, that leads them to be perceived as enemies of society.

The right-wing terrorism practiced by Timothy McVeigh was based on the notion that rather than protecting individual rights, the federal government trampled on them, as it did at Waco. For Theodore Kaczynski, the Unabomber, technology was a dehumanizing force that was incompatible with personal freedom. Aum Shinrikyo took the persecutive delusions of one man and turned it into a global apocalyptic theory.

In the new era of global religious based terrorism, the fringe terrorists do not represent the same level of threat. Their activities are disruptive in part because they add a level of confusion to the growing picture of violence. For example, the recent anthrax attacks may be the work of extremist right-wing groups or an Aum Shinrikyo style paranoid. The very fact that peripheral groups are marginal and do not generally take credit for their acts makes them all the more difficult to find. The fringe terrorists' failure to attract a continuous stream of new recruits and the obvious inconsistencies of their ideas eventually lead to their dissolution. But these groups have to be taken seriously, in part because they may be driven to compete with or may be used by more powerful terrorist groups in an ever-escalating spiral of hostility.

The International Jew
by Henry Ford

This shocking excerpt by auto magnate Henry Ford, originally run in a
Dearborn, Michigan, newspaper and later collected in a book, demonstrated the supposed financial advantage of anti-Semitism. Ford, one of
the world's richest men, saw the Jews as competition, particularly in
the rapidly growing cultural sector. His response was to attack their collective character, perhaps as a way of weakening their hold on certain
markets or encouraging individuals to boycott their products. This
approach was consistent with strategies employed by the Nazis (whom
Ford supported until the war made his position treasonous). Having
seized Jewish property without compensation, turning it over to
Christian businessmen, the Nazis left the markets intact, nationalizing
only those industries necessary for the outfitting of the war machine.
The Turner Diaries, the *Mein Kampf* of the current extremist right and a
book that heavily influenced Timothy McVeigh, advocates a similar
approach, keeping everything about the market system except the participation of the Jews. It has a strong appeal to the lower-middle-class
followers of the militia mentality living on the margins of today's afflu-
ence. As Hitler realized, dividing up Jewish assets would go a long way
toward solving Germany's financial problems. The creation of a "pure"
or all-white nation would have a silver lining.

Theater and Cinema

The Theater has long been a part of the Jewish program for the guidance of public taste and the influencing of the public mind. Not only is the theater given a special place in the program of the Protocols, but it is the instant ally night by night and week by week of any idea which the "power behind the scenes" wishes to put forth. . . .

Not only the "legitimate" stage, so-called, but the motion picture industry—the fifth greatest of all industries—is also entirely Jew-controlled. . . .

Every night hundreds of thousands of people give from two to three dollars to the Theater, every day literally millions of people give up from 30 minutes to 3 hours to the "Movies"; and this simply means that millions of Americans every day place themselves voluntarily within range of Jewish ideas of life, love and labor; within close range of Jewish propaganda, sometimes cleverly, sometimes clumsily concealed. This gives the Jewish masseur of the public mind all the opportunity he desires; and his only protest now is that exposure may make his game a trifle difficult. . . .

The screen, whether consciously or just carelessly, is serving as a rehearsal stage for scenes of anti-social menace. There are no uprisings of revolutions except those that are planned and rehearsed. Revolutions are not spontaneous uprisings, but carefully planned minority actions. There have been few popular revolutions. Civilization and liberty have always been set back by those revolutions which subversive elements have succeeded in starting. Successful revolution must have a rehearsal. It can be done better in the motion pictures than anywhere else: this is the "visual education" such as even the lowest brow can understand. Indeed, there is a distinct disadvantage in being "high-brow" in such matters. Normal people shake their heads and pucker their brows and wring their hands, saying, "We cannot understand it." Of course, they cannot. But if they understood the low-brow, they would understand it, and very clearly. There are two families in this world, and on one the darkness dwells. . . .

Popular Music

Many people have wondered whence come the waves upon waves of musical slush that invade decent homes and set the young people of this generation imitating the drivel of morons. *Popular music is a Jewish monopoly.* Jazz is a Jewish creation. The mush, slush, the sly suggestion, the abandoned sensuousness of sliding notes, are of Jewish origin.

Monkey talk, jungle squeals, grunts and squeaks and gasps suggestive of calf love are camouflaged by a few feverish notes and admitted in homes where the thing itself, unaided by "canned music," would be stamped out in horror. The fluttering music sheets disclose expressions taken directly from the cesspools of modern capitals, to be made the daily slang, the thoughtlessly hummed remarks of school boys and girls.

Is it surprising that whichever way you turn to trace the harmful streams of influence that flow through society, you come upon a group of Jews? In baseball corruption—a group of Jews. In exploitative finance—a group of Jews. In theatrical degeneracy—a group of Jews. In liquor propaganda—a group of Jews. In control of national war policies— a group of Jews. In control of the Press through business and financial pressure—a group of Jews. War profiteers, 80 per cent of them—Jews. Organizers of active opposition to Christian laws and customs—Jews. . . .

The "song-pluggers" of theater, vaudeville and radio, are the paid agents of the Yiddish song agencies. Money, and not merit, dominates the spread of the moron music which is styled Jewish jazz and swing. Non-Jewish music is stigmatized as "high-brow." The people are fed from day to day on the moron suggestiveness that flows in a slimy flood out of "Tin-Pan-Alley," the head factory of filth in New York which is populated by the "Abies," the "Izzies," and the "Moes" who make up the composing staffs of the various institutions. . . . Flocks of young girls who thought they could sing, and others who thought they could write song poems, came to the neighborhood allured by the dishonest advertisements that promised more than the budding Yiddish promoters could fulfill. Needless to say, scandal became rampant, as it always does when so-called "Gentile" girls are reduced to the necessity of seeking favors from the Jew. It was the constant shouting of voices, the hilarity of "parties," the banging of pianos and the blaring of trombones that gave the district the name of "Tin-Pan-Alley." All America is now one great Tin-Pan-Alley, its entertainment, its youth, its politics, a blare of moronic Judaism. . . .

LIQUOR

The claim made for the Jews that they are a sober race may be true, but that has not obscured two facts concerning them; namely, that they usually constitute the liquor dealers of countries where they live in numbers, and that in the United States they were the only race exempted from the operations of the Prohibition Law. In general, the Jews are on the side of liquor and always have been. . . .

BASEBALL

Whether baseball as a first-class sport is killed and will survive only as a cheap-jack entertainment; or whether baseball possesses sufficient intrinsic character to rise in righteous wrath and cast out the danger that menaces it, will remain a matter of various opinion. But there is one certainty, namely, that the last and most dangerous blow dealt baseball was curiously notable for its Jewish character. . . .

To begin with, the Jews are not sportsmen. This is not set down in complaint against them, but merely as analysis. It may be a defect in their character, or it may not; it is nevertheless a fact which discriminating Jews unhesitatingly acknowledge. Whether this is due to their physical lethargy, their dislike of unnecessary physical action, or their cast of mind, others may decide; the Jew is not naturally an out-of-door sportsman; if he takes up golf it is because his station in society calls for it, not that he really likes it; and if he goes in for collegiate athletics, as some of the younger Jews are doing, it is because so much attention has been called to their neglect of sports that the younger generation thinks it necessary to remove that occasion of remark. . . .

WRESTLING

Wrestling is so tightly controlled by Jewish managers that a real wrestler is absolutely barred out, for fear he will be able to show that the handful of wrestlers hired by the Jewish Sports Trust are not wrestlers at all, but only impositions on the good nature of the public. The rottenness of the ancient sport of clean wrestling has surfaced in such disgusting orgies as "all in" and "mud" wrestling and, lately, wrestling contests between screaming viragos of the female sex. Wrestling is as much a Jewish *business* controlled in its every part as the manufacture of clothing. . . .

excerpt from:

Armed and Dangerous
by James Coates

There is a long history of a fringe element of American white
Protestants hating other religious groups, including Catholics. In this
excerpt from James Coates's work we learn that the bigotry of current
Christian Identity right-wing movements makes them a logical if
extreme inheritor of this unhappy tradition. Coates is an investigative
reporter who writes about extremist movements.

For the purpose of understanding the Survival Right's historical
roots and gaining a glimmer of its potential as a political force as
well as a seedbed of terrorism, one needs to go back to the anti-
Catholic tradition that the country's English colonists brought to the New
World along with beads and blankets to trade with the Indians. Then the
target was the Papists instead of the Jews and the conspiracy was directed
by the "Pope of Rome" instead of the "Elders of Zion."

The English colonists who first settled the Americas were molded by
the profound forces of the Protestant Reformation. These colonists were
the grandchildren of men and women who had been alive when Henry
VIII bolted the Church of Rome and established the Anglican tradition
by attacking "Popery" and claiming that an evil cabal of Jesuits was
secretly in control of world economic activity.

Throughout colonial times Catholics were a tiny minority in the
Americas, with openly practicing congregations only in Rhode Island and
Maryland until after the Revolution. And their fellow colonists wanted to
keep it that way. In 1704 the Maryland legislature enacted an "Act to
Prevent the Growth of Popery," which imposed a heavy fine for attending

Catholic religious services. In 1750 Harvard College offered lectures "for detecting and convicting and exposing of the idolatry of the Romish church, their tyranny, usurpations, damnable heresies, fatal errors, abominable superstitions and other crying wickedness in her high places." After the American Revolution, New Jersey incorporated in its state constitution a clause stipulating that Catholics might not hold state offices. Similar measures were included in the constitutions of North Carolina and Georgia in 1776. The 1777 Vermont constitution required all holders of state offices to swear they were Protestants.

Generally called the nativist movement by social historians, the American anti-Catholics were holding rallies as early as 1814 to talk about how the Pope was planning to take over the New World by infiltrating Catholics in such numbers that they would rise up on orders from Rome, shoulder the guns they stored under the altars of their churches and visit havoc on their Protestant neighbors. Posters were tacked on the sides of barns showing a bitch nursing a teeming litter of pups representing immigrants from Europe with the caption: "Catholics in search of their dog-ma."

By the late 1820s, nativist mobs were harassing convents and beating up nuns and priests all along the eastern seaboard. In 1834 Samuel F. B. Morse, inventor of the telegraph, wrote a series of twelve anti-Catholic letters to the New York *Observer* entitled "A Foreign Conspiracy against the Liberties of the United States," which warned that the Pope was about to send hordes of his henchmen into America under the guise of immigrants to establish a Romish kingdom in the Mississippi Valley. Once established, the Papists would rise up and take over the entire nation and turn it over to Rome. Morse explained to the *Observer's* readers:

> The conspirators against our liberties, who have been admitted from abroad through the liberality of our institutions, are now organized in every part of the country; they are all subordinates, standing in regular steps of

slave and master from the most abject dolt that obeys the commands of his priest, up to the great masterslave [Austrian Count] Metternich, who commands and obeys his illustrious master, the Emperor [of Austria] . . . Every unlettered Catholic emigrant, therefore, that comes into the country, is adding to a mass of ignorance which it will be difficult to reach by any liberal instruction; and however honest (and I have no doubt most of them are so), yet, from the nature of things, they are but obedient instruments in the hands of their more knowing leaders out to accomplish the designs of their foreign masters.

The same year that Morse launched this attack, a mob of "No Popery" activists stormed the Ursuline Sisters' Mount Benedict, the largest convent in Boston, and burned it to the ground after chasing the nuns and priests until they found refuge in the Irish shanties of Charlestown. Such attacks against Catholic churches became commonplace over the next two decades. A dozen churches were burned in 1853–55 alone, according to one survey of newspapers by scholar Ray Allen Billington. Far more churches were vandalized, their crosses stolen, their altars violated and windows broken. Churches in Sidney, Ohio, and Dorchester, Massachusetts, were bombed. A New York mob laid siege to the Cathedral of St. Peter and St. Paul. When the Pope sent a block of Leonardo da Vinci's marble as a Vatican contribution to the Washington Monument, a nativist mob stole it from a shed and tossed it into the nearby Potomac River.

Nativist preachers took to their pulpits to warn that the events unfolding in America as a result of Catholic emigration from Europe were foretold in the New Testament Book of Revelation, which ends in the final battle on a field called Armageddon when the forces of God and goodness do battle with Satan and his evil seed in the person of "the Beast."

Over twenty-two symbol-laden chapters, St. John tells of the last seven years of humanity when a tremendous "Tribulation" is visited on humankind as God fulfills all his stern Old Testament warnings with a series of plagues, natural calamities and wars until the Second Coming of Christ. Wrote John in Revelation 13:18:

> Let him that hath understanding count the number of
> the beast: for it is the number of a man; and his number
> is six hundred threescore and six.

The nativist sermonizers produced labored computations to associate the papacy with the number 666. One popular formula dwelled upon the Latin name assumed by the Pope, "Vicar General of God upon Earth" or "Vicarius Generalis Dei in Terris," to reach 666. Yet another found that by turning the printed words "Pius the Ninth (9th)," the Pope of the time, upside down one could produce the dreaded 666. More than a century later, doomsayers on the American Fundamentalist Right were noting with far more easily comprehensible zeal that the words Ronald, Wilson and Reagan each contained six letters.

From the nativists who burned the Ursuline convent in 1834 up to the neo-Nazis who slaughtered Alan Berg, American hate movements have been inspired by and driven by those last few pages of the New Testament in which John describes the revelations that came to him toward the end of his days while living as a hermit on the Aegean island of Patmos shortly after the Crucifixion. Here the Four Horsemen ride across a sky rendered blood red while sinners gnash their teeth in hopeless despair. Here 200 million infidels from the East die at the hands of avenging angels while, at the same time, God marks 144,000 of his chosen people on the forehead so that they can escape the "Tribulations" and carry the message of salvation to the rest of humanity's beleaguered survivors.

Just as it was a century ago in the heyday of American anti-Catholicism, the Book of Revelation is absolutely crucial to the chemistry that pits much of today's Survival Right against the rest of the world. In scores of fundamentalist, anti-Semitic congregations of the modern-day religious movement called Identity Christianity, a new generation of haters uses this biblical prophetic book to explain a Jewish conspiracy and to justify their hatred. These Scriptures likewise drive large segments of what may be the nation's largest single segment of the Survivalist Right, the loosely structured Posse Comitatus tax protest, underground.

Later in this book we will deal at some length with how the Survival Right is driven by Revelation's prophesies of slaughter for millions of Jews and forecasts of the final, world-ending battle between the forces of good and evil. Here it suffices to explain that these are the holy writings that foretell the nuclear nightmare of the Survivalists and that the biblical interpretations sounded by Identity Christians, such as the Idaho-based Aryan Nations' Reverend Richard Butler, are virtually the same as those proffered by the anti-Catholic forces after the battle was joined in 1840 over the King James Version of the Bible. But in the 1840s the cancer had not yet progressed to the stage of advocating genocide. The nativists would have settled for a few laws keeping the Irish with their whiskey and the Germans with their beer at home.

In that quest, the nineteenth-century anti-Papist crusaders had seized upon the unwillingness of the American Catholic clergy to accept the Protestant King James Version of Scripture as evidence that the Pope of Rome had forbidden his immigrant followers to read the unadulterated word of God out of fear that once exposed to the holy writ they would bolt the Romish Church and become loyal Americans. Protestant Bible Societies were formed in most states to press legislatures to incorporate the King James Version into the school curricula and force Catholic children to read it. Protestants accused the Catholics of not allowing the true Bible in their homes. The Catholic Douay Version of Scripture was edited to permit such lurid abuses as the sex orgies and child stealing that the fundamentalist nativists charged went on behind the doors of convents and monasteries. Some priests made the staggering public relations error of responding by publicly burning King James volumes. The bonfires proved that Holy Scripture was more than the satanic Pope of Rome could bear, argued the nativists. The Papists were burning Bibles because the Holy Book of Revelation shows that the Pope is the Antichrist, the demon who bears the mark of the Beast—666.

Then, in 1844, the Irish potato blight struck, America opened its doors to the world's starving masses, and the nativists became a force to reckon with in U.S. politics. They became the American Party, known popularly as the Know-Nothings because that was what members of the secretive "native Protestant" group were instructed to tell anyone who asked them what they knew about the party.

The founding force behind the Know-Nothings was E. Z. C. Judson, the flamboyant writer of more than four hundred dime novels under the pseudonym Ned Buntline whose florid fictions transformed an obscure Indian scout named William Cody into the American archetype Buffalo Bill. Buntline's Know-Nothings too were archetypes, archetypes for all the hate groups to follow. Their platform was simple and uncompromising: No Catholic whether foreign-born or native to the United States could hold any form of public office. No foreign-born Protestant could hold office. No person could apply for naturalization until he or she had lived inside the United States for at least twenty-one years, instead of the five years that the law prescribed.

The waves of emigration that followed the potato blights in Europe produced an ample supply of newcomers for the Know-Nothings to hate. In 1845 the United States accepted 100,000 immigrants. In 1853, 300,000 were admitted. In addition to establishing religious intolerance as a basis for an American political movement, the social dynamics of the period pitted secretive, "populist" rural Americans directly against their urban counterparts, a dichotomy that can still be seen today in the Survivalist phenomenon with its compounds in rural pockets. The immigrants whom the nativists hated did not live among the Know-Nothings; they gravitated instead to the cities, where they became major forces in the urban Democratic machines.

Just as the neo-Nazis of Idaho have to drive all the way to Denver to find a Jew to hate, the rural Know-Nothings often had to take a trip to town to find an Irish Catholic. In fact, a key element in the chemistry of scapegoat hatred is that the targeted minorities tend either to be very small ones or else to have very few members living in close proximity to the people doing the hating. It is very difficult to live around large numbers of Jews or blacks or whatever and maintain the fictions that fuel the hatred. In 1856, the year of peak political influence by the nativists, the U.S. government estimated that only 7 percent of its residents were immigrants, with most of them, particularly the Irish, clustered in a few major cities such as New York, Boston and New Orleans.

Nevertheless, a widely quoted passage by the American historian Ray Allen Billington explained the Know-Nothings' rather stunning political successes during the 1850s in terms of urban citizens' reaction to the newcomers about them:

> The average American had only to look about him to find tangible evidence of the propagandists' worst fears. He could see quiet city streets transformed into unsightly slums by the foreigners' touch. He could see corrupt political machines thriving upon foreign votes and deadlocked political parties struggling for the support of untrained aliens. He could see the traditional policy of American isolation threatened by immigrant blocs seeking to embroil the United States in the affairs of their homelands. He could see intemperance, illiteracy, pauperism, and crime all increase with the coming of the

foreigner. He could see alien labor, content with a lower standard of living, taking over more and more of the work which American hands had formerly performed. Here were arguments which required no propagandist embroidery.*

Ultimately the Know-Nothings sent seventy-five members to Washington to serve in Congress and controlled several state legislatures, including that of Massachusetts, where anti-Irish hatred allowed the nativists to control the entire state government. In 1856 the American Party's candidate for the presidency, Millard Fillmore, won 21 percent of the vote, a showing that no domestic hate group has ever approached since. Fillmore had served as President between 1850 and 1853 as a Whig and attempted to regain power in 1856 via the anti-Catholic route. It was a turbulent era in American politics as conflicting views over economic issues and slavery had forced the breakdown of the traditional Democrat versus Whig political system. The time was ripe for the Know-Nothings, and they seized it. In addition to the 21 percent turnout for Fillmore, the party won congressional races in New York, Massachusetts, Rhode Island, New Hampshire, Connecticut, Pennsylvania, Delaware, Maryland and California.

By 1860 the Know-Nothings were once again just another bitter minority. Most of the people who had voted for Fillmore on the American Party ticket had moved into the ranks of the Republican Party—founded in 1854.

The Civil War followed. The South lost and, because it lost, the saga of America's haters resumed in 1867 in room 10 of the Maxwell House Hotel in Nashville, Tennessee. In that room, shortly before Independence Day, 1867, Confederate general Nathan Bedford Forrest, second only to

* From *The Protestant Crusade: A Study of the Origins of American Nativism* (New York: Macmillan, 1938).

Robert E. Lee as a hero of the South, presided over the inauguration of the racist, xenophobic hate group that today is the one still point in the otherwise changing universe of America's extreme right—the Invisible Empire of the Ku Klux Klan.

The Kluxers actually had started around Pulaski, Tennessee, in 1865, when six young Confederate veterans returned home and decided to start a "club" to cheer up their friends and neighbors who still hadn't shaken off the gloom of Appomattox. As legend has it, the six original Klansmen decided to dress up in costumes because it was faddish at the time to masquerade. With the South ravaged by the war, however, the only costumes they could find were the stiff linen sheets and bedding that their womenfolk had carefully husbanded. When the "pranksters" and their horses—also covered in white linen—rode about the Tennessee countryside on their revels, the racist legend has it, blacks became terrified, thinking they were being visited by the ghosts of rebel war dead.

In 1867, however, General Forrest joined the Klan, took its reins, and transformed the group into a guerrilla cadre dedicated to opposing "Northern oppression." Since the rules imposed for Reconstruction called for granting blacks the vote and allowing majority governments to form, much of the Klan's efforts focused on keeping former slaves from going to the polls. To that end Forrest and his troops developed the tactics of hate that latter-day Klansmen emulate today. Crosses were burned; blacks were told not to vote; lynchings were held in the dark of night.

The Klan was anti-black for obvious reasons. After all, for Klansmen the Civil War never ended. It also was anti-Catholic because so much of the political power in the North was wielded by the urban Catholic immigrants who had been the targets of the Know-Nothings. Born in the fundamentalist Baptist South, the Ku Klux Klan proclaimed itself a white Christian movement. By the early 1870s the Klan was another template for the modern-day hate groups that are the subject of this book.

Like the neo-Nazi Silent Brotherhood (Bruder Schweigen), the Klan had a complex and highly secret rule book full of hidden meanings. It was called the Invisible Empire, for example, because the day Forrest held his seminal meeting at the Maxwell House he had presented a letter from Robert E. Lee saying that Lee supported the Klan but desired to remain "invisible" in its affairs.

The leader was designated the Imperial Wizard because General Forrest had been nicknamed the "horse wizard" while a cavalry officer. Grand Dragons were named, each to head a different Realm in one of the Southern states. Each Realm or state was divided into Provinces headed by Grand Giants, while each locality in a Province was headed by a Cyclops. Each Cyclops headed a Den composed of twelve Terrors and two Night Hawks, who were couriers and guides. A code of secrecy demanded that no Klansman disclose how the group was structured. While the mumbo jumbo sounds like nothing more than a bunch of schoolboys forming a secret club in their backyard tree house, it has proven to be far more long-lasting—to this day neophytes are given a fifty-four-page Kloran (Klan + Koran) that outlines the elaborate pecking order. Ironically, the Kloran and the Klan's "secret" membership oath were both copyrighted and filed at the Library of Congress, where anybody interested in reading them can obtain a copy.

The original Klan was to continue with its structure largely unchanged down to the present, thanks largely to the efforts of one of America's legendary moviemakers—D. W. Griffith—and the genius of a canny fundamentalist snake-oil seller, Colonel William J. Simmons, who saw that the global tension that gripped Americans on the eve of World War I could be exploited by appeals to the old racial and religious hatreds.

In 1905 Thomas Dixon, Jr., a Southern minister who had grown to manhood during Reconstruction, was so enamored of what he considered the knightly exploits of the Klansmen that he published what turned out to be a best-selling novel, *The Clansman: An Historic Romance of the Ku Klux*

Klan. Dixon had captivated oil baron John D. Rockefeller, a fellow Baptist, who offered to build Dixon a church of his own. Dixon's other famous friend was President Woodrow Wilson, the Virginian who had attended graduate school with him at Johns Hopkins University in Baltimore.

The Clansman revolved around two beautiful examples of white Southern womanhood—young girls who were so attractive that animalistic Negroes could not resist the urge to ravish them sexually. Egged on by sneering carpetbaggers, black men surround the first Baptist virgin on a mountainside, giving her the chance to throw herself to death over a cliff rather than be raped by a race mixer. The second belle is trapped in a ramshackle cabin, blocking windows and doors as sexually obsessed black men relentlessly try to invade even as the Klan rides to the rescue.

One of the great embarrassments of Hollywood to this day is the fact that the pioneer filmmaking genius David Wark Griffith chose *The Clansman* as the subject of the first full-length dramatic motion picture ever made. He transformed *The Clansman* into the film *The Birth of a Nation*, the first effort to go beyond the slapstick short subjects that had been the staple of the aborning entertainment medium up to then. It was a success to rival today's blockbusters by George Lucas, Steven Spielberg or Francis Ford Coppola. In 1915, when a nickel bought dinner, a penny bought a daily newspaper and two cents covered a passable breakfast, *The Birth of a Nation* premiered in theaters that charged two dollars for a ticket. It grossed $18 million and was seen by an estimated 50 million people.

Film historians, almost universally a subset of humanity cut from liberal cloth, nevertheless reluctantly rate the movie's climactic scenes a masterpiece both of propaganda and of cinematic dramatic technique. With the theater organ blaring Grieg's "In the Hall of the Mountain King," a posse of white-robed Klansmen rides furiously toward the cabin where the heroine faces imminent rape by a rutting black demon emboldened by his carpetbagger mentors. She swoons; he looms. The camera pans to the crashing hooves of the robed rescuers' horses, then back to the lust-crazed former slave and his trembling victim. The music builds, the black man presses ever harder, the beleaguered virgin's terror grows even as the hooves crash to earth faster and faster. The camera work, the music and the theme were more than many a true-blue son of the South could bear. Movie screens in Knoxville and Greensboro were shot to shreds by audiences who couldn't stand the suspense.

Two weeks before *The Birth of a Nation* opened in Atlanta, William Simmons, a showman and a bitter racist from Alabama, staged a rally just outside of town to mark the revival of the Ku Klux Klan. A professional organizer of fraternal clubs, Simmons saw the Klan as a moneymaking enterprise as well as an ideological goal.

His timing was impeccable. The film was a national box office hit and Simmons's fellow Georgians and Alabamans flocked to join his revived edition of the "Hooded Order." With a ritualistic cross burning in sight of the Atlanta theater where *The Birth of a Nation* played, Simmons wrote the first chapter in the history of the modern-day Klan. It was he who composed the Kloran (and copyrighted it) and outlined the structure of Titans, Kleagles, Cyclopes, etc., that is followed to this day.

Between 1915 and 1920, Simmons became moderately wealthy as membership in his new Klan blossomed. He charged each member an entry fee and monthly dues. He also sold members a group insurance policy and even peddled the requisite white robes, Confederate flags and other regalia. But the organization remained confined to the Deep South. In fact, there was little Klan activity outside Georgia and Alabama until after 1920, when Simmons hired two publicists, Edward Young Clarke and Elizabeth Tyler, to help him take the organization nationwide after membership had reached the saturation point in those two states.

Clarke and Tyler had handled successful membership drives for the Salvation Army and the Anti-Saloon League, which, with their focus on saving humanity from the liquor sold by immigrant Irish and German tavernkeepers, were two of the major anti-Catholic organizations in America at the time. The consultants offered a lopsided deal by which they would get 80 percent and Simmons would get 20 percent of all new membership fees. With new membership virtually at a stop, the racist "colonel" agreed and the savvy, if cynical, public relations wizards went to work.

The Klan needed somebody else to hate, they advised Simmons. It was no longer enough just to target blacks and appeal to people's patriotism. The Klan needed other scapegoats. And they needed to find a conspiracy to attack. Clarke and Tyler explained how World War I had left many people frustrated and frightened. It was clear that it had been far from the "war to end all wars" that President Wilson had promised. The Bolsheviks had seized control of Russia, and once again droves of foreigners were passing through Ellis Island.

Clarke and Tyler went back to the Know-Nothing campaigns for inspiration and advised Simmons to expand his list to include Jews and Catholics to take advantage of the fact that much of the immigration had shifted from German and Irish Catholics to Jews from Poland and Russia as well as Italians and Slavs.

Until the late nineteenth century the Jewish population in the United States had been minuscule, a fact that protected it from much of the outrageous prejudice that flourished in Europe. There were only an estimated 1,000 Jews in the United States at the end of the Revolution, and their numbers only grew to perhaps 200,000 by the late 1800s. Then the wave of emigration from Eastern Europe swelled their numbers to several million and allowed the Klan to bolster its ranks by adopting anti-Semitism.

On the advice of Clarke and Tyler, the Klan declared itself "100 percent American, 100 percent Christian and 100 percent Protestant," and Simmons developed a particularly galling act to open each of his recruiting rallies. He would stride out on the stage, remove a heavy Colt pistol from one pocket and slam it on a table. He would pull an even longer Remington sidearm from the other pocket, toss it alongside the Colt, then draw his bowie knife from a boot and drive its tip into the table between the two guns. With the blade still quivering he would shout, "Now let the niggers, Catholics, Jews and all the others who disdain my Imperial Wizardry come on."

In the first fifteen months of the 1920–21 membership drive, 85,000 people signed up at ten dollars per head. In each town Clarke and Tyler first sent their recruiters to see the local fundamentalist minister and deliver the same Know-Nothing message about the Antichrist prophesied in the Book of Revelation. The recruiters would then make a ten- or fifteen-dollar donation to the church—a windfall for many a hardscrabble-poor country preacher—and ask permission to speak to the congregation.

Recruiters often would pass out broadsides, such as one that read:

> Every criminal, every gambler, every thug, every libertine, every girl ruiner, every home wrecker, every wife beater, every dope peddler, every moonshiner, every crooked politician, every pagan Papist priest, every shyster lawyer, every Knight of Columbus, every white slaver, every brothel madam, every Rome-controlled newspaper, every black spider—is fighting the Klan. Think it over. Which side are you on?

While the Klan never reached the lofty political powers attained by the Know-Nothings in the mid-1850s, it did score some brief triumphs around the country, particularly during the 1920s in Oregon and Indiana, where Klan-backed candidates dominated both state legislatures and Klan forces controlled large numbers of state and local offices as well.

Probably the high point for Klan political power came in July 1923, when 100,000 people turned out in Kokome, Indiana, for the inauguration of Hoosier Daniel Clarke Stephenson as the group's Grand Dragon, second in command only to the Imperial Wizard himself. It was estimated that at its peak in the late 1920s Simmons's new Klan had raised $75 million and had as many as 4 million members.

But the United States soon was undergoing sea changes that deflated the Klan ranks even faster than they had swelled. Notably, a number of leading newspapers became incensed at the lynchings and cross burnings and launched anti-Klan drives. The legendary Herbert Bayard Swope of the New York *World* devoted a twenty-one-day series to exposing Klan outrages.

The story of how Clarke and Tyler connived to expand the Klan by adding Jews and Catholics to the list of conspirators came out after it was disclosed by the *World* that both of them had been arrested while "less than fully clad and less than fully sober" in a 1919 police raid on a Birmingham whorehouse.

The sensational disclosures won the newspaper the Pulitzer Prize, and Swope boasted that his circulation jumped 60,000 copies because of the series. Predictably, the *World*'s success led to numerous other newspapers around the country taking on the Klan, attempting to infiltrate its secret ranks and warning about its credo of hatred. In 1985 Roland Wood, an exasperated neo-Nazi Klansman in Greensboro, North Carolina, told the author, "I don't go to cross burnings or rallies anymore because the only people who are there are FBI agents and reporters wearing white sheets tryin' to win the Pulitzer Prize."

But far more devastating to the Klan's prospects for becoming a political force than the antagonistic news media were the two major historical developments of the Great Depression and World War II.

As Fred J. Cook notes in his book *The Ku Klux Klan: America's Recurring Nightmare*, "With banks failing, with millions upon millions unemployed, with factories idle and all business life at a stand-still, the Klan's anti-Catholic, anti-Semitic, and anti-black rhetoric seemed unrealistic. It had nothing to do with the great issues of the day."

When the German-American Bund, an arm of Hitler's Nazi Party operating in the United States, became active in the late 1930s, the already beleaguered Klan leadership made the mistake of getting into bed with the Nazis. The two groups shared many of the same ideologies and Klan leaders watched with envy and glee as Hitler's power grew. At an August 18, 1940 rally in Bund-operated camp near Andover, New Jersey, several hundred robed Klansmen joined a like number of Bundists to hear Arthur Bell, Grand Dragon of the Realm of New Jersey, tell them that "God Bless America" was a "Semitic song fit only for Bowery taverns and brothels" because it was written by a Jew named Irving Berlin.

It is hard to imagine a bigger public relations error at a time when the Nazi blitzkrieg already was moving across Europe and causing great anxiety among Americans. A crowd of angry New Jerseyites gathered outside the Bund camp gates to shout "Put Hitler on your crosses" and sing "The Star-Spangled Banner," and in doing so spoke for most of their fellow citizens.

From the 1940s on, the Klan has declined as any sort of significant national electoral force. Nevertheless, it has had a tremendous impact on the national psyche from World War II to the present. A raft of horrors has been visited upon the American scene by subsequent generations of the "Hooded Order," even while the Klan itself has degenerated into a disjointed agglomeration of feuding splinter groups, an alphabet soup overstocked with K's. There is the United Klans of America Knights of the Ku Klux Klan, Inc.; the Knights of the Ku Klux Klan, Invisible Empire; the National Knights of the Ku Klux Klan; the Knights of the Ku Klux Klan; the Original Knights of the Ku Klux Klan; the Dixie Klans; the National Alliance—and many more.

Yet despite the diversity among the internally warring hate groups, the Klan's connection to Nazism remains firm. Robert Matthews, the commando who founded the Silent Brotherhood, started out as a Klansman before gravitating to the neo-Nazi movement. Robert Miles, one of those who federal prosecutors charged had been sent money from the Silent Brotherhood's armored car robberies, was the Klan's Grand Dragon in Michigan before he joined the neo-Nazi movement and set a half dozen school buses on fire in Pontiac, Michigan, in 1971. Others who allegedly received money from the Silent Brotherhood were the Carolina Knights of the KKK, a splinter group led by Glenn Miller that received national attention after the bloody clash in 1979 in Greensboro when they were filmed shooting five members of the Communist Worker's Party.

excerpt from:

Targets of Hatred
by Patricia Baird-Windle and Eleanor J. Bader

This chilling book thoroughly documents the extreme element of the anti-abortion movement, which has been responsible for seven murders, seventeen attempted murders, forty bombings, one hundred sixty-three arson attacks, one hundred fifteen cases of assault and battery and countless incidents of harassment and physical intimidation. It also clearly analyzes and categorizes the responsible groups and relates anti-abortion violence to a larger movement of intimidation of minorities by linking some of the right-to-life extremists to the other right-wing extremist sects. Patricia Baird-Windle was an abortion provider for more than two decades. Eleanor J. Bader is a social worker and journalist who writes on topics of interest to women.

WHO, WHAT, WHEN AND WHERE: THE ANTI-ABORTION MOVEMENT

Hundreds of anti-abortion groups, many of them church- or community-based, currently exist; all want to reverse *Roe v. Wade* and recriminalize abortion. While most engage in legal protest—lobbying legislators, pro-choice lawmakers and feminist organizations—many of those remaining at clinics have tested or crossed the line into illegal activities. Quiet, peaceful pickets are largely a thing of the past, say providers, because most moderates have left the field due to increasing violence. The extremists who remain employ actions spanning a broad continuum, from the increasingly nasty pestering of patients as they enter and leave reproductive health centers, to harassing clinic workers and their families; from tampering with or destroying medical equipment, to brutal violence against clinic property or personnel. Arson, chemical attacks, firebombings, kidnappings, stabbings, shootings, vandalism and murder—all have occurred because some extreme anti-abortionists are frustrated that legal efforts to outlaw abortion have so far failed.

Who are these anti-abortion groups? What distinguishes those who do and do not engage in terrorism, violence or other illegal actions? The following roster, beginning with the most moderate group and ending with what many consider the most extreme, is meant to introduce the major anti-choice organizations operating in the United States and Canada:

The **Pro-Life Action League** (PLAL; www.prolifeaction.org) was founded in 1980 by former Roman Catholic (Benedictine) seminarian and journalist Joseph Scheidler. Eager for tangible victories, Scheidler opted to bypass the NRTLC and has, for twenty years, organized in-your-face demonstrations, sit-ins and blockades. His 1985 book, *Closed: 99 Ways to Stop Abortion*, is a classic text for anti-choice zealots and would-be saboteurs. Aggressive "sidewalk counseling" meant to stop women from ending unwanted pregnancies; amplified demonstrations, often using bullhorns, outside operating rooms; "rescue" missions, the precursors of blockades, at clinics; confrontations with doctors at their homes, offices, churches and at restaurants, funerals and social functions; the taunting of pro-choice politicians and organizational representatives—these are the stock-in-trade of PLAL.

The group purports to engage in only aboveboard activities; nonetheless, it was found liable for extortion, a violation of the Racketeer Influenced Corrupt Organizations (RICO) Act, in 1998 and has been ordered to pay damages to two clinics represented by the National Organization for Women (NOW) and the National Women's Health Organization (NWHO). PLAL is currently appealing the decision.

• • •

Operation Rescue/Operation Rescue National/Operation Save America (OR or OSA; www.operationsaveamerica.org; www.orn.org), a group founded by fundamentalist preacher Randall Terry in 1986, changed its name from Operation Rescue National to Operation Save America in the spring of 1999, presumably to reflect its growing interest in denouncing not just abortion but family planning, homosexuality, pornography and the lack of prayer in public school classrooms. (Most pro-choice activists believe that the change had a more sinister motive: to confuse the courts and dodge attempts to trace the organization's financial assets and potential liabilities. Patricia Baird-Windle states that "the name change fits the Operation Rescue pattern of making public threats, overtly or covertly carrying out these threats, then denying that they did anything. OR members distance themselves from their actions by frequent name changing and denials, maintaining the pretense that they were never involved in illegal activities.")

The OR/OSA Web page states its purported—if ambiguous—purpose: "OR unashamedly takes up the cause of pre-born children in the name of Jesus Christ. We employ only Biblical principles. The Bible is our foundation; the cross of Christ is our strategy; the repentance of the church of Jesus Christ is our ultimate goal.")

During its brief heyday, 1988 to 1994, OR/OSA's sole focus was on "ending the slaughter of innocent babies" by blocking clinic doors. Terry says that this was a tactical decision. "From the beginning when I founded OR, the vision was not only to end child killing; the vision was to recapture the power bases of America, for child killing to be the first domino, if you will, to fall. Once we mobilize the momentum, the manpower, the money and all that goes with that to make child killing illegal, we will have sufficient moral authority and moral force and momentum to get the homosexual movement back in the closet, to get the condom pushers in our schools to go back to the fringes of society where they belong."

OR/OSA is currently headed by the Reverend Philip "Flip" Benham, a former bar owner who was "saved" in 1976. Under his leadership, the group has continued to protest at abortion clinics and leads a "God is Going to School" project to promote daily prayer and the posting of the Ten Commandments in educational settings. OR/OSA has also demonstrated against the sale of "pornographic" books by Barnes & Noble Booksellers. In addition, in 1998 and 1999 the group picketed the annual June Gay Days gathering at Disney theme parks and has assailed the diversity and tolerance that Gay Days celebrates.

Although OR/OSA has pursued only minor efforts against contraception, Randall Terry has repeatedly exhorted his followers to oppose human interference with God's reproductive plan. "We should trust God with how many children we should have," he wrote in an article reprinted in *Life Advocate Magazine.* "At its core birth control is anti-child. When we use birth control we are saying, 'No, I don't want children.' If you are on the pill or using an IUD, stop immediately. They are abortifacients. . . . Leave the number of children you have in God's hands. . . . Our children are the only eternal possession we have except our souls."

While OR-sponsored "rescues" often involve low-level violence, the group publicly condemns the concept of "justifiable homicide" against providers.

Missionaries to the Pre-Born (MTP; www.execpc.com/~restore/mtp/mtp) was founded in 1990 by fundamentalist Matt Trewhella, a former Detroit gang member. An avid supporter of armed resistance and Christian militias, Trewhella has great contempt for reformist groups such as the National Right to Life Committee. MTP castigates the incremental approach to ending abortion demonstrated by the push to ban so-called partial-birth abortions and sees the campaign as a move from "a half-measure to a minuscule-measure strategy." It further opposes the gradual winnowing away of reproductive options. For the Missionaries, it is all or nothing.

• • •

The Lambs of Christ (www.thelambsofchrist.com) are best known for organizing mass sit-ins at clinics and pushing junker cars into entryways to prevent ingress and egress and then encouraging participants not to divulge their names to arresting police officers. Once incarcerated, Lambs often show their "oneness with the unborn" by refusing to bathe and defecating and urinating on themselves. Lambs founder Father Norman Weslin, a retired military officer, was married and raised two adopted children before being called to the ministry as a middle-age adult.

A member of the Roman Catholic Oblates of Wisdom, Weslin was ordained in the late 1980s. Since founding the Lambs, he has been arrested between sixty and seventy times for anti-abortion protests. He is rumored to support himself—and at least partially finance the Lambs—through donations supplemented by a substantial military pension.

The Lambs' Web page, complete with funereal music, includes articles about abortion, morality and political doctrine. "One Nation Under Satan," for example, advises readers that "all the severe problems which the administration of our beloved country is now experiencing are not so much because of the sexual abuse of young women, perjury, obstruction of justice or tampering with witnesses, but the reason for evil that prevails in the United States is because our president kills Jesus Christ's babies. This is no longer 'One Nation Under God.' This is now 'One Nation Under Satan.' " Another piece depicts "unborn babies" as ' "America's most despised minority."

December 25: Pensacola, Florida

Linda Taggart, administrator of the Community Healthcare Center of Pensacola, Inc. (formerly The Ladies Center), first noticed the feelings of free-floating anxiety on the evening of December 24. Still, it was

Christmas Eve, and as always, she took her place with the Trinity Presbyterian Church choir.

"I got to bed around midnight," Taggart recalls. "At 4:00 a.m. the phone rang. No one had to tell me. I knew. I had to wake my daughter up since I didn't want to leave her home alone and we drove five miles an hour through pea-soup thick fog to get to the clinic. The fire truck was there and I wondered why since I'd been told by the police that there had been a break-in. A policeman finally came over to me and said he thought there had been an explosion. We still could not see a thing; I have rarely been in fog that thick even though Pensacola is on the Gulf of Mexico and is frequently fogged-in."

The damage was confined to several rooms at one end of the site; as a result, that section of the building was cordoned off until repairs could be made. The clinic was closed for several days, but was quickly made minimally functional.

Two other Pensacola abortion providers were not as lucky. The bombers, later identified as Matthew Goldsby, James and Kathren Simmons and Kaye Wiggins, had hurled incendiary devices at three facilities in a two-mile radius over a twenty-minute period. Only three walls remained at Dr. William Permenter's office, and windows and cornices were blown out of his building. Dr. Bo Bagenholm's office was also badly damaged. All told, the bombs caused $706,000 in damages at the three locations.

Dr. Permenter never rebuilt and left the field of medicine. Likewise, Dr. Bagenholm ceased providing abortions in July 1985.

Matthew Goldsby, his girlfriend Kaye Wiggins and James and Kathren Simmons belonged to the Assemblies of God, a fundamentalist denomination that researchers say is characterized by the belief that God speaks directly to the believer. "Both [Matt Goldsby and James Simmons] felt God was calling them to end abortion. Since two of them felt this compulsion, they concluded that it must have been a specific direction from

God," wrote sociologists Dallas Blanchard and Terry Prewitt in their 1993 book, *Religious Violence and Abortion.* In addition, the men called their activities The Gideon Project because Gideon "had laid low the altars of Baal, on which first born children were sacrificed."

Goldsby, a construction worker, and Simmons, a glass cutter—both in their early twenties—were charged with conspiracy to create firearms or explosive devices to damage or destroy a business engaged in interstate commerce; building three firearm or explosive devices; and using those devices to maliciously destroy three separate buildings. Wiggins and Kathren Simmons were charged with aiding and abetting.

The bombers' defense attorneys opened the case by arguing that the men were suffering from severe psychiatric disorders that fueled their anti-abortion furor. Defense witness Dr. Nancy Mullen told the court that "Goldsby experienced grandiose delusions that led him to identify with God. Jesus to Matt is an imaginary friend." She further testified that James Simmons suffered from borderline personality disorder, an emotional condition characterized by emotional instability and impulsive and unpredictable behavior. In addition, she revealed that in her interview with him, Simmons confessed that he obsessed about abortion between five and eight hours a day. Worse, after viewing the film *Assignment Life*, he told her he felt as if "a piece of me was taken out. A piece of me instead of the kid. Like being stuck with a knife."

Dr. Daniel Dansak countered Mullen, contending that both men were sane, able to hold down jobs and engage in normal social interactions. Dansak held sway, and on April 23 the pair were found competent to stand trial.

The abortion battlefield reflected society's polarities. While OR and the Lambs of Christ continued to block clinic doors, and The National Right to Life Committee continued to lobby for abortion restrictions, other activists were looking for a more permanent solution to what they saw as the sin of "baby killing." Michael Bray, pastor of the Reformation Lutheran Church in Bowie, Maryland, and a convicted clinic firebomber, was one of many who argued that outright violence was the best means to end legal abortion.

In *A Time to Kill*, a 1994 treatise on "justifiable homicide" against abortion doctors, Bray expressed his viewpoint. "What if the first 10 aborturaries built had been set ablaze? What if, after the first abortionist was shot, the pastors of God's churches had sent out news releases saying, 'Amen'? What if Christians individually had simply recognized that a defense was being raised similar to what they would want for their own children?"

Bray's philosophical justification of violence dovetailed with the previously published *Army of God Manual*, a tactical how-to guide that was discovered by law enforcement and the women's health community in 1993. A virtual celebration of arson, chemical attacks, invasions and bombing, the manual offers chilling, practical instructions on bomb making, purchasing and using butyric acid and many forms of general sabotage.

Alongside an array of anti-abortion films and videos, pro-choice activists quickly grasped that these books heralded the arrival of a highly volatile wing of the anti-abortion movement, a movement they feared would physically assault clinic staff. Although the BATF, the FBI and the Department of justice largely ignored their concerns, by the time the *Army of God Manual* was discovered, one doctor had been killed and several people had been shot.
Murdered? Wounded?

Despite clear warnings that these tactics were in the offing, shock waves rocked the pro-choice community when, on March 10, 1993, Dr. David Gunn was assassinated—shot in the back—as he entered Pensacola Medical Services, a northwest Florida clinic. Within the next twenty months, four others—James Barrett, Dr. John Bayard Britton, Shannon Lowney and Leanne Nichols—would also be killed by anti-abortion fanatics. (Dr. George Wayne Patterson, owner of Pensacola Medical Services, was murdered in August 1994. Although his former colleagues remain skeptical, police blame his death on a bungled robbery and not anti-abortion violence. The pro-choice community continues to point out that Patterson's wallet, cellular phone and Cadillac were untouched by the "robbers.")

More than half a dozen others in the United States and Canada would be wounded and "hit lists" of medical workers slated for death would be compiled by anti-abortion zealots.

December 28: Springfield, Missouri

A man in a ski mask walked into the Central Health Center for Women and asked to see a doctor. When he was told that the physician had already gone for the day, the man pulled out a sawed-off shotgun and fired it. He seriously wounded the clinic receptionist and the owner of the building. The gunman was not apprehended, and the clinic closed its doors in early 1992. The pair were the first victims of an abortion-related shooting.

March 10: Pensacola, Florida

Jeanne Singletary, assistant to the clinic administrator at Pensacola Medical Services (PMS), knew something was wrong the second she arrived at her office. Although she had worked at the clinic for two years, she had never before seen picketers at the facility. In fact, the closest she had ever come to anti-abortion protestors was driving past The Ladies Center or viewing photos of disruptions on television or in newspapers.

"I usually got to work at the crack of dawn and our doctor, David Gunn, usually got here between 8:30 and 9:00," she says. "That day I walked among the protestors and watched them. What made me wonder was that they were all dressed up, in church clothes, so I knew something was up. Donny Gratton, John Burt and young women from Burt's group home were marching out front. There were about fifteen of them. The staff thought we should try to stop Dr. Gunn from coming in. We wanted to let him know that protestors were here. We beeped him but he did not answer the page. He probably thought, 'I'm on my way. We'll talk when I get in.'"

Shortly thereafter, Singletary remembers hearing an explosive noise. Another staffer went upstairs to look out a window and when she screamed, Singletary says she instinctively knew what had occurred. "David was lying near the rear entrance out back. We got blood pressure cuffs out and worked on him. I went crazy. I was screaming and screaming," she says. "Meanwhile, the protestors out front didn't even come to the back of the building to see what had happened. They knew. I started screaming at Burt and Gratton: 'You killed him. What kind of people are you?' The cops were out front and patients were in the building. The police got us all in one room and made us close the curtains and windows. The six of us working that day were questioned one at a time, all day long. Calls were forwarded to a clinic in Mary Esther [Florida] that was owned by the same doctor who owned PMS. We reopened two days later."

Although David Gunn was rushed to the hospital, the forty-seven-year-old doctor from Eufaula, Alabama, was pronounced dead later that day, the first fatality in the one-sided war against abortion.

"When we found out that he had been shot, we tried to reach his family," says Linda Taggart, administrator of Community Healthcare Center of Pensacola, Inc., the second Pensacola clinic that employed Gunn. "CNN broadcast it before we notified them. By the time they called the hospital he had died. That was no way for the family to hear."

"We had begged David to get a car phone," she continues. "It might have saved his life; at least it might have stopped the antis that day." Tears stream down her face as she describes the impact of losing both a friend and colleague, and she repeatedly points to the many photographs of Gunn decorating her office. "David worked with us from 1986 or '87. As soon as he came it was as if family had arrived," she says. "He was funny, flirtatious, interesting. Every Friday when we were through he'd come into my office and we'd discuss all the problems in the world. He was very political. He wanted to help women maintain pregnancies when they wanted to be pregnant or help them when they did not. He would ask every patient on the table if she was registered to vote. If she was not he gave her a lecture. David was five foot five and about 125 pounds. He'd had polio as a child and had been tormented because of this affliction and because he had to wear a brace on his leg. Maybe it made him more sensitive. He was one of the best physicians I have ever known. He could do anything. He was our only doctor, and we closed for about two weeks after he died, until we could find another. For the first three or four weeks after we reopened we had temporary doctors step in."

August 19: Wichita, Kansas
Dr. George Tiller, one of the country's premier providers of second- and third-trimester abortions, had just completed an application to the World Population Council to request that Women's Health Care Services be allowed to participate in a study of RU-486, a chemical abortifacient. "It was 7:00 p.m. on a Thursday night. I had just finished the paperwork and was all pumped up," he recalls. "As I drove out I noticed five, six, seven antis and remember thinking, 'Gee, the spooks are here late tonight.' Then someone approached my car. She had something in her hand and I

thought she was going to give me a leaflet. It turned out she was holding a gun. As she got closer I gave her the finger and turned the car to the right. If I hadn't given her the finger I might have gotten the bullet in the chest. Instead, I was hit in both arms."

Tiller knew that he had been shot. Nonetheless, he tried to chase his assailant as she attempted to flee from the clinic's parking lot. "She was on foot," he says, "and I wanted to stop her. I was looking at her through the window she'd shot out. But after a few minutes I realized that I was pretty woozy so I went back to the clinic. I recall saying I'd drive myself to the hospital but there was a police officer standing there and he told me to lie down and wait for the ambulance so I did. It seemed like suddenly everybody and their brother was around. I had no idea why these people were there. My time perception was way off."

A clinic nurse, who had also been working late, saw the woman who fired at Tiller and had the presence of mind to write down the license tag number and physical description of the car she was driving. The shooter turned out to be Oregon activist Rachelle "Shelley" Shannon, the woman who had mailed the first issue of *The Brockhoeft Report* as a favor for incarcerated pal John Brockhoeft and in whose yard the *Army of God Manual* was found. She was apprehended when she returned a car she had rented days earlier to an Oklahoma airport.

The Brookline shootings marked the first time that nonphysicians were killed by anti-abortion violence. "Before 1994 it was not on our radar screen that someone could walk in and murder receptionists," said Nicki Nichols Gamble, former president of the Planned Parenthood League of Massachusetts. "We knew physicians were targets, but after December 30 we found out that they weren't the only targets."

As the story unfolded, Verhoeven and Nichols Gamble learned that a man, later identified as John Salvi III, had come into the clinic and asked if it was Planned Parenthood. When he was told that it was, he leveled his rifle and shot Lowney in the neck. He then fired several more times and fled the scene. Salvi apparently drove two miles down the street and at approximately 10:30 a.m. entered Preterm Health Services, another Brookline clinic. There he shot thirty-eight-year-old receptionist Leanne Nichols to death while shouting, 'This is what you get. You should pray the rosary.' He then shot and wounded twenty-nine-year-old office worker Jane Sauer and forty-five-year-old security guard Richard J. Seron.

Despite being hurt, Seron fired back at Salvi from the Preterm entranceway; although he did not hit the gunman, he scared him, and in his haste to leave the, clinic Salvi dropped a black gym bag he had been carrying. The bag contained receipts for the gun and the ammunition he had purchased, as well as a .22 caliber Colt handgun, bullets and a detachable magazine that held more than five rounds.

excerpt from:

American Terrorist
by Lou Michel and Dan Herbeck

The bombing of the Murrah Building in Oklahoma City by Timothy
McVeigh with the resulting loss of 168 lives was, until September 11,
the bloodiest terrorist event on American soil. A great deal is known of
the details of the attack and its aftermath, but little about McVeigh's
character or his motivations. In this way he falls into the cipher tradition of Lee Harvey Oswald and Sirhan Sirhan. An ex-G.I. and a Gulf War
combat veteran, McVeigh was cold-blooded and systematic in his
preparation for and execution of the bombing, as this minute-by-
minute account demonstrates. *American Terrorist* is based on extensive
interviews with the incarcerated McVeigh by Lou Michel and Dan
Herbeck, two reporters from McVeigh's hometown newspaper, *The
Buffalo News*. Gaining his trust, they get him to speak in minute detail
about the events before and after the bombing. In the first excerpt we
read about the morning of that fateful day up to and including the
explosion. The second selection has McVeigh becoming friendly with his
cellblock mate Theodore Kaczynski on the "bombers row" of the maximum security wing of a Colorado Federal prison, where Ramzi Yousef
(see p. 378), is also housed.

It was after 7 a.m. when Timothy McVeigh pulled out of the parking lot where he'd passed the night. By nine o'clock he would be closing in on his target in Oklahoma City.

On this day McVeigh would not drive with his usual abandon, sliding through turns with no regard for speed limits. He would take special care to keep the Ryder truck safely on the highway. Of course, the main reason was caution; with seven thousand pounds of explosives behind him, he could hardly afford a traffic accident.

But McVeigh had another reason—a tactical reason—for taking his time. He did not want to get there too early, before the Alfred P. Murrah Building filled up with people. He wanted his body count.

It was an issue to which McVeigh had devoted considerable thought. He knew that the vast majority of workers in the building—more than five hundred of them—worked during the day. He had considered setting off his bomb at 11 p.m., or even at 3 a.m., when the only fatalities would be a few security guards, maybe some cleaning people. With any luck, he thought, a federal agent or two might be lingering in the building, perhaps listening to a wiretap or filling out a report.

But that wouldn't accomplish what he wanted, McVeigh felt. The feds would just dip into their endless reserves of cash and put up another building. "The government could give a shit about a building," he concluded. "They've got bottomless pockets of cash to build a new one." The federal juggernaut would hardly lose a step. His entire purpose was to make a statement that could not be ignored; he had no interest in mounting an action that would be little more than a footnote in history.

To McVeigh, a serious loss of human life was the only way to put a sufficiently powerful exclamation point behind his message to the American government.

The American military had been using the same philosophy for years, he would argue. American bombing raids were designed to take lives, not just destroy buildings. The atom bombs that brought a bloody end to World War II—the bombs in whose image he saw his own—were designed to kill not just hundreds, but hundreds of thousands of people. He claimed to take no pleasure from killing. But in his mind, McVeigh had no trouble justifying what he was about to do.

At least two of the agencies he most despised—the ATF and the DEA—would be affected by the blast, as would the Secret Service. As for the other agencies in the building—such as the Social Security Administration, the Department of Housing and Urban Development, and the Department of Agriculture—they were all part of a government he regarded as evil and out of control.

Many of the people he planned to kill today had nothing to do with the law-enforcement agencies that were involved in the deaths at Waco and Ruby Ridge. And to justify this to himself, McVeigh summoned an image that had remained with him since his childhood: the destruction of the Death Star in the 1977 motion picture *Star Wars*.

McVeigh saw himself as a counterpart to Luke Skywalker, the heroic Jedi knight whose successful attack on the Death Star closes the film. As a kid, McVeigh had noticed that the *Star Wars* movies showed people sitting at consoles—Space-Age clerical workers—inside the Death Star. Those people weren't storm troopers. They weren't killing anyone. But they were vital to the operations of the Evil Empire, McVeigh deduced, and when Luke blew up the Death Star those people became inevitable casualties. When the Death Star exploded, the movie audiences cheered. The bad guys were beaten: that was all that really mattered. As an adult, McVeigh found himself able to dismiss the killings of secretaries, receptionists, and other personnel in the Murrah Building with equally cold-blooded calculation. They were all part of the Evil Empire.

"I didn't define the rules of engagement in this conflict," he said later. "The rules, if not written down, are defined by the aggressor. It was brutal, no holds barred. Women and kids were killed at Waco and Ruby Ridge. You put back in [the government's] faces exactly what they're giving out."

Aside from constructing the bomb itself, McVeigh had performed careful reconnaissance in preparing for every aspect of his plan. On one of his previous trips to Oklahoma City he had scouted the exact route he would take to get there, looking for speed traps, highway construction, possible road hazards, and, especially, underpasses too low for the truck. On the morning of the nineteenth, McVeigh was careful to stay at or below the speed limits, and to signal all his turns and lane changes. Even with his precautions, though, McVeigh eventually noticed that a marked police car had fallen in behind him. The cop stayed behind McVeigh for several miles, riding his tail as he neared the city.

Again and again McVeigh glanced at his rearview mirrors, trying his best to look unconcerned. The cop was still there.

"At this point, I'm thinking, *Why is he following me?*" McVeigh recalls. "*I know it's not my driving. Is there some problem with the truck?*"

Like a soldier, he began running scenarios through his head. What would he do if the cop tried to pull him over? If the stop was for some traffic infraction, would the cop ask to look into the cargo area?

He wasn't that far from Oklahoma City. McVeigh decided that if the cop tried to pull him over, he would ignore him and head straight for the Murrah Building. McVeigh resolved he "would run the cop off the road if I had to."

He was also prepared to use the black Model 21 semiautomatic .45-caliber Glock pistol he was wearing in his shoulder holster. The gun was loaded, and McVeigh was ready to draw the weapon and start firing if he needed to. In the chamber, the handgun had a Black Talon bullet, sometimes known as a cop-killer. Once it penetrates a human body, the Black Talon mushrooms, ripping apart the victim's internal organs. In the clip of the gun were thirteen more bullets, standard high-velocity rounds.

But the problem with the police car took care of itself. Just as McVeigh was thinking about how he would run him off the road, the officer veered off down another road.

McVeigh rolled on, focusing on the mission ahead.

The nubs of the two fuses he had installed the day before were sticking into the cab of the truck, just behind his left shoulder. McVeigh planned to light the two fuses, park the truck in the small parking area in front of the Murrah Building, and walk away. "If I needed to, I was ready to stay in the truck and protect it with gunfire until the bomb blew up," McVeigh says.

And although McVeigh considered his an essentially military mission, he had not neglected to carry with him the evidence of the apocalyptic political ideology that had first triggered his plan.

The date he chose for the bombing was significant in two ways. Not only was it the second anniversary of the Waco raid; just as important to McVeigh, April 19, 1995, was the 220th anniversary of the Battle of Lexington and Concord, the "shot heard 'round the world" that began the war between American patriots and their British oppressors. To McVeigh, this bombing was in the spirit of the patriots of the American Revolution, the stand of a modern radical patriot against an oppressive government.

As a token of his defiance, McVeigh was wearing his favorite Patriot T-shirt—the one with a drawing of Abraham Lincoln and the phrase SIC SEMPER TYRANNIS—"Thus ever to tyrants"—that was shouted by John Wilkes Booth after he shot Lincoln in the head in a Washington, D.C., theater in 1865. On the back of the shirt was the jolting image of a tree with droplets of red blood dripping off the branches, and superimposed on the tree, McVeigh's favored quote from Thomas Jefferson: THE TREE OF LIBERTY MUST BE REFRESHED FROM TIME TO TIME WITH THE BLOOD OF PATRIOTS AND TYRANTS.

McVeigh was expecting to be either captured or killed after the bombing, and he had packed a plain white envelope with articles he hoped would be found in the old Mercury. He was counting on police to leak details of the articles to the news media, and on the media to gobble up the leaks and pass his message on in turn to the public.

The collection of documents inside the envelope offered a varied and disturbing window into McVeigh's philosophy. There was a bumper sticker that read, WHEN THE GOVERNMENT FEARS THE PEOPLE, THERE IS LIBERTY. WHEN THE PEOPLE FEAR THE GOVERNMENT, THERE IS TYRANNY. Under the printed slogan—a quote from the Revolutionary War patriot Samuel Adams—McVeigh had scrawled, "Maybe now, there will be liberty!"

Also included was a pamphlet, "The American Response to Tyranny," equating the American militia movement with the colonists who rose up against the British 220 years earlier.

"At sunrise, on Wednesday April 19, 1775," it read,

> 400 government troops arrived in Lexington, Massachusetts, to disarm the citizens, so as to destroy any potential resistance to the growing tyranny of government in that time. About 100 colonists, none of whom had any strictly personal reason for becoming involved in what was about to occur, gathered with their assault rifles on the green just above the bridge. No family members were in jail, neither had they been shot by the British. No economic gain motivated these men to stand against the British forces. No monetary value could have been placed on their risk to life that they feared. They stood, and fought, on principle for their rights and for liberty.

The pamphlet's author contended that most modern-day Americans lacked that kind of courage. But men who belonged to militia groups two centuries ago were different.

"The motto of many American militias was, 'Don't tread on me,' which was symbolized by a coiled rattlesnake—an animal which, when left to exist peaceably, threatens no one, but when trodden upon, strikes as viciously and with as deadly an effort as any creature on earth." McVeigh used a marker to highlight this section about the rattlesnake striking. He considered his bombing to be a strike for the greater good of the American people, rather than a crime motivated by greed.

The packet, more than a quarter-inch thick, also included articles criticizing the government's handling of the Waco siege. Some of the articles referred to federal agents as "Gestapo" or "Terrorist Goon Squads." One article made the same link between the Waco raid and Adolf Hitler's attacks on German Jews that militia groups had been making since the event itself.

And there were dozens of other items: quotes about liberty from Jefferson, Patrick Henry, Winston Churchill, and John Locke, whose writings about big government helped inspire the American Revolution. "I have no reason to suppose that he who would take away my liberty, would not, when he had me in his power, take away everything else," Locke wrote, in a famous passage McVeigh copied and stashed in his sampler. "Therefore, it is lawful for me to treat him as one who has put himself into a 'state of war' against me, and kill him if I can."

Another document quoted Samuel Adams's challenge that those who value wealth more than liberty should "crouch down and lick the hands which feed you."

There was even a copy of the Declaration of Independence; on the back, McVeigh had written: "Obey the Constitution of the United States, and we won't shoot you."

Perhaps most telling, though, was the inclusion of a quote from Earl Turner, the protagonist of *The Turner Diaries*, whose protest of gun laws and political correctness culminated in the bombing of the FBI headquarters and other government buildings.

"The real value of our attacks today lies in the psychological impact, not in the immediate casualties," Turner writes in his diary. "More important, though, is what we taught the politicians and the bureaucrats. They learned this afternoon that not one of them is beyond our reach. They can huddle behind barbed wire and tanks in the city, and they can hide behind the concrete walls of their country estates, but we can still find them and kill them."

McVeigh was fully expecting to be stopped in his tracks by the end of the day of the bombing—whether killed by the bomb, killed in a shootout with police, or arrested in his getaway car. Indeed, even the simple gesture of leaving the license plate off the Mercury, he knew, would make it easier for cops to apprehend him.

McVeigh was not suicidal, but he had developed an indifference to life, his own in particular. Like Earl Turner, McVeigh had decided his cause was more important than his life. And he knew that once he was stopped, the news media would swoop in and tell the public every detail of his arrest, his trial, his life story, and his politics.

About 8:50 a.m., McVeigh entered Oklahoma City, a proud community of 440,000 people. The weather was warm and sunny, the sky a brilliant blue. Most people in the downtown area were just settling into what promised to be an ordinary workday. McVeigh wore no expression as he sat at the wheel of the truck. He was devoting every ounce of energy to scanning his surroundings, running over in his head every contingency he might face in the next few minutes.

At the first stoplight he encountered in the downtown area, he reached into his pocket and pulled out a pair of green foam earplugs. Someone had given McVeigh the plugs a couple of years earlier, when he was working security at a Monster Truck show back home. He crammed them into his ears.

Nobody in downtown Oklahoma City took much notice of the yellow rental truck as it rumbled up NW 5th Street a few minutes before 9 a.m. Ryder trucks drove through the city all the time. It was one reason McVeigh picked the Ryder.

He was surprised how little traffic there was on NW 5th.

Keeping his eyes peeled for onlookers, McVeigh pulled the truck briefly over to the side of the road, just long enough to pull out a disposable lighter and ignite the five-minute fuse to his bomb. The sizzling fuse began to fill the truck cab with smoke and the acrid smell of burning gunpowder. As he continued along NW 5th Street, McVeigh had to roll down both windows to let some of the smoke out.

Just past the Regency Towers apartment complex, a block from the target building, McVeigh had to stop for a traffic light. Now, he lit the shorter bomb fuse—the one he had measured at approximately two minutes.

For the longest thirty seconds of his life, McVeigh sat watching the red light, with both fuses burning. His fingers tight on the steering wheel, he glared up at the light, willing it to change.

The light turned green. McVeigh made sure to ease away from the intersection. No stomping on the gas pedal. No frantic movements.

He approached the building carefully. As his eyes fell upon it, the enormity of what he was about to do hit Timothy McVeigh as if for the first time.

Just as quickly, he pushed the thought aside.

McVeigh finally spotted the location he had chosen for the bomb—a drop-off point, several car lengths long, cut into the sidewalk on the north side of the structure. Not one car was pulled up there when he arrived, and when he realized that fact, McVeigh breathed a sigh of relief. If the drop-off spots had been filled with cars, he'd decided, he would drive onto the sidewalk and crash his truck into the building. That would not be necessary now.

As calmly as any delivery-truck driver making a routine drop-off, McVeigh parked right below the tinted windows of the America's Kids Day Care Center on the second floor.

McVeigh looked over his creation one last time. The fuses were still burning, the shorter of the two nearly complete. The vehicle was parked exactly where he wanted it, its back end facing the building.

He grabbed his envelope full of antigovernment articles, locked up the truck, and walked away.

In the next half-minute, perhaps a dozen people saw McVeigh walking away from the Murrah Building. He was wearing a nondescript blue windbreaker over his Abe Lincoln T-shirt, with a black baseball cap, Army boots, and faded black jeans.

Looking straight ahead, McVeigh walked at deliberate speed toward the nearby YMCA building, across NW 5th at the intersection of Robinson Avenue.

He never looked back.

From his earlier visits to downtown Oklahoma City McVeigh knew he could make it behind the YMCA building in plenty of time to avoid the blast, even walking at normal speed.

As he crossed NW 6th Street, a block from the Murrah Building, he noticed a police car parked on the side of the street. Looking out the corner of his eye, McVeigh couldn't tell if there was an officer inside the car, and he wasn't about to stop for a closer look. He wondered whether the cop would be looking right at him when the moment came.

He kept walking.

McVeigh counted off the seconds to himself as he walked north into an alley off NW 6th Street. He was now about 150 yards from ground zero, the spot where he had left his truck. Now, with the police car out of view, McVeigh broke into a jog for the first time.

That bomb should have blown by now, he thought. For an instant he wondered if something might have gone wrong.

Oh man, am I going to hate to walk back there and shoot that damn truck?

Then he heard the roar.

And felt it.

The Murrah Building's explosion lifted McVeigh a full inch off the ground. Even muffled by earplugs, with the YMCA and other buildings forming a buffer, the sound was deafening. It was the equivalent of three tons of TNT. When he looked up, McVeigh could see buildings wobbling from side to side, plate glass showering down into the street around him. He felt the concussion buffeting his cheeks.

The brick facade tumbled down from one of the buildings. A live power line snapped and whipped toward McVeigh. Some falling bricks struck him in the leg, but he was able to hop out of the way of the power line. Smoke and dust billowed high into the air. Fires erupted.

Just like at Waco, McVeigh thought. *Reap what you sow.*

The blast had rocked hundreds of downtown buildings. Every one of the structures in a sixteen-block area surrounding the blast was damaged, some so badly they would have to be demolished.

Fragments of the Ryder truck had rocketed in every direction. A mangled piece of truck frame, four feet long, soared skyward and landed on the roof of a building nearly two blocks away. Another piece of the vehicle, its 250-pound rear axle, whirled like a boomerang the distance of two football fields before crashing down on the hood of a red Ford Festiva near the Regency Towers Apartments, narrowly missing a man named Richard Nichols, his wife, and their young nephew.

McVeigh refused to look behind him, never stopped to gaze at his handiwork. He kept walking, eyes straight ahead, toward his beat-up getaway car, still parked in a lot several blocks from the blast site, its PLEASE DO NOT TOW sign still in the windshield.

He almost bumped into a man rushing in the other direction, toward the rising smoke at the Murrah Building. The shaken man, dressed in a dark uniform, looked to McVeigh like he worked for some kind of delivery company.

For a few seconds they were just a couple of strangers, sharing their nervous observations after the horrific experience.

"Man," said the delivery worker. "I thought that was us blowing up!"

"Yeah," McVeigh said. "Me too."

Minutes later McVeigh was at his Mercury. He gave the car a quick look. The piece of tissue he'd left in the gas tank had not been disturbed; no one had messed with it.

But when he got behind the wheel, his eighteen-year-old getaway car wouldn't start.

He tried several times; the engine wouldn't turn over. McVeigh smelled gasoline.

He stomped the gas pedal to the floor. No luck.

He tried again, and again.

Finally, the old engine coughed to life. McVeigh put the pedal to the floor. His tires squealed as he hauled ass out of the parking area. *I do not want to get caught in Oklahoma City,* he thought.

The automatic transmission in the old car was slipping badly as McVeigh headed north. By 9:10 a.m., eight minutes after the bombing, he had regained his composure and was driving under the speed limit.

An observer watching the scene from a helicopter would have seen many of the people of Oklahoma City rushing toward their crippled federal office building. They would have seen drivers abandoning their cars on the road and running toward the blast scene to provide what help they could. They would have seen the flashing emergency lights on dozens of police cars, fire trucks, and ambulances, all heading toward the rising dust and smoke.

And if they looked closely, they would have noticed an old yellow sedan heading slowly in the other direction. After delivering his ghastly wake-up call to the American government, McVeigh was cruising out of town.

He did not go back and look at what his bomb had done to the Murrah Building. The sound of the explosion told him all he needed to know. *With a noise like that,* he figured, *the whole building must have gone down.*

He was certain that many had died, and he had no regrets. In fact, he could feel the anxiety leaving his body.

It's over, he thought.

As McVeigh headed north, Oklahoma City was reeling from the worst disaster in the state since the Dust Bowl storms of the 1930s. That morning, not a single Oklahoman could have known or cared about the reasons behind the bombing, or about the life and obsessions of the as-yet-unknown bomber. They were dealing with a firestorm, a real-life nightmare so bloody and horrifying that thousands of people would be haunted by it the rest of their days.

McVeigh's bomb did not take down the entire nine-story building, as he hoped it would, but it punched a gaping horseshoe-shaped hole in the north side of the structure. As the northern face came crashing down, employees and visitors to the building tumbled down with it.

The blast killed 167 people; 163 of those killed were inside the building at the time of the blast. A 168th victim, a nurse who rushed to the scene trying to help the injured, died while assisting in the rescue efforts. One woman was killed across the street in the Athenian Building, which housed a Greek restaurant. A man and a woman died in the Oklahoma Water Resources Building, also across the street. Another woman was killed as she walked through a nearby parking lot. And at least 509 people were injured, many of them seriously. McVeigh's bomb killed twenty more people than the 148 Americans killed in combat during the Gulf War.

Eight of the victims were federal law-enforcement agents, and five others were law-enforcement support personnel.

Many of the dead, as McVeigh knew to expect, were employees of other federal agencies—non-law-enforcement agencies such as the Social

Security Administration, the Federal Highway Administration, the Agriculture Department, and the Department of Housing and Urban Development. Although McVeigh considered those agencies part of the federal juggernaut, he did not consider them his targets.

And some of the victims, such as the children in the day-care center and the civilians who were in the Murrah Building that morning to inquire about government services, were people McVeigh would regret killing. He would regard their deaths as "collateral damage."

Some were annihilated instantly. Some fell several floors to their deaths. Some were crushed beyond recognition, mangled, or decapitated. Some lost arms or legs. Some bled to death while rescuers tried to find them. Some were horribly burned or disfigured.

Ninety-nine of the dead worked for the federal government. The other sixty-nine did not.

The dead ranged in age from three months to seventy-three years.

The bomb killed nineteen children, ages five and younger. Four of the children were visitors to the building; the fifteen others were babies and young children from the day-care center. Their bodies were carried out of the building and laid on the pavement outside, covered with blankets; their playground behind the building was pressed into use as a temporary morgue.

Soon after, the medical examiner's office brought two refrigerated trucks to the blast scene to store the bodies until they could be taken to the morgue. One by one, technicians put the bodies through X-rays, fingerprinting, dental examinations, and blood tests, all for identification purposes.

Three unborn children were killed, including the unborn son of Carrie Ann Lenz, a Drug Enforcement Administration employee who, just before the blast, had been showing her co-workers an ultrasound video-tape of her baby.

The bomb killed a cross section of Americans—one hundred twenty-five Caucasians, thirty-four African-Americans, five Hispanic-Americans, two Asian-Americans, one Native American, and one Pacific Islander. Five married couples, all of whom were nearing retirement age and had gone to the Murrah Building to get information about Social Security, were also among the victims.

McVeigh's former colleagues in the Army were hit hard. The Army had personnel working on the third and fourth floors of the Murrah Building, on the devastated north side. Seven employees of an Army recruiting office were killed.

Also killed there was three-year-old Kayla Marie Titsworth, who was visiting the fourth-floor Army office with her family. Her father, Sergeant William Titsworth, her mother, Chrissie Titsworth, and her sister, Katie, five, were all injured in the blast. The family had driven in from Fort Riley just that morning, and had parked their car outside the Murrah Building only minutes before McVeigh arrived with his bomb. Thirteen other Army employees were injured.

The fatalities included Secret Service agents Donald Ray Leonard, Alan G. Whicher, and Mickey B. Maroney, veteran agents who had faced danger all over the world protecting presidents, popes, and other dignitaries.

Three of the slain victims were close relatives of Oklahoma City resident Daina Bradley, who did not work for the government. Bradley had come to the Murrah Building to get a Social Security card for her baby boy, three-month-old Gabreon D. L. Bruce. Bradley and the baby were accompanied by her mother, Cheryl E. Hammon, her sister, Felicia Bradley, and her daughter, Peachlyn Bradley, three.

Bradley noticed a Ryder truck as it parked outside, and saw the driver get out of the vehicle. Soon after, she saw a flash of light come over a desk in the Social Security office. The next thing she knew, Bradley was lying in six inches of water. Her leg was buried under a huge mound of rubble. Her mother, son, and daughter were dead, her sister terribly burned. Bradley was trapped beneath the rubble for five hours. The rescuers who finally freed her had to cut off her right leg at the knee to do it.

Similar stories abounded, as the world would learn in the coming days and weeks. Patti Hall, a veteran employee of the Federal Employees Credit Union, was another who experienced a brush with death. Hall, fifty-eight, worked on the third floor. As McVeigh was driving up to the Murrah Building, she was stepping out of her office into a hallway with a can of air freshener in her hand. She had gone out with the air freshener because a man with terrible body odor had just passed through the hallway.

Just as Hall pressed down on the button of the air freshener, the Murrah Building blew up. For a fraction of a second, before she blacked out, she wondered in astonishment whether there was some kind of connection between the explosion and her spraying the air freshener.

Hall suffered cuts, bruises, and broken bones all over her body; she was in a coma for five weeks before recovering. But she was luckier than Robbin Ann Huff, thirty-seven, her co-worker in the credit union. When Hall walked out of her office, Huff sat down at Hall's desk to talk for a minute with another employee. Pregnant with her first child, Huff was killed.

Richard E. Williams, the assistant building manager for the General Services Administration, knew virtually every federal employee who was killed or injured in the blast. Williams, fifty, had worked in the building since it opened in 1977. Working his way up from maintenance mechanic, at one time or another he had been around to every single office in the building.

Williams was standing in his first-floor office, less than one hundred feet from McVeigh's ground zero, when the bomb hit. Hundreds of pieces of broken glass, stone, and metal pummeled the right side of his body as if they'd been shot from a cannon. He fell, nearly unconscious. Two of his closest friends in the office, Steve Curry and Mike Loudenslager, were killed.

As he lay in a haze, with his right hand broken and his right ear hanging on by a flap of skin, Williams heard a voice call out: "Hang on. I'll be right back." An Oklahoma City policeman, Terry Yeakey, had noticed Williams's arm rising from a pile of rubble. Yeakey, six-feet-four and built like a bull, carried the 225-pound Williams out of the building on his back.

Williams had served in the Air Force in Vietnam. The Oklahoma City bombing, he said, was a hundred times worse than anything he witnessed during the war. "In the war, you knew the enemy was coming after you. You were prepared. You could defend yourself," he said. "We had no warning for this."

Most of the dead would not be positively identified for several days. For some, it took weeks.

All Oklahoma—indeed, all of America—was in shock.

As he headed north in his Mercury, McVeigh says, he felt the satisfaction of a mission accomplished. In his mind, he had watered the tree of liberty—with the blood of Oklahoma City.

McVeigh maintains that he was not nervous as he drove away. He knew the toughest part of the job was behind him. And he didn't care whether he got caught.

Still, he was on high alert, scanning the highway intently.

He was an hour's drive north of Oklahoma City, heading toward the Kansas border, giving little thought to the implications of what he'd done. He wasn't following the news on the radio; the Mercury didn't even have a radio. He had access to a police scanner, but hadn't bothered to bring it. He just wanted to drive, to see what happened.

He did think back to how he had dealt with his first killing, back in the Gulf War. When he blew away the two Iraqis, he didn't dwell on it right away. "In a combat situation," he said, "you do your duty and set your feelings aside. It's like saving your emotions in a memory bank for later access."

He looked for helicopters and police cars, marked or unmarked. He drove at what he considered the normal speed for motorists, about two miles per hour above the speed limit. He signaled all his turns and obeyed all traffic signs and signals.

So far, the only complication had been a construction project that squeezed traffic into a single lane for a few miles. He'd been stuck behind a bus for a while. Otherwise, the drive was incident-free. After pulling off the bloodiest attack on American territory since Pearl Harbor, he was driving away a free man.

But McVeigh figured he might run into trouble soon enough. He'd left his future in the hands of fate by leaving the license plate off his car. And if he did get stopped, the envelope of clues on the seat beside him would help police tie him to the crime in Oklahoma City. Indeed, though McVeigh wasn't exactly eager to get caught, there was a part of him that was curious to see how things would play out if he did.

Ultimately, McVeigh figured, some officer would pull him over for the missing plate, but it would probably happen somewhere in Kansas. Cops in Oklahoma, he was sure, would be too busy dealing with the bombing.

And if no officer stopped him? McVeigh's rough plan was to head up to Kansas and clear out the storage shed in Herington. He might put the license plate back on the Mercury and camp out at Geary Lake for a day or two. After that, McVeigh imagined he might wind up in Arizona or the forests of the Northwest, and continue his war against the federal government.

He wasn't planning more bombings, but he would find other ways to be a thorn in the government's side. It occurred to him that he might select individual targets—federal agents, perhaps—and pick them off one by one. "If I was out in the woods with those jackboots," he would boast in a later interview, "I could take them out by the dozens. No exaggerating. Warfare in the woods is what I was trained for."

As McVeigh rolled through the Oklahoma countryside along Interstate 35, he noticed an oncoming vehicle, a nondescript red sedan. It was rocketing toward Oklahoma City. McVeigh figured it had to be doing 110 miles per hour.

That's a government car, McVeigh thought. *Federal agents. On their way to the Murrah Building.*

Sixty miles north of Oklahoma City McVeigh noticed a marked Oklahoma Highway Patrol car by the side of the road. A trooper stood outside the patrol car, looking over a minivan. *Probably a speeding arrest,* McVeigh thought. He wondered why Oklahoma troopers would be bothering with speeders at a time like this.

About twenty minutes later, at 10:20 a.m., McVeigh saw what looked like the same state trooper in his rearview mirror, coming up fast, at a good ninety-five miles per hour. He was in the passing lane, roaring up alongside McVeigh.

McVeigh pretended not to notice, but his peripheral vision was locked in on the trooper.

The trooper's car was almost past him when McVeigh noticed the front end of the vehicle dip slightly. The police cruiser slowed down and fell in alongside McVeigh's car. The trooper at the wheel was Charles J. Hanger, a nineteen-year police veteran known for his ability to bird-dog traffic violators.

For Hanger, the morning had already been hectic. The first televised reports of the bombing had been noticed at his troop headquarters a few minutes after it happened. Hanger and other troopers were directed to hurry to Oklahoma City and report to the command post near the Murrah Building.

Hanger took off toward Oklahoma City at more than a hundred miles per hour. With his siren blaring and emergency lights flashing, he'd traveled about ten minutes toward the bombing site when his radio broadcast an order to return. They already had enough help at the command post.

Hanger was indeed the trooper McVeigh had seen by the side of the road near a minivan, but he wasn't stopping speeders. He'd been helping two women get assistance for their disabled vehicle. Right around the time McVeigh had driven by one of the women had told Hanger that her husband was an Oklahoma City firefighter. She was worried that he might get hurt at the bombing scene.

"I'm sure he'll be okay," Hanger told her.

Now Hanger was heading back north when he happened to glance at an old Mercury with a big primer spot on the left rear quarter panel. It was McVeigh's junker getaway car, sans license plate.

As he drove wheel-to-wheel with the Mercury, Hanger glanced over and gave McVeigh a little nod. McVeigh nodded back. Now the trooper fell in behind McVeigh and turned on his emergency flasher, directing McVeigh to pull over.

McVeigh complied. He slowed down, pulled over, and parked on the shoulder of I-35, easing the right tires of his car onto the grass, a few inches off the pavement.

Hanger parked behind him. They were about twenty minutes out of Perry, a small town south of the Kansas border.

McVeigh sat in his vehicle. It was decision time.

For a moment, he considered the option of pulling out his Glock and killing the trooper.

As Hanger stepped out of his patrol car, McVeigh emerged from his. McVeigh sized up the trooper. He noticed that Hanger was alone, and had no bulletproof vest. McVeigh sized up his options. If he drew on the trooper, he figured the element of surprise—plus McVeigh's expertise— would put Hanger at a severe disadvantage.

If I want him, I can take him, McVeigh thought. But then he thought again: *No, not a state trooper. Stand down.*

If Hanger had been a federal agent, McVeigh would probably have started shooting. But McVeigh had a grudging respect for local and state cops and sheriffs, and their right to do their jobs. McVeigh felt no hatred for a state trooper stopping a car without a license plate. He would not draw his gun on this officer of the law.

Hanger was wondering what McVeigh was up to as he watched the younger man step out of the battered Mercury. Most people just sat in their cars, nervously waiting for the trooper to approach. By stepping out of his car, McVeigh put Hanger on edge.

This seemed like a fairly routine traffic stop, just a missing license plate. But during another seemingly routine traffic stop exactly two weeks earlier, twelve miles north of this spot, a motorist had pulled out a gun and fired at another Oklahoma trooper. That incident—which ended with the trooper firing back and wounding the motorist—had Hanger and other Oklahoma cops on guard.

Now, Hanger stood behind his open car door, watching McVeigh's hands closely as he approached his patrol car. Cautiously, Hanger began walking toward McVeigh.

Hanger looked at the Mercury, then back at McVeigh.

"You don't have a license plate," he said.

McVeigh glanced at the rear bumper of his car.

"Huh. No," McVeigh said.

Hanger began making notes in a book he was carrying, but the trooper kept a wary eye on McVeigh.

"Do you have insurance?" Hanger asked.

"No, I just bought the car."

"You have a registration? Do you have a bill of sale?"

"Not yet, but I have a license."

McVeigh reached back into his pants pocket and pulled out his camouflage wallet.

As McVeigh took out his Michigan state driver's license, Hanger noticed a bulge under McVeigh's windbreaker.

"What's that?" Hanger asked.

"I have a gun," McVeigh said.

McVeigh spoke calmly. He wanted to avoid showing any signs of aggression or inflaming the situation.

Hanger reached out toward McVeigh and felt for the Glock. Then he pulled out his own gun and pointed it at McVeigh.

"Move your hands away, slowly," Hanger instructed. "Get both hands up in the air."

Hanger pointed his gun at the back of McVeigh's head. He directed him to put his hands on the trunk of the Mercury, bend over, and spread his legs. The trooper was having a bit of trouble removing the Glock from McVeigh's shoulder holster.

"My gun is loaded," he warned the trooper, so there wouldn't be any accidents removing the gun.

"So is mine," Hanger said.

McVeigh told Hanger he would also find a clip of ammunition and a knife attached to his belt. Keeping his gun at the back of McVeigh's head, Hanger took away the Glock, the knife, and the ammo clip, tossing them onto the shoulder a few feet away. He then patted McVeigh down for any additional weapons and cuffed his hands behind his back.

Hanger asked McVeigh why he was carrying a weapon.

McVeigh answered that he felt it was his legal right to carry it.

"You know, when you carry a gun around like that, one wrong move could get you shot," Hanger told McVeigh.

"Possible," McVeigh said.

Hanger marched his handcuffed prisoner toward the police cruiser and put McVeigh in the front seat on the passenger side. He clicked McVeigh into a seat belt and went to retrieve the weapons and ammo he'd just seized.

Hanger unloaded the gun, briefly examining the deadly Black Talon bullet he took from the chamber. He put the knife and the ammo in the trunk of his patrol car, then got back into his cruiser and called his dispatcher on his cell phone. (Troopers had been asked to confine their use of the radio to emergencies and matters related to the bombing.)

Examining the Michigan driver's license McVeigh gave him, Hanger asked the dispatcher to run a computer check to find out whether McVeigh had a criminal history, or if there were any arrest warrants out for him. The dispatcher quickly reported back: no warrants, no record. Tim McVeigh had never been arrested in his life.

Hanger also wanted the dispatcher to run a computer check on the Glock, to see whether it had been stolen. He was turning the unloaded gun around in his hand, looking for the serial number, when McVeigh spoke up.

"The serial number is VM769," McVeigh said.

Just as McVeigh spoke, Hanger was finding the serial number for himself.

"Well, you're close," he told McVeigh. "It's VW769."

"I knew it was an M or a W," McVeigh said.

That's unusual, Hanger remarked. He didn't know many people who memorized the serial numbers of their guns.

"Well, I do," McVeigh said.

The gun was not stolen, the dispatcher reported. Hanger read McVeigh his Miranda rights. McVeigh said he understood his rights and told the trooper that it would be okay to ask him some questions.

Hanger wanted to know why McVeigh was driving without a license plate.

McVeigh said he'd bought the car only a few days ago, from a Firestone dealer named Tom up in Junction City. McVeigh said he had an Arizona plate from his former car, but that he hadn't put it on the Mercury. He'd figured he'd be better off driving without a plate than using the old one.

Hanger asked for a second time why McVeigh was carrying a gun.

"For personal protection," McVeigh said. "I have a concealed-weapon permit for it in New York."

"That's not valid here," Hanger said.

"Yeah," McVeigh said, "I know."

He told Hanger he'd been in the military and had done some work as a security guard back in New York State. He had a security guard's badge in his wallet, which Hanger confiscated. McVeigh explained that he was in the middle of a move from Kansas to Arkansas, and was on his way to Kansas to pick up some of his belongings.

McVeigh gave Hanger permission to search the Mercury. Leaving the prisoner alone in the police car, Hanger examined the car.

Inside the car, on the front seat, he found McVeigh's baseball cap, his PLEASE DO NOT TOW sign, and the white legal-sized envelope. The envelope was sealed and had no writing on the outside. In the trunk, Hanger found a small toolbox with a few tools inside, some soiled rags, and a few leaves and twigs. Hanger locked up the Mercury, leaving all the items inside.

Back in the patrol car, McVeigh had an idea. The handcuffs, he found, weren't that tight. They allowed him some movement. He was able to reach into his back pocket and pull out a business card, which he left in the folds of the car seat.

The card was from Dave Paulsen, a young military supply dealer from the Chicago area, whom McVeigh had met at a gun show in late 1994. On the back of Paulsen's card, McVeigh had written "TNT $5/stick need more." Next to Paulsen's phone number, McVeigh had scrawled, "Call after 01 May, see if I can get some more."

Leaving the business card in Hanger's car was a dirty trick McVeigh was playing on Paulsen. McVeigh was upset that Paulsen had talked with him about the possibility of selling McVeigh some dynamite, strung him along for weeks, and had failed to go through with the deal. McVeigh had also tried to sell Paulsen some blasting caps.

McVeigh had made a special point to carry Paulsen's card with him on the day of the bombing. He knew Paulsen would face some hard questions if police found the card.

Dirty for dirty, McVeigh thought.

Sure enough, as it turned out, FBI agents did wind up going to Illinois, questioning Paulsen at length, and searching his residence. Paulsen later admitted to agents that he spoke to McVeigh about selling him some dynamite but was just "stringing him along."

As the trooper walked back to his patrol car, he noticed McVeigh squirming around in the front seat.

"Why were you fidgeting?" Hanger asked.

"The cuffs get kind of tight," McVeigh said.

"I wouldn't know," Hanger said. "I've never been in handcuffs."

They were ready to ride to Noble County Jail in Perry, where McVeigh would be booked. Hanger wanted to know if McVeigh was willing to pay to have his car towed to Perry, the county seat, or if he preferred to leave it locked up on the shoulder of the road until he could get bailed out and retrieve it.

Just leave it, McVeigh said.

Hanger wondered whether there might be something valuable to McVeigh in that sealed envelope on the front seat. He asked whether McVeigh wanted him to go and get it for him.

"No," McVeigh said. "Leave it there."

They chatted a bit on the way to Perry—a cop and his prisoner, making small talk. Always fascinated by firearms and fast cars, McVeigh asked Hanger what kind of gun he carried.

"A Sig Model two-two-eight," Hanger said.

"Oh," McVeigh said, "a nine-millimeter."

Noticing that Hanger's police cruiser was almost brand-new, McVeigh tried to coax the trooper into showing him how fast the car would go. Hanger declined.

The trooper told McVeigh that a lot of police officers from this part of the state were on their way to Oklahoma City because of a big explosion in the federal office building. He asked McVeigh whether he'd heard about the tragedy.

"No," McVeigh said, "I don't have a radio in my car."

It was nearly 11 a.m. when they pulled into the parking lot of the Noble County Jail in Perry. McVeigh took off his jacket, and Hanger got his first look at the odd and unsettling T-shirt his prisoner was wearing. Hanger didn't look too closely, but it registered in his mind that he'd never seen a shirt like this before, with its picture of Abe Lincoln on the front and illustration of a tree on the back. But Hanger didn't really read the slogans that captioned the drawings.

Hanger and Marsha Moritz, the jailer, booked McVeigh on four misdemeanor charges: transporting a loaded firearm in a motor vehicle, unlawfully carrying a weapon, failing to display a current license plate, and failing to maintain proof of insurance.

She had the prisoner empty out his pockets, which yielded two commemorative Revolutionary War coins, four .45-caliber bullets, a pair of Fit to Be Tried–brand earplugs, a small bottle of aspirin substitute, and $255 McVeigh was carrying in his wallet.

Moritz took the new prisoner's mug shot against a height-measurement poster; in his thick-soled combat boots, McVeigh was well over six feet two. His face betrayed no emotion as he stood and held a card in front of his chest, showing his prisoner number, 95–057, and the date, 04–19–95.

The prisoner-screening process went routinely until Moritz told McVeigh she needed to know his next of kin, in case he got sick or something happened to him in the jail.

McVeigh didn't answer at first. After an awkward silence, he gave the name of James Nichols. McVeigh's Michigan driver's license listed the James Nichols farm in Decker as his home address.

Other than that, McVeigh was surprisingly loose for a man being arrested for the first time. As Hanger prepared to fingerprint him, he asked McVeigh to wipe the perspiration off his hands.

"Most people I arrest are sweaty," Hanger said.

"No problem," McVeigh said. "My hands are dry."

McVeigh smiled and raised his eyebrows when he saw Moritz bring out a pair of rubber gloves.

"What are you going to do with those?" he wisecracked.

"You never know, do you?" McVeigh remembers her kidding back.

But the light mood didn't last long. There was a TV set in the office, and the continuing broadcast about the bombing cast a pall over everyone in the Noble County Sheriff's Department.

Moritz and Hanger exchanged a few words about the tragedy—how terrible it was that so many people had been killed and injured, how sad it was that it all happened in their backyard, just about sixty miles away.

McVeigh pretended to pay little attention to the television, but he was watching and listening to every word. This was his first opportunity to see what his bomb had done to the Murrah Building.

His initial reaction was disappointment. *Damn,* he thought, *the whole building didn't come down.*

But McVeigh says how that even that revelation had a silver lining for him: with part of the Murrah Building still standing, in its ruined state, the American public would be left with its carcass, standing as a symbol.

McVeigh then heard someone in the office mention how horrible it was that the blast had destroyed a day-care center in the building, killing a group of children.

This news hit McVeigh harder. He had never intended for children to be among his victims; though he had no feeling at all for the government workers he had slain, the presence of children among his victims did cause him a moment's regret. Yet even that sliver of humanity was matched with a more coldblooded reaction: within a moment he recognized that the deaths of innocent children would overshadow the political message of his bombing. In the court of public opinion, he figured, this would be a disaster for his cause. *The media's going to latch on to that,* McVeigh thought. *Everybody's going to say, "He's a baby killer."* "The day-care center," he would later say. "If I had known it was there, I probably would have shifted the target."

Everyone in the sheriff's office was listening closely as a TV reporter gave the first sketchy descriptions of a possible suspect: a white male, somewhere between five feet nine and six feet one.

A deputy who was listening to the report looked over and eyeballed McVeigh.

"Gee, you're a recent arrival," he remarked.

"That ain't me," McVeigh said, laughing off the suggestion. "I'm six-two. Listen to that description."

There was no further talk about the description. For the next two days, McVeigh would linger in the jail in this peaceful little town of fifty-three hundred people, awaiting his court appearance. As a first-time offender charged with a few misdemeanors, he stood a good chance of getting a quick release on low bail.

He had been stopped eighty miles north of the bombing, seventy-eight minutes after it occurred, carrying earplugs in his pocket and wearing a T-shirt celebrating the assassination of an American president. But so far, no one had any inkling that he might have anything to do with the bombing.

Marsha Moritz thought McVeigh was an unusually cooperative and polite prisoner. But she noticed one odd thing about him: the T-shirt. She mentioned it to Hanger after McVeigh had removed his personal clothes and put on an orange jailhouse jumpsuit to be taken to the cellblock. The T-shirt had already been stored in a paper bag with McVeighs other personal effects.

"Wasn't that a strange T-shirt he had on?" Moritz said to Hanger.

"What do you mean?"

"Well, it had a strange saying on it."

"I didn't read it."

As he sat contemplating his fate within the walls of the Supermax, it occurred to McVeigh that he could be considered the poster child for Generation X. Look up the dictionary definition of the Gen-X slogan "No

Fear," McVeigh quipped, and you'd find his picture beside it. He some-times found himself wishing the final moment would come sooner, rather than later. "I'll be glad to leave this fucked-up world," he said. "Truth is, I determined mostly through my travels that this world just doesn't hold anything for me." But as the weeks rolled by, the isolated hours he spent in the four-cell special disciplinary unit at Supermax provided time for self-examination, and he would come to realize that he was not immedi-ately suicidal. "I figure, why not take a few years in retirement. Sit in my cell; write letters, make peace with everyone. What does that make the death penalty, if that's what it is?" In McVeigh's opinion, it was nothing more than state-assisted suicide. "I knew I wanted this before it happened. I knew my objective was a state-assisted suicide and when it happens, it's in your face, motherfuckers. You just did something you're trying to say should be illegal for medical personnel."

McVeigh also contended that the experience of prison, while it lasted, wasn't that difficult to bear. "These guys do my laundry. I lay in bed all day and watch cable television. I don't even pay the electric or cable bills. Is that torture?" McVeigh even found himself reminded of his old dream of becoming a survivalist. Looking at the concrete and steel-reinforced walls of the ultramodern Supermax, McVeigh thought, *I've always wanted to live in a bunker, and now here I am.*

In truth, though, during his first few months there McVeigh hated life in the Supermax. The lights in his cell never turned off, and at night, he found it next to impossible to sleep. To make matters worse, the prison staff delivered breakfast at 4:30 a.m.—*to fuck with you,* McVeigh was convinced.

Suffering from sleep deprivation, he experienced increased paranoia and aggression. In those first few months, when he would go to an outside cage for recreation, McVeigh claims he would return to find his cell had been ran-sacked in searches conducted by the correctional officers. He believed that the officers were making him pay a price for taking his recreation.

Worst of all, there was virtually no opportunity to talk with any other inmates. Each cell had a double set of doors to prevent voices from carrying. Yelling or knocking on walls to communicate was impractical. Each of the cells was separated by an empty room, which absorbed and deadened sounds.

McVeigh tolerated the conditions for several months before blowing his top one day at the warden and another prison official who were inspecting the disciplinary unit. He spared no energy in telling Warden Hurley and the other official exactly how he felt. Screaming and cursing, McVeigh told the warden that he was playing by the institution's rules. In return, he wanted to be treated like a human being.

"I make my bed, and do everything you ask me to do!" McVeigh hollered, following up with a barrage of profanity.

"Tim, it does you no good to call my workers motherfuckers," Hurley said calmly.

McVeigh noticed a man standing next to Hurley. "Who's that?" he asked.

"This man is my regional supervisor," Hurley answered.

McVeigh expressed immediate remorse for causing a scene. He hadn't lost his military respect for chain of command.

McVeigh shared the disciplinary unit with extraordinary company. The three other cells were occupied by three of the few men alive whose record rivaled his own: Theodore Kaczynski, Ramzi Ahmed Yousef, and Luis Felipe.

Kaczynski, better known as the Unabomber, had been the last of the four to arrive at the Colorado prison. He was serving four consecutive life sentences in connection with sixteen mail bombings and attempted bombings he had perpetrated in seven states between 1978 and 1995. The bombings injured ten [twenty-three—ed.] people and killed three—a computer-store owner, a public-relations executive, and an official of the California Forestry Association. He pleaded guilty to bombing and murder charges in January 1998, and was sent to the Supermax the following May.

Kaczynski, who graduated from high school early and entered Harvard at age sixteen, was mainly protesting the advancement of technology, but he also shared some of McVeigh's concerns about the loss of personal freedoms in America. Many of his bombs bore the initials FC, which stood for "Freedom Club." Kaczynski even embodied the survivalist principles McVeigh so ardently admired, having spent years alone in a secluded ten-by-twelve-foot Montana cabin before being captured by federal agents.

Ramzi Yousef was serving a 240-year sentence for his conviction as the mastermind of the 1993 World Trade Center bombing. In addition to the bombing, which killed six people, injured a thousand, and caused hundreds of millions of dollars in damage, Yousef was also convicted of plotting to bomb eleven airliners as they crossed the Pacific Ocean with American passengers. He belonged to a terrorist group whose members were suspected of planning an attack on Pope John Paul II, and he was suspected of plotting to kidnap and kill U.S. diplomats in Pakistan. In sending him to prison, a federal judge in New York City had called him an "apostle of evil."

At his sentencing, Yousef had made a long and angry speech denouncing the American government and its overseas policies. Like McVeigh, Yousef considered leaders of the American government the world's ultimate terrorists; his words might have come from McVeigh's lips. "You killed civilians and innocent people—not soldiers—innocent people [in] every single war. . . . You went to more wars than any country in this century, and then you have the nerve to talk about killing innocent people.

"Yes, I am a terrorist, and I am proud of it. And I support terrorism so long as it was against the United States Government and against Israel. . . . You are butchers, liars and hypocrites."

Luis Felipe was a native of Cuba who had been in and out of prison since age nine. The founder of the New York City chapter of the ultraviolent Latin Kings street gang, he had led a life that could not have been more different from McVeigh's. Known by the nickname "King Blood," Felipe had brought his own form of terror to the prison system. While serving time for various crimes of violence in New York State prisons, Felipe had used coded letters to continue managing his gang. Using code teens like "T.O.S.," for "terminate on sight," Felipe from his prison cell had ordered the beatings and murders of several people on the outside— including one beheading. In October 1997 Felipe was sentenced to life in prison, plus forty-five years; federal officials had relegated him to the Supermax to enforce his isolation from society.

With McVeigh added to the mix, the four constituted one of the most fearsome groups of prisoners ever housed in one facility at one time, let alone one disciplinary wing. One day McVeigh received a newspaper clipping in the mail that featured color photographs of him, Kaczynski, Yousef, and Felipe. The letter writer asked McVeigh to autograph the article. McVeigh happily obliged, signing it "The A-Team! T.J.M."

Some at the prison called the disciplinary wing "Celebrity Row"; to others it was "Bomber Row." When the four were first assembled at the Supermax, they were completely isolated from the rest of the prison population—and from each other. Confined to their cells at least twenty-three hours a day, their only relief was one hour of caged outdoor exercise twice a week—alone. When prison officials eased some of the restrictions on the four men some months later, they were finally allowed to take their outdoor exercise at the same time. And, through the walls of cages placed about ten feet apart, the four terrorists would exchange conversation.

With Felipe, McVeigh found he shared an appetite for women, and the two began trading pornography—"smut books," as they called them. With Yousef, McVeigh found himself involved in deep political discussions; Yousef even made frequent, unsuccessful attempts to convert him to the Muslim faith. With Kaczynski, McVeigh shared his fondness for the outdoors and wilderness.

Of all the inmates McVeigh came to know at the Supermax, he found he had the most in common with the fifty-seven-year-old Kaczynski. Initially Kaczynski had refused to speak with McVeigh. "He fell for the propaganda against me," McVeigh believed. In truth, Kaczynski had some misgivings about the way McVeigh had executed the Oklahoma City bombing. Kaczynski's bombings had targeted carefully selected individuals, people he blamed for the ills of America. Kaczynski felt the Oklahoma City blast, killing scores of low-level government employees, was a "bad action" because it was unnecessarily inhumane. In time, though, Kaczynski came to believe that his fellow bomber had, like him, been demonized by false media reports. There was more than just a mutual appreciation for the outdoors between them; their political views often coincided.

One important link between the two men was their mutual disdain for federal agents and prosecutorial misconduct. McVeigh once gave Kaczynski a copy of *Tainting Evidence: Inside the Scandals at the FBI Crime Lab*, by John F. Kelly and Phillip K. Wearne, a book about the alleged manufacture of evidence by federal agents. The book struck a nerve in Kaczynski, who genuinely came to like McVeigh.

"You were in the Persian Gulf War?" Kaczynski asked one day.

"Yes, sir," McVeigh answered. "Ironic, isn't it? In Desert Storm I got medals for killing people."

Like McVeigh, Kaczynski preferred the idea of execution to life in prison. But when Kaczynski made his preference public, McVeigh thought his fellow prisoner had made a big mistake—particularly since Kaczynski was seeking a retrial. "Ted messed up," he said. "They're not going to want to seek death now because they know he's being tortured with life. . . . They won't give the opportunity for the death penalty again, either with a federal retrial or state trial. If one is serious about it, you never show your hand."

Kaczynski laid out his feelings about McVeigh and the bombing at Oklahoma City in an eleven-page letter to the authors of this book.

"On a personal level I like McVeigh and I imagine that most people would like him," Kaczynski wrote.

. . .

He was easily the most outgoing of all the inmates in our range of cells and had excellent social skills. He was considerate of others and knew how to deal with people effectively. He communicated somehow even with the inmates on the range of cells above ours, and, because he talked with more people, he always knew more about what was going on than anyone else on our range. . . . Here at the ADX [prison] my senses and my mind are turned inward most of the time, so it struck me as remarkable that even in prison McVeigh remained alert and consistently took an interest in his surroundings.

Kaczynski said it was his impression that McVeigh was "very intelligent": "He thinks seriously about the problems of our society, especially as they relate to the issue of individual freedom, and to the extent that he expressed his ideas to me they seemed rational and sensible."

Like others who had known McVeigh throughout his adult life, Kaczynski noticed that even in his thirties McVeigh still seemed affected by his experience in the Gulf War. "I do recall his mentioning that prior to the Gulf War, he and other soldiers were subjected to propaganda designed to make them hate the people they were going to fight, but when he arrived in the Persian Gulf area, he discovered that the 'enemies' he was supposed to kill were human beings just like himself, and he learned to respect their culture."

Kaczynski said the two spoke about firearms, and McVeigh once told him that he liked a particular type of gun because it could be used with armor-piercing ammunition.

I said, "So what would I need armor-piercing ammunition for?" In reply McVeigh indicated that I might some day want to shoot at a tank. . . . I think McVeigh knew well that there was little likelihood that I would ever need to shoot at a tank—or that he would either, unless he rejoined the Army. My speculative interpretation is that McVeigh resembles many people on the right who are attracted to powerful weapons for their own sake and independently of any likelihood that they will ever have a practical use for them. Such people tend to invent excuses, often far-fetched ones, for acquiring weapons for which they have no real need.

But McVeigh did not fit the stereotype of the extreme right-wingers. I've already indicated that he spoke of respect for other people's cultures, and in doing so he sounded like a liberal. He certainly was not a mean or hostile person, and I wasn't aware of any indication that he was super patriotic. I suspect that he is an adventurer by nature, and America since the closing of the frontier has had little room for adventurers.

excerpt from:

The Unabomber's Manifesto
by Theodore Kaczynski

Theodore Kaczynski, the Unabomber, was at the top of the FBI's most
wanted list for a decade. During a seventeen-year period ending in
1997 he mailed seventeen letter bombs that killed three people and
injured twenty-three. Kaczynski's victims were individuals whom he
saw as part of a totalitarian technological machine that was destroying
personal freedom and our natural environment. These people included
research scientists and forestry executives. Kaczynski offered to stop
sending letter bombs if his manifesto was published in its entirety by
major publications. The *New York Times* and the *Washington Post*
printed all fifty-six pages. His brother David recognized the writing style
and went to the FBI, offering to turn in Kaczynski in exchange for the
government agreeing to waive the death penalty. What is unusual
about the manifesto is that it exists at all. This lengthy document is
probably the most extensive public statement ever issued by a terrorist.
In a rambling style Kaczynski rails against Leftists whom he sees as
knee-jerk moralists. But he directs most of his venom at technology,
stating that it is impossible to have modern devices without enslaving
the individual to an arbitrary logic. In this respect Kaczynski is firmly a
part of the Luddite tradition that originated in England in the 19th
Century, wherein workers sabotaged the machines in their factories,
leaving unchallenged other aspects of their servitude. Kaczynski is
serving life without the possibility of parole. These excerpts deal with
the core of his argument: the unreformable nature of technology and
its incompatibility with freedom.

INDUSTRIAL-TECHNOLOGICAL SOCIETY
CANNOT BE REFORMED

111: There has been a consistent tendency, going back at least to the Industrial Revolution for technology to strengthen the system at a high cost in individual freedom and local autonomy. Hence any change designed to protect freedom from technology would be contrary to a fundamental trend in the development of our society. Consequently, such a change either would be a transitory one—soon swamped by the tide of history—or, if large enough to be permanent would alter the nature of our whole society. . . . Moreover, since society would be altered in a way that could not be predicted in advance . . . there would be great risk. Changes large enough to make a lasting difference in favor of freedom would not be initiated because it would realized that they would gravely disrupt the system. So any attempts at reform would be too timid to be effective. Even if changes large enough to make a lasting difference were initiated, they would be retracted when their disruptive effects became apparent. Thus, permanent changes in favor of freedom could be brought about only by persons prepared to accept radical, dangerous and unpredictable alteration of the entire system. In other words, by revolutionaries, not reformers.

112. People anxious to rescue freedom without sacrificing the supposed benefits of technology will suggest naive schemes for some new form of society that would reconcile freedom with technology. Apart from the fact that people who make suggestions seldom propose any practical means by which the new form of society could be set up in the first place, it follows . . . that even if the new form of society could be once established, it either would collapse or would give results very different from those expected.

• • •

113. So even on very general grounds it seems highly improbably that any way of changing society could be found that would reconcile freedom with modern technology.

117. In any technologically advanced society the individual's fate MUST depend on decisions that he personally cannot influence to any great extent. A technological society cannot be broken down into small, autonomous communities, because production depends on the cooperation of very large numbers of people. When a decision affects, say, a million people, then each of the affected individuals has, on the average, only a one-millionth share in making the decision. What usually happens in practice is that decisions are made by public officials or corporation executives, or by technical specialists, but even when the public votes on a decision the number of voters ordinarily is too large for the vote of any one individual to be significant. . . . Thus most individuals are unable to influence measurably the major decisions that affect their lives. Their is no conceivable way to remedy this in a technologically advanced society. The system tries to "solve" this problem by using propaganda to make people WANT the decisions that have been made for them, but even if this "solution" were completely successful in making people feel better, it would be demeaning.

118. Conservatives and some others advocate more "local autonomy." Local communities once did have autonomy, but such autonomy becomes less and less possible as local communities become more enmeshed with and dependent on large-scale systems like public utilities, computer networks, highway systems, the mass communications media, the modern health care system. Also operating against autonomy is the fact that technology applied in one location often affects people at other locations far away. Thus pesticide or chemical use near a creek may contaminate the

water supply hundreds of miles downstream, and the greenhouse effect affects the whole world.

119. The system does not and cannot exist to satisfy human needs. Instead, it is human behavior that has to be modified to fit the needs of the system. This has nothing to do with the political or social ideology that may pretend to guide the technological system. It is the fault of technology, because the system is guided not by ideology but by technical necessity. . . . Of course the system does satisfy many human needs, but generally speaking it does this only to the extent that it is to the advantage of the system to do it. It is the needs of the system that are paramount, not those of the human being. For example, the system provides people with food because the system couldn't function if everyone starved; it attends to people's psychological needs whenever it can CONVENIENTLY do so, because it couldn't function if too many people became depressed or rebellious. But the system, for good, solid, practical reasons, must exert constant pressure on people to mold their behavior to the needs of the system. Too much waste accumulating? The government, the media, the educational system, environmentalists, everyone inundates us with a mass of propaganda about recycling. Need more technical personnel? A chorus of voices exhorts kids to study science. No one stops to ask whether it is inhumane to force adolescents to spend the bulk of their time studying subjects most of them hate. When skilled workers are put out of a job by technical advances and have to undergo "retraining," no one asks whether it is humiliating for them to be pushed around in this way. It is simply taken for granted that everyone must bow to technical necessity and for good reason: If human needs were put before technical necessity there would be economic problems, unemployment, shortages or worse. The concept of "mental health" in our society is defined largely by the extent to which an individual behaves in accord with the needs of the system and does so without showing signs of stress.

...

120. Efforts to make room for a sense of purpose and for autonomy within the system are no better than a joke. For example, one company, instead of having each of its employees assemble only one section of a catalogue, had each assemble a whole catalogue, and this was supposed to give them a sense of purpose and achievement. Some companies have tried to give their employees more autonomy in their work, but for practical reasons this usually can be done only to a very limited extent, and in any case employees are never given autonomy as to ultimate goals—their "autonomous" efforts can never be directed toward goals that they select personally, but only toward their employer's goals, such as the survival and growth of the company. Any company would soon go out of business if it permitted its employees to act otherwise. Similarly, in any enterprise within a socialist system, workers must direct their efforts toward the goals of the enterprise, otherwise the enterprise will not serve its purpose as part of the system. Once again, for purely technical reasons it is not possible for most individuals or small groups to have much autonomy in industrial society. Even the small-business owner commonly has only limited autonomy. Apart from the necessity of government regulation, he is restricted by the fact that he must fit into the economic system and conform to its requirements. For instance, when someone develops a new technology, the small-business person often has to use that technology whether he wants to or not, in order to remain competitive. . . .

TECHNOLOGY IS A MORE POWERFUL SOCIAL FORCE THAN THE
ASPIRATION FOR FREEDOM

125. It is not possible to make a LASTING compromise between technology and freedom, because technology is by far the more powerful social force and continually encroaches on freedom through REPEATED

compromises. Imagine the case of two neighbors, each of whom at the outset owns the same amount of land, but one of whom is more powerful than the other. The powerful one demands a piece of the other's land. The weak one refuses. The powerful one says, "OK, let's compromise. Give me half of what I asked." The weak one has little choice but to give in. Some time later the powerful neighbor demands another piece of land, again there is a compromise, and so forth. By forcing a long series of compromises on the weaker man, the powerful one eventually gets all of his land. So it goes in the conflict between technology and freedom.

128. While technological progress AS A WHOLE continually narrows our sphere of freedom, each new technical advance CONSIDERED BY ITSELF appears to be desirable. Electricity, indoor plumbing, rapid long-distance communications . . . how could one argue against any of these things, or against any other of the innumerable technical advances that have made modern society? It would have been absurd to resist the introduction of the telephone, for example. It offered many advantages and no disadvantages. Yet . . . all these technical advances taken together have created world in which the average man's fate is no longer in his own hands or in the hands of his neighbors and friends, but in those of politicians, corporation executives and remote, anonymous technicians and bureaucrats whom he as an individual has no power to influence. The same process will continue in the future. Take genetic engineering, for example. Few people will resist the introduction of a genetic technique that eliminates a hereditary disease. It does no apparent harm and prevents much suffering. Yet a large number of genetic improvements taken together will make the human being into an engineered product rather than a free creation of chance (or of God, or whatever, depending on your religious beliefs).

...

129. Another reason why technology is such a powerful social force is that, within the context of a given society, technological progress marches in only one direction; it can never be reversed. Once a technical innovation has been introduced, people usually become dependent on it, unless it is replaced by some still more advanced innovation. Not only do people become dependent as individuals on a new item of technology, but, even more, the system as a whole becomes dependent on it. (Imagine what would happen to the system today if computers, for example, were eliminated.) Thus the system can move in only one direction, toward greater technologization. Technology repeatedly forces freedom to take a step back—short of the overthrow of the whole technological system.

130. Technology advances with great rapidity and threatens freedom at many different points at the same time (crowding, rules and regulations, increasing dependence of individuals on large organizations, propaganda and other psychological techniques, genetic engineering, invasion of privacy through surveillance devices and computers, etc.) To hold back any ONE of the threats to freedom would require a long different social struggle. Those who want to protect freedom are overwhelmed by the sheer number of new attacks and the rapidity with which they develop, hence they become pathetic and no longer resist. To fight each of the threats separately would be futile. Success can be hoped for only by fighting the technological system as a whole; but that is revolution not reform. . . .

excerpt from:

Underground

by Haruki Murakami

This excerpt begins with an account of the Tokyo nerve gas attack. On
March 20, 1995, five members of the Aum Shinrikyo cult carried out a
chemical attack on the subway system using sarin, a nerve gas twenty-
six times more lethal than cyanide. Twelve subway riders died. The
fanatical Aum Shinrikyo cult and its leader Shoko Asahara had previously been investigated for numerous crimes, including the murder and
torture of several of the group's own members. But they were not seen
as a serious threat, capable of making good on their apocalyptic vision,
until it was too late. Next, we read a survivor's account of the attack
that demonstrates how resilient the Japanese civilians were. The next
day the subway was up and running on a normal schedule. In conclusion, we discover that the scars on the national consciousness go
deeper than the Japanese themselves acknowledge, as Murakami
points out in his analysis. Haruki Murakami is a leading Japanese novelist. This is his only nonfiction work.

Two men were assigned to drop sarin gas on the Chiyoda Line: Ikuo Hayashi and Tomomitsu Niimi. Hayashi was the principal criminal, Niimi the driver-accomplice.

Why Hayashi—a senior medical doctor with an active "frontline" track record at the Ministry of Science and Technology—was chosen to carry out this mission remains unclear, but Hayashi himself conjectures it was to seal his lips. Implication in the gas attack cut off any possibility of escape. By this point Hayashi already knew too much. He was devoted to the Aum cult leader Shoko Asahara, but apparently Asahara did not trust him. When Asahara first told him to go and release the sarin gas Hayashi admitted: "I could feel my heart pounding in my chest—though where else would my heart be?"

Boarding the front car of the southwestbound 7:48 a.m. Chiyoda Line, running from the northeast Tokyo suburb of Kita-senju to the western suburb of Yoyogi-uehara, Hayashi punctured his plastic bag of sarin at Shin-ochanomizu Station in the central business district, then left the train. Outside the station, Niimi was waiting with a car and the two of them drove back to the Shibuya *ajid*—Aum local headquarters—their mission accomplished. There was no way for Hayashi to refuse. "This is just a yoga of the Mahamudra," he kept telling himself, Mahamudra being a crucial discipline for attaining the stage of the True Enlightened Master.

When asked by Asahara's legal team whether he could have refused if he had wanted to, Hayashi replied: "If that had been possible, the Tokyo gas attack would never have happened."

Born in 1947, Hayashi was the second son of a Tokyo medical practitioner. Groomed from middle and secondary school for Keio University, one of Tokyo's two top private universities, upon graduating from medical school he took employment as a heart and artery specialist at Keio Hospital, after which he went on to become head of the Circulatory

Medicine department at the National Sanatorium Hospital at Tokaimura, Ibaragi, north of Tokyo. He is a member of what the Japanese call the "superelite." Clean-cut, he exudes the self-confidence of a professional. Medicine obviously came naturally to him. His hair is starting to thin on top, but like most of the Aum leadership, he has good posture, his eyes focused firmly ahead, although his speech is monotonous and somehow forced. From his testimony in court, I gained the distinct impression that he was blocking some flow of emotion inside himself.

Somewhere along the line Hayashi seems to have had profound doubts about his career as a doctor and, while searching for answers beyond orthodox science, he became seduced by the charismatic teachings of Shoko Asahara and suddenly converted to Aum. In 1990 he resigned from his job and left with his family for a religious life. His two children were promised a special education within the cult. His colleagues at the hospital were loath to lose a man of Hayashi's caliber and tried to stop him, but his mind was made up. It was as if the medical profession no longer held anything for him. Once initiated into the cult, he soon found himself among Asahara's favorites and was appointed Minister of Healing.

Once he had been called upon to carry out the sarin plan, Hayashi was brought to Aum's general headquarters, Satyam No. 7, in Kamikuishiki Village near Mt. Fuji, at 3 a.m. on March 20, where, together with the four other principal players, he rehearsed the attack. Using umbrellas sharpened with a file, they pierced plastic bags filled with water rather than sarin. The rehearsal was supervised by Hideo Murai of the Aum leadership. While comments from the other four members indicate that they enjoyed this practice session, Hayashi observed it all with cool reserve. Nor did he actually pierce his bag. To the 48-year-old doctor, the whole exercise must have seemed like a game.

"I did not need to practice," says Hayashi. "I could see what to do, though my heart wasn't in it."

After the session, all five were returned by car to the Shibuya *ajid*, whereupon our physician Hayashi handed out hypodermic needles filled with atropine sulphate to the team, instructing them to inject it at the first sign of sarin poisoning.

On the way to the station, Hayashi purchased gloves, a knife, tape, and sandals at a convenience store. Niimi, the driver, bought some newspapers in which to wrap the bags of sarin. They were sectarian newspapers—the Japan Communist Party's *Akahata* (*Red Flag*) and the Soka Gakkai's *Seikyo Shimbun* (*Sacred Teaching News*)—"more interesting because they're not papers you can buy just anywhere." That was Niimi's little in-joke. Of the two papers, Hayashi chose *Akahata:* a rival sect's publication would have been too obvious and therefore counterproductive.

Before getting on the subway, Hayashi donned a gauze surgical mask, of the sort commonly worn by many commuters in winter to prevent cold germs from spreading. The train number was A725K. Glancing at a woman and child in the car, Hayashi wavered slightly. "If I unleash the sarin here and now," he thought, "the woman opposite me is dead for sure. Unless she gets off somewhere." But he'd come this far; there was no going back. This was a Holy War. The weak were losers.

As the subway approached Shin-ochanomizu Station, he dropped the bags of sarin by his right foot, steeled his nerves, and poked one of them with the end of his umbrella. It was resilient and gave a "springy gush." He poked it again a few times—exactly how many times he doesn't remember. In the end, only one of the two bags was found to have been punctured; the other was untouched.

Still, the sarin liquid in one of the bags completely evaporated and did a lot of damage. At Kasumigaseki two station attendants died in the line of duty trying to dispose of the bag. Train A725K was stopped at the next station, Kokkai-gijidomae—the stop for the Japanese National Assembly—all passengers were evacuated, and the cars were cleaned.

Two people were killed and 231 suffered serious injuries from Hayashi's sarin drop alone.*

"I'm not a sarin victim, I'm a survivor"
Toshiaki Toyoda

Born in Yamagata Prefecture in northeastern Japan, Mr. Toyoda joined the Subway Authority on March 20 in 1961—thirty-four years to the day before the gas attack. "After graduating I came to Tokyo with literally just a futon to sleep on," *he recalls. He wasn't particularly interested in the subway, but a relative's introduction landed him the job. He has worked in Tokyo as a station attendant ever since, but he still has a slight Yamagata accent.*

Talking to Mr. Toyoda is a lesson in professional ethics. Or perhaps that should be civic ethics. Thirty-four years on the job have done him proud and made him someone people can depend upon. Just to look at him is to see the very model of a good citizen.

From what Mr. Toyoda tells us I would venture a guess that, to a greater or lesser degree, his two colleagues—who unfortunately sacrificed their lives while trying to dispose of the sarin—both shared his ethical stance.

Even at his age he jogs twice a week so that he has no problem doing the more physical tasks around the station.

---

*Ikuo Hayashi was sentenced to life imprisonment. At the time of going to press, he was serving time in prison and Tomomitsu Niimi was still on trial. [Tr.]

He even takes part in interstation sports events. "It's good to forget about the job and work up a good sweat," *he says.*

We talked for at least four hours. Not once did he complain. "I want to conquer my own weak spirit," *he says,* "and put the gas attack behind me." *Surely easier said than done.*

Since interviewing Mr. Toyoda, every time I'm on the subway I look very carefully at all the station attendants. They really do have a tough job.

I want to say first of all that I'd really rather not talk about this whole thing. I spent the night before the gas attack at the station along with Takahashi, who died. I was on monitor duty that day for the Chiyoda Line, and two colleagues died while I was responsible. Two men who ate in the same canteen as me. If I must speak, that's what comes to mind. To tell the truth, I'd rather not remember it.

MURAKAMI: *Understood. I appreciate how difficult this must be, and I certainly don't mean to open up wounds that are only now beginning to heal. However, for my part, the more living testimonies I can bring together in writing, the more accurate the picture I can put across to everyone of just what happened to the people who found themselves in the Tokyo subway on March 20, 1995.*

Well, all right, then, I'll do my best . . .

That day I had round-the-clock duty, so I'd stayed overnight and was working on Platform 5 until 8:00 a.m. About 7:40 I handed over to Okazawa, the assistant stationmaster, saying, "Everything's in order." Then I went around to check the ticket barriers and other parts of the station before returning to the office. Takahashi was there. When I'm out on the platforms, Takahashi has to stay in the office; when Takahashi's out on the platforms, I'm in the office—that's how our shift alternated.

Before 8 a.m. Hishinuma also came out to see an out-of-service train. Hishinuma was from the Transport department, so he was supervising the drivers and conductors. It was good weather that day and he was joking as we drank our tea: "Train's never late when it's my duty." Everyone was in good spirits.

About the same time Takahashi went to the platform upstairs, while I stayed in the office relaying the day's messages to those just reporting for work. Pretty soon Okazawa came by again, picked up the intercom, and said: "There was an explosion or something at Tsukiji Station, so they've stopped the train." Stopping the Hibiya Line train meant that we were going to be rushed off our feet, because if something happens at Tsukiji, they send the train back to Kasumigaseki. Next came a phone call from Central Office: "Suspicious item sighted on board. Please verify." It was Okazawa who took the call, but I said, "I'll go and have a look, you wait here," and headed out to the platform.

But when I got to Train A725K, all the doors were closed. It seemed ready to depart. I noticed there were spots all over the platform, almost like paraffin or something. There are ten cars and each car has four doors. Up toward the front of the train, I could see where this paraffin stuff must have dripped out of the second door of one of the cars. And around the base of a pillar were seven or eight big wads of newspaper. Takahashi was on the platform—he'd been trying to mop up the stuff.

Hishinuma had boarded the cab and was talking with the driver, but there seemed to be no particular operational problems. Just then a train pulled in on the opposite platform and maybe the breeze dispersed the sarin.

It didn't look as if an ordinary dustpan could collect all the wads of newspaper, so I called out to Takahashi, "I'll go get plastic bags," and went back to the office. I told the station attendants: "Paraffin or something's spilled all over the platform, so get a mop. Any free hands come along for backup." Okazawa let someone else take over and followed me. Around this time they announced over the station PA that the Hibiya Line had been shut down.

I got covered in sarin, so my memory's a bit vague on the order of things, but on the way back to the platform someone must have handed me a mop. Now, a mop's something we use every day. If we don't mop up muck and standing water immediately, a passenger could fall and get hurt. If someone spills a drink on the platform, it's the mop straightaway. Sprinkle sawdust over it, wipe it clean. Just comes with the job.

As I said, there were these bundles wrapped in newspaper placed at the base of the pillar. I crouched down, picked them up, and put them in a plastic bag that Okazawa held open for me. I didn't know what was in them, but whatever it was they were sticky with some kind of oily substance. The draft from the train hadn't budged them, so they must have been on the heavy side. After that Hishinuma came along, and all three of us gathered up the newspaper into plastic bags. Initially I'd had it in my head that this was paraffin, but there wasn't any paraffin or petrol smell. Hmm, how would I describe the smell? Very difficult.

I only heard this later, but apparently the smell disgusted Okazawa, so he kept looking away. I also thought it was pretty horrible. I once witnessed a cremation in the country and the smell was a bit like that, or else like a dead rat. A real stink.

I can't remember if I was wearing gloves or not. I always carry gloves (*he pulls out gloves*) just in case, but you can't open plastic bags very well with gloves on. So I can't have been wearing them. Later on Okazawa told me: "Toyoda, your hands were bare. That stuff was dripping from your fingers." I didn't think much about it at the time. But as it turned out, no gloves was better. They would have soaked up the sarin and carried the poison around with you. Bare hands let it drip off.

We managed to bag up all the newspaper, but still there was the paraffin stuff on the platform. At the time I was scared it might explode. The staff at Tsukiji had mentioned explosives, and only a few days before, on March 15, they'd found a booby-trapped attaché case at our station, on the Marunouchi Line, which they say was probably Aum's doing as well. It had *boccilinus* bacteria in it or something. The assistant member of staff who carried the attaché case out of the trash can over to an exit said: "For a second there, I felt sure my number was up."

Fringe Terrorism

In my line of work, I always tell my wife: "Remember, I may not come back tonight." You never know what's going to happen on the job. Maybe they'll plant sarin, or maybe there'll be a fight and somebody'll have a knife. Or then again, there's no telling when some psycho might suddenly come up from behind and push an assistant onto the tracks. Or if there's explosives, I can't very well tell a subordinate, "You take care of it." Maybe it's my character, but I just can't; I have to do it myself.

The bags were clear plastic trash-can liners. We closed them as best we could, but then we were thinking about where to take the stuff, so we probably forgot to tie them. Me and Okazawa carried them back to the office staffroom. Takahashi stayed on the platform, cleaning.

Sugatani was at the office, ready to start his shift. I was trembling all over by then. I tried to check the train timetable, but couldn't read the numbers. He said, "It's okay, I'll put the call into Central for you." Then, for want of a better place, I put the plastic bags at the foot of a chair in the office staffroom.

Meanwhile, Train A725K had already gone. They'd removed the suspicious items, swept out the cars, and just let it carry on. That was Hishinuma's department, so he'd probably been in touch with Central Office and asked for the go-ahead to continue to the next station.

Takahashi always stood on the platform at the front of the train, so naturally when a passenger tells him, "There's something strange inside," he'll try to deal with it as quickly as possible. I didn't actually see it—this is just a guess—but I'll bet Takahashi took it upon himself to remove the stuff. He was the nearest, after all.

There was a trash can on the opposite platform, so that must be where Takahashi got the newspapers to swab the car floor. It was probably just him and Hishinuma. If there'd been mops handy they'd have used them, of course, but they had to use newspaper. They had to think fast. It was the middle of rush hour, after all, with about two and a half minutes, more or less, between trains.

After that I checked the office clock, thinking to jot down a memo. In my work, I make a habit of making memos straightaway. Later I have to enter everything in the record book, so reminders are a must. It was 8:10, I remember, I was trying to write an "8" but my pen was shaking too much. I was trembling all over, but I couldn't just sit idly by. That's when my eyesight went. I couldn't make out the numbers. My field of vision got smaller and smaller.

Just then word came in that Takahashi had collapsed on the platform. An attendant who was helping clean up went to get a stretcher, and together with another staff member they tried to give Takahashi first aid. I was in no shape to go and help. I was shaking too much. It was all I could do to touch-dial the subway phone. I tried to call in to Central Office—"Takahashi's collapsed. Send support."—but I was trembling uncontrollably and my voice wouldn't come.

I felt so bad it seemed doubtful I would make work the next day, so I started to check over my paperwork and things. I thought it best to tidy up while I could. They'd already called an ambulance to take us to the hospital and I didn't know when I'd be back. Tomorrow was out of the question. That's what I was thinking, shaking all over as I tried to pack up. All the time those bundles of sarin-soaked newspapers were right there at my feet.

Takahashi was unconscious when they took him away on the stretcher, and I called out, "Hang in there, Issho!" But he didn't move. All I could see in my narrowed field of vision was a woman passenger. She was in the office. That's when I thought I'd better do something about the plastic bags. If the stuff blew up here, it'd endanger the passengers and staff, too.

Word came in that Takahashi's teeth were chattering, just like an epileptic. I lifted the plastic bags, hoping to get rid of them, but knew I had to do something about Takahashi first. I issued instructions: "Stuff a handkerchief in his mouth. Careful he doesn't bite your hand." I'd heard that's what you're supposed to do during epileptic seizures. By then my nose was running, my eyes were sore. I was in a terrible state, though I was completely unaware of this. I only learned that later.

I told an attendant who had just arrived: "Take these plastic bags over there," to a bunk room in the back where they'd be less dangerous if they exploded. There they'd be sealed off behind a stainless steel door.

The woman, I learned later, was the one who'd spotted the suspicious object on board and had come to inform us. She had begun to feel sick and got off one station before at Nijubashi, then caught the next train to Kasumigaseki.*

Hishinuma returned from the platform. "What the hell was that stuff we brought in here?" he said. "I've never had the shakes so bad. In all my years on the subway, I never saw anything like it." He had come off the platform along with Takahashi on a stretcher. Hishinuma had lost his eyesight too, but now he had to signal the next train, because the station attendant was out of commission.

"Okay for now," I thought, "I've done my job. Cleaned away the unidentified stuff. Hishinuma and Takahashi are both back inside. I've done the immediate tasks at hand." And I'd instructed a member of the support staff to meet the ambulance at Exit A11, the Trade Ministry exit. That's the most convenient place for an ambulance pickup. "We've done our jobs, so it's just a matter of the ambulance getting here"—I was focused on that. So I had them bring Takahashi on the stretcher into the office to wait.

I went to wash my face. Nose running, eyes watering, not a pretty sight. Have to make myself a bit more presentable, I thought. I stripped off my jacket and washed my face at the sink. I always take off my uniform when I wash so as not to get it wet. Sheer habit. Only later did I find out that taking my uniform off was a good thing, because it was soaked with sarin. Same goes for washing my face.

Just then I started to tremble really badly. Not like shivering from

---

* This woman refused to be interviewed.

a chill or something, this was much worse. I wasn't cold, but my body wouldn't stop shaking. I tried to hold my stomach in tight, but it didn't help. I headed over to the lockers to grab a towel, was wiping my face as I walked back, when I just couldn't stand any more. I went faint and collapsed.

I felt like throwing up, couldn't breathe. Me and Hishinuma had dropped at the same time, more or less. We complained of pains almost simultaneously. I can still hear his voice in my ear: "Agh, it hurts!" I can also hear others around us saying, "Hang in there, they've called the ambulance" and "Hold on, it's on its way." After that I don't remember a thing.

I didn't think I was going to die. I'll bet even Takahashi didn't think he was going to die. After all, an ambulance was coming to take us to the hospital. I was more worried about my work, what I needed to do.

I was foaming at the mouth. My hands just wouldn't let go of the towel. That's when one of the staff members did a smart thing. There were respirators in the office, which Konno took out and put on me and Hishinuma. I couldn't even hold the mouthpiece in place. My eyes were wide open. Hishinuma somehow managed to hold his own mouthpiece, so my symptoms were worse at that point.

They'd used the only stretcher to carry Takahashi, so there was nothing left for us. Someone went to the Uchisawaicho office to fetch a stretcher from there, and as my symptoms were more serious, they carried me out first. They laid Hishinuma on some sheets and carried him out like that. Then we all waited at the exit for the ambulance.

I was taken to Jie Medical University Hospital, but it was 11:00 the next morning before I came around. I had two tubes shoved in my mouth for oxygen and to keep my lungs working. I couldn't talk. And I had drips in my neck, feeding something into both arteries. My family was all around.

After that, four of the Kasumigaseki staff came to visit. I still couldn't speak, so I borrowed a pen. I couldn't hold it properly, so I clutched it in my hand and somehow managed to write ISSHO, Takahashi's first name, two simple characters. One of the guys just crossed his hands in an "X." I knew it was bad news. "Takahashi didn't make it," he said. I wanted to ask about Hishinuma, but his name wouldn't come. I had a mental block. So I scrawled TRANS for "transport staff." Another two-handed "X." That's how I knew he'd lost his life too.

After that I wrote KASUMI. Had any other station attendants been hurt? But they said everyone was okay; I was the one in the most serious condition.

"So it's only me who survived," I realized. I still had no idea what on earth had happened, but here I'd been close to death and had survived. The more people worried over me and came to see me, the stronger the realization grew that I'd been saved. I felt happy to have survived and ashamed for what had happened to the others. This put me on edge and that night—the twenty-first, when I regained consciousness—I couldn't get to sleep. Kids get all excited and can't sleep the night before a school trip—well, it was like that. I'd been spared, thanks to everyone. They'd pitched in and come to the rescue quick, which saved my life.

I was hospitalized until March 31, after which I convalesced at home for a while, then returned to work on May 2. I gradually got my strength back, but it was a lot harder to get a grip on my mental state. First, I was hardly sleeping. Barely two or three hours, then—bang!—I'd wake up and not be able to get back to sleep. It went on like that for days. And that was the good part.

After that came the anger. I was irritable, irrational, got upset at everything. It was clearly some sort of hyperexcited condition. I didn't drink, obviously, so I was short of any psychological release. I couldn't concentrate, either. I feel a lot more relaxed now, but this rage sometimes flares up over nothing.

At first my wife was really careful with me, but it seems I was so demanding over every little thing it became aggravating for her. It was time to get back to work. I wanted to put on my uniform again and be back on the platform. Returning to the job was the first step.

I have no physical symptoms, but psychologically there's this burden. I've got to get rid of it somehow. Of course, when I first went back to work I was scared the same thing might happen again. It takes positive thinking to overcome fear, otherwise you'll carry around this victim mentality forever.

There were ordinary passengers who unfortunately lost their lives or suffered injuries just because they were traveling on the subway. People who are still suffering mentally or are in pain. When I consider their lot, I don't have the luxury to keep seeing myself as a victim. That's why I say: "I'm not a sarin victim, I'm a survivor." Frankly, there are some latent symptoms, but nothing to keep me bedridden. I'm just glad I survived.

The fear, the mental wounds are still with me, of course, but there's no way to flush them out of my system. I could never find words to explain it to the families of those who died or who sacrificed their lives on the job.

I try not to hate Aum. I leave them to the authorities. I've already gone beyond hatred. My hating them wouldn't help anyway. I don't follow the news reports on the Aum trial—what would be the point? I know what's what without looking. Going back over the circumstances won't solve anything. I've no interest in the verdict or the punishment. That's for the judge to decide.

MURAKAMI: *What exactly do you mean, you know "what's what without looking"?*

I already knew society had gotten to the point where something like Aum had to happen. Dealing with passengers day after day, you see what you see. It's a question of morals. At the station, you get a very clear picture of people at their most negative, their downsides. For instance, if we're sweeping up the station with a dustpan and brush, just when we've finished, someone will flick a cigarette butt or a piece of litter right on the spot where we've cleaned. There are too many self-assertive people out there.

There's an upside to passengers too. A guy around 50, always travels on the first train of the day, always used to greet me, he probably thought I'd died until I returned to the job. Yesterday morning when we met, he said: "Alive and well means you've still got things to do. Don't give up the fight!" It's such an encouragement just to get a cheerful greeting. Nothing comes of hatred.

The Handed-Down Self: the Allocated Narrative

To quote from the Unabomber manifesto, published in *The New York Times* in 1995:

> The system reorganizes itself so as to put pressure on those who do not fit in. Those who do not fit into the system are "sick"; to make them fit in is to "cure." Thus, the power process aimed at attaining autonomy is broken and the individual is subsumed into the other-dependent power process enforced by the system. To pursue autonomy is seen as "disease."*

Interestingly enough, while the Unabomber's modus operandi almost exactly parallels Aum's (when, for instance, they sent a parcel bomb to

---

*The document that became known as the Unabomber's manifesto was sent to *The New York Times* and *The Washington Post* in April 1995 by a person called "FC," identified by the FBI as the Unabomber and implicated in three murders and sixteen bombings. The author threatened to send a bomb to an unspecified destination "with intent to kill" unless one of the newspapers published this manuscript, entitled "Industrial Society and Its Future." The attorney general and the director of the FBI recommended publication and it appeared in a special supplement in both papers in September 1995. This led David Kaczynski to draw a comparison between the Unabomber and his estranged brother Theodore, who was arrested in April 1996. He was sentenced to life imprisonment in 1998. [Tr.]

Tokyo City Hall), Theodore Kaczynski's thinking is even more closely linked to the essence of the Aum cult.

The argument Kaczynski puts forward is fundamentally quite right. Many parts of the social system in which we belong and function do indeed aim at repressing the attainment of individual autonomy, or, as the Japanese adage goes: "The nail that sticks up gets hammered down."

From the perspective of the Aum followers, just as they were asserting their own autonomy, society and the state came down on top of them, pronouncing them an "antisocial movement," a "cancer" to be cut out. Which is why they became more and more antisocial.

Nonetheless, Kaczynski—intentionally or unintentionally—overlooked one important factor. Autonomy is only the mirror image of dependence on others. If you were left as a baby on a deserted island, you would have no notion of what "autonomy" means. Autonomy and dependency are like light and shade, caught in the pull of each other's gravity, until, after considerable trial and error, each individual can find his or her own place in the world.

Those who fail to achieve this balance, like Shoko Asahara perhaps, have to compensate by establishing a limited (but actually quite effective) system. I have no way of ranking him as a religious figure. How does one measure such things? Still, a cursory look at his life does suggest one possible scenario. Efforts to overcome his own individual disabilities left him trapped inside a closed circuit. A genie in a bottle labeled "religion," which he proceeded to market as a form of shared experience.

Asahara surely put himself through hell, a horrific bloodbath of internal conflicts and soul-searching until he finally arrived at a systematization of his vision. Undoubtedly he also had his satori, some "attainment of paranormal value." Without any firsthand experience of hell or extraordinary inversion of everyday values, Asahara would not have had such a strong, charismatic power. From a certain perspective, primitive religion always carries its own associated special aura that emanates from some psychic aberration.

In order to take on the "self-determination" that Asahara provided, most of those who took refuge in the Aum cult appear to have deposited all their precious personal holdings of selfhood—lock and key—in that "spiritual bank" called Shoko Asahara. The faithful relinquished their freedom, renounced their possessions, disowned their families, discarded all secular judgment (common sense). "Normal" Japanese were aghast: How could anyone do such an insane thing? But conversely, to the cultists it was probably quite comforting. At last they had someone to watch over them, sparing them the anxiety of confronting each new situation on their own, and delivering them from any need to think for themselves.

By tuning in, by merging themselves with Shoko Asahara's "greater, more profoundly unbalanced" Self, they attained a kind of pseudo-self-determination. Instead of launching an assault on society as individuals, they handed over the entire strategic responsibility to Asahara. We'll have one "Self-power versus the system" set menu, please.

Theirs was not Kaczynski's "battle against the system to attain the power process of self-determination." The only one fighting was Shoko Asahara: most followers were merely swallowed up and assimilated by his battle-hungry ego. Nor were the followers unilaterally subjected to Asahara's "mind control." Not passive victims, they themselves actively sought to be controlled by Asahara. "Mind control" is not something that can be pursued or bestowed just like that. It's a two-sided affair.

If you lose your ego, you lose the thread of that narrative you call your Self. Humans, however, can't live very long without some sense of a continuing story. Such stories go beyond the limited rational system (or the systematic rationality) with which you surround yourself; they are crucial keys to sharing time-experience with others.

Now a narrative is a story, not logic, nor ethics, nor philosophy. It is a dream you keep having, whether you realize it or not. Just as surely as you breathe, you go on ceaselessly dreaming your story. And in these stories you wear two faces. You are simultaneously subject and object. You are the whole and you are a part. You are real and you are shadow. "Storyteller" and at the same time "character." It is through such multilayering of roles in our stories that we heal the loneliness of being an isolated individual in the world.

Yet without a proper ego, nobody can create a personal narrative, any more than you can drive a car without an engine, or cast a shadow without a real physical object. But once you've consigned your ego to someone else, where on earth do you go from there?

At this point you receive a new narrative from the person to whom you have entrusted your ego. You've handed over the real thing, so what comes back instead is a shadow. And once your ego has merged with another ego, your narrative will necessarily take on the narrative created by that other ego.

Just what kind of narrative?

It needn't be anything particularly fancy, nothing complicated or refined. You don't need to have literary ambitions. In fact, rather, the sketchier and simpler the better. Junk, a leftover rehash will do. Anyway, most people are tired of complex, multilayered scenarios—they are a potential letdown. It's precisely because people can't find any fixed point within their own multilayered schemes that they're tossing aside their self-identity.

A simple "emblem" of a story will do for this sort of narrative, the same way that a war medal bestowed on a soldier doesn't have to be pure gold. It's enough that the medal be backed up by a shared recognition that "this is a medal," no matter that it's a cheap tin trinket.

Shoko Asahara was talented enough to impose his rehashed narrative on people (who for the most part came looking for just that). It was a risible, slapdash story. To unbelievers it could only be regurgitated tripe. Still, in all fairness, it must be said that a certain consistency runs through it all. It was a call to arms.

From this perspective, in a limited sense, Asahara was a master storyteller who proved capable of anticipating the mood of the times. He was not deterred by the knowledge, whether conscious or not, that his ideas and images were recycled junk. Asahara deliberately cobbled together bits and pieces from all around him (the way that Spielberg's ET assembles a device for communicating with his home planet out of odds and ends in the family garage) and brought to them a singular flow, a current that darkly reflected the inner ghosts of his own mind. Whatever the deficiencies in that narrative, they were in Asahara himself, so they presented no obstacle to those who chose to merge themselves with him. If anything, these deficiencies were a positive bonus, until they became fatally polluted. Irredeemably delusional and paranoiac, a new pretext developed, grand and irrational, until there was no turning back . . .

Such was the narrative offered by Aum, by "their" side. Stupid, you might say. And surely it is. Most of us laughed at the absurd off-the-wall scenario that Asahara provided. We laughed at him for concocting such "utter nonsense" and we ridiculed the believers who could be attracted to such "lunatic fodder." The laugh left a bitter aftertaste in our mouths, but we laughed out loud all the same. Which was only to be expected.

But were we able to offer "them" a more viable narrative? Did we have a narrative potent enough to chase away Asahara's "utter nonsense"?

That was the big task. I am a novelist, and as we all know a novelist is someone who works with "narratives," who spins "stories" professionally. Which meant to me that the task at hand was like a gigantic sword dangling above my head. It's something I'm going to have to deal with much more seriously from here on. I know I'm going to have to construct a "cosmic communication device" of my own. I'll probably have to piece together every last scrap of junk, every weakness, every deficiency inside me to do it. (There, I've gone and said it—but the real surprise is that it's exactly what I've been trying to do as a writer all along!)

So then, what about you? (I'm using the second person, but of course that includes me.)

Haven't you offered up some part of your Self to someone (or something), and taken on a "narrative" in return? Haven't we entrusted some part of our personality to some greater System or Order? And if so, has not that System at some stage demanded of us some kind of "insanity"? Is the narrative you now possess *really and truly* your own? Are your dreams *really* your own dreams? Might not they be someone else's visions that could sooner or later turn into nightmares?

CONFRONTING TERRORISM

Confronting Terrorism

The current thinking on how to confront terrorism falls into two camps. The government approach is limited, pragmatic, and multifaceted. It comprises a series of aggressive military, political, and economic actions, including armed assaults, interdiction of funding to terrorist groups, legal prosecution, pressure on state sponsors, and prevention of future threats through heightened security measures. The second approach sees the battle against terrorism principally as a war over the minds of terrorisms' current and future constituency, because whether or not to engage in terrorism is ultimately a conscious choice made by individuals.

Confronting terrorism requires, first of all, asking the right questions. This process can only be successful if those posing the questions are honest about their own contributions to the current social dynamic (see *Cruelty and Silence: War, Tyranny, Uprising and the Arab World*, page 537). What kinds of people join terrorist groups, and why do they join them? (See *Understanding Terrorist Behavior*, page 516.) What message are terrorists communicating, explicitly and implicitly? What conditions have made some receptive to that message? In what circumstances does terrorism decline?

Historically, terrorism has had little impact when it has attempted to
an agenda on representative democracies such as Germany, the U.
States (see *Fugitive Days,* page 227), and Spain (see *ETA: Profile*
Terrorist Group, page 154). But the growing deadliness of arms availal
today and the fervor of the extremist fundamentalist groups makes it cei
tain that terrorists will continue to seek to change the policies of the
United States and other industrialized nations by violent means. This state
of affairs makes it imperative that terrorism and the social realities that
create and support it be examined with unswerving determination.

Terrorist Behavior

force
ited
a
le

. to relate terrorism to psychological motives,
profile as an investigative tool. As Walter Reich, a
psychiatrist at the National Institute of Health, points out,
_n is problematic. It's susceptible to overgeneralization and
ism, it fails to grasp the significance of the group dynamic,
s the historical context for these acts, overcomplicates simple moti-
ions, and ignores state terrorism. In this article, Reich poses a number
of avenues of research that avoid these pitfalls and lead to the posing of
important questions about terrorism and the world that creates it.

Several aspects of terrorism seem susceptible to psychological inquiry—the effects of terrorism on its victims, for example, and the behaviors of both terrorists and authorities during hostage negotiations. But the aspect of terrorism that seems most susceptible of all to such inquiry—that, for better or worse, almost begs for it—is the psychology of the terrorists themselves: their developments, motivations, personalities, decision-making patterns, behaviors in groups, and, some would argue, psychopathologies. Certainly, the public has turned to psychiatrists and psychologists regularly, particularly after witnessing especially violent terrorist acts, to explain this aspect of terrorist behavior; and psychiatrists and psychologists, just as regularly, have rushed to give explanations, sometimes without even being asked.

But susceptible as terrorists' motivations and personalities may be, in principle, to psychological inquiry, such inquiry, in practice, is regularly beset by problems that, in devious but powerful ways, limit, undermine, or even vitiate it—problems that, in the main, stem from too exclusive a focus on psychology itself or too narrow a definition of it. This chapter focuses on some of those problems and, when possible, suggests ways in which they can be avoided or overcome.

Overgeneralization

Persons and groups have carried out terrorist acts for at least two thousand years. During that considerable span of human experience, such acts have been carried out by an enormously varied range of persons with an enormously varied range of beliefs in order to achieve an enormously varied range of ends—including, in the case of at least one terrorist group, as I note later, no end at all. Even if we are careful to include in our historical catalogue of terrorist acts only those that satisfy one contemporary, restrictive definition of the term—let's choose, for our purposes here, the State Department's definition, which, in recent years, has been "premeditated, politically-motivated violence perpetrated against noncombatant targets by subnational groups or clandestine state agents, normally intended to influence an audience"— the list we can produce is breathtaking in its variety and scope. Given this variety and scope, it would be foolish to believe that many psychological principles can be adduced that apply to and explain all of the entries on the list.

To be sure, terrorism is not nearly so broad and universal a phenomenon as, say, violence or war—phenomena that occur under such astonishingly varied circumstances and for such astonishingly varied reasons that few would even dream of offering a single, overarching psychological theory to explain them all. Still, terrorism is so varied and complex a phenomenon that it should give pause to anyone whose aim it is to understand it—or, to be more precise, whose aim it is to understand the many different terrorisms that the deceptively singular term covers.

Yet psychological accounts of terrorism are replete with explanations that ignore or blur the variety and the complexity.[1] Blanket statements, some of which will be cited later, tend to be made that attribute certain characteristics to "terrorists" with the implication that all terrorists, of whatever variety, possess them. In part, it is a problem of semantics: It is always hard for writers to remind readers that only one particular group of terrorists is being discussed and not all of them through recorded history. But that is probably too generous an explanation for this penchant for psychological overgeneralization about terrorism. Too often overgeneralization is a product of loose and weak thinking, a disregard for the need for evidence, and the habit, unfortunately endemic in so many areas of psychological discourse, of having a single idea and applying it to everything.

Even the briefest review of the history of terrorism reveals how varied and complex a phenomenon it is, and therefore how futile it is to attribute simple, global, and general psychological characteristics to all terrorists and all terrorisms.

Some of the earliest terrorist campaigns were carried out in an arena that has seen so many of them in recent years, the zone now known as the Middle East. Perhaps the most striking of these campaigns was the one carried out by two Jewish groups during the first century A.D., the Zealots and the Sicarii. Their primary goal was to inspire popular insurrection among Judea's Jews against its Roman occupiers, an insurrection that would result not in a compromise with the occupiers but in total rebellion. A second purpose, perhaps no less assiduously pursued, was to cleanse Jewish religious institutions and society of persons too closely aligned with Roman and Hellenistic ways. The method used by the Sicarii, or daggermen, was assassination. As Josephus describes it:

• • •

---

[1] See H. H. A. Cooper, "What Is a Terrorist: A Psychological Perspective," *Legal Medical Quarterly* 1 (1997): 16–32; H. H. A. Cooper, "Psychopath as Terrorist: A Psychological Perspective," *Legal Medical Quarterly* 2 (1978): 188–97.

The Sicarii committed murders in broad daylight in the heart of Jerusalem. The holy days were their special seasons when they would mingle with the crowd carrying short daggers concealed under their clothing with which they stabbed their enemies. Thus, when they fell, the murderers joined in cries of indignation, and through this plausible behavior, were never discovered. The first assassinated was Jonathan, the high-priest. After his death there were numerous daily murders. The panic created was more alarming than the calamity itself; nearly everyone, as on the battlefield, hourly expected death. Men kept watch at a distance on their enemies and would not trust even their friends when they approached.[2]

The goals of the Zealots and of the Sicarii were clearly political—they wanted an end to Roman subjugation—and depended on the belief that extraordinary actions were necessary in order to rouse a passive or corrupted populace. But their goals were also religious, and depended on the belief that such actions not only were justified on religious grounds but would even bring on divine intervention.

Another early terrorist movement in the Middle East, that of the Assassins, also had political goals, but these were ultimately designed to serve primarily religious ends. Active from the eleventh through the thirteenth century A.D., the Assassins, whose origins were in Shia Islam,

---

[2] Josephus, *The Jewish War*, in *Works* (London: Heinemann [Loeb Classical Library], 1926), quoted in David C. Rapoport, "Fear and Trembling: Terrorism in Three Religious Traditions," *American Political Science Review* 78, no. 2 (1984): 658–77. On the Zealots and Sicarii, see also S. J. D. Cohn, *Josephus in Galill and Rome* (Leiden: Brill, 1979); David C. Rapoport, "Introduction: Religious Terror," in *The Morality of Terrorism: Religious and Secular Justification*, edited by David C. Rapoport and Yonah Alexander (New York: Pergamon, 1982); and M. Smith, "Zealots and Sicarii: Their Origins and Relations," *Harvard Theological Review* 64 (1971): 1–19.

believed that Islam had been corrupted; and, also using daggers, they assassinated Muslim leaders who, they believed, represented and propagated that corruption. They sought not only the death of their enemies but also the publicity that the assassinations excited—publicity that, they hoped, would result in attention to their cause, recognition that it was just, and the bringing about of a new, cleansed, and revitalized theological and social order.[3]

The era of modern terrorism is usually said to have begun in the nineteenth century with the rise, in Russia, of the *Narodnaya Volya* (People's Will). In 1879, that party's program spoke of "destructive and terroristic activity," and its methods, which involved assassination of Tsarist officials in the hope of provoking Russian society into revolution, were opposed by later Russian revolutionaries, particularly the Bolsheviks, who believed that revolution could be attained successfully not by "individual terror" carried out by a small elite of intellectuals but by class struggle carried out by the masses. Such individual terror came to be called "propaganda by the deed"[4]—that is, the method, using extreme acts, by which the masses would be stirred not only to understand the depth of their subjugation but also the vulnerability of the authorities. As Peter Kropotkin puts it:

> By actions which compel general attention, the new idea seeps into people's minds and wins converts. One such act may, in a few days, make more propaganda than thousands of pamphlets. Above all, it awakens the spirit of revolt; it breeds daring. . . . Soon it becomes apparent that

---

[3] See Rapoport, "Fear and Trembling," 658–77. See also Bernard Lewis, *The Assassins: A Radical Sect in Islam* (London: Weidenfeld and Nocholson, 1967).

[4] This term was probably first used in the declaration of the Italian Federation of the Anarchist International of 3 December 1876. See Ze'ev Iviansky, "Individual Terror: Concept and Typology," *Journal of Contemporary History* 12 (1977): 43–63.

the established order does not have the strength often supposed. One courageous act has sufficed to upset in a few days the entire governmental machinery, to make the colossus tremble. . . . The people observe that the monster is not so terrible as they thought . . . hope is born in their hearts.[5]

But repression, such a terrorist hopes, is born in the hearts of the authorities. They react fiercely, Kropotkin predicts; the masses suffer terribly, become enraged, and respond with revolution.

For many anarchists, terror itself was an end; indeed, one anarchist group in Russia during the revolution of 1905–7 advocated *bezmotivniy terror* (unmotivated terror).[6] For anarchists, the invention of dynamite introduced an era of exciting destructive possibilities in which individuals could be, in their actions, as powerful as governments. Some anarchists advocated violence aimed not just at authorities but also at the general public, particularly those parts of it, such as the bourgeoisie, who could be identified as supporting the existing order merely because they profited from it. "There are no innocents," Emile Henry, the young French anarchist, said at his trial for throwing a bomb into the Café Terminus.

For the early Russian revolutionaries who advocated terror, however, it was to be carried out with discrimination and with clear purposes in mind. Authorities were the targets, not ordinary citizens. But even then the method had to be justified. And the justification was that the authorities' monopoly on power gave the revolutionaries no other choice, and that, in overturning mass tyranny, which was responsible for mass deaths,

[5] Peter Kropotkin, "The Spirit of Revolt," in *Revolutionary Pamphlets* (New York, 1968), 35–43, quoted in Iviansky, "Individual Terror," 43–63.

[6] See Walter Reich, "Serbsky and Czarist Dissidents," *Archives of General Psychiatry* 40 (1983): 697–8.

assassinations were actually life-saving and moral. Such terrorists, usually intellectuals, spent a great deal of time worrying about, and seeking justifications for, the moral dilemmas provoked by the method they had adopted.

During the early part of this century, as revolutionary, ideological terrorism grew strong, so did terrorism aimed at nationalist ends. Such terrorism developed great prominence in Ireland, but it was also evident in the Balkans, Armenia, and elsewhere. Between the wars, especially in the 1920s, right-wing terrorism, particularly by the Nazis and the Italian Fascists, was used to intimidate enemies and create publicity; a number of right-wing groups in Eastern Europe devolved into little more than criminal gangs.

After World War II, guerrilla warfare related to decolonization predominated, although terrorism occurred in a number of areas; for example, it was used by the Irgun and the Stern Gang in mandate Palestine. But in the 1960s and 1970s terrorism of several varieties once again became a frequent occurrence in a number of geographic zones. In Western Europe and Latin America it was, and remains, heavily left wing; one 1986 communiqué by a Belgian left-wing terrorist group, the Fighting Communist Cells, restated, for the thousandth time, and in the same apocalyptic, incendiary language used in previous ideological iterations, such terrorism's goal: the resumption of combat so that "the spark sets the plain ablaze, so that the class struggle burns down history."[7] Elsewhere, nationalist-separatist terrorism was prominent among the Palestinians, Basques, Armenians, Croatians, Sikhs, Tamils, and others. And the IRA continued its campaign against the British, now the oldest terrorist campaign in the world. Recently, in the 1980s, terrorism in the name of another cause, religion, reemerged with particular force and ardor in the

---

[7] James M. Markham, "Terrorists Put Benign Belguim Under Mental Seige," *New York Times*, 6 February 1986, p. A-2.

Middle East, primarily in Lebanon and Iran, with its special characteristics and justifications, thus bringing the history of terrorism full circle to its beginnings in that convulsed corner of the world.

Certainly, a number of themes and characteristics are shared by many of the terrorist groups and movements mentioned in this short history; the goals of achieving terror and publicity for the cause are shared by nearly all of them. But one searches with difficulty, and probably in vain, for psychological qualities that are shared by all or nearly all of the terrorists and terrorist groups mentioned here. The constellation of psychological qualities that may characterize West European terrorists, such as the Red Army Faction of West Germany, Direct Action of France, and the Red Brigades of Italy, is probably quite different from the ones that characterize or characterized, say, the followers of Abu Nidal or the members of the Palestinian Front for the Liberation of Palestine, the Armenian ASALA, the Basque ETA, the Shi'ite groups, the Croats, or even the leftist terrorists in Latin America, such as the Tupamaros of Uruguay, the Shining Path of Peru, the Montoneros of Argentina, or the M-19 of Colombia. Indeed, even within the United States, the qualities that may have characterized the Weatherman group were no doubt different from the ones that characterized the black members of the Symbionese Liberation Army. And regarding fundamental attitudes toward one of the central facets of terrorism—violence—different terrorist groups, even those that have shared the "left wing" designation, have, across the decades, varied enormously. Thus, the *Narodnaya Volya* tortured themselves about the snuffing out of any life, even that of a hated government official, whereas modern-day leftist terrorists, as well as most others both now and in the past, have managed to justify easily almost any killings, even of the most indubitably innocent souls.

Moreover, the terrorist groups themselves shift in character. Some terrorist groups that were once on the right have ended up on the left, and vice versa; and most are, in fact, mixtures of types, such as leftist nationalists, rightist nationalists, religious nationalists, and so on. In terrorism, there are many mixed and borderline conditions.[8]

The lesson that the psychological researcher must draw from the long history of the terrorist enterprise, and especially from its variety and complexity, applies not only to the study of individual terrorists but also to the study of the terrorist groups themselves. Like individual terrorists, the groups to which they belong, and ultimately the communities from which those groups arise, are not necessarily alike in their psychological characteristics, even if they share certain goals or orientations.

Religiously oriented or nationalist terrorists, for example, are driven by forces and shaped by circumstances that are usually specific to particular religious or nationalist experiences—experiences that lend powerfully determining characteristics to those particular groups. Why else have some nationalities with deep feelings of having been wronged by history or by other nationalities, such as the Palestinians, Basques, Armenians, and Croatians, given rise to groups that carry out terrorism in order to right those wrongs, whereas other nationalities that have been wronged, such as the Germans who were displaced from Eastern Europe after World War II and many other nationalities that lost parts of their homeland or were never permitted a homeland, have not? And why have some terrorist movements persisted in their efforts for decades whereas others have not?

Clearly, differences in the political circumstances surrounding those groups, as well as in the responses given to their grievances and actions, have played important roles in determining the nature, momentum, and success of their terrorist efforts. But no less important have been the particular characteristics of terrorist groups themselves. However similar such groups may be, they are usually, in significant ways, also very different;

---

[8] For an extended and rich discussion of the many varieties of terrorism and of the way in which various terrorist movements have undergone radical changes over time, see Walter Laqueur, *The Age of Terrorism* (Boston: Little, Brown, 1987).

and, as in the cases of individual terrorists, the differences are probably at least as telling as the similarities.

Reductionism

Closely related to the problem of overgeneralization is the problem of reductionism: Just as it is easy, and usually unjustified, to attribute specific characteristics to a wide range of terrorists and terrorist groups, so it is easy, and usually unjustified, to attribute all or much of terrorist behavior to one or another specific cause. Yet this has often been done, and occasionally it still is.

In the 1870s, as terrorism was gaining strength not only in Russia but also in Italy, Cesare Lombroso, who believed that criminality in general was a congenital condition, attributed terrorist behavior, and in particular bomb throwing, to pellagra and other vitamin deficiencies. At the same time, other authorities examined the connection between terrorism and barometric pressure, moon phases, alcoholism, droughts, and cranial measurements.[9]

A century later, some authors have returned to biological causes to explain terrorist violence. David G. Hubbard, a psychiatrist, has suggested that there may be a connection between inner-ear vestibular function and terrorism.[10] He has also suggested that terrorism may be partly a result of the levels of certain chemicals in the brains of terrorists, specifically norepinephrine, acetylcholine, and endorphins.[11] Paul Mandel, a biochemist at the Center for Neurochemistry in Strasbourg, having studied the

---

[9]Cesare Lombroso and R. Laschi, *Le Crime Politique et les Révolutions* (Paris, 1982), passim. The ideas of Lombroso regarding the physical causes of terrorism, as well as those of others, are discussed in Laqueur, *Age of Terrorism*, 151.

[10] David G. Hubbard, "Terrorism and Protest," *Legal Medical Quarterly* 2 (1978): 188–97.

[11] David G. Hubbard, "The Psychodynamics of Terrorism," in *International Violence*, edited by Y. Alexander and T. Adeniran (New York: Praeger, 1983), 45–53. For research on the relationship between dopamine, norepinephrine, acetylcholine, and aggression in animals, see Louis J. West, "Studies of Aggression in Animals and Man," *Psychopharmacology Bulletin* 13 (1977): 14–25.

inhibitory effects of gamma-aminobutyric acid (GABA) and serotonin on violence in rats, extrapolated his findings to terrorism. He suggested recently, in a newspaper interview, that emotional self-stimulation can lower brain serotonin levels so as to promote the violence associated with religious fanaticism, and that the Ayatollah Khomeini "suppressed his GABA and serotonin levels through religious excitation. . . . and now there's no inhibition." According to the newspaper, Mandel believes that the ayatollah would have benefited from drug treatment.[12]

Presumably, not only would the ayatollah have benefited if he had taken drugs, but so would Iraq, Kuwait, the whole Persian Gulf, the thousands of Iranian Revolutionary Guards reportedly blown up while holding their plastic keys to Paradise, and, not least, the Western hostages who fell into the hands of the Iranian-inspired Hizballah in Lebanon.

Less reductionistic but still problematic efforts have been made to attribute much of terrorism to mental illness—efforts reviewed by Corrado.[13] Two authors, for example, have expressed the view that terrorists are psychopaths.[14] Certainly, terrorist groups reside at the fringes of the societies they inhabit, and it stands to reason that those groups might

---

[12] Quoted in Jon Franklin, "Criminality Is Linked to Brain Chemistry Imbalances," *Baltimore Evening Sun*, 30 July 1984. For both animal and human studies on the relationship between GABA, serotonin, and aggression in both animals and human beings, see Gerald L. Brown and Frederick K. Goodwin, "Human Aggression—A Biological Perspective," in *Unmasking the Psychopath*, edited by W. H. Reid et al. (New York: W. W. Norton, 1986); Gerald L. Brown, Frederick K. Goodwin, and William E. Bunney, Jr., "Human Aggression and Suicide: The Relationship to Neuropsychiatric Diagnosis and Serotonin Metabolism," in *Serotonin in Biological Psychiatry*, edited by B. T. Ho et al. (New York: Raven Press, 1982), 287–307.

[13] R. R. Corrado, "A Critique of the Mental Disorder Perspective of Political Terrorism," *International Journal of Law and Psychiatry* 4 (1981): 293–310. Heskin has come to this conclusion also regarding IRA terrorists; see K. Heskin, *Northern Ireland: A Psychological Analysis* (New York: Columbia University Press, 1980).

[14] See Cooper, "What Is a Terrorist," 16–32, and K. I. Pearce, "Police Negotiations," *Canadian Psychiatric Association Journal* 22 (1977): 171–4.

preferentially attract persons with various mental illnesses so that the proportion of their membership that is made up of the mentally ill might be higher than that proportion in the general population. It seems clear, however, that the proportion is not strikingly high, and that terrorists do not, in general, suffer from mental illnesses either of a psychotic or other type.[15] To be sure, Ferracuti and Bruno, in studying the prevalence of mental illness among Italian terrorists during the 1970s, found more among members of right-wing groups than among members of left-wing groups;[16] but even among those terrorists, psychopathology does not appear to be the primary source of terrorist motivation or activity.

Nor does that constellation of characteristics long sought but still not found, the "terrorist personality," appear to account for terrorist behavior; indeed, it almost certainly does not exist. The most exhaustive interview studies of terrorists ever carried out, sponsored by the West German Ministry of the Interior and involving 227 left-wing West German terrorists and 23 right-wing extremists, revealed a number of patterns in the personal histories of the subjects that seemed significantly more common among them than among other West Germans of their age—patterns such as the loss, at an early age, of one or both parents, severe conflicts with authorities, and frequent episodes of school and work failures.[17] But other patterns—in particular, two personality constellations, one consisting of extreme dependence on the terrorist group, extroversion, a parasitic

[15] W. Rasch, "Psychological Dimensions of Political Terrorism in the Federal Republic of Germany," *International Journal of Law and Psychiatry* 2 (1979): 79–85.

[16] F. Ferracuti and F. Bruno, "Italy: A Systems Perspective," in *Aggression in Global Perspective*, edited by A. P. Goldstein and M. H. Segall (Elmsford, N.Y.: Pergamon, 1983).

[17] G. Schmidtchen, "Terroristische Karrieren: Soziologische Analyse anhand von Fahndungsunterlagen und Prozessakten" ["Terrorist Careers: Sociological Analysis Based on Investigation and Trial Documents"], in *Analysen zum Terrorismus [Analysis of Terrorism]*, edited by H. Jäger, G. Schmidtchen, and L. Süllwold (Opladen: Westdeutscher Verlag, 1981), vol. 2, *Lebenslauf-Analysen [Biographical Analysis]*.

lifestyle, and stimulus seeking and the other consisting of hostility, suspiciousness, aggressiveness, and self-defensiveness—also are described in the study[18] and are difficult to compare with the patterns for other persons of the same age who live at society's edge.

In any case, these patterns of individual history or personality, even if they could be demonstrated to be characteristic of these particular kinds of terrorists—a demonstration that has not been accomplished—are unlikely to be characteristic of other terrorists from other groups. The paths to a life of terrorism appear to be quite different in different societies and different types of groups. If any "terrorist personality" reliably could be found among West German leftists, it probably would be very different from the typical personalities (if such typical personalities were in fact to exist) of Middle Eastern terrorists of the nationalist or religious sort, and even different from leftist terrorists in Latin America.

Other attempts at attributing terrorist behaviors, in some blanket way, to particular psychological mechanisms, processes, or characteristics also seem to be without foundation. It is unlikely, for example, as Corrado has noted, that "narcissism" explains the terrorism of even a small number of ideologically radical groups,[19] or that the death wish does, either.[20]

Even attempts to explain, on the basis of one or another motivation, certain very stylized, specific terrorist acts by specific populations in specific

---

[18] Süllwold, "Stationen in der Entwicklung von Terroristen: Psychologische Aspekte Biographischer Daten" [Stages in the Development of Terrorists: Psychological Aspects of Biographical Data], in *Analysen zum Terrorismus*, edited by Jäger, Schmidtchen, and Süllwold, vol. 2.

[19] See Christopher Lasch, *The Culture of Narcissism* (New York: W. W. Norton, 1979), 154, and Gustave Morf, *Terror in Quebec: Case Studies of the F.L.Q.* (Toronto: Clarke, Irwin, 1970), 107, quoted in R. R. Corrado, "A Critique," 293–310

[20] See Cooper, "What Is a Terrorist," 16–32, and "Psychopath as Terrorist," 253–62.

places—in particular, suicide car bombings by Shi'ites against Israelis in southern Lebanon—ultimately have been shown to be wrong, or only partly true. To be sure, some of those bombers probably were quite ready to blow themselves up in a holy act of explosive, Paradise-seeking martyrdom. But in the case of at least one such about-to-be suicide car bomber, a sixteen-year-old Shi'ite from Beirut's southern suburbs who was apprehended by the Israelis just before he was about to drive the lethal car that had been prepared for him, the motivation was not religious. Rather, he was coerced by officials of the Shi'ite militia, who used threats against his family. The last thing the secular boy wanted to do, it turns out, was to kill himself—either for Allah or for anyone or anything else.[21]

Inadequate appreciation of the palpable and psychic rewards of belonging to terrorist groups

Just as there is a psychology of needs, so there is a psychology of rewards. Certainly, a life of terrorism can satisfy needs such as support and approval from other members of the terrorist group, opportunities for violence, lashing out against the world of one's parents, and many others of which most of us would not be proud.

But there are other things that a life of terrorism can provide that, although they may also be things of which most of us would not be proud, may play a significant role in the decision of some terrorists to join terrorist groups—things such as power, prestige, privilege, and even wealth. These things, described pungently in an essay by Conor Cruise O'Brien,[22] are attractive to young people from impoverished backgrounds—backgrounds of the sort that are common in many zones of terrorist conflict, such as the

---

[21]Thomas J. Friedman, "Boy Says Lebanese Recruited Him as Car Bomber," *New York Times*, 14 April 1985, p. 1. For a general discussion of the motivations of suicide bombers, see Chapter 10 in this volume.

[22] Conor Cruise O'Brien, "Thinking About Terrorism," *Atlantic Monthly* (June 1986), 62–6.

Middle East and Northern Ireland—and together serve as a powerful impetus for many of these people to join terrorist groups. They are especially accessible to terrorists in cultures that have a long and persistent revolutionary tradition—cultures in which terrorist traditions have popular roots.

And the rewards of joining can be enormously satisfying. In some groups, terrorism can provide a route for advancement, an opportunity for glamour and excitement, a chance at world renown, a way of demonstrating one's courage, and even a way of accumulating wealth.[23] No small advantages, these, and almost totally unstudied by researchers seeking to understand why terrorists become terrorists, and why they continue to do what they do.

Psychologizing motivations that are understandable enough when discussed in everyday language

"Hatred," "revulsion," "revenge"—these terms characterize precisely the feelings and motivations of many terrorists. Somehow, they seem too human for psychiatrists and psychologists to use in scientific discourse. But used they should be. Using them brings us closer to the psychological states of many

---

[23] The annual budgets of a number of terrorist organizations now exceed the budgets of some small states. According to Laqueur (*The Age of Terrorism*, 102), in 1975 the annual budget of Fatah was $150 million to $200 million (in 1980 dollars), with other Palestinian factions gathering their own millions; the IRA's budget was, in the same year, $1 million to $3 million; and the budgets of each of several South American groups, raised from the sales of illicit drugs, were $50 million to $150 million in 1985. With such sums changing hands in clandestine ways, significant amounts are bound to reach the pockets of people at least as interested in comforts as in selfless causes. Even George Ibrahim Abdullah, the Christian Lebanese terrorist for whose release from a French prison his friends and relatives engineered a wave of Paris bombings in September 1986, devolved, according to his neighbors in the Lebanese village of Qobayat, from a nationalist idealist into a fighter not for a cause but for wealth. Referring to Abdullah's group, one neighbor told a reporter, "They were once idealists and now they do it all for money." See Nora Boustany, "The Christian Village That Spawned the Paris Bombers," *Washington Post*, 26 October 1986. On the tendency that develops among some terrorists to accumulate precisely the material goods whose accumulation they despise in others, see Michael Baumann, *Terror or Love: Bommi Baumann's Own Story of His Life as a West German Urban Guerrilla* (New York: Grove Press, 1979), p. 104.

terrorists, and to what they want, than using the milder terms with which we may feel more comfortable, such as "anger" or "frustration"—terms that convey a lesser sense of some terrorists' moods and convictions.[24]

These nonprofessional but accurate descriptive terms should be used in psychiatric discourse because they are true, and because they can help explain, in some cases, the continuation of terrorism even after significant demands have been satisfied. Terrorists' frustration may be lessened by such achievements, but the hatred, the revulsion, and especially the desire for revenge may not. Therefore, these motivations may continue to spur the terrorist enterprise even after many demands have been satisfied.

Even psychiatrists and psychologists accustomed to professional language should, in this very human arena, use the most powerfully human

---

[24] For examples of what appear to be hatred, revulsion, and revenge as the primary goals of various terrorist groups and acts, see Thomas L. Friedman, "Armed and Dangerous: A Mideast Consumed by the Politics of Revenge," *New York Times*, 5 January 1986, sec. 4, p. 1, about Abu Nidal and some other Palestinian groups.

In the case of Abu Nidal and his organization, Jerrold Post's theses that "the cause is not the cause" seems apt. . . . According to this theses, the official, political goals of the organization, as publicized as they may be, are less important than the goal of maintaining the existence of the terrorist organization itself. Post's thesis is strengthened, I think, by an appreciation of the central roles that such feelings as hatred and revenge have come to play in the ethos of some terrorist groups—roles that have displaced, and even rendered irrelevant, most of the original nationalist ones. However, whereas Abu Nidal might not stop terrorism even if the Palestinians were to achieve a state that displaced not only all of Israel but also every other country in the Middle East, most terrorist groups probably ultimately could be satisfied enough by the achievement of their goals to stop their terrorism, despite their current feelings of hatred and vengefulness—although what they might consider satisfactory achievements may require from their adversaries comprises that, for them, would add up to nothing less than political or national suicide. Thus, feelings of hatred and desire for revenge are shared by many terrorists, and these feelings probably increase the difficulty the terrorists may have, for other reasons, in stopping their terrorism. For a small percentage of these terrorists, however, those feelings probably constitute the residue of the nationalist and idealist goals for which they adopted a life of terrorism in the first place.

For a specific example of terrorist actions that appeared to observers to be explicable only in terms of a logic of hatred, revenge, and the need to commit violence, see Don Podesta, "Terror for Terror's Sake: Motive Missing in Egyptair Hijacking," *Washington Post*, 1 December 1985, p. A-1.

terms. The words we use in discussing a subject affect the way in which we think about it. If we use words like "hatred," "revulsion," and "revenge" rather than "anger," "opposition," and "desire for political change," we may better understand the kinds of responses that need to be constructed to contend with the impulse and reality of terrorism.

Our own impulses—the preference for compromise, say, and for reason—may produce pallid rejoinders to demands that are, in many cases, apocalyptic. The language we use in discussing and examining terrorist groups should reflect with fidelity the reality of their members' inner lives and provide us with a realistic sense of which responses, in which cases, might be effective in reducing terrorism, and which might not.

Ignoring rational reasons for choosing a terrorist strategy

Many terrorist groups routinely offer strategic, logical reasons to explain their use of terrorism; and many people who study terrorism just as routinely prefer to believe that those reasons are only covers for the real reasons, which must derive solely or primarily from deep needs. Sometimes they do—but rarely solely, and sometimes not even primarily.

Numerous declarations and memoirs by terrorists going back to the nineteenth century provide rationales for the adoption of terrorist strategies, such as the assertion that terrorism is an efficient revolutionary method, and perhaps the only one, that can be used by a weak force against a powerful regime.[25] Many of these rationales are summarized by

[25] See, for example the following documents and works: Peter Kropotkin, "Programma Ispolnitel'novo Komiteta" [Program of the Executive Committee], in *Literatura Sotsial'no Revolutsionnoi Partii 'Narodnoi Voli'* [Literature of "The People's Will" Social Revolutionary Party] (Paris, 1905); Nikolai Morozov, *Terroristicheskaya Bor'ba [The Terrorist Struggle] (London, 1880); Michel Confino,* Violence dans la Violence (Paris: F. Maspero, 1973); Carlos Marighella, *Mini Manual of the Urban Guerilla* (London, 1971); Menachem Begin, *The Revolt* (Los Angeles: Nash, 1972); Leila Kadi, *Basic Political Documents of the Armed Palestinian Resistance Movement* (Beirut: Palestine Liberation Organization Research Center, 1969); and Charles Foley (ed.), *Memoirs of General Grivas* (London: Longman's, 1964).

Martha Crenshaw in ["The Logic of Terrorism"] and elsewhere.[26] In general, it should be remembered that, although these rationales are the rationales of terrorists, and although what they often rationalize is acts of indiscriminate murder, the rationales may make strategic sense. To the extent that they do, psychological research should not ignore them. Strategic logic can spur actions no less powerfully than emotional logic.

Inaccessibility to direct research on terrorists

Many terrorists believe, for good reason, that any attempt to explain their motivations in psychological terms diminishes the validity of their ideas, their actions, and their beings. If they are serious in their commitment to their causes and have no illusions that they can convert to their views the researcher who asks to meet with them—a researcher who is likely to be seen as a representative of the government, society, or class against which they have organized their actions—they are likely to refuse to meet with that researcher, even if they are languishing in prison with nothing else to do. Agreement to meet with a psychiatrist or psychologist is more likely to occur when the terrorists have already begun to have doubts about their decision to adopt a terrorist career; and, in such cases, the information provided, as rich as it may be, is inevitably affected by the change in psychological orientation.

Ignoring state terrorism and the destructive acts of Western governments

Critics, especially critics on the political left, object to terrorist studies in part on the grounds that they tend to ignore (for reasons of ideological convenience, they often argue) the kind of terrorism that has produced more destruction than any other: the terrorism carried out by states

---

[26]See Martha Crenshaw, . . . "The Strategic Development of Terrorism," a paper prepared for delivery at the 1985 annual meeting of the American Political Science Association, New Orleans.

against their own people. These critics often argue that terrorism researchers have insufficient sympathies for the sources of most modern terrorist movements—the aspirations of the poor and the oppressed to shake off the yoke of colonial or capitalist rule or to end the occupation of their homelands by nations or peoples or governments that are supported by Western colonial interests.

As a result of this lack of sympathy, those critics argue, terrorism specialists tend to see terrorism in purely negative terms. In addition, the critics argue, because the terrorism researchers are generally members of Western societies, they are inclined to support the regimes and types of polities—namely, liberal democracies—that are the targets of so many terrorist groups, and fail to see the ways in which those regimes oppress certain minorities, classes, or national groups or support other countries that do so. Such oppression, the critics argue, constitutes a form of terrorism, a terrorism that is often far worse in its effects, scope, and ruthlessness than the acts of the substate terrorists.[27]

These arguments cannot be dismissed outright. State terrorism has certainly been the most potent and destructive form of terrorism the world has seen: Nazi Germany and the Soviet Union, to name the two regimes that have engaged in it most egregiously, have indeed amassed deaths that a near eternity of conventional substate terrorist actions could not hope to accomplish. Whether substate terrorist actions have become the focus of terrorism specialists because of an ideological preference for Western values and interests and whether such a preference distorts the effort to understand terrorism in psychological terms are, however, different matters.

For some terrorism specialists, including some who concern themselves

---

[27] A vigorously argued formulation of much of this position is contained in a 1977 review of eleven books on terrorism by Anthony Arblaster, "Terrorism: Myths, Meaning and Morals," *Political Studies* 25, no. 3 (1977): 413–24.

with the psychology of terrorism, Western interests and concerns probably *are* paramount. This may be due, in part, to the fact that most of these specialists are Westerners themselves, as well as to the fact that they are well acquainted with the ravages that substate terrorism has caused. In addition, some of these specialists have been employed by their governments in the military, the police, or the foreign-affairs bureaucracies, or have worked as consultants to these organizations. In those roles they have had, as their primary responsibility, the theoretical or operational task of combating terrorist activities—a responsibility whose exercise is not promoted by the readiness to feel empathy for terrorist aspirations, whether of the revolutionary or the third-world variety.

Many researchers interested in the psychology of terrorism, however, appear to be genuinely interested in terrorism as a human activity—as a product of individual and group motivation, thinking, and interaction. Although capable of recognizing, and even having empathy for, terrorist needs and feelings, most of them also recognize the human toll exacted by those needs and feelings as they are expressed through terrorist behavior. They are accustomed to working with individuals and groups, and so find it natural to work with substate terrorists. But they tend to feel unprepared—as a result of a lack of theory and experience, rather than ideological bias—to deal with the psychologies of leaders and nations that carry out terrorism against their own or other peoples or that are accused by one or another terrorist group, or by people sympathetic to those groups, of doing so.

In the main, the kinds of actions carried out by terrorist individuals and groups differ in character, strategy, scope, and motivation from the kinds of actions carried out by states against persons or populations who oppose, or are considered undesirable by, those states. The nature of terrorist behavior, and perhaps also the nature of the moral and psychological questions raised by that behavior, differs in the cases of state and substate terrorism and requires different methods of analysis.

The complaint that terrorism specialists, including those who study the psychology of terrorism, have a selective preference for studying one kind of terrorism rather than another is not utterly without merit. But that criticism does not necessarily render impossible the valid study of the one, and it does not facilitate the successful study of the other.

excerpt from:

Cruelty and Silence

by Kanan Makiya

Kanan Makiya is an Iraqi dissident who ranks high on Saddam's most wanted list. Openly repudiating the blame game that characterizes much of current Middle Eastern social and political analysis, Makiya focuses on the mindset of certain influential Arab intellectuals. He also analyzes recent events in the Muslim world to lay bare the causes of the region's current paralysis and the accompanying cynicism, despair and defensiveness that dominate intellectual and moral life and that give tacit support to terrorism. In this excerpt from Makiya's book, written in 1993, he lays the blame for the current social crisis in the Middle East squarely on the shoulders of the educated elite.

Human life was not always held in such low regard in the Arab world. Until the 1967 war, Arab sensitivity to human rights abuses was not worse than that of any other people in the developing world. That is not to imply that it was adequate, simply that it was in keeping with other parts of Asia or Latin America. Since 1975, and the beginning of the Lebanese civil war, the Arab world east of Egypt has become an exceptionally nasty place. The forerunners for Lebanon were the glorification of violence, armed struggle, and ideas of revolution, all born decades earlier in Iraq and Syria. The result is that Arab human rights sensibilities today lag behind other parts of the developing world like India and Latin America. Powerful despotisms and populist lawlessness are accompanied by an intelligentsia with no liberal or "rights-centered" critique of either. Meanwhile, wealth on an unprecedented scale has been flowing into the Middle East, even as Arabs themselves have been running away from the region in ever-growing numbers. They run away not because there are no economic opportunities, but because cruelty has everywhere become the rule.

This cruelty is a highly specific phenomenon of the 1970s and 1980s, with no general implications for "the Arabs" or "Islam." The critical moment in the change from a set of political and intellectual preoccupations typical of much of the Third World to the current extraordinary brutality of the Mashriq was, paradoxically, one of the most intellectually innovative interludes in modern Arab politics. I am thinking of the 1967–75 interregnum between the Six Day War and the outbreak of the Lebanese civil war.

For a few short years after 1967 a handful of intellectuals like Sadiq Jalal al-'Azm and Adonis, along with journals like *Mawaqif* subjected everything around them to searching criticism. The titles of 'Azm's books alone tell the story: *A Critique of Religious Thought, Self-Criticism After the Defeat, A Critique of the Thought of the Palestinian Resistance.* The importance of these books is not that they were "correct" in some timeless sense. There is no such thing in culture. Nor did they "accept" Israeli or Western meddling in the affairs of the region; they were still "rejectionist" works, in the Arab political lexicon. Their importance lies in the fact that they looked inwardly, into Arab and Muslim political-cultural defects, without seeking outsiders to blame. A current was emerging in Arab thought that did not swing between triumphalism and breast-beating, the twin poles of contemporary Arab discourse. Many passages from these writings retain a striking relevance:

> Merely to use the expression, *al-nakba*, the catastrophe, with reference to the June [1967] war and its outcome carries to a certain degree an apologetic logic along with a running away from responsibility. For one upon whom a catastrophe has befallen cannot be held responsible for

it. Or, if he was responsible, then that responsibility is very partial in relation to the enormity and magnitude of the event. For this reason we [Arab] have become used to attributing catastrophes to fate, time and nature, in other words, to factors over which we have no control.

The most important and long-lasting legacy of the 1967–75 period was the emergence of the Palestinian Resistance movement. During those crucially important (and still inadequately studied) years, Arab political discourse went through cycles of euphoria, renewal, and reaching out for new ideas, followed by hopelessness, despair, and the beginnings of retrenchment into tradition. But the 1967 war was a test, which, in the end, even the inwardly reflective, secular stance of al-'Azm and Adonis failed. Israel was still there, stronger than ever, still an unfathomable entity in Arab eyes. *Self-Criticism After the Defeat* did not go far enough; it remained trapped inside the limitations of underlying assumptions like: What is wrong with us such that *they* succeeded in defeating us so overwhelmingly? How can *we* change so that we can do to *them* what they did to us the next time around?

The ground was now left clear for radical ideologies of every description: Ba'thism, vulgar Marxism, Islamic political activism, Arab socialism, and militant local nationalisms (Palestinian, Lebanese, Greater Syrian, etc.). None of these ideologies—for all their important other differences— is capable of evolving a view of the world centered on a conception of human rights or the inviolability of the human person as the central principle of a modern vision of Arabness. Moreover, in spite of the great multiplicity of post-1967 voices, in the end it turned out everyone had only "anti-imperialism" and "anti-Zionism" in common. You could always get quite far in Arab politics by blaming everything on the West or on Israel. There used to be mitigating ideas in the post-independence Arab political experience which complicated this simplemindedness. It is important to remember that there were liberals and democrats in the Arab world in the 1940s and 1950s. Tragically, 1967 blew what was left of their ideas away. As cruelty spread, feeding on itself all through the 1980s, every kind of variety in Arab politics was choked off. Sickly thought-killing resentment was all that remained. It is as though we had regressed since al-'Azm wrote *Self-Criticism After the Defeat.*

The anti-Western rhetoric of the Arab intelligentsia during the 1990–91 Gulf crisis is a fossilized restatement of the same evasion of responsibility that al-'Azm was criticizing in the wake of the 1967 war. The rhetoric had grown cynical and bitter with age, losing the only things it had going for it: hope in a new and better order, and the fervor of belief that one was capable of changing. A quarter of a century has passed since June 1967, and a new generation of much more sophisticated Arab writers and thinkers today edit journals and occupy chairs in famous universities throughout the Western world. On the surface they are so different from the Ahmad Shuqairis and Muhammad Hasanain Haikals of a previous generation. They argue about modernism and tradition, about democracy and Islam, about representations and counterrepresentations of East and West. They write in English, French, and Arabic, publishing simultaneously all over the world. But when it comes to cruelty in their own backyard, committed by "their own" people, the strange thing is they are more infantile than their predecessors. Ever-increasing denial of ever-growing cruelty has created a completely untenable gap between the way these intellectuals talk and the way their world really is. When Saddam Husain invaded Kuwait, all these people fell headlong into that gap—a gap which is in the final analysis one of their own making.

My generation, which includes many of the intellectuals I have been quoting in this book, was formed politically in the crucible of the 1967 war. Edward Said, for instance, although born in Jerusalem, became acutely conscious of his Palestinian-Arab identity after the defeat of Nasser's armies and the emergence of Palestinian hope. We all went through broadly similar kinds of experiences, whether we were living in Beirut, in London, or in New York. I started off in politics as a young activist supporter of the same Palestinian organization as both Said and al-ʿAzm. As I worked virtually full time in support of the Palestinian movement, I became aware of myself as an Arab for the very first time. Even as the Baʿth were legitimizing their power in Iraq on the grounds of the ideology of Pan-Arabism, I was being attracted to their old idea of an "Arab revolution." But it was not Michel ʿAflaq's formulation of the 1940s that was attracting me; it was a new version articulated by Palestinian intellectuals and fired by the example of the rising Palestinian movement. My sense of myself as an Iraqi, which was never something I had been anxious about, receded into the background. Nor was I changing in isolation from everyone else. Wherever you looked, identities were being re-imagined, wrapped up in bright new ideas which had come shooting out of the darkness like lightning bolts.

The onset of the Lebanese civil war tested this instant mental universe of young Arabs against reality, where it really counted. In this test, the halo of the Palestinian organizations lost its aura completely. In Lebanon these organizations exercised power and, consequently, stopped being just "resistance" organizations. It now became clear that they had become as corrupt and as nasty in their practices as all the others around them. Palestinian organizations ran their protection and taxation rackets just like everyone else. They looted and sniped and kidnapped and muscled in on ordinary Lebanese and on helpless Palestinian civilians. They invented ingenious new ways of killing and hurting other Arabs, just like everyone else. What difference was there, to the ordinary Lebanese, between a Palestinian "mafioso" and his counterpart from the Murabitoun or the Phalange? The very ground had been taken away from under their feet by gangs of thugs. What difference did it make whether the ones who were doing the taking belonged to this gang or that? In Lebanon, it all boiled down to killing over little bits of other people's turf. Everyone sold their soul to "their" little mafia for a piece of protection. So it happened that stagnation, hopelessness, cynicism, and despair took over where grand revealed truths once used to beckon.

With the onset of the Lebanese civil war, the intellectual renovation that had started in 1967 ground virtually to a complete halt. Nowhere was the stagnation as noticeable as among the Palestinian intelligentsia. Understandably, this intelligentsia was completely preoccupied with defining its newly discovered "Palestinianness" vis-à-vis an Israel that was itself being corrupted by the experience of occupation (of territories and people captured in 1967). Israeli politicians had in the meantime picked up a nasty trick or two from their Arab counterparts: deny that any such thing as a Palestinian existed, and call occupied territories "Judea and Samaria." In the Mashriq, all through the 1980s, everyone made the worst choices, Palestinian intellectuals included. Wedded as they were to the leadership of the very same organizations that had behaved so abominably in Lebanon, they did not even attempt to claim the moral high ground that was opening up for them all through the 1970s and 1980s. At a time when South Africa was producing a Nelson Mandela, Czechoslovakia a Václav Havel, and Poland a Lech Walesa, Palestinian intellectuals stuck to "their" Yasser Arafat. In such choices, the failings of an entire generation are summed up. Are such a gifted people as the Palestinians—with the largest, most cosmopolitan, and best-educated intelligentsia in the Arab world—unable to improve on Yasser Arafat as their leader in all these years of organized political activity?

The mere act of putting such questions down on paper frightens me. I have no answers. All I can do is point to the glaring collective failure of an intelligentsia to evolve a language of rights and democracy to supplement the language of nationalism. It is as though the two were perceived by Arabs to be theoretically as irreconcilable as they have practically proven to be nonexistent in the Mashriq. Words like "freedom," "democracy," "justice," "human dignity," and "human rights" have lost all meaning in the hands of the same intellectuals who go on and on about Western "hypocrisy." They no longer believe in the very things that they so vociferously denounce the West for not believing in.

Those lost old meanings need to be reconquered and reappropriated. But not in the form of "alternative" definitions, nor in the shape of simply stating that "we are all" against the nastiness of the Baʿth. These are just not good enough. All too often, the language of denial and rejection is an excuse for inaction; even worse, it can become a justification for cruelty. That is what it proved to be in that "crisis of exposure" which began on the day Saddam Husain invaded Kuwait. Only new ways of thinking, founded on the deepest kind of unreasoning revulsion against the cruelty and intolerance that has been perpetrated by Arabs against their fellow Arabs, or against Kurds and other national minorities of the Middle East, can carry conviction and hope to the long-suffering peoples of this part of the world. A new self-critical discourse is needed, one that is rooted in a thoroughgoing insistence upon the inviolable sanctity of human life and the subordination of everything else to this criterion. To the extent that Palestinian intellectuals rightly expect all Arabs to join hands in fighting against their oppression, they must start to understand that they have morally failed all Arabs in this respect more than anyone else.

At a time when large chunks of the rest of the world (Eastern Europe, Latin America, China, South Africa) were beginning to discover human rights/democracy and struggling with home-grown tyrannies and Stalinist bureaucracies, the best and most gifted Palestinians were writing learned books that rested on statements such as:

> . . . all academic knowledge about India and Egypt is somehow tinged and impressed with, violated by, the gross political fact [of imperialism] . . . *that is what I am saying* in this study of Orientalism . . .

543

It is therefore correct that every European, in what he
could say about the Orient, was consequently a racist, an
imperialist, and almost totally ethnocentric.

Orientalism as an intellectual project influenced a whole generation of
young Arab scholars, and it shaped the discipline of modern Middle East
studies in the 1980s. The original book was never intended as a critique of
contemporary Arab politics, yet it fed into a deeply rooted populist politics
of resentment against the West. The distortions it analyzed came from the
eighteenth and nineteenth centuries, but these were marshaled by young
Arab and "pro-Arab" scholars into an intellectual-political agenda that was
out of kilter with the real needs of Arabs who were living in a world characterized by rapidly escalating cruelty, not ever-increasing imperial domination. The trajectory from Said's *Orientalism* to his *Covering Islam: How the
Media and the Experts Determine How We See the Rest of the World* is
premised on the morally wrong idea that the West is to be blamed in the
here-and-now for its long nefarious history of association with the Middle
East. Thus it unwittingly deflected from the real problems of the Middle East
at the same time as it contributed more bitterness to the armory of young
impressionable Arabs when there was already far too much of that around.

As cruelty grew, there was less and less objective reason for that bitterness by comparison with any other period in the long and thorny history of the Arabs and the West. There is an aging, declining West out there,
not a crusading, imperial one. American foreign policy had been decisively defeated in Vietnam, routed by Khomeini in Iran, and seemed to
have been made by buffoons in the Lebanon (when a lone suicide bomber
dispatched more than two hundred Marines in one blow). Israel had been
forced out of Egypt. Iran was "lost" to the West for a whole historical
period. Arab financial power was without precedent. In these conditions,
the most interesting intellectual question to reflect upon was no longer
how omniscient and omnipotent American power was in the world, but

how *ineffectual* it had become when it did do something (which was rare) in the face of the intractability of the problems of the politically independent countries of Middle East. The classic instance of this, ironically, is the Gulf war—a war financed by Arab states to resolve an inter-Arab conflict. If, from an Iraqi point of view, this war was left unfinished, that was not for lack of American initiative. Iraq was destroyed and Saddam Husain remained in power not because the West wanted him to stay on, but because the Allied forces were terrified of inheriting the responsibilities that necessarily accompanied finishing the job.

The argument implicit in the agenda of Arab and "pro-Arab" intellectuals based in the West was that *only the West* could do something about a regional problem like the Arab-Israeli conflict because that problem was "historically" of its own making. "We Palestinians are not responsible," the thinking goes, "because we are always and only history's victims." The Israeli invasion of southern Lebanon and the murder of some twenty thousand innocent Lebanese and Palestinian civilians by indiscriminate shelling was seen by the Palestinian-Arab and "pro-Arab" intelligentsia as *caused by* American policies in the first place, just like Saddam Husain's invasion of Kuwait. Not until after the Gulf war could you talk to Israelis or fight for your rights inside Israel; you had to address yourself constantly to Americans. The very notion of waging a fight for "rights" addressed directly to Israeli public opinion (where the evidence suggests it might have found support) was deemed compromising. Why is it that Nelson Mandela can talk to Pik Botha, but a Palestinian intellectual cannot talk to his Israeli counterparts, the best of whom would fall over themselves at the opportunity? Instead of directly grasping at this central core of the problem, Palestinian intellectuals during the 1980s indulged in one doomed war after the other directed at the "biases" of the U.S. government or American media networks. In fact, the one Palestinian who espoused a radical redirection of political priorities lived inside Israel-Palestine, and was well and truly ostracized by those of his peers who did not.

Like the poem of Nizar Qabbani, "Abu Jahl Buys Fleet Street," *Orientalism* operates through a populist ethos of Arab prejudice built up over a very long time; it does nothing to reshape Arab stereotypes of the West, even though its author is probably the most perfectly situated Arab to do so. The book makes Arabs feel contented with the way they are, instead of making them rethink fundamental assumptions which so clearly haven't worked. Maybe that was never the book's original intention. But books have a life of their own which is independent of the intentions of those who write them. I am addressing myself to the young Arab readers of *Orientalism*, who remain to this day its biggest fans. They desperately need to unlearn ideas such as that "every European" in what he or she has to say about their world is or was a "racist." The very adoption of the book in academic institutions of learning in the West—at a time when empires had long since collapsed (Britain and France) or were in a state of terminal decline (the United States)—suggests the irrelevance of its guiding thesis to modern Western scholarship on the Middle East. The ironical fact is that the book was given the attention it received in the "almost totally ethnocentric" West largely because its author was a Palestinian, just as *Republic of Fear* was taken seriously only after Saddam Husain had invaded Kuwait, and because its author was an Iraqi. It is time we faced up to such home truths.

Silence is not born out of fear; it is born out of the poverty of thought. Our vacuum turned out to be a spiritual vacuum, but one that could never be filled by religious belief alone. Silence is what Salman Rushdie, in *Midnight's Children*, called the "hole in my heart." The politics of silence is that bizarre state of affairs that allowed a Lebanese leftist (Trabulsi), a Jordanian newspaper editor (Khouri), a Tunisian historian (Djaïet), a Syrian literary critic (Abu Deeb), and a Palestinian human rights activist

(Kuttab), all to meet under one umbrella in defense of "the rights" of a tyrant that not one of them would ever dream of living under. The fact that such a meeting place not only exists but has become so vast, holding in one terrifying embrace so many different and well-educated Arabs, is the principal obstacle to the emergence of a less violent or more tolerant politics in this part of the world.

The Gulf crisis revealed Arab silence to mean first and foremost a loss of empathy with the other, a retreat from the public realm into the comforting but suffocating embrace of smaller and smaller units of identity like tribe, religion, sect, and family allegiances. Silence is a synonym for the death of compassion in the Arab world; it is the politics of not washing your dirty laundry in public while gruesome cruelties and whole worlds of morbidity unfold all around you. Silence is choosing, ostrichlike, not to know what Arab is doing to fellow Arab, all in the name of a knee-jerk anti-westernism which has turned into a disease. Health "is infinite and expansive in mode," reaching out "to be filled with the fullness of the world," writes Oliver Sacks. If so, then Arab silence is like a sickness, "finite and reductive in mode." Silence is the language of a narcissistic inwardness, endeavoring always to reduce the world to reflections of oneself. Silence in the Arab world is silence over cruelty.

In the end, the contention of this book is very simple: the politics of keeping silent over escalating cruelties inside the Arab world, cruelties inflicted for the most part by one Arab on another, is principally responsible for an Arab moral collapse which has today reached epidemic proportions. Leaders like Saddam Husain thrive on the silence of the Arab intelligentsia toward cruelty. They are also *created by that silence.* Intellectuals created the discourse of silence. Silence is a way of talking, of writing; above all, it is a way of thinking that obfuscates and covers up for the cruelty that should today be a central preoccupation of those people who make talking, writing, and thinking their business. Breaking with this silence is the moral obligation of every Arab, in particular the "intellectuals" among us. Nothing else is of comparable importance—not even the "struggle against Israel." For all of us who love and identify with this corner of the world, it isn't easy or nice to say such things. That doesn't make them any the less true.

I did not attempt to grapple with the very complicated question of how we got into such a terrible state. That kind of a project needs distance and takes years. Meanwhile, the dead are still accumulating in the Arab world; the stench of their bodies is overwhelming; I no longer have the stomach for "scholarship" on such questions. This book was never about scholarship in the first place. Maybe it isn't possible for the proper distance to be obtained by anyone today. It is enough to know that things didn't have to turn out this way, and it is enough to know that we still hold in our own hands the key to reversing silence. The first step out of the morass is the ruthless and radical one of uprooting, from deep within our own sensibilities, the intellectual and moral authority that blaming someone else still carries today among us Arabs. If I have bent that stick as far as I know how in the opposite direction, it is because I firmly believe that only upon its demise can a healthy, multi-dimensional, and pluralist meaning to Arabness be born.

The second step is to "put cruelty first." This wonderfully simple aphorism has the great quality of being deeply anti-ideological in its disregard for the idea of sin, whether in its religious form (transgression of divine rules), or in its modern form of "historical blame." The two forms are interlinked and go to the roots of the modern Arab malaise. One can only inflict physical pain on a living creature, an individual being weaker than oneself. As Judith Shklar points out, when this activity is judged as "the supreme evil,"

> it is judged so in and of itself, and not because it signifies a denial of God or any other higher norm. It is a judgement made from within the world in which cruelty occurs as part of our normal private life and our daily

public practices. By putting it unconditionally first, and with nothing above us to excuse or to forgive acts of cruelty, one closes off any appeal to any order other than that of actuality. To hate cruelty with utmost intensity is perfectly compatible with . . . religiosity [and all ideologies], but to put it first . . . is a purely human verdict upon human conduct.

Change for the better will only come in the Arab world when a new generation of young Arabs become incensed at the unacceptably cruel state of their world; they need to become so revolted as to lose every vestige of shame, speaking out without caring who is listening, or to what nefarious use some people will inevitably put their words. It is a terrible and an exciting time to be a young Arab. Pan-Arabism as a political creed is dead for now, but "Arabness" is in greater flux than at any time since the end of the first centuries of Islam. If the principal task of this book was not scholarship, then it was the simpler one of identifying a malaise and trying to find new ways of describing it. History and scholarship can wait for better days, which I am certain will come. But when?

Acknowledgments

Thanks to the following people at Thunder's Mouth Press
and Avalon Publishing Group:

Neil Ortenberg for being decisive.
Will Balliett for being reasonable.
Kristen Couse for being calm.
Simon Sullivan for being methodical.
Maria Fernandez for being consistent.
Linda Kosarin for being subtle.

Photo Credits

Page 1
Leon Czolgosz assassinates President McKinley in Buffalo, New York,
on September 6, 1901.
Copyright © Corbis

Page 43
Leila Khaled, Palestine-born Fatah hijacker, with an AK-47
Copyright © Corbis

Page 235
An Osama bin Laden supporter
Copyright © Corbis

Page 413
The mountain cabin of Theodore Kaczynski
Copyright © AP Wide World Photos

Page 513
Mohamed Atta passes through airport security in Portland, Maine,
on his way to Boston Logan International Airport.
Copyright © AP Wide World Photos

Permissions

Excerpt from *A History of Terrorism* by Walter Laqueur. Copyright © 2001 by Transaction Publishers. Reprinted by permission of Transaction Publishers. ❧ Excerpt from *The Wretched of the Earth* by Franz Fanon. Copyright © 1963 by Presence Africaine. Used by permission of Grove Atlantic, Inc. ❧ Excerpt from *No One A Neutral* by Norman Antokol and Mayer Nudell. Copyright © 1990 by Norman Antokol and Mayer Nudell. Reprinted by permission of the authors. ❧ Excerpt from *Televisionaries: The Red Army Faction Story 1963-1993* by Tom Vague. Reprinted by permission of AK Press. ❧ Reprinted from *Jackal: The Complete Story of the Legendary Terrorist, Carlos the Jackal* by John Follain. Copyright © 1998 by John Follain. Published by Arcade Publishing Company, New York, New York ❧ Martin Dillon, excerpts from *The Dirty War: Covert Strategies and Tactics Used in Political Conflicts*. Copyright © 1999. Reprinted with the permission of Routledge, Inc., part of The Taylot & Francis Group. ❧ Excerpt from *ETA: Profile of a Terrorist Group* by Yonah Alexander, Michael S. Swetnam and Herbert Levine. Copyright © 2001 by Transnational Publishers. Reprinted by permission of Transnational Publishers. ❧ Excerpt from *The Autobiography of a Revolutionary* by Leila Khaled. Copyright © 1973 by George Hajjar. Reprinted by permission of Bantam Books. ❧ Patrick Seale, excerpt from *Abu Nidal: A Gun for Hire*. Copyright © 1992 by Patrick Seale. Reprinted with the permission of Random House, Inc. ❧ Reprinted from *One Day in September* by Simon Reeve. Copyright © 2000 by Simon Reeve. Published by Arcade Publishing, New York, New York ❧ Excerpt from *Fugitive Days* by William Ayers. Copyright © 2001 by William Ayers. Reprinted by permission of Beacon Press, Boston. ❧ Excerpt from The Introduction to *Social Justice in Islam* by Hamid Alger. Copyright © 2000 by Islamic Publications International. Reprinted by permission of Islamic Publications International. ❧ From *The New Terrorism* by Walter Laqueur. Copyright © 1999 by Walter Laqueur. Used by permission of Oxford University Press, Inc. ❧ The Diversity of Bio Weapons by Joshua Lederberg (pp. 18-22) from *Super Terrorism: Biological, Chemical and Nuclear* (Yonah Alexander, ed.). Copyright © 2001 by Transnational Publishers. Reprinted by permission of Transnational Publishers ❧ Benjamin R. Barber, excerpt from *Jihad vs. McWorld*. Copyright © 1995 by Benjamin R. Barber. Reprinted with the permission of

Permissions

Bibliography

Alexander, Yonah & Levine, Herbert M & Swetnam, Michael. *ETA: Profile of a Terrorist Group*: Ardsley, New York: Transnational Publishers, 2001.

Algar, Hamid. Introduction. In Sayyid Qutb, *Social Justice in Islam.* Oneonata, New York: Islamic Publications International, 2000.

Antokol, Norman and Nudell, Mayer. *No One Neutral: Political Hostage Taking in the Modern World,* Medina Ohio: Alpha Publications of Ohio, 1990.

Ayers, Bill. *Fugitive Days.* Boston: Beacon Press, 2001

Bader, Eleanor J. and Windle, Patricia Baird. *Targets of Hatred: Anti-Abortion Terrorism*, New York; Palgrave, 2001.

Barber, Benjamin R. *Jihad Vs. McWorld*. New York: Ballantine Books, 1995.

Bin Laden, Osama. (1996) Declaration of War Against the Americans Occupying the Land of the Two Holy Places. In Yonah Alexander and Michael S. Swetnam, *Usama bin Laden's Al-Qaida: Profile of a Terrorist Network.* Ardsley, New York: Transnational Publishers.

Coates, James. *Armed and Dangerous: The Rise of the Survivalist Right.* New York: Hill and Wang, 1987.

Conrad, Joseph. *The Secret Agent: A Simple Tale.* New York: Oxford Classics, 1998.

Cooley, John K. *Unholy Wars.* London: Pluto Press, 2000.

Dillon, Martin. *The Dirty War.* New York: Routledge, 1998.

Fanon, Franz. *The Wretched of the Earth.* New York: Grove Press, 1963.

Follain, John. *Jackal: The Complete Story of the Legendary Terrorist, Carlos the Jackal.* New York: Arcade Publishing, 1998.

Ford, Henry. (November, 1920) The International Jew. *The Dearborn Independent*

Hamas from http://www.palestine-info.com/hamas/index.htm.

Herbeck, Dan and Michel, Lou. *American Terrorist: Timothy McVeigh and the Oklahoma City Bombing*, New York: Regan Books, 2001.

Kaczyinski, Theodore. The Unabomber Manifesto from http://www.panix.com/~clays/Una/

Katz, Samuel M. *The Hunt for the Engineer: How Israeli Agents Tracked the Hamas Master Bomber.* New York: Fromm International, 1999.

Khaled, Leila. *My People Shall Live.* London: Hodder and Staughton, 1973.

Bibliography

Kramer, Martin. (2000) The Moral Logic of Hizballah. In Walter Reich (ed.), *Origins of Terrorism* (pp.131-160) Washington, D.C.: Woodrow Wilson Center Press.

Labeviere, Richard. *Dollars for Islam: The United States and Islam.* New York: Algora Publishing, 2000.

Laqueur, Walter. *A History of Terrorism.* New Jersey: Transaction Publishers, 2001.

Laqueur, Walter. *The New Terrorism.* New York: Oxford University Press, 1999.

Lederberg, Joshua, (2000) The Diversity of Bio Weapons. In Yonah Alexander (ed.), *Super Terrorism: Biological, Chemical and Nuclear,* (pp. 18-22). Ardsley, New York: Transnational Publishers.

Makiya, Kanan. *Cruelty and Silence: War, Tyranny, Uprising and the Arab World.* New York: W.W. Norton & Company, 1993.

Most, Johann. *The Science of Revolutionary Warfare.* London: Freedom Press, 1996.

Marighella, Carlos. *Mini-Manual of the Urban Guerilla,* Havana: Tricontinental, 1970.

Murakami, Haruki, *Underground,* New York: Vintage Books, 2001.

"President McKinley Shot, The Trial and Execution of Leon Czolgosz" from intotem.buffnet.net/bhw/panamex/assassination/assassin.htm

Rashid, Ahmed, *Taliban,* New Haven: Yale University Press, 2001.

Reeve, Simon. *The New Jackals, Ramzi Yousef, Osama Bin Laden and the Future of Terrorism.* Boston: Northeastern University Press, 1999.

One Day In September: the Full Story of the 1972 Munich Olympic Massacre and the Israeli Revenge Operation "Wrath of God." New York: Arcade Publications, 2000.

Reich, Walter. (2000) Understanding Terrorist Behavior: The Limits and Opportunities of Psychological Inquiry.. In Walter Reich (ed.), *Origins of Terrorism* (pp. 261-280) Washington, D.C.: Woodrow Wilson Center Press.

Sanguinetti, Gianfranco. *On Terrorism and the State.* London: Aldgate Press, 1982.

Seale, Patrick. *Abu Nidal: A Gun for Hire,* New York: Random House, 1992.

Vague, Tom. *Televisionaries: The Red Army Faction Story.* London: AK Press, 1994.

Yardley, Jim (October 10, 2001) *A Portrait of the Terrorist from Shy Child to Singleminded Killer,* the *New York Times,* Section B, Page 1.

Suggestions for Further Reading

Pre-History

Adamic, Louis, *Dynamite*. London: Rebel Press, 1985. Class violence in America, 1830-1930.

Avery, Paul, *Bakunin and Nechaev*. London: Freedom Press. Anarchists and nihilists in conflict in Russia in 1881.

Conquest, Robert. *The Great Terror*. New York: Oxford University Press, 1990. The classic war on Stalinist state terror.

Dostoyevsky, Fyodor. *The Devils*. Penguin USA, 1954. Same territory as Avery's book from a fictional point of view.

Schama, Simon. *Citizen*. New York: Alfred A. Knopf, 1989. The terror of the French Revolution.

Political Terrorism

Anonymous, *Handbook for Volunteers of the Irish Republican Army*. Boulder, Colorado: Paladin Press, 1985. How to fight the British militarily for new recruits to this organization.

Baumann, Bommi. *How it All Began: The Personal Account of a West German Urban Guerrilla*. Edinburgh: AK Press, 1988. Auto-biography of a German anarchist bomb thrower.

Chomsky, Noam. *The Culture of Terrorism*. Boston: South End Press, 1988. State sponsored terror in Latin America and elsewhere with analysis of methodology of distortion.

Coogan, Tim Pat. *The IRA*. New York: St. Martin's Press, December 2001. General history.

Curtis, Liz. *Ireland: the Propaganda War*. London: Pluto/InBook, 1985. Account of manipulation of events by British media.

Feraoun, Mouloud. *Journal 1955-1962: Reflections on the French Algerian War*. Lincoln, Nebraska: University of Nebraska Press, 2000. State terror during the Algerian war for independence.

Guevara, Che. *Guerilla Warfare*. Wilmington: Scholarly Resources, 1997. Rural warfare manual. Inspired Marighella.

Lenin, V.I. *Imperialism the Highest Stage of Capitalism*. Moscow: International
    Publishers, 1990. The theory behind the war against colonialism.
Powell, William F. *The Anarchist Cookbook*. Fort Lee, New Jersey: Barricade
    Books, 1972. Practical recipes for mayhem. A must read for the American
    Left of the 1970s.
Tse-Tung, Mao. *On Guerrilla Warfare*. Chicago: University of Illinois Press,
    2000. A key text of anti-colonialist warfare along with Marighella and
    Guevara.
Thornton, Lawrence. *Imagining Argentina*. New York: Bantam Books, 1987.
    Novel about the disappearing of Argentinians during the 1970s.

Religious Terrorism
Bamford, James. *Body of Secrets*. New York: Doubleday, 2001. Indictment of
    Sharon's murderous practices during the Arab-Israeli war of 1967 by
    intelligence agencies reporter.
Begin, Menachem. *The Revolt*. New York: Nash Publishing, 1977. How Israel was
    founded on terrorism against the British colonial rulers.
Bergen, Peter. *Holy War, Inc*. New York: The Free Press, 2001. Solid biography on
    Osama Bin Laden.
Borovik, Aatyom. *The Hidden War*. New York: Grove Press, 1990. The Dispatches
    of the Russian war in Afghanistan.
Carey, Roane. *The New Intifada*. New York: Verso Books, 2001. The human cost
    of the war from the Palestinian side.
Cossery, Albert. *Men God Forgot*. San Franciso, City Lights Books, 1963. Novel
    of the crushing poverty of Cairo.
Hamzah, Khidr Abd Al-Abbas. *Saddam's Bombmaker: The Daring Escape of the
    Man Who Built Iraq's Secret Weapon*. New York: Touchstone Books, 1997.
    Iraq's weapons program from the inside.
Herzl, Theodor. *The Jewish State*. New York: Dover Publications, 1989. Founding
    document of modern Zionism.
Hroub, Khaled. *Hamas: Political Thought and Practice*. Washington, D.C.: Insti-
    tute for Palestine Studies, 2000. Detailed presentation of their ideology
    with an emphasis on the possibilities for a political solution to the conflict
    in the Middle East.

Irgun, *Psychological Warfare and Propaganda*. Yonah Alexander (ed.). Wilmington: Scholarly Resources, Inc., 1982. Documents of the Resistance movement against the British in Palestine.

Jaber, Hala. *Hezbollah*. New York: Columbia University Press, 1997. Detailed account of this organization.

Naipul, V.S. *Beyond Belief*. New York: Vintage Books, 1998. Sober evaluation of Islam in non-Arabic countries.

Fringe Terrorism

Abbey, Edward. *The Monkeywrench Gang*. New York: HarperCollins Books, 1975. The bible of eco-activists and an influence on Kaczynski.

Army of God. *99 Covert Ways to Stop Abortion*. http://www.armyofgod.com/AOGhistory.html Right wing frat boy manual with sinister implications.

Chalmers, David. *Hooded Americanism*. Durham, North Carolina: Duke University Press, 1987. History of the Ku Klux Klan.

Coulson, Danny O. *No Heroes*. New York: Pocket Books, 1999. Terrorism from the FBI perspective.

Dee, Morris. *Gathering Storm: America's Militia Threat*. New York: HarperCollins Book, 1996. History of Christian Identity movement from one of its fiercest and most effective opponents.

Lifton, Robert Jay. *Destroying the World to Save It*. New York: Metropolitan Books: New York, 1999. Psychological portrait of Aum Shinrikyo.

Macdonald, Andrew. *The Turner Diaries*. Fort Lee, New Jersey: Barricade Books, 1996. Racist novel that inspired Timothy McVeigh.

General Interest

Cole, Benjamin and Gurr, Nadine, *The New Face of Terrorism*. New York: I.B. Taurus, 2000. Detailed histories of chemical, nuclear and biological terrorism incidents.

Rand Institute. *The Rand St. Andrews Chronology of International Terrorist Incidents, 1995*. Santa Monica, California: The Rand Institute, 1998. Every terrorist incident of that year.

Schaffer, Martin. *The Missile Threat to Civilian Aviation*. Santa Monica, California: The Rand Institute, 1997. Shoulder guided missles as a threat to commercial air travel.

Suggestions for Further Reading

U.S. Department of State."Terrorist Group Profiles: Index of Groups". All the groups on the U.S. watch list. http://web.nps.navy.mil/~library/tgp/tgpndx.htm